Expert Android

Satya Komatineni
Dave MacLean

Apress·

Expert Android

ISBN 978-1-4302-4950-4

ISBN 978-1-4302-4951-1 (eBook)

President and Publisher: Paul Manning
Lead Editor: Steve Anglin
Developmental Editor: Douglas Pundick
Technical Reviewer: Rick Boyer
Editorial Board: Steve Anglin, Mark Beckner, Ewan Buckingham, Gary Cornell, Louise Corrigan, Morgan Ertel, Jonathan Gennick, Jonathan Hassell, Robert Hutchinson, Michelle Lowman, James Markham, Matthew Moodie, Jeff Olson, Jeffrey Pepper, Douglas Pundick, Ben Renow-Clarke, Dominic Shakeshaft, Gwenan Spearing, Matt Wade, Tom Welsh
Coordinating Editor: Jill Balzano
Copy Editor: Carole Berglie
Compositor: SPi Global
Indexer: SPi Global
Artist: SPi Global
Cover Designer: Anna Ishchenko

Distributed to the book trade worldwide by Springer Science+Business Media New York, 233 Spring Street, 6th Floor, New York, NY 10013. Phone 1-800-SPRINGER, fax (201) 348-4505, e-mail orders-ny@springer-sbm.com, or visit www.springeronline.com. Apress Media, LLC is a California LLC and the sole member (owner) is Springer Science + Business Media Finance Inc (SSBM Finance Inc). SSBM Finance Inc is a Delaware corporation.

For information on translations, please e-mail rights@apress.com, or visit www.apress.com.

Apress and friends of ED books may be purchased in bulk for academic, corporate, or promotional use. eBook versions and licenses are also available for most titles. For more information, reference our Special Bulk Sales–eBook Licensing web page at www.apress.com/bulk-sales.

Any source code or other supplementary materials referenced by the author in this text is available to readers at www.apress.com. For detailed information about how to locate your book's source code, go to www.apress.com/source-code/.

To my 10-year-old son Narayan Komatineni, who teaches me to think fearlessly on a daily basis.

To my wife Rosie, for her patience and support, and mostly for keeping me sane.
And to my son Mike, who makes me a prouder Dad every day.

Contents at a Glance

Contents

About the Authors

Satya Komatineni has been programming for more than 20 years in the IT and Web space. He has had the opportunity to work with Assembly, C, C++, Rexx, Java, C#, Lisp, HTML, JavaScript, CSS, SVG, relational databases, object databases, and related technologies. He has published more than 30 articles touching on many of these areas, both in print and online. He has been a frequent speaker at O'Reilly Open Source Conference, speaking on innovations around Java and the Web. Satya has done a considerable amount of original work in creating Aspire, a comprehensive open-source Java-based Web framework, and has explored personal Web productivity and collaboration tools through his open-source work for KnowledgeFolders.com. Satya holds a Master's degree in Electrical Engineering from Indian Institute of Technology, New Delhi, and a Bachelor's degree in Electrical Engineering from Andhra University, India. You can find his website at SatyaKomatineni.com. His current research is Mobile, Cloud, and the Web.

Dave MacLean is a Technical Architect living and working in Orlando, Florida. He has been writing software for over 30 years, and Android programs, books, and magazine articles since 2009. His career has been mostly in IT at large and small companies, with some robotics sprinkled in. He loves to learn new things, and Google provides a never-ending supply of new stuff to play with. You can reach him at davemac327@gmail.com.

About the Technical Reviewer

 **Rick Boyer** is a Senior Software Engineer with over 20 years of experience ranging from desktop and Web to mobile development. Ever since his first experience with a PDA, he has had a passion for mobile development, which has included Windows CE, Windows Phone, and Android. He was the technical reviewer for two other Android books, and he runs a consulting business, NightSky Development. NightSky Development provides Android consulting services to startup companies. You can contact him at about.me\RickBoyer.

Acknowledgments

Writing a technical book is a team effort, and we'd like to thank this team in particular. The folks at Apress were great, including Steve Anglin, Douglas Pundick, Jill Balzano, Carole Berglie, and Anna Ishchenko. We'd also like to graciously thank our technical reviewer Rick Boyer, who worked tirelessly to catch our goofs and who made this book so much better.

We have also been ably assisted by the various Android forums that have provided answers to our questions as well as valuable advice. And finally, but certainly not least, we extend our thanks to our readers. We greatly appreciate your picking up our books, asking us questions, and keeping us on our toes. We are better for it, and we hope our work can somehow help you achieve your goals.

We especially want to thank the readers of our books, as you give us reason to write and excel. We worked very hard on this *Expert Edition* of Android. We really hope you will learn a lot from it, as we did. If you are not fully satisfied just hang on, as we are committed to gain your laurels by working twice as hard for the next book on Android, which we would like to see in your hands as well.

Introduction

As a programmer, designer, or architect, you may be lulled into thinking that the Android API is merely what you use to write mobile programs for the Android mobile platform—which, of course, is true. However, we believe that the Android architecture has an undercurrent that makes it a key pillar in the cloud-based Google computing era that is beckoning all of us! When you learn deeply about the Android API, you are gaining a pass to the future of Google, and perhaps to the future of all of us.

This book, *Expert Android*, is our fifth book on Android in the last four years. In the first four books, published under the Pro Android name, we covered increasingly new material on the core Android API. *Expert Android* Is the outcome of our deepest desire and commitment to bring you the essentials for writing compelling and impactful Android applications at a faster pace.

In *Expert Android*, you will find more difficult topics that are not covered anywhere else. You will discover ways that help you extend Android and companion topics that will enhance your Android mobile applications. You also will find information that is applicable for any release of Android.

Is This Book for You?

As authors, the first question we want to answer is whether this book is for you. Yes, this book is for you if you are transitioning from learning about Android and writing stock applications to writing applications that are impactful. Yes, it's for you if you also want to release those applications to the market quickly.

A key focus of *Expert Android* is to write components that extend Android, especially UI components. This is important, for two reasons. First, you can write reusable components that are specific to your suite of applications or problem space. Second, there are increasingly reusable open-source components that you can borrow along with their source codes. Often, or even only occasionally, you will need to tweak these components to meet your needs. You will then need to understand how the source codes of these custom components work. This book will guide you through the details of these customized components. The first three chapters on customizing views, and the fourth chapter on OpenGL, serve this Android UI customization goal.

There is an advantage in the mobile space if you can release applications quickly into the marketplace, a topic that we address in *Expert Android*. The chapter on JSON shows you a really cool and quick way to use persistence, which is so essential for all mobile applications.

Additionally, many mobile applications are form based. The chapter on advanced form processing makes writing form-based applications really easy. And the three chapters on Parse will further expedite your writing of collaborative mobile applications in record time.

Yes, this book is for you if you want to push the mobile programming practice to the next level, using the best tools and approaches available.

What You Need to Know Before You Begin

Expert Android assumes that you are familiar with Java and Android. The basis for most of Android programming is Java. However, if you know any high-level object-oriented programming language, you should be able to pick up Android programming fairly quickly. Having experience with Eclipse or IntelliJ would be quite helpful. This book further assumes that you know the basics of Android and that you have written a few simple applications. There are a number of books to get you to this stage, including our Pro Android series from APress. In short, we assume you will have worked with Java, Eclipse or IntelliJ, and Android for a year or two. With that said, here's a brief, quick overview of what is in *Expert Android*, chapter by chapter.

What's in This Book

We start *Expert Android* by documenting in depth how you can customize Android UI by customizing the views, controls, and layouts. You will see over 100 pages of this material spread over the first three chapters.

In Chapter 4, we provide a practical way to persist the application state with JSON. This allows you to write small to medium mobile applications really quickly, as it makes persistence super-simple. Just quickly browse through this chapter if you are skeptical.

In Chapter 5, we address an essential question of how to write a mobile application that works well on multiple mobile form factors.

Continuing the theme of practical guidance for mobile applications, in Chapter 6 we present an advanced form-processing framework to write form-based mobile applications using really simple principles.

A mobile device is a phone too, which we tend to forget. Chapter 7 covers the telephony API of Android.

With the memory and power consumption of mobile devices always at a premium, you want your applications to run as efficiently as possible. In Chapter 8, we cover the debugging approaches and tools available for ensuring this is the case.

OpenGL has a come a long way on Android, now with substantial support for the new generation of programmable GPUs. Android has been supporting ES 2.0 for sometime. In Chapter 9, we have over 100 pages covering OpenGL. With this chapter on OpenGL, we start at the begining and explain all the concepts without needing to refer to external books, although we do provide an extensive bibliography on OpenGL. We cover ES 2.0, and we provide guidance to combine OpenGL and regular views to pave the way for 3D components.

Federated search protocol of Android is powerful, as you can use it in quite a few imaginative ways. The search experience is also shifting and pivoting with each release of Android so as to reach its full potential. Chapters 10, 11, and 12 fully explore the fundamentals of the search protocol and also offer some alternative ways to optimally use this Android facility.

And if our intuitions are correct, mobile applications will increasingly be collaborative, so they will need to store data in the cloud and also collaborate among users. Chapters 13, 14, and 15 present Parse-related material. In short, we have taken a successful cloud platform called Parse, and have engaged it for user management, cloud storage, and push notifications. With Parse now being part of Facebook, this coverage of Parse is a valuable addition to our book, for two reasons: its synergy with Facebook, and how easy it is to take collaborative applications to the marketplace. Mobile in the cloud is the future. We are proud to have taken a good first step toward exploring this potential in *Expert Android*.

How to Prepare for Expert Android

Although we have used the latest Android release (4.2) to write and test *Expert Android*, the contents of this book are fairly independent of any Android release. Most, if not all, sample programs and code should work even in future releases. Expecially, the concepts and approaches presented here should be valid across all Android releases.

To heighten the readability of these chapters, among other improvements we have reduced the typical pages and pages of source code. Instead, the source code for each chapter is available both on Apress.com and at our supporting site, androidbook.com. You will be able to download each chapter's source code and load it into Eclipse directly. If you are using IntelliJ or another editor, you can unzip each chapter and build the code by importing the projects manually into your favorite IDE.

Furthermore, we have broken some of the bigger topics into more manageable shorter chapters. For example, we have the discussion of custom views spread out in three chapters. Coverage of Parse.com is spread across three chapters as well. We've done the same to explain Android Search. Although most chapters are self-contained in terms of their examples, you may occasionally need to refer to the earlier chapters on that topic.

If you are programming using any of the topics that we have covered in any of our books, including *Expert Android*, remember that our websites androidbook.com and satyakomatineni.com have dedicated knowledge folders for each topic. These knowledge folders document various items in each topic. For example, you will see in this book the Android API links you will need as you develop code in that context. In short, we use these sites often to grab code snippets and also quickly get to the Android API links.

We have written *Expert Android* in such a way that we expect you will read through it like a novel, chapter by chapter, and grasp an idea before implementing it. You can then come back to the book for clarification or additional reference when you start implementing these ideas.

How to Reach Us

We can be reached readily via our respective e-mail addresses: Satya Komatineni at satya.komatineni@gmail.com, and Dave MacLean at davemac327@gmail.com. Also, keep this URL in your bookmarks: http://androidbook.com/expertandroid. Here you will find links to source code, links to downloadable projects, key feedback from readers, full contact information, future notifications, errata, news on our future projects, a reading guide, additional resources—even some future alpha chapters and perhaps more.

Exploring Custom Views

Your understanding of Android SDK is not vigorous until you master the architecture of Android's Views. So it is appropriate that we begin *Expert Android* by exploring the power of Android's custom views. Our goal in this and the next two chapters is to unwrap the architecture of Android's Views by customizing them. In Android you can customize views in three ways:

- Custom views (by extending the View class)

- Compound views/controls (by composing other existing controls through extending one of the existing Layout classes) (Note that in this and the next few chapters we are using custom views and custom components synonymously)

- Custom layouts (by extending the ViewGroup class)

We have learned a lot in researching each of these topics. We are eager to share with you this information on custom components, presented in this and the next two chapters. We believe custom components hold the key to unlocking the full potential of the Android SDK.

We start this chapter by covering the custom views. This chapter also forms the basis for the next two chapters: Compound views/controls and Custom layouts.

To demonstrate custom views, in this chapter we:

- Create a custom view called CircleView and explain the theory and mechanics of customizing a View.

- Present the entire source code of CircleView in order to guide you to write your own custom views.

- Show how to embed the CircleView in any of Android layouts.

- Show how the CircleView responds to touch events by changing the size of the circle. (Note that we are using "click" and "touch" synonymously in much of the book!)

- Show how the CircleView remembers state (such as the size of the circle) as you rotate the device.

- Show how to use custom attributes in layout files to initialize the CircleView.

Planning a Custom View

Before we explain the implementation of a custom view like the `CircleView`, let us show you the expected look, feel, and behavior of the `CircleView`. This, we believe, will make it easier for you to follow the subsequent explanation and code.

Let's begin by examining the `CircleView` in Figure 1-1. In Figure 1-1, the `CircleView` is between two text views in a linear layout. The width of the view is set to `match_parent`. The height of the `CircleView` is set to `wrap_content`.

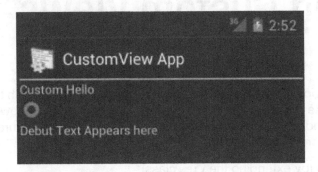

Figure 1-1. Custom CircleView with wrap_content

When we design this `CircleView`, we make the circle stroke color and width configurable in the layout file using custom attributes. To test responding to events, we use click events to expand the circle and redraw. Figure 1-2 shows what the `CircleView` would look like after a couple of clicks. Each click expands the circle by 20 percent.

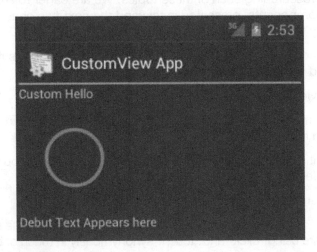

Figure 1-2. Custom CircleView expanded with clicks

We then implement state management to the `CircleView` so that when we flip the device to landscape, the view retains its magnification. Figure 1-3 shows the rotated device with `CircleView` maintaining its expansion.

Figure 1-3. Custom CircleView retaining state after rotation

Let's get started and cover all the essential things (there are a lot of them) about custom views so that you can design and code the CircleView that is shown in Figures 1-1, 1-2, and 1-3.

Nature of Drawing in Android

To understand how to draw in Android, you have to understand the architecture of the following classes:

```
View
ViewParent (interface)
ViewGroup (extends View and implements ViewParent)
ViewRoot (implements ViewParent)
```

View is the fundamental class that all of the visible components in Android are derived from. It defines a number of callbacks to customize its behavior, like the ability to define size, draw, and save state.

A ViewParent defines the protocol for any object (including another view) that wants to play the role of a parent to other views. There are two important view parents. Of those, ViewGroup is the key one. In addition to being a ViewParent, a ViewGroup also defines the protocol for a collection of child views. All layouts like the FrameLayout and LinearLayout in the Android SDK extend this class ViewGroup. ViewGroup plays a central role in defining these layouts in XML files and in placing the controls (views) at the right place. A ViewGroup also controls the background and animation of its child views.

The other key ViewParent, the ViewRoot is implementation centric and is not a public API. In some releases it is called ViewRoot, and in some implementations it is called ViewRootImplementation—and it may even be changed in the future to something else. However, this class is important for understanding how drawing is done in Android.

We advise you to keep tabs on the source code of these three classes (View, ViewGroup, ViewParent) to refer back to, should you have questions that were not answered anywhere else. For instance, if you want to look up the source code for View.java, Google that name and you will see a number of places on the Web that has this source code. The source code may not match the latest release, but for understanding what this class does, it is sufficient. I tend to download the latest android.jar source code and keep it in eclipse, then quickly locate a file in the source using CTRL-SHIFT-R (*R* stands for "resource").

Being a root parent of all views in the activity, the ViewRoot schedules traversals of all the views in order to first lay them out at the right place with the right size; this is called the layout phase. The ViewRoot then traverses the view hierarchy to draw them; this phase is called the drawing phase. We will talk about each of these phases now.

Layout Phase: Measurement and Layout

The goal of the layout phase is to know the position and size of each view in the view hierarchy owned by a parent such as the ViewRoot. To calculate the position and size of each view, the ViewRoot initiates a layout phase. However, in the layout phase, the view root does a traversal of only those views that reported or requested a layout change. This conditional measurement is to save resources and improve response time.

The trigger to initiate the layout phase may come from multiple events. One trigger may be the very first time everything is being drawn. Or one of the views, while reacting to an event like a click or touch, could report that its size has changed. In such an event, the view that got clicked on calls the method requestLayout(). This call walks up the chain and gets to the root view (ViewRoot). The root view then schedules a layout traversal message on the main thread's queue.

The layout phase has two passes: a measure pass and a layout pass. The measure pass is implemented by the measure() function of the View class. The signature of this function is

```
public final void measure(int widthMeasureSpec, int heightMeasureSpec)
```

Make a note of this method's signature. This signature will help you to easily locate this method measure() in the source code of the large View.java source file. This method, measure(), does some housekeeping and calls the onMeasure() of the derived views. The derived views need to set their dimensions by calling setMeasuredDimension(). These measured dimensions set on each view are then subsequently used in the layout pass. In this context, your primary override is View.onMeasure(). Keep in mind that there is a default implementation for onMeasure(). The default implementation of onMeasure() decides the size of your view based on suggestions from the layout files, including an exact size passed in. We will cover this later in the chapter.

Although it is the onMeasure() that you care about when you are a creating custom view like the CircleView, there are times when measure() is important as well. If the inherited custom view is a collection of other views, as in a ViewGroup, then you need to call measure() on child views in your onMeasure() method. The signature of measure() earlier clearly supports the idea that you can't override it by being final, but you are expected to call it by being public. We will cover the measure() method arguments widthMeasureSpec and heightMeasureSpec when we work with onMeasure() later in this chapter.

After the measure pass, each view knows its dimensions. The control then passes to the layout pass. This layout pass is implemented in the layout() method, whose signature in the base View class is:

```
public void layout(int left, int top, int right, int bottom)
```

Again, we are giving the full signature of the layout() method because this signature will help you to locate this method in the base View class source file. Much like the measure() method, the layout() method carries out an internal protocol for the base View and result in calling the overridden methods in Listing 1-1, in that order.

Listing 1-1. Overridden Methods Called by a View's Layout() Method

```
protected void onSizeChanged(int w, int h, int oldw, int oldh);
protected void onLayout(boolean changed, int left, int top, int right, int bottom)
```

The layout pass, implemented in layout(), will take the dimensions measured by the measure pass into account and give out the starting position for each view and the dimension each view needs to use. The base layout() method actually sets these dimensions on the view on which it is called. It then calls the onSizeChanged() if there is actually a change in size or position. The default implementation of onSizeChanged() exists in the View class but it is a no-op.

After calling the onSizeChanged() method, the layout() method calls the onLayout() to allow for something like a view group to call layout() on its children. The default implementation for onLayout() exists but it is a no-op. To apply this to our CircleView, we don't need to do anything in the onLayout() because our position and dimensions are already fixed, and we have no children to advise their layouts by calling their layout() method.

Once both of the passes of the layout phase are completed, the traversal initiated by the view root will move to the drawing phase.

Drawing Phase: Mechanics of onDraw

The draw traversal is implemented in the View's draw() method. The protocol implemented by this method is:

```
Draw the background
Draw view's content by delegating to onDraw()
Draw children by delegating to dispatchDraw()
Draw decorations such as scroll bars
```

Because the draw traversal happens after the layout traversal, you already know the position and the size of your views. If your view like the CircleView doesn't have children, you don't care much about dispatchDraw(). The default implementation for this method in the base View class exists but is empty.

You could ask: If my custom view has children, why am I not choosing to draw them in onDraw? Perhaps because, in a framework, the base class View's fixed protocol of draw() may choose to do something between your onDraw() and your children's onDraw(). So, it is suggested to the programmer, by dispatchDraw() of the View, that the View's drawing is complete and the derived implementation could choose whatever is needed.

In a sense, the programmer could even treat dispatchDraw() as a post onDraw(). We suggest you examine the source code for the draw() method of the View class. You can use the following method signature to search for it in the source code of the View class.

```
public void draw(...)
```

Although draw() is a public method that you could override, you shouldn't. It implements a protocol and a contract defined by the base View. Your choices are to override its suggested methods:

```
public void onDraw(...)
public void dispatchDraw(...)
```

This idea of a dispatch... pattern is used often in Android to do things for children after you have done them for yourself.

As the trigger for the layout phase is requestLayout(), the trigger for the draw phase is invalidate(). When you invalidate a view, it goes up the chain and results in scheduling of the traversal from the view root. It is possible that if a view did not request an invalidate or if its position and size haven't changed then the onDraw() may not be called for that View.

However if size or position has changed for a view, the base view will call invalidate on that view. So it is probably not necessary to invalidate things in your onSizeChanged(). When you are in doubt, call invalidate() after a requestlayout() as the performance impact is minimal because all these calls get aggregated for a traversal at the end of current main thread cycle.

Let us recap and look at the methods available to customize a view:

```
onMeasure
onSizeChanged

onLayout
onDraw
dispatchDraw
```

All of these are callbacks. Especially interesting are onMeasure(), onLayout(), and onDraw(). All three of them have their equivalent "protocol" or "template" methods: measure(), layout(), draw().

This pattern is often called a *template/hook*. For example, draw() is the template method that fixes the behavior in a certain manner while relying on the hook onDraw() to specialize itself. Another way to look at this is that a template method is like an "HTML template with substitution fillers" and a hook or hooks are the data that goes there and get substituted to complete the whole web page.

You could even further call this pattern *template/hook/children*. The idea is:

```
measure()
   onMeasure()
       for(child in children) child.measure()
```

or

```
template()
   hook()
       for(child in children) child.hook()
```

So, draw() breaks this mold a little, but measure() and layout() follow the mold. This is a good rule of thumb to avoid getting lost in the sea of callback names when customizing components.

When you are customizing views that don't have any children, the methods that are usually overridden are:

```
onMeasure(...)
onDraw(...)
```

The method that might also be overrridden once in a while is onSizeChanged().

This concludes the coverage on how drawing is done in Android. To quickly summarize in order to lead you to the next section, note that we have established the following:

- There is a layout phase where a measure pass happens and we need to override onMeasure().

- There is a drawing phase where we need to implement onDraw().

Let us now show you the mechanics of implementing onMeasure().

Implementing Measure Pass

In the measure pass, a custom view needs to return the size that it wants (or dictated to) when it gets painted in the subsequent draw pass. The view needs to set its dimensions in the overriden onMeasure(). Setting the size of a view is not straightforward. Your view size depends on how your view is going to fit with the rest of the views. It is not as simple as saying your view is 400 pixels by 200 pixels. Android passes something called a mode bit to onMeasure() to give context to calculating the size of the view.

This mode bit can be one of three: AT_MOST, UNSPECIFIED, and EXACT. For example, if the mode bit is EXACT, your view should use the size passed in and no calculation is necessary. You will have a full understanding of these mode bits by the end of this section.

The key responsibility of onMeasure() is to recognize how it is called (mode) and then calculate the view size, if that is an option (based on mode), and then set that size using setMeasuredDimension(). Another wrinkle in onMeasure() is that it may be called multiple times depending on how the parent layout is coordinating space for all its children. There is a brief protocol of negotiation that needs to be implemented in this method. You will know this protocol as well by the end of this section.

Sometimes you may be able to use the default implementation of onMeasure() from the base View class. But first we will explain what we did in this method and then go into why we didn't use the default implementation for the CircleView. Listing 1-2 shows how we implemented onMeasure().

Listing 1-2. How to Override a Views onMeasure() Method

```
protected void onMeasure(int widthMeasureSpec, int heightMeasureSpec)
{
    logSpec(MeasureSpec.getMode(widthMeasureSpec));
    Log.d(tag, "size:" + MeasureSpec.getSize(widthMeasureSpec));

    setMeasuredDimension(getImprovedDefaultWidth(widthMeasureSpec),
            getImprovedDefaultHeight(heightMeasureSpec));
}
```

Let's elaborate on our implementation of the onMeasure() method in Listing 1-2, point by point. Note that this implementation in Listing 1-2 relies on two other methods we have specialized, namely: getImprovedDefaultWidth() and getImprovedDefaultHeight(). We will cover them shortly.

Let's start with the arguments in Listing 1-2: the width and height measure specifications. We know that our CircleView could be part of a layout. This means a developer can specify a dimension like height in three different ways in a layout file. Listing 1-3 provides an example of a layout file.

Listing 1-3. Providing Layout Sizes in a Layout File that Could Impact onMeasure

```
<com.androidbook.custom.CircleView
    android:id="@+id/circle_view_id"
    android:layout_width="match_parent"
    android:layout_height="wrap_content"
    circleViewPkg:strokeWidth="5"
    circleViewPkg:strokeColor="@android:color/holo_red_dark"
    />
```

The argument android:layout_height can be one of:

```
wrap_content
match_parent
or exact width in pixels like: 30dp
```

In each case, the onMeasure() gets called differently. The widthMeasureSpec is actually two arguments rolled into one integer. The class that encapsulates this behavior is View.MeasureSpec.

Listing 1-4 shows how you get to their individual parts.

Listing 1-4. Deciphering Through MeasureSpec

```
int inputMeasureSpec;
int specMode = MeasureSpec.getMode(inputMeasureSpec);
int specSize= MeasureSpec.getSize(inputMeasureSpec);
```

Listing 1-5 shows how you can print the various modes that a measure spec can come in.

Listing 1-5. Understanding MeasureSpec Modes

```
private void logSpec(int specMode)
{
    if (specMode == MeasureSpec.UNSPECIFIED) {
        Log.d(tag,"mode: unspecified");
        return;
    }
    if (specMode == MeasureSpec.AT_MOST) {
        Log.d(tag,"mode: at most");
        return;
    }
    if (specMode == MeasureSpec.EXACTLY) {
        Log.d(tag,"mode: exact");
        return;
    }
}
```

If the layout specification says match_parent, then onMeasure() will be called with a specification of EXACT. The size will be equal to the size of the parent. Then, onMeasure() will need to take that exact size and set it on the same view by calling setMeasuredDimension (as shown in Listing 1-2)

If the layout specification says exact pixels, then the onMeasure() will be called with a specification of EXACT. The size will be equal to the size of the specified pixels. Then onMeasure() will set this size using setMeasuredDimension.

Now comes the harder mode. If you set the dimension to wrap_content, then the mode will be AT_MOST. The size that gets passed could be much larger, taking up the rest of the space. So it might say, "I have 411 pixels. Tell me your size that doesn't exceed 411 pixels." The question then to the programmer is: What should I return?

In your circle, you can take all the size that is given to you and draw a circle big enough. But if you do that, the rest of the views will not have any space. (We're not sure why Android does this, but that's what happens.) So, you should give a "reasonable" size. In our case, we chose to return minimum size, like a well-meaning conservative who dispatches cash.

To see how we handled each of these measuring modes, let's return to the getImprovedDefaultHeight() and getImprovedDefaultWidth() that were cited previously in Listing 1-5. Listing 1-6 has the implementation of these methods showing how they handle onMeasure() modes.

Listing 1-6. *Implementing onMeasure() Properly*

```
private int getImprovedDefaultHeight(int measureSpec) {
    int specMode = MeasureSpec.getMode(measureSpec);
    int specSize =  MeasureSpec.getSize(measureSpec);

    switch (specMode) {
    case MeasureSpec.UNSPECIFIED:
        return hGetMaximumHeight();
    case MeasureSpec.EXACTLY:
        return specSize;
    case MeasureSpec.AT_MOST:
        return hGetMinimumHeight();
    }
    //you shouldn't come here
    Log.e(tag,"unknown specmode");
    return specSize;
}

private int getImprovedDefaultWidth(int measureSpec) {
    .... identical to getImprovedDefaultHeight
    .... but of course uses the width as opposed to height
}

//Override these methods to provide a maximum size
//"h" stands for hook pattern
abstract protected int hGetMaximumHeight();
abstract protected int hGetMaximumWidth();
```

```
protected int hGetMinimumHeight() {
    return this.getSuggestedMinimumHeight();
}
protected int hGetMinimumWidth() {
    return this.getSuggestedMinimumWidth();
}
```

Notice how we are calling the getSuggestedMinimumHeight() from the base View class to get the minimum size for this view. This means the derived view must call setMinimumHeight() and setMinimumWidth(). If a derived view like CircleView calls these set methods in its constructor, then the size of the widget for wrap_content will use the minimum dimension. If your intention is to return an average width, as opposed to a minimum width, change this code accordingly.

From Listing 1-6 you also see that we have used maximum size for UNSPECIFIED mode. So when does this get called? Documentation says that this mode is passed in when the layout wants to know what the true size is. True size could be as big as it could be; layout will likely then scroll it. With that thought, we have returned the maximum size for our circle. You will see this when we show you the full source code for CircleView, later in this chapter.

Also notice that, to satisfy onMeasure() (in Listings 1-2 and 1-6), we have used two built-in functions:

```
setMeasuredDimension()    //from view class
getSuggestedMinimumWidth() //from view class
```

Let's see now what the default implementation of onMeasure() does (Listing 1-7) and why we didn't choose it.

Listing 1-7. *Default Implementation of onMeasure() by the View Class*

```
protected void onMeasure(int widthMeasureSpec, int heightMeasureSpec) {
    setMeasuredDimension(getDefaultSize(getSuggestedMinimumWidth(), widthMeasureSpec),
            getDefaultSize(getSuggestedMinimumHeight(), heightMeasureSpec));
}
public static int getDefaultSize(int size, int measureSpec) {
    int result = size;
    int specMode = MeasureSpec.getMode(measureSpec);
    int specSize = MeasureSpec.getSize(measureSpec);

    switch (specMode) {
    case MeasureSpec.UNSPECIFIED:
        result = size;
        break;
    case MeasureSpec.AT_MOST:
    case MeasureSpec.EXACTLY:
        result = specSize;
        break;
    }
    return result;
}
```

Notice that this implementation will result in taking the entire remaining space when the mode is wrap_content! That is why we have overridden the class. If you don't anticiapte wrap_content on your widget (meaning it has no natural size), then you can use the default implementation and you don't allow wrap_content in the layout file.

Most of the work in understanding custom views is in the measure pass and how you implement the onMeasure(). Now that it is behind us, let us turn to onDraw().

Implementing Drawing through onDraw()

Unlike onMeasure(), there is no confusion about onDraw(). For starters, the default implementation does nothing. It is your job to draw. Here is how we implemented it in Listing 1-8:

Listing 1-8. Overriding onDraw()

```
...
private int defRadius;
private int strokeWidth;
private int strokeColor;

...
//Called by the constructor
public void initCircleView()
{
    //Set the minimum width and height
    this.setMinimumHeight(defRadius * 2);
    this.setMinimumWidth(defRadius * 2);

    //Say we respond to clicks
    this.setOnClickListener(this);
    this.setClickable(true);

    //allow for statmanagement
    this.setSaveEnabled(true);
}

//we don't use the defRadius variable here
//we just use the dimensions that are passed
//defRadius is used to set the minimum dimension
@Override
public void onDraw(Canvas canvas) {
    super.onDraw(canvas);
    Log.d(tag,"onDraw called");

    int w = this.getWidth();
    int h = this.getHeight();
    int t = this.getTop();
    int l = this.getLeft();
```

```
        int ox = w/2;
        int oy = h/2;
        int rad = Math.min(ox,oy)/2;
        canvas.drawCircle(ox, oy, rad, getBrush());
}
private Paint getBrush()
{
        Paint p = new Paint();
        p.setAntiAlias(true);
        p.setStrokeWidth(strokeWidth);
        p.setColor(strokeColor);
        p.setStyle(Paint.Style.STROKE);
        return p;
}
```

Simple. You get the canvas. You ask the view for width, height, left, and top. Left and top are relative to the parent view, starting at 0. The width and height also include padding. Use the getPadding...() series of methods to get padding coordinates, if you choose to use them.

In Listing 1-8, there are no surprises at all. Of course, as you start using canvas in inventive ways, then you get into the wonderful world of 2D graphics. But the focus of this chapter is on the plumbing of custom views and not on the gravity-defying 2D graphics programming.

To get the bare-bones custom view up and running, the only two methods that need to be overwrittern are onMeasure() and onDraw(). With some thought you can continue to use the same implementation of onMeasure() for a whole class of custom components. Once you understand the basics of these methods, writing a custom view that draws to the canvas is a cinch.

Responding to Events

As a next step for our custom view, we want to exercise the requestLayout() and invalidate() methods. To demonstrate these two methods in Listing 1-9, we make our circle respond to a touch.

Listing 1-9. Custom Views Responding to Events

```
public class CircleView
extends implements OnClickListener {
....other stuff
    public void initCircleView() {
        ...other stuff
        this.setOnClickListener(this);
        this.setClickable(true);
        ...other stuff
    }
    ....other stuff
    public void onClick(View v) {
        //increase the radius
        defRadius *= 1.2;
        adjustMinimumHeight();
        requestLayout();
        invalidate();
    }
```

```
    private void adjustMinimumHeight() {
        this.setMinimumHeight(defRadius * 2);
        this.setMinimumWidth(defRadius * 2);
    }
....other stuff
}
```

To respond to a click, our custom control implements the click listener and overrides the onClick method. It also tells the base View class that this is the click listener and clicking is enabled for this view. In the onClick() method, we increase the default radius and use that radius to change the minimum height and width.

Because the onClick event has caused the dimensions to change, our view needs to become bigger and take more space. How do we express that need to Android? Well, we requestLayout(). This method goes up the chain, marking every view parent that it needs to be remeasured. When the final parent gets this request (the view root), the parent schedules a layout traversal. A layout traversal may or may not result in onDraw, although in this case it should. As a good programming practice, we also call the invalidate() to ensure the drawing phase as well.

It is possible that a particular event will detect no change to the size but just the color of the circle; in that case, we just need to do invalidate() and not call the requestLayout().

If you are in the layout phase, you shouldn't call methods that could potentially result in a requestLayout(). Say, you added a background image in onSizeChanged(). You shouldn't call requestLayout again from the same phase. It won't take effect, as the view root resets these flags at the end of the current cycle. But you can do that in the painting phase. Alternatively, you can post an event to the queue that calls the requestLayout().

There is another method on a view called forceLayout(). The difference between this and requestLayout() is that the latter goes up the chain and results in a scheduling of layout pass. Nothing makes this more clear than looking at the source code (taken from API 14) for these two methods in the View class (shown in Listing 1-10):

Listing 1-10. Difference Between forceLayout() and requestLayout()

```
public void forceLayout() {
    mPrivateFlags |= FORCE_LAYOUT;
    mPrivateFlags |= INVALIDATED;
}

public void requestLayout() {
    if (ViewDebug.TRACE_HIERARCHY) {
        ViewDebug.trace(this, ViewDebug.HierarchyTraceType.REQUEST_LAYOUT);
    }

    mPrivateFlags |= FORCE_LAYOUT;
    mPrivateFlags |= INVALIDATED;

    if (mParent != null) {
        if (mLayoutParams != null) {
            mLayoutParams.resolveWithDirection(getResolvedLayoutDirection());
        }
```

```
        if (!mParent.isLayoutRequested()) {
            mParent.requestLayout();
        }
    }
}
```

Please note that the methods in Listing 1-10 are internal methods and are not part of the public API, so they may change with newer releases. However, the underlying protocol would remain the same.

In Listing 1-10, it is easier to first tell what forceLayout() is. It is like a touch command in build environments. Usually when a file hasn't changed, the build dependencies will ignore it. So, you force that file to be compiled by "touch"ing, and thereby updating its time stamp. Just like touch, the forceLayout() will not invoke any build commands by itself (unless your build environment is too sophisticated to kick off right away). The effect of touch is that, when a build is requested, you don't ignore this file.

So, when you forceLayout() a view, you are marking that view (only that one) as a candidate for measuring. If a view is not marked, then its onMeasure() will not be called. You can see this in the measure() method of the view. The measure() method checks to see if this view is marked for layout.

The behavior of requestLayout() is (only) slightly different. A requestlayout touches the current view as does forceLayout(), but it also walks up the chain touching every parent of this view until it reaches ViewRoot. ViewRoot overrides this method and schedules a layout pass. Because it is just a schedule to run, it doesn't start the layout pass right away. It waits for the main thread to complete its chores and attend the message queue.

You may wonder, *Still, explain to me when I use* forceLayout()*! I understand the* requestLayout() *because I end up scheduling a pass. What am I doing with* forceLayout()*?* Obviously if you are calling a requestLayout on a view, there is no point in calling forceLayout on that view. What is "force" anyway?

Recall that a "force" is like a "touch" for build! So, you are "forcing" the file to compile. Although it may look like it is going to run the layout pass right away, it does not.

When a view gets its requestLayout called, neither its siblings nor its children are touched. They don't have this flag up. So, if the view that is touched is a view group (as when you delete a view or add a view), the view group doesn't need to calculate the sizes of its children because their sizes haven't changed. There's no point in calling their onMeasure. But if for some reason the view group decides that these children need to be measured, it will call forceLayout on each of them, followed by measure(), which now correctly calls onmeasure(). It won't call requestLayout on children because there's no need to trigger another pass when you are in the middle of the current pass. (It's a "Don't interrupt me while I am interrupting" kind of deal.)

That introduces the question, then, of what happens the very first time. Who touched all the views to begin with, so that they are measured? When a view is added to a view group, the view group makes sure the view is marked for measurement and it calls a request layout for that view. More important, when does one call each of these methods?

Developers typically have more occasions to call requestLayout. For example, when you respond to a click on a view to increase its size, you do that and then you say requestLayout on that view. For whatever reason, if that doesn't do anything, you are inclined to call forceLayout, as the name is quite misleading. Based on what we know, that is like yelling twice. If the first yell is a no-op, the second yell will get the same response.

If a target view is changing size, and if you believe the size of your sibling view will get impacted, then call requestLayout on yourself and call forceLayout on your sibling. Of course, you can call the siblings requestLayout as well, but that adds a few more cycles to the CPU; if youknow what you are doing, a simpler forceLayout would do the trick. It is possibly also common in complex layouts that are derived from view groups, where a change to a single sibling may need a measurement of its siblings, so you want to explicitly decide if they need to remeasure again or not.

Saving View State

By now, you know this about working in Android: When you flip a phone or your device, you go from portrait to landscape or the other way around. This is called, at large, a configuration change to the device. A configuration change will stop the activity and remove it, and recreate a new instance using the new configuration. So, all memory variables held by the activity are gone and are recreated.

If you have a view that has local variables, they are gone and reinitialized as well. If you have transient data that you have created since the view was initialized, and was not written to a permanent store, that data is gone, too.

In order to retain the transient state, you use an activity or a fragment to save and restore instance data. "Instance data" refers to the local variables maintained by classes such as Activity, Fragment, or View. Activity and Fragment have a predefined protocol to manage this method. We are not going to cover that in detail in this chapter; our focus is on how to manage the instance state of the view.

There are three ways to manage the view state:

- Have the Activity use save and restore instance methods to explicitly call the view to save and restore its state.
- Use the built-in functionality of a View to save and restore its state.
- Use the built-in functionality of a View to save and restore its state, as in item above, but use a BaseSavedState protocol.

We will discuss the pros and cons of each way, and recommend that the third way is the best for industrial-strength components.

Rely on Activity Methods

Pseudo code in Listing 1-11 shows how an Activity can locate and call the View to save and restore the transient state.

Listing 1-11. View State Management Through an Activity

```
YourActivity
{
    @Override
    protected void onSaveInstanceState(Bundle savedInstanceState) {
        super.onRestoreInstanceState(savedInstanceState);
```

```
    //locate your view component
    CircleView cv = findViewById(R.id.circle_view_id);

    //call a custom method and get a bundle
    Bundle b = cv.saveState();

    //Put the bundle to be saved
    savedInstanceState.putBundle("circle_view_bundle",b);
}
@Override
protected void onRestoreInstanceState(Bundle savedInstanceState) {
    super.onRestoreInstanceState(savedInstanceState);

    //locate your view component
    CircleView cv = findViewById(R.id.circle_view_id);

    //call a custom method
    cv.restoreState(savedInstanceState.getBundle("circle_view_bundle"));
}
}
```

This is the approach used in some of the Android SDK API samples, like the SnakeView. Listing 1-12 shows a snippet of the source from the SnakeView example:

Listing 1-12. Example of Saving and Restoring State

```
public Bundle saveState() {
    Bundle map = new Bundle();
    map.putIntArray("mAppleList", coordArrayListToArray(mAppleList));
    map.putInt("mDirection", Integer.valueOf(mDirection));
    ....more
    return map;
}
public void restoreState(Bundle icicle) {
    mAppleList = coordArrayToArrayList(icicle.getIntArray("mAppleList"));
    mDirection = icicle.getInt("mDirection");
    ....more
    mSnakeTrail = coordArrayToArrayList(icicle.getIntArray("mSnakeTrail"));
}
```

This approach is really simple, and that is its charm. However, if the activity contains a lot of views, then we have to save and restore the state for each view in Listing 1-12. We also have to define string constants for each view and make sure they don't collide. That will be lot of code, not to mention being a bit error-prone. This approach as shown in Listing 1-12 is nevertheless useful for simple scenarios.

Enabling the View for Self State Management

If you could have the view do its own state management, then you don't need to do the bookkeeping in higher-level components, like fragments and activities. You could tell Android that a view does its own state management by calling:

```
view.setSaveEnabled();
```

This will call the following methods, shown in Listing 1-13, on the view (as long as the view definition in the layout file has a unique ID defined; this is a limitation and requirement for the view to manage its own state).

Listing 1-13. Overriding a View's Save and Restore State Methods

```
@Override
protected void onRestoreInstanceState(Parcelable p)
{
    //Code for these two methods are presented a little later
    this.onRestoreInstanceStateSimple(p);
    this.initCircleView();
}
@Override
protected Parcelable onSaveInstanceState()
{
    //Code for this method is presented a little later
    return this.onSaveInstanceStateSimple(p);
}
```

The caveat with this approach is that the view has to have a unique ID to trigger these two methods. This is not a problem when the view like CircleView stands by itself and is independently hooked to a layout. But if the CircleView becomes part of a compound component, and if that compound component is specified multiple times in a layout, then the IDs will collide. We will cover this topic in more detail in the next chapter, when we tell you how to program compound controls.

In Listing 1-13, we have only showed what methods are called by the view to save and restore state. We haven't shown how to actually save the state. There is a simple way to do this, and there is a standard way to do it. We will cover the simple approach first, as presented in Listing 1-14.

Listing 1-14. A Simple Approach to Managing View State

```
private Parcelable onSaveInstanceStateSimple()
{
    Parcelable p = super.onSaveInstanceState();
    Bundle b = new Bundle();
    b.putInt("defRadius",defRadius);
    b.putParcelable("super",p);
    return b;
}
```

```
private void onRestoreInstanceStateSimple(Parcelable p)
{
    if (!(p instanceof Bundle))
    {
        throw new RuntimeException("unexpected bundle");
    }
    Bundle b = (Bundle)p;
    defRadius = b.getInt("defRadius");
    Parcelable sp = b.getParcelable("super");

    super.onRestoreInstanceState(sp);
}
```

In this method shown in Listing 1-14, the super class View is passing an object during onSave and wants it back during onRestore. If the objects don't match, the super class View will throw an exception. To get around that, we take the object that is passed in and place it in our own bundle during save, then unwrap it and send it back during restore.

This is a middle-of-the-road solution, and is simple as well, suitable for demo purposes. The primary drawback is that if you expect your view to be inherited, then these bundles can have colliding names that have to be managed. We will discuss the right approach now.

BaseSavedState Pattern

To save state for the built-in UI controls, Android uses a pattern based on BaseSavedState class of the View. It is a bit roundabout and requires a chunk of code. The good news, though, is that you can just replicate this code and change a couple of things for each derived view, and you have a rock-solid framework that works well with the core state management for views.

In this method, in your most derived custom view, like CircleView, you need to create an inner static class, as shown in Listing 1-15.

Listing 1-15. *Implementing View-Specific SavedState Class for Managing View State*

```
public class CircelView extends View
{
....other stuff
public static class SavedState extends BaseSavedState {
    int defRadius;

    SavedState(Parcelable superState) {
        super(superState);
    }
    @Override
    public void writeToParcel(Parcel out, int flags) {
        super.writeToParcel(out, flags);
        out.writeInt(defRadius);
    }
```

```
    //Read back the values
    private SavedState(Parcel in) {
        super(in);
        defRadius = in.readInt();
    }

    @Override
    public String toString() {
        return "CircleView defRadius:" + defRadius;
    }

    @SuppressWarnings("hiding")
    public static final Parcelable.Creator<SavedState> CREATOR
            = new Parcelable.Creator<SavedState>() {
        public SavedState createFromParcel(Parcel in) {
            return new SavedState(in);
        }
        public SavedState[] newArray(int size) {
            return new SavedState[size];
        }
    };
}//eof-state-class
....other stuff
}//eof-custom-view-class
```

The only thing different for this inner SavedState class for each derived view is the internal variables you are saving. In this case, it is defRadius. This SavedState class ultimately derives from Parcelable. So, by contract of that class Parcelable, SavedState needs to have a static CREATOR object to create these SavedState parcelable objects from a parcel stream. This code, shown in Listing 1-15, is a standard template for every one of your derived views that intend to manage their state.

In SavedState, you also need to override writeToParcel() method to write the local variables to the parcel. You read them back in your SavedState constructor from the passed in Parcel.

Once you have this inner SavedState class, Listing 1-16 shows how you use this inner class SavedState to save and restore state for the CircleView. See Listing 1-13 for how the methods in Listing 1-16 are called from the View's save and restore callbacks.

Listing 1-16. Using View-Specific SavedState Object to Maintain View State

```
private Parcelable onSaveInstanceStateStandard()
{
    Parcelable superState = super.onSaveInstanceState();
    SavedState ss = new SavedState(superState);
    ss.defRadius = this.defRadius;
    return ss;
}
```

```
private void onRestoreInstanceStateStandard(Parcelable state)
{
    //If "state" object is not yours doesn't mean it is BaseSavedState
    //You may have a parent in your hierarchy that has their own
    //state derived from BaseSavedState.
    //It is like peeling an onion or opening a Russian doll
    if (!(state instanceof SavedState)) {
        super.onRestoreInstanceState(state);
        return;
    }
    //it is our state
    SavedState ss = (SavedState)state;
    //Peel it and give the child to the super class
     super.onRestoreInstanceState(ss.getSuperState());

    defRadius = ss.defRadius;
}
```

This approach of employing the SavedState pattern removes the need for inventing string names for saving and restoring your local variables. This pattern also has a protocol to recognize your view's bundle from the bundles belonging to your super view's in the inheritance hierarchy.

Custom Attributes

This brings us to the last detail in the implementation of custom views. Say, your custom view has special attributes you want to read. Listing 1-17 shows a linear layout where you indicate our custom attributes: strokeWidth and strokeColor of the circle we are drawing.

Listing 1-17. Specifying Custom Attributes

```
<LinearLayout xmlns:android="http://schemas.android.com/apk/res/android"
    xmlns:circleViewPkg="http://schemas.android.com/apk/res/com.androidbook.custom"
....
<com.androidbook.custom.CircleView
    android:id="@+id/circle_view_id"
    android:layout_width="wrap_content"
    android:layout_height="wrap_content"
    circleViewPkg:strokeWidth="5"
    circleViewPkg:strokeColor="@android:color/holo_red_dark"
    />
</LinearLayout>
```

Notice the two custom attributes in Listing 1-17:

```
strokeWidth
strokeColor
```

To be able to place these custom variables in a layout (as in Listing 1-17), you need to declare these custom attributes to Android in /res/values/attrs.xml file, as shown in Listing 1-18.

Listing 1-18. *Defining Custom Attributes in attrs.xml*

```
<resources>
<declare-styleable name="CircleView">
    <attr name="strokeWidth" format="integer"/>
    <attr name="strokeColor" format="color|reference" />
</declare-styleable>
</resources>
```

The filename `attrs.xml` can be anything, but convention is to use that name. There are a couple of things worth noting about the attributes in Listing 1-18. First, for your entire package, your attributes have to be unique. If you have another component called `CircleView1`, you cannot do this as shown in Listing 1-19.

Listing 1-19. *Showing the Uniqueness of Custom Attributes at the Package Level*

```
<resources>
<declare-styleable name="CircleView">
    <attr name="strokeWidth" format="integer"/>
    <attr name="strokeColor" format="color|reference" />
</declare-styleable>
<declare-styleable name="CircleView1">
    <attr name="strokeWidth" format="integer"/>
    <attr name="strokeColor" format="color|reference" />
</declare-styleable>
</resources>
```

You will get errors saying that those attribute names are already used. So, the name space for attributes is your entire package! The styleable name `CircleView` in the `attrs.xml` is merely a convention; you could use any name. You could also define the attributes outside of a styleable group, like `CircleView`. (See Listing 1-20.)

Listing 1-20. *Showing Custom Attributes Can be Defined Outside of Styleable Tags*

```
<resources>
<declare-styleable name="CircleView">
    <attr name="strokeWidth" format="integer"/>
    <attr name="strokeColor"/>
</declare-styleable>
    <attr name="strokeColor" format="color|reference" />
</resources>
```

Second, Listing 1-20 demonstrates that attributes can be defined as stand alone and can stay independent of `declare-styleable` grouping; `declare-styleable` is merely a grouping of attributes. You can also group an attribute into multiple groups as long as you don't redefine its format. You see that in Listing 1-20, where we have reused `strokeColor`.

Third, if attributes can be independently defined, then why are we grouping them into `declare-styleable` and giving it a name called `CircleView`? Because this grouping makes it easy for `CircleView` to read these custom attributes. With this grouping in place, `CircleView` class would say "Read all the variables in that group from the layout file!"

We have left one more detail concerning use of custom attributes, as shown in Listing 1-17. In that listing, we have declared the namespace for `strokeWidth`:

xmlns:**circleViewPkg**="http://schemas.android.com/apk/res/com.androidbook.custom"

Although namespace values are arbitrary, the tooling in Android wants your trailing piece `/apk/res/com.androidbook.custom` to match your package name. This is how it locates and allocates ids for your attributes.

Given the `attrs.xml` in Listing 1-18, Android generates the following IDs:

```
R.attr.strokeWidth (int)
R.attr.srokeColor (int)
R.styleable.CircelView (an array of ints)
R.styleable.CircleView_strokeWidth (offset into the array)
R.styleable.CircleView_strokeColor (offset into the array)
```

We use these constants, as shown in Listing 1-21, to read the custom attribute values from the layout XML file.

Listing 1-21. Using TypedArrays to Read Custom Attributes

```
public CircleView(Context context, AttributeSet attrs, int defStyle) {
    super(context, attrs, defStyle);
    //Use the array constant to read the bag once
    TypedArray t = context.obtainStyledAttributes(attrs,
                    R.styleable.CircleView,
                    defStyle, //if any values are in the theme
                    0); //Do you have your own style group

    //Use the offset in the bag to get your value
    strokeColor = t.getColor(R.styleable.CircleView_strokeColor, strokeColor);
    strokeWidth = t.getInt(R.styleable.CircleView_strokeWidth, strokeWidth);

    //Recycle the typed array
    t.recycle();

    //Go ahead and initialize your class.
    initCircleView();
}
```

In Android, attributes, styleables, styles, and themes are linked. To fully understand how layouts are read and custom attributes are initialized, you have to understand this connection. Although you can mechanicaly repeat this pattern of reading custom attributes, it is good to know why you read these custom attributes this way. A quick primer on this connection is necessary.

Attributes, as you saw here, are a unique set of names tied to a package. Objects like TextView, say, pick and choose some of those attributes for its use. Styleable (also as you saw here) is a grouping for a given custom component to choose what attributes it cares about. A style is a named collection (bag) of values for a set of attribute names. You can attach a style to an Activity or a View. When you do that, the call obtainStyledAttributes will walk up the chain and pull all attributes that this component cares about. (We have included URLs for the author's notes on custom attributes, styles, and themes in the Refererences, at the end of this chapter.)

Taking all this into account, Listing 1-22 shows how a custom view class is constructed.

Listing 1-22. Designing Constructors for the Custom View

```java
public class CircleView extends View implements OnClickListener
{
//Local variables
public static String tag="CircleView";
private int defRadius = 20;
private int strokeColor = 0xFFFF8C00;
private int strokeWidth = 10;

//for using it from java cdoe
public CircleView(Context context) {
    super(context);
    initCircleView();
}
//for using it from java cdoe
public CircleView(Context context, int inStrokeWidth, int inStrokeColor) {
    super(context);
    strokeColor = inStrokeColor;
    strokeWidth = inStrokeWidth;
    initCircleView();
}
//Invoked by layout inflater
public CircleView(Context context, AttributeSet attrs) {
    //Delegate this to a more general method.
    //we don't have any default style we care about
    //so set it to 0.
    this(context, attrs,0);
}
//Meant for derived classes to call if they care about defStyle
//Not called by the layout inflater
public CircleView(Context context, AttributeSet attrs, int defStyle) {
    super(context, attrs, defStyle);
    TypedArray t = context.obtainStyledAttributes(attrs,R.styleable.CircleView, defStyle,0);
    strokeColor = t.getColor(R.styleable.CircleView_strokeColor, strokeColor);
    strokeWidth = t.getInt(R.styleable.CircleView_strokeWidth, strokeWidth);
    t.recycle();
    initCircleView();
}

//See how all constructors swoop in on this one initialization
public void initCircleView()
{
    this.setMinimumHeight(defRadius * 2);
    this.setMinimumWidth(defRadius * 2);
    this.setOnClickListener(this);
```

```
        this.setClickable(true);
        this.setSaveEnabled(true);
    }
    ...You will see other methods when we present the full source code
    ...very soon after this section.
}//eof-class
```

Read the comments in Listing 1-22 for an explanation of how the constructor methods tie together and are used to read custom attributes from layout files.

Complete Source Code for the Custom View

We have covered all the theory (and code snippets) necessary to write production-ready custom views. In this section, we show you the complete source code for CircleView in one place. This ties up any loose ends that we felt were not all that important but that you might want to see in the context of a full implementation.

That implementation of the CircleView has been broken here into two classes. The first is a base abstract class that you could reuse for other custom views. The second is the CircleView itself, specializing the base abstract View class to complete the implementation. We will also present any dependent files, such as the attrs.xml, that go with the implementation.

Implementing a Base Abstract View Class

Instead of coding CircleView directly, we first want to create a base class that outlines what methods are overridable from a view. We list each method of a View and comment on how it makes sense to override it. We also implement in this base class if there is a default behavior that makes sense. For example, we know that we can do a better job of onMeasure() and relieve that responsibility from derived classes, like the CircleView.

This abstract base view class is shown in Listing 1-23. With everything we have covered so far, albeit in segments, you should be able to read through the comments without further explanation. Here, you now have all the code in one place.

Listing 1-23. Implementing AbstractBaseView

```
public abstract class AbstractBaseView
extends View
{
    public static String tag="AbstractBaseView";
    public AbstractBaseView(Context context) {
        super(context);
    }
    public AbstractBaseView(Context context, AttributeSet attrs) {
        super(context, attrs);
    }
    public AbstractBaseView(Context context, AttributeSet attrs, int defStyle) {
        super(context, attrs, defStyle);
    }
```

```java
@Override
protected void onMeasure(int widthMeasureSpec, int heightMeasureSpec)
{
    logSpec(MeasureSpec.getMode(widthMeasureSpec));
    Log.d(tag, "size:" + MeasureSpec.getSize(widthMeasureSpec));

    setMeasuredDimension(getImprovedDefaultWidth(widthMeasureSpec),
            getImprovedDefaultHeight(heightMeasureSpec));
}
private void logSpec(int specMode) {
    if (specMode == MeasureSpec.UNSPECIFIED) {
        Log.d(tag,"mode: unspecified");
        return;
    }
    if (specMode == MeasureSpec.AT_MOST) {
        Log.d(tag,"mode: at most");
        return;
    }
    if (specMode == MeasureSpec.EXACTLY) {
        Log.d(tag,"mode: exact");
        return;
    }
}
@Override
protected void onSizeChanged(int w, int h, int oldw, int oldh) {
    super.onSizeChanged(w,h,oldw,oldh);
}
@Override
protected void onLayout (boolean changed, int left,
                         int top, int right, int bottom)
{
    Log.d(tag,"onLayout");
    super.onLayout(changed, left, top, right, bottom);
}
@Override
public void onDraw(Canvas canvas) {
    super.onDraw(canvas);
    Log.d(tag,"onDraw called");
}
@Override
protected void onRestoreInstanceState(Parcelable p) {
    Log.d(tag,"onRestoreInstanceState");
    super.onRestoreInstanceState(p);
}
@Override
protected Parcelable onSaveInstanceState() {
    Log.d(tag,"onSaveInstanceState");
    Parcelable p = super.onSaveInstanceState();
    return p;
}
```

```java
    private int getImprovedDefaultHeight(int measureSpec) {
        //int result = size;
        int specMode = MeasureSpec.getMode(measureSpec);
        int specSize =  MeasureSpec.getSize(measureSpec);

        switch (specMode) {
        case MeasureSpec.UNSPECIFIED:
            return hGetMaximumHeight();
        case MeasureSpec.EXACTLY:
            return specSize;
        case MeasureSpec.AT_MOST:
            return hGetMinimumHeight();
        }
        //you shouldn't come here
        Log.e(tag,"unknown specmode");
        return specSize;
    }
    private int getImprovedDefaultWidth(int measureSpec) {
        //int result = size;
        int specMode = MeasureSpec.getMode(measureSpec);
        int specSize =  MeasureSpec.getSize(measureSpec);

        switch (specMode) {
        case MeasureSpec.UNSPECIFIED:
            return hGetMaximumWidth();
        case MeasureSpec.EXACTLY:
            return specSize;
        case MeasureSpec.AT_MOST:
            return hGetMinimumWidth();
        }
        //you shouldn't come here
        Log.e(tag,"unknown specmode");
        return specSize;
    }
    //Override these methods to provide a maximum size
    //"h" stands for hook pattern
    abstract protected int hGetMaximumHeight();
    abstract protected int hGetMaximumWidth();

    //For minimum height use the View's methods
    protected int hGetMinimumHeight() {
        return this.getSuggestedMinimumHeight();
    }
    protected int hGetMinimumWidth() {
        return this.getSuggestedMinimumWidth();
    }
}
```

CircleView Implementation

Listing 1-24 shows the full implementation of the CircleView that extends the AbastractBaseView (see previous Listing 1-23).

Listing 1-24. Source Code for Custom CircleView Implementation

```
public class CircleView
extends AbstractBaseView
implements OnClickListener
{
    public static String tag="CircleView";
    private int defRadius = 20;
    private int strokeColor = 0xFFFF8C00;
    private int strokeWidth = 10;

    public CircleView(Context context) {
        super(context);
        initCircleView();
    }
    public CircleView(Context context, int inStrokeWidth, int inStrokeColor) {
        super(context);
        strokeColor = inStrokeColor;
        strokeWidth = inStrokeWidth;
        initCircleView();
    }
    public CircleView(Context context, AttributeSet attrs) {
        this(context, attrs,0);
    }
    //Meant for derived classes to call
    public CircleView(Context context, AttributeSet attrs, int defStyle) {
        super(context, attrs, defStyle);
        TypedArray t = context.obtainStyledAttributes(attrs,R.styleable.CircleView, defStyle,0);
        strokeColor = t.getColor(R.styleable.CircleView_strokeColor, strokeColor);
        strokeWidth = t.getInt(R.styleable.CircleView_strokeWidth, strokeWidth);
        t.recycle();
        initCircleView();
    }
    public void initCircleView()    {
        this.setMinimumHeight(defRadius * 2);
        this.setMinimumWidth(defRadius * 2);
        this.setOnClickListener(this);
        this.setClickable(true);
        this.setSaveEnabled(true);
    }
    @Override
    public void onDraw(Canvas canvas) {
        super.onDraw(canvas);
        Log.d(tag,"onDraw called");
```

```java
        int w = this.getWidth();
        int h = this.getHeight();
        int t = this.getTop();
        int l = this.getLeft();

        int ox = w/2;
        int oy = h/2;
        int rad = Math.min(ox,oy)/2;
        canvas.drawCircle(ox, oy, rad, getBrush());
    }
    private Paint getBrush() {
        Paint p = new Paint();
        p.setAntiAlias(true);
        p.setStrokeWidth(strokeWidth);
        p.setColor(strokeColor);
        p.setStyle(Paint.Style.STROKE);
        return p;
    }
    @Override
    protected int hGetMaximumHeight() {
        return defRadius * 2;
    }
    @Override
    protected int hGetMaximumWidth() {
        return defRadius * 2;
    }
    public void onClick(View v) {
        //increase the radius
        defRadius *= 1.2;
        adjustMinimumHeight();
        requestLayout();
        invalidate();
    }
    private void adjustMinimumHeight() {
        this.setMinimumHeight(defRadius * 2);
        this.setMinimumWidth(defRadius * 2);
    }
    /*
     * ************************************************************
     * Save and restore work
     * ************************************************************
     */
    @Override
    protected void onRestoreInstanceState(Parcelable p) {
        this.onRestoreInstanceStateStandard(p);
        this.initCircleView();
    }
    @Override
    protected Parcelable onSaveInstanceState() {
        return this.onSaveInstanceStateStandard();
    }
```

```java
private void onRestoreInstanceStateStandard(Parcelable state) {
    //If it is not yours doesn't mean it is BaseSavedState
    //You may have a parent in your hierarchy that has their own
    //state derived from BaseSavedState
    //It is like peeling an onion or a Russian doll
    if (!(state instanceof SavedState)) {
        super.onRestoreInstanceState(state);
        return;
    }
    //it is our state
    SavedState ss = (SavedState)state;
    //Peel it and give the child to the super class
    super.onRestoreInstanceState(ss.getSuperState());

    defRadius = ss.defRadius;
}
private Parcelable onSaveInstanceStateStandard() {
    Parcelable superState = super.onSaveInstanceState();
    SavedState ss = new SavedState(superState);
    ss.defRadius = this.defRadius;
    return ss;
}
/*
 * ************************************************************
 * Saved State inner static class
 * ************************************************************
 */
public static class SavedState extends BaseSavedState {
    int defRadius;

    SavedState(Parcelable superState) {
        super(superState);
    }
    @Override
    public void writeToParcel(Parcel out, int flags) {
        super.writeToParcel(out, flags);
        out.writeInt(defRadius);
    }
    //Read back the values
    private SavedState(Parcel in) {
        super(in);
        defRadius = in.readInt();
    }
    @Override
    public String toString() {
        return "CircleView defRadius:" + defRadius;
    }
    @SuppressWarnings("hiding")
    public static final Parcelable.Creator<SavedState> CREATOR
            = new Parcelable.Creator<SavedState>() {
        public SavedState createFromParcel(Parcel in) {
            return new SavedState(in);
        }
```

```
            public SavedState[] newArray(int size) {
                return new SavedState[size];
            }
        };
    }//eof-state-class
}//eof-main-view class
```

All of this code in Listing 1-24 has been presented earlier in this chapter. Having it all in one place now should give you the context for implementation.

Defining Custom Attributes for the CircleView

Listing 1-25 shows the attrs.xml that goes with this code.

Listing 1-25. Attrs.xml for the Custom CircleView

```
<resources>
<declare-styleable name="CircleView">
    <attr name="strokeWidth" format="integer"/>
    <attr name="strokeColor" format="color|reference" />
</declare-styleable>
</resources>
```

Using the CircleView in a Layout

Listing 1-26 shows how you can use the CircleView custom component in a linear layout to produce the image you saw in Figure 1-1.

Listing 1-26. Using CircleView in a Linear Layout

```
<?xml version="1.0" encoding="utf-8"?>
<LinearLayout xmlns:android="http://schemas.android.com/apk/res/android"
    xmlns:circleViewPkg="http://schemas.android.com/apk/res/com.androidbook.custom"
    android:orientation="vertical"
    android:layout_width="fill_parent"
    android:layout_height="match_parent">
<TextView
    android:id="@+id/text1"
    android:layout_width="fill_parent"
    android:layout_height="wrap_content"
    android:text="Custom Hello" />
<com.androidbook.custom.CircleView
    android:id="@+id/circle_view_id"
    android:layout_width="wrap_content"
    android:layout_height="wrap_content"
    circleViewPkg:strokeWidth="5"
    circleViewPkg:strokeColor="@android:color/holo_red_dark"/>
```

```
<TextView
    android:id="@+id/text1"
    android:layout_width="fill_parent"
    android:layout_height="wrap_content"
    android:text="Debut Text Appears here" />
</LinearLayout>
```

References

We have a lot of good references for supplementing the information provided in this chapter. You will find these resources below immensely helpful.

- Our research log on custom components. Includes not only our research but also references to everything else you saw in this chapter. You will also see here source code links to View.java, ViewGroup.java, and ViewRoot.java: http://androidbook.com/item/4148.

- A series of articles on our complete research on custom components: http://androidbook.com/customcomponents.

- Complete code snippets for this chapter: http://androidbook.com/item/4330.

- Android SDK documentation on custom components: http://developer.android.com/guide/topics/ui/custom-components.html.

- Android SDK documentation on how drawing happens in Views: http://developer.android.com/guide/topics/ui/how-android-draws.html.

- An excellent video on custom layouts from Android graphics developers Romain Guy and Chet Haase: http://www.parleys.com/#st=5&id=2191&sl=3.

- An excellent presentation on custom components from Chiu-Ki Chan: http://www.sqisland.com/talks/android-custom-components.

- Key API links: API docs for the View class are at: http://developer.android.com/reference/android/view/View.html. The other key API links to look up, following this pattern, are ViewGroup, Paint, and Canvas.

- Some Android-specific quick code snippets that one of the authors keeps handy: http://androidbook.com/item/3838.

- Android code snippets from Java2s: http://www.java2s.com/Code/Android/CatalogAndroid.htm.

- Techniques and approaches for managing View state: http://androidbook.com/item/4327.

- Understanding custom attributes. At this link you will also find links to how attributes, styles, and themes are defined at the Android SDK level: http://androidbook.com/item/4169.

- To understand Android styles and themes: http://androidbook.com/item/3864.

- Download the test project dedicated for this chapter at www.androidbook.com/expertandroid/projects. The name of the ZIP file is ExpertAndroid_Ch01_CustomViews.zip.

Summary

Understanding custom components broadens your reach with the Android SDK. It makes you more confident to borrow and download custom components from others. We have showed you how to measure your components. We have also showed you how to correctly manage view state. We have explained the differences between requestLayout(), forceLayout(), and invalidate(). We have comprehensively covered custom attributes and their relationship to styles and themes. This chapter lays a solid foundation not only for the next two chapters but also for furthering your expertise with Android.

Review Questions

The following questions should further act as landmarks for determining what you have learned in this chapter:

1. What are the differences between requestLayout(), invalidate(), and forceLayout()?

2. Why is ViewRoot important?

3. What is meant by scheduling of a traversal?

4. What is a template/hook/child pattern?

5. What do you do in onMeasure()?

6. What methods do you use to override for a custom view?

7. How do you correctly manage view state?

8. What are the limitations of view state management in Android?

9. What constructor method is called from the layout inflater?

10. What is the name space for attributes?

11. How are attributes, styles, and themes connected?

12. What are measure spec modes and how do they correlate to layout sizes?

Chapter 2

Exploring Compound Controls

In Chapter 1, we said that one of the ways to customize views in Android is to compose (or put together) existing controls as a new compound control. In this chapter, we talk about how to create these custom compound controls.

There are a number of similarities between writing custom compound controls (the topic of this chapter) and directly customizing a standalone view (as what we did in Chapter 1). Managing custom attributes is identical in both types of customization. However, there are subtle but important differences in managing the view state of the custom compound control when compared to a custom view. Also, unlike custom views in which you do your own drawing, in the compound controls you don't deal with measuring, layout, or drawing. This is because you are using existing controls and those controls (such as text view, buttons, etc.) know how to measure and draw themselves.

Moving beyond these high-level similarities and differences between custom views and compound controls, you'll learn that creating a well-behaved compound control involves the following steps.

1. Derive the custom compound control from an existing layout like `LinearLayout`, `RelativeLayout`, etc.

2. Place the child controls you want to compose in a layout XML file. Then load that layout XML file in the constructor of the custom compound control as its layout.

3. Use `merge` as the root node of your custom layout XML file so that the composed child components in the layout XML file become the direct children of the custom control.

4. If you intend to invoke fragment dialogs from your child controls (like clicking or touching a button), you might need to assume your context for the fragment dialog as an activity.

5. From step 4, you will be able to derive a fragment manager and use fragment dialogs.

6.   If you are going to use a fragment dialog, you need to create a fragment class to work with your fragment dialog.

7.   When using fragment dialogs, to allow for device rotation, you need to pass the view ID of the parent compound control in the argument bundle of the fragment dialog. This ID is needed so that your fragment dialog can communicate with the parent compound control.

8.   On device rotation, you need to restore view pointers to the parent compound control in your dialog fragments in the fragment method onActivityCreated().

9.   To overcome the "ID" dependence of the views for view state management, the compound control needs to take over view state management for child views.

10.   Of course, as in Chapter 1, you can use custom attributes.

We are going to explain each of these steps along with annotated code snippets. First, we present the custom compound control that we are using to illustrate all of these steps.

Planning a Duration Compound Control

For our custom compound control, we will use two dates and see how many days or weeks are between these two dates. Figure 2-1 shows what this control may look like when embedded in the layout of an activity.

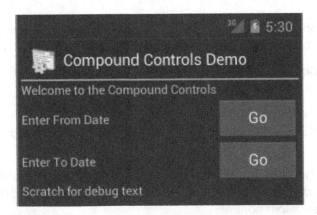

Figure 2-1. A compound control: DurationControl

Our custom duration component is embedded between two text controls, one that starts with "Welcome…" and the other at the bottom that starts with "Scratch for debug…."

We have two dates on this control: a "from" date and a "to" date. When we press GO against the from date, we invoke a date picker dialog (a fragment dialog) and replace the text "Enter From Date" with the "from" date. When we press GO against the to date, we invoke the same date picker dialog and replace the text "Enter To Date" with the "to" date. The compound DurationControl can then calculate the duration in either days or weeks (based on a custom attribute).

Figure 2-2 shows what the date picker fragment dialog looks like in portrait mode when you click GO.

Figure 2-2. Invoking a fragment dialog from a compound control

Once you pick a date from Figure 2-2, that date will be populated in the date text box, as shown in Figure 2-3.

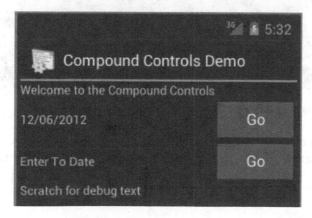

Figure 2-3. Saving the date from a date picker fragment dialog

In Figure 2-3, notice that the "from" date text is replaced with the date chosen. At this point, you want to make sure the data stays intact when you flip the device. Say, you start out with the date dialog in portrait mode. You flip the phone to landscape. Then, Figure 2-4 shows what this dialog should look like. You shouldn't have to reclick GO to see this dialog if the device is flipped.

Figure 2-4. Demonstrating device rotation with fragment dialogs

It is not that simple to retain dialogs on device flips. We will cover how to do this well later in the chapter. Figure 2-5 shows the view of the compound DurationControl in landscape when you pick the date from Figure 2-4 and set the "to" date.

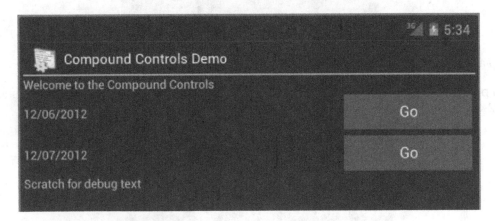

Figure 2-5. DurationControl state in landscape mode

Now, you want to flip the device to make sure the compound control can maintain its state (the two selected dates and their values). Figure 2-6 shows the DurationControl view after a flip back to portrait.

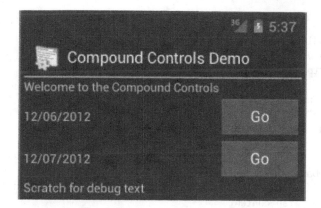

Figure 2-6. Duration control state in portrait mode

Now that you have a full understanding of the custom compound DurationControl, let's get started exploring each of the steps required to implement the full suite of functionality as listed at the beginning of the chapter.

Deriving from an Existing Layout

Listing 2-1 shows the first step required on your way to creating your custom compound control. In this listing, we will have our DurationControl extend the LinearLayout to produce the layout in Figure 2-1.

Listing 2-1. DurationControl Extending an Existing Layout

```
public class DurationControl
extends LinearLayout
implements android.view.View.OnClickListener
{
...
```

In addition to extending the LinearLayout, the control also implements an onclick listener. This listener is there to hear for the two buttons and kick off the fragment dialog to gather the dates.

Creating the Layout file for the Compound Control

Listing 2-2 shows the layout file required to produce the layout for the DurationControl as shown in Figure 2-1. As illustrated in Figure 2-1, this listing has (a) the two text views that show the selected date values, and (b) the two buttons that invoke the date picker dialogs. We used two inner LinearLayouts to accomplish the DurationControl view, as in Figure 2-1. Perhaps you can get innovative and use a single RelativeLayout to accomplish or arrive at the layout in Figure 2-1. (RelativeLayout is the preferred mechanism when compared to nested LinearLayouts for production code.)

Listing 2-2. DurationControl Custom Layout file

```xml
<?xml version="1.0" encoding="utf-8"?>
<!--/res/layout/duration_view_layout.xml -->
<merge xmlns:android="http://schemas.android.com/apk/res/android">
<LinearLayout
    android:orientation="horizontal"
    android:layout_width="fill_parent"
    android:layout_height="wrap_content"
>
<TextView
    android:id="@+id/fromDate"
    android:layout_width="0dp"
    android:layout_height="wrap_content"
    android:text="Enter From Date"
    android:layout_weight="70"
    />
<Button
    android:id="@+id/fromButton"
    android:layout_width="0dp"
    android:layout_height="wrap_content"
    android:text="Go"
    android:layout_weight="30"
    />
</LinearLayout>
<LinearLayout
    android:orientation="horizontal"
    android:layout_width="fill_parent"
    android:layout_height="wrap_content"
>
<TextView
    android:id="@+id/toDate"
    android:layout_width="0dp"
    android:layout_height="wrap_content"
    android:text="Enter To Date"
    android:layout_weight="70"
    />
<Button
    android:id="@+id/toButton"
    android:layout_width="0dp"
    android:layout_height="wrap_content"
    android:text="Go"
    android:layout_weight="30"
    />
</LinearLayout>
</merge>
```

You need to place this layout in an XML file under the layout resource directory. This will generate the layout ID you will use in the constructor of `DurationControl` to read in this custom layout. We will show you how this is done very shortly.

Notice that the root of this layout file is not <LinearLayout>but, instead, is <merge>. This is important because the custom control is already a LinearLayout (see Listing 2-1), and you want to have the children just in Listing 2-2 attached directly to DurationControl, which itself is a LinearLayout. If you don't do this and instead place a LinearLayout as a root node in Listing 2-2, your DurationControl will have an additional unnecessary LinearLayout as its child. This becomes evident when you see the constructor of the DurationControl in Listing 2-3, attaching these nodes of Listing 2-2 to itself as the parent view.

Listing 2-3. Loading Custom Layout in DurationControl Constructors

```
//Constructor for Java
public DurationControl(Context context) {
  super(context);
  initialize(context);
}

...other constructors that are there to read custom attributes
...Which also call initialize(context)

private void initialize(Context context)  {

  //Get the layout inflater
  LayoutInflater lif = (LayoutInflater)
  context.getSystemService(Context.LAYOUT_INFLATER_SERVICE);

  //inflate the custom layout of listing 2-2
  //Use the second argument to attach the layout
  //as a child of this layout
  lif.inflate(R.layout.duration_view_layout, this);

  //Initialize the buttons
  Button b = (Button)this.findViewById(R.id.fromButton);
  b.setOnClickListener(this);
  b = (Button)this.findViewById(R.id.toButton);
  b.setOnClickListener(this);

  //Allow view state management
  this.setSaveEnabled(true);
}
```

Listing 2-3 is typical of how compound controls load their custom layouts.

All inheriting views, including those inheriting from layouts, have multiple constructors. You have seen this in Chapter 1. There is one constructor that is used for instantiating the class directly from Java. There are two additional constructors that are used by Android to instantiate the view as part of exploding the layout. In Listing 2-3, we have only showed one constructor to demonstrate how the DurationControl loads its custom layout. We will show the rest of the constructors in this class later in the chapter, when we discuss the custom attributes for this class.

Either way, all of these constructors of DurationControl ultimately call the initialize() method in Listing 2-3. This initialization method gets a layout inflater from the activity and uses it to load the layout from Listing 2-2 using the generated ID for this custom layout file. Assuming that the layout in Listing 2-2 is in the file /res/layout/duration_view_layout the ID we will use is R.layout.duration_view_layout.

The initialization routine of Listing 2-3 then locates the buttons in the custom layout of Listing 2-2 and sets the DurationControl as the target for their onClicks.

You now have a custom layout (Listing 2-2). You have loaded that custom layout in your DurationControl constructor (Listing 2-3). Let us see now how the custom DurationControl is used in an activity's layout. This is an important point to fully appreciate the effect of merge in the custom layout file.

Specifying DurationControl in an Activity Layout

Notice that the merge in Listing 2-2 has no additional attributes in it other than the xmlns specification. Where do you say the controls in the layout Listing 2-2 (or in Figure 1-1) need to be laid out vertically? This is not done at the merge node, but instead is done when you specify the DurationControl in an activity's layout, as shown in Listing 2-4. Listing 2-4 is the layout that you see in the activity shown in Figure 1-1.

Listing 2-4 DurationControl in an Activity Layout

```xml
<?xml version="1.0" encoding="utf-8"?>
<LinearLayout xmlns:android="http://schemas.android.com/apk/res/android"
    xmlns:cc="http://schemas.android.com/apk/res/com.androidbook.compoundControls"
    android:orientation="vertical"
    android:layout_width="fill_parent"  android:layout_height="match_parent">
<TextView
    android:id="@+id/text2"
    android:layout_width="fill_parent" android:layout_height="wrap_content"
    android:text="Welcome to the Compound Controls"/>
    />
<com.androidbook.compoundControls.DurationControl
    android:id="@+id/durationControlId" android:orientation="vertical"
    android:layout_width="fill_parent" android:layout_height="wrap_content"
    cc:durationUnits="weeks"
    />
<TextView
    android:id="@+id/text1"
    android:layout_width="fill_parent" android:layout_height="wrap_content"
    android:text="Scratch for debug text"
    />
</LinearLayout>
```

Notice how the second node in this layout is your custom control DurationControl. See how the DurationControl node is specified just like a linear layout.

So far you have gotten the look and feel of our custom control right to match it with what is in Figure 1-1. We now will focus on its behavior. This leads us to a discussion of fragment dialogs, as we need them to capture the "from" and "to" dates.

Working with Fragment Dialogs

It so happens that our compound control uses fragment dialogs like the date picker to figure out "from" and "to" dates. It is not that straightforward to work with fragment managers if you want to isolate this functionality in a view so that this behavior is hidden outside of the compound custom view. In this section, we present, step by step, how to work with fragment dialogs from a self-contained compound control such as DurationControl.

Getting Access to a Fragment Manager

We know that we want to invoke a date picker dialog. The new approach to invoking dialogs in Android is by using fragments. To use these dialog fragments, you need access to a fragment manager. But because views don't have direct access to a fragment manager, you need an activity to get a fragment manager associated with that activity. Even to do that—getting an activity from a view—there is no direct way.

A view has access to only its context and not to an activity. Although an activity is a type of context, it is possible that a view may be operating in a context that is not an activity. So, you need to make some assumptions if you want to use fragment dialogs. This particular control heavily relies on fragment dialogs. It won't work at all if you can't get a fragment manager. So you assume that you work only in the context of an activity. Once you go with this argument, Listing 2-5 shows how to obtain a fragment manager from the view.

Listing 2-5. Getting Access to a Fragment Manager

```
Public class DurationControl...{

private FragmentManager getFragmentManager() {
     Context c = getContext();
     if (c instanceof Activity) {
         return ((Activity)c).getFragmentManager();
     }
     throw new RuntimeException("Activity context expected instead");
   }
...} //end-of-class DurationControl
```

As you design custom compound controls, you may or may not be required to use fragment dialogs. It depends on the need and nature of the compound control. In this chapter, we cover the more difficult case of using the fragment dialogs. Because this component is using fragment dialogs, we are in the predicament of assuming that the context available in the View class is an activity. You could have a compound control that doesn't invoke fragment dialogs, and you won't need to make this assumption; in that case, you don't need to make this unnecessary assumption.

Invoking Fragment Dialogs

Now that you have a way to get the fragment manager, you can invoke the fragment dialogs using the code in Listing 2-6. The onclick in Listing 2-6 will be invoked when any of the GO buttons in Figure 1-1 are touched/pressed. Based on the button pressed, you invoke the date picker fragment dialog and also pass the button ID along. This button ID allows the date picker dialog to send the button ID back to DurationControl to know which date ("from" or "to") to set.

Listing 2-6. Invoking Fragment Dialogs

```java
public class DurationControl {
...
    public void onClick(View v)
    {
        Button b = (Button)v;
        if (b.getId() == R.id.fromButton)
        {
          DialogFragment newFragment = new DatePickerFragment(this,R.id.fromButton);
          newFragment.show(getFragmentManager(), "com.androidbook.tags.datePicker");
          return;
        }

        //Otherwise - to button
        DialogFragment newFragment = new DatePickerFragment(this,R.id.toButton);
        newFragment.show(getFragmentManager(), "com.androidbook.tags.datePicker");
        return;
    }//eof-onclick
...
}//eof-class DurationControl
```

If you are following Listing 2-6, you will have noticed that we haven't showed you the code for fragment dialog DatePickerFragment. However, you will have seen that DatePickerFragment needs a fragment manager to work (see the call to the show() method in Listing 2-6). In the previous section, we showed how to obtain the fragment manager with reasonable assumptions. We now show the DatePickerFragment class.

Creating DatePickerFragment Class

Listing 2-7 shows the code for the DatePickerFragment. This custom class encapsulates the SDK-provided DatePickerDialog. It is the standard mechanism for showing dialogs in the new Android SDK (starting with Android release 3).

Listing 2-7. Source Code for DatePickerFragment

```java
public class DatePickerFragment extends DialogFragment
implements DatePickerDialog.OnDateSetListener
{
    public static String tag = "DatePickerFragment";
    private DurationControl parent;
    private int buttonId;

    public DatePickerFragment(DurationControl inParent, int inButtonId)
    {
        parent = inParent;
        buttonId = inButtonId;
        Bundle argsBundle = this.getArguments();
```

```java
        if (argsBundle == null)
        {
            argsBundle = new Bundle();
        }
        argsBundle.putInt("parentid", inParent.getId());
        argsBundle.putInt("buttonid", buttonId);
        this.setArguments(argsBundle);
    }

    //Default constructor for device rotation
    public DatePickerFragment(){}

    @Override
    public Dialog onCreateDialog(Bundle savedInstanceState)
    {
        //this.establishParent();
        // Use the current date as the default date in the picker
        final Calendar c = Calendar.getInstance();
        int year = c.get(Calendar.YEAR);
        int month = c.get(Calendar.MONTH);
        int day = c.get(Calendar.DAY_OF_MONTH);

        // Create a new instance of DatePickerDialog and return it
        return new DatePickerDialog(getActivity(), this, year, month, day);
    }

    public void onDateSet(DatePicker view, int year, int month, int day) {
    // Do something with the date chosen by the user
        parent.onDateSet(buttonId, year, month, day);
    }

    @Override
    public void onActivityCreated(Bundle savedInstanceState) {
        super.onActivityCreated(savedInstanceState);
        Log.d(tag,"DatePickerFragment onActivity created called");
        this.establishParent();
    }

    private void establishParent()    {
        if (parent != null) return;
        Log.d(tag, "establishing parent");
        int parentid = this.getArguments().getInt("parentid");
        buttonId =  this.getArguments().getInt("buttonid");
        View x = this.getActivity().findViewById(parentid);
        if (x == null)    {
            throw new RuntimeException("Sorry not able to establish parent on restart");
        }
        parent = (DurationControl)x;
    }
} //eof-class-DatePickerFragment
```

Although this is the standard approach for showing dialogs, there are a couple of things we have done to make these fragment dialogs work well for a custom compound control like ours. As we indicated in the beginning of the chapter, the device can be rotated while this fragment dialog is displayed. We need to design `DatePickerFragment` class so that it takes into account the device rotation.

Constructing the DatePickerFragment

Referencing Listing 2-8, let's take a focused look at the constructor of the `DatePickerFragment`. We have a few things to point out.

Listing 2-8. Using Bundles in a Fragment Constructor

```
public DatePickerFragment(DurationControl inParent, int inButtonId)
{
  parent = inParent;
  buttonId = inButtonId;
  Bundle argsBundle = this.getArguments();
  if (argsBundle == null)  {
    argsBundle = new Bundle();
  }
  argsBundle.putInt("parentid", inParent.getId());
  argsBundle.putInt("buttonid", buttonId);
  this.setArguments(argsBundle);
}

//Default constructor for device rotation
public DatePickerFragment(){}
```

Because `DatePickerFragment` is a dialog fragment, it needs to tell the invoker (our custom compound view, `DurationControl`) that the dialog is completed with the picking of the date. To facilitate this communication back to the `DurationControl`, we passed a reference to the `DurationControl` through a parent argument to `DatePickerFragment` during its construction.

The `DatePickerFragment` then saves this reference as a local variable. This parent reference is used later to call back the dialog fragment when the dialog is finished. We also took the button ID as an input to the constructor of `DatePickerFragment`. We will pass the button ID to the callback so that the `DurationControl` knows which date field to set.

Once we store the `DurationControl` and the button ID as local variables in the `DatePickerFragment`, we do something interesting, at least uncharacteristic (especially if you are new to Android and fragments!). We take the view ID of `DurationControl` and the button ID that was passed in, and stuff them in the argument bundle of the `DatePickerFragment`.

> **Note**   Refer to the literature on fragments, including our own Pro Android 4, on how argument bundles work for fragments in managing their state when the device rotates.

You would have also noticed in Listing 2-8 a default constructor to the fragment dialog. When does the default constructor get called? Why is this default constructor empty? What happens to all the important local variables parent and buttonid when the default constructor is called? Who sets them? We answer these questions in the next section.

Restoring the Dialog Fragment State

The default constructor for the dialog fragment in Listing 2-8 is called when the device rotates. Android removes the activity and all its fragments, and reinstantiates them. Android calls default constructors during this reinstantiation phase. It relies on a number of state-related callbacks to reinitialize these objects.

When this default constructor is called, there is an incomplete dialog fragment class: the parent reference to the DurationControl and the button ID are not filled in yet. To set these variables, you need to look for a callback on the dialog fragment class that tells you when all the views in the activity have been recreated. The callback on the fragment you are looking for is onActivityCreated(). Although a fragment has a number of callbacks during it reinitialization phase, it is this onActivityCreated() method that gurantees that all views have been created.

When a fragment is recreated, it remembers the argument bundle that you have originally set on this fragment. In the onActivityCreated callback, you will use the IDs from the argument bundle to locate the parent DurationControl by using its view ID. Listing 2-9 shows how this is done.

Listing 2-9. Reestablishing Pointers during a Fragment Rebirth

```
@Override
public void onActivityCreated(Bundle savedInstanceState) {
  super.onActivityCreated(savedInstanceState);
  this.establishParent();
}

private void establishParent()
{
  if (parent != null) return;
  //get parent view id from the arguments bundle
  int parentid = this.getArguments().getInt("parentid");
  buttonId =  this.getArguments().getInt("buttonid");

  //Look for the parent view in the activity
  View x = this.getActivity().findViewById(parentid);
  if (x == null) {
     throw new RuntimeException("Sorry not able to establish parent on restart");
  }
  //Get back our DurationControl parent
  parent = (DurationControl)x;
}
```

Calling the Parent Back

Once the date picker dialog fragment has the parent reestablished, as shown in Listing 2-9, the dialog fragment is in a good constructed state. It has access to the button ID and the parent view DurationControl. Now if a date is chosen from date picker dialog (as in Figure 2-4), the DatePickerFragment will call the onDateSet method of the parent. Here is that callback method of DurationControl as shown in Listing 2-10.

Listing 2-10. Implementing Fragment Dialog Callback in a Compound Control

```
public class DurationControl...{
...
    public void onDateSet(int buttonId, int year, int month, int day)    {
        Calendar c = getDate(year,month,day);
        if (buttonId == R.id.fromButton) {
            setFromDate(c);
            return;
        }
        setToDate(c);
    }
    private void setFromDate(Calendar c)    {
        if (c == null) return;
        this.fromDate = c;
        TextView tc = (TextView)findViewById(R.id.fromDate);
        tc.setText(getDateString(c));
    }
    private void setToDate(Calendar c)    {
        if (c == null) return;
        this.toDate = c;
        TextView tc = (TextView)findViewById(R.id.toDate);
        tc.setText(getDateString(c));
    }
    private Calendar getDate(int year, int month, int day)    {
        Calendar c = Calendar.getInstance();
        c.set(year,month,day);
        return c;
    }
    public static String getDateString(Calendar c)    {
        if(c == null) return "null";
        SimpleDateFormat df = new SimpleDateFormat("MM/dd/yyyy");
        df.setLenient(false);
        String s = df.format(c.getTime());
        return s;
    }
...more
}//eof-class-DurationControl
```

This key callback method onDateSet of the DurationControl is highlighted in Listing 2-10. Now you can see why we have taken the effort of passing the button ID to the dialog fragment. In this onDateSet callback method, we interrogate to see whether the button that invoked the fragment dialog is a "from" date button or a "to" date button. In Listing 2-10, also see how we then locate the text view belonging to the corresponding date control and set its text.

This concludes the intricacies involved in using fragment-based dialogs in compound controls. To summarize, (a) you have to get a fragment manager, (b) you have to pass callback objects to the fragment dialogs, (c) you have to use argument bundles to save state, and (d) you have to use onActivityCreated to reestablish callback pointers. With that finished, we turn to the next topic in compound controls: managing view state.

Managing the View State for a Compound Control

We covered view state management in detail in Chapter 1 when we talked about custom views. Managing view state for a compound control is similar, but there are some differences.

If you use a compound control like our DurationControl multiple times in an activity, then the IDs for the text views and the button views will get repeated. This will not work for managing their own view state based on the protocol laid out by Android's view class, which requires a unique view ID in the context of a given activity.

To overcome this, you use a compound control to block its children from managing their view state and instead manage their state for them. To understand this approach to view state management, you need to understand four base class methods from the ViewGroup class. These are shown in Listing 2-11.

Listing 2-11. Relevent APIs for ViewGroup View State Management

```
dispatchSaveInstanceState
dispatchFreezeSelfOnly
dispatchRestoreInstanceState
dispatchThawSelfOnly
```

A ViewGroup uses dispatchSaveInstanceState to first save its own state by calling super (view's) dispatchSaveInstanceState, which in turn triggers onSaveInstanceState on itself and then calls the dispatchSaveInstanceState for each of its children. If the children are plain views and not ViewGroups, this will result in having their onSaveInstanceState called. Listing 2-12 presents the pseudo code for how these key methods are meshed together.

Listing 2-12. Psuedo Code for How Dispatch Save Instances Work

```
ViewGroup.dispatchSaveInstanceState() {
        View.dispatchSaveInstanceState()
           ...ends up calling its own ViewGroup.onSaveInstanceState()
        Children.dispatchSaveInstanceState()
           ...ends up calling children's onSaveInstanceState()
}

View.dispatchSaveInstanceState() {
        onSaveInstanceState()
}

ViewGroup.dispatchFreezeSelfOnly() {
        View.dispatchSaveInstanceState()
           ...ends up calling ViewGroup.onSaveInstanceState()
}
```

Notice the wrinkle here with the dispatchFreezeSelfOnly. This method on the ViewGroup simply invokes the semantics of saving state for itself as it ends up calling the onSaveInstanceState of the current view group. The same thing happens during the restore phase with equivalent methods.

Knowing this, albeit intricate, protocol, you can override proper methods of the ViewGroup as shown in Listing 2-13 to suppress the state saving of the child views and implement the state management in the view group itself.

Listing 2-13. Overriding dispatchSaveInstanceState for a Compound Control

```
@Override
protected void dispatchSaveInstanceState(SparseArray<Parcelable> container)
{
  //Don't call this so that children won't be explicitly saved
  //super.dispatchSaveInstanceState(container);
  //Call your self onsavedinstancestate
  super.dispatchFreezeSelfOnly(container);
}
```

When you do this, you are calling onSaveInstanceState on your self but not on your children. You do the same for dispatchRestoreInstanceState, as shown in Listing 2-14.

Listing 2-14. Overriding dispatchRestorInstanceState for a Compound Control

```
@Override
protected void dispatchRestoreInstanceState(
    SparseArray<Parcelable> container)
{
  //Don't call this so that children won't be explicitly saved
  //super.dispatchRestoreInstanceState(container);
  super.dispatchThawSelfOnly(container);
}
```

By overriding these two methods (Listings 2-13 and 2-14), you have supperessed the child state management. We now show you the code for onSaveInstanceState and onRestoreInstanceState on our DurationControl, which is responsible for managing the state of its four children: the two text views and the two buttons. Of course, the buttons don't have a state, but the two text views do. Before showing you the code for onSaveInstanceState and onRestoreInstanceState, however, we show you how this DurationControl implements its own SavedState class, which is required for these two methods. (Refer to Chapter 1 for this type of BaseSavedState pattern of saving state.)

Implementing the SavedState Class for DurationControl

Listing 2-15 shows the SavedState class that holds the state for DurationControl and its children. It follows the same pattern as laid out in the "BaseSavedState Pattern" section of Chapter 1. The two variables we are interested in saving are the two dates: the "from" date and the "to" date.

Listing 2-15. SavedState Class Implementation for the Custom DurationControl

```java
public static class SavedState extends BaseSavedState {
    //null values are allowed
    private Calendar fromDate;
    private Calendar toDate;

    SavedState(Parcelable superState) {
        super(superState);
    }
    SavedState(Parcelable superState, Calendar inFromDate, Calendar inToDate) {
        super(superState);
        fromDate = inFromDate;
        toDate = inToDate;
    }
    @Override
    public void writeToParcel(Parcel out, int flags) {
        super.writeToParcel(out, flags);

        if (fromDate != null) {
            out.writeLong(fromDate.getTimeInMillis());
        }
        else {
            out.writeLong(-1L);
        }
        if (fromDate != null) {
            out.writeLong(toDate.getTimeInMillis());
        }
        else {
            out.writeLong(-1L);
        }
    }

    @Override
    public String toString() {
        StringBuffer sb  = new StringBuffer("fromDate:"
                    + DurationControl.getDateString(fromDate));
        sb.append("fromDate:" + DurationControl.getDateString(toDate));
        return sb.toString();
    }

    @SuppressWarnings("hiding")
    public static final Parcelable.Creator<SavedState> CREATOR
            = new Parcelable.Creator<SavedState>() {
        public SavedState createFromParcel(Parcel in) {
            return new SavedState(in);
        }
        public SavedState[] newArray(int size) {
            return new SavedState[size];
        }
    };
```

```
//Read back the values
private SavedState(Parcel in) {
    super(in);

    //Read the from date
    long lFromDate = in.readLong();
    if (lFromDate == -1) {
        fromDate = null;
    }
    else {
        fromDate = Calendar.getInstance();
        fromDate.setTimeInMillis(lFromDate);
    }
    //Read the from date
    long lToDate = in.readLong();
    if (lFromDate == -1) {
        toDate = null;
    }
    else {
        toDate = Calendar.getInstance();
        toDate.setTimeInMillis(lToDate);
    }
}
}//eof-state-class
```

We represent the two dates that need to be saved and restored as Java calendar objects. When we store them in the parcelable, we store them as longs (milliseconds) and retrieve them as longs and convert them back to calendar objects. Other than doing that, this code Listing 2-15 is super-similar to what was given in Chapter 1. Let us see now how to use this SavedState class to restore the child text views.

Implementing Save and Restore State on Behalf of Child Views

Listing 2-16 shows the implementation of save and restore methods for our DurationControl, using the SavedState class designed in Listing 2-15. You retrieve dates from the SavedState parcelable and use the set methods to set the value of the text views. The dates are available on the SavedState class (Listing 2-15) as public variables. The methods to set the dates on DurationControl are available in the DurationControl class. We haven't shown you these two setdate methods yet, but we include them in the entire source code for the DurationControl presented toward the end of the chapter (Listing 2-19). The methods onRestoreInstanceState and onSaveInstatanceState in Listing 2-16 are also on the DurationControl class. These two state methods are originally defined on the base ViewGroup class, and in Listing 2-16 you are overriding those methods in the DurationControl class. You could also see these methods in their full context in Listing 2-19.

Listing 2-16. Using SavedState to Manage Child View State

```
@Override
protected void onRestoreInstanceState(Parcelable state) {
  if (!(state instanceof SavedState)) {
      super.onRestoreInstanceState(state);
      return;
  }
  //it is our state
  SavedState ss = (SavedState)state;
  //Peel it and give the child to the super class
  super.onRestoreInstanceState(ss.getSuperState());
  this.setFromDate(ss.fromDate);
  this.setToDate(ss.toDate);
}

@Override
protected Parcelable onSaveInstanceState() {
   Parcelable superState = super.onSaveInstanceState();
   SavedState ss = new SavedState(superState);
   ss.fromDate = this.fromDate;
   ss.toDate = this.toDate;
   //Or you can do this
   //SavedState ss = new SavedState(superState,fromDate,toDate);
   return ss;
}
```

This brings us to the last topic in creating custom compound controls: defining and using custom attributes. We cover that now.

Creating Custom Attributes for DurationControl

Defining and using custom attributes is identical to what we have presented in Chapter 1 for a custom view. Listing 2-17 shows the single custom attribute we have defined for this class.

Listing 2-17. attrs.xml for DurationControl

```
<resources>
<declare-styleable name="DurationComponent">
    <attr name="durationUnits">
      <enum name="days" value="1"/>
      <enum name="weeks" value="2"/>
    </attr>
</declare-styleable>
</resources>
```

The custom attribute durationUnits indicates whether you want the custom control to return duration in days or weeks. (We agree; it is a lame custom attribute, but we just wanted to show you how this is done and you have an example to follow for coding your own custom attributes.)

Once you have the custom attribute defined, Listing 2-18 shows how you read this attribute in the constructor of the DurationControl.

Listing 2-18. Initializing DurationControl with Custom Attributes

```
public DurationControl(Context context) {
  super(context);
  initialize(context);
}

public DurationControl(Context context, AttributeSet attrs, int defStyle) {
    super(context, attrs, defStyle);
    TypedArray t = context.obtainStyledAttributes(attrs,
                            R.styleable.DurationComponent,0,0);
    durationUnits = t.getInt(
        R.styleable.DurationComponent_durationUnits, durationUnits);
    t.recycle();
    initialize(context);
}

public DurationControl(Context context, AttributeSet attrs) {
  this(context, attrs,0);
}

private void initialize(Context context)  {
  LayoutInflater lif = (LayoutInflater)
    context.getSystemService(Context.LAYOUT_INFLATER_SERVICE);
    lif.inflate(R.layout.duration_view_layout, this);
    Button b = (Button)this.findViewById(R.id.fromButton);
    b.setOnClickListener(this);
    b = (Button)this.findViewById(R.id.toButton);
    b.setOnClickListener(this);
    this.setSaveEnabled(true);
}
```

That concludes our presentation of the details for creating custom compound controls. See the section "Implementation Detail of DurationControl" later in this chapter for all the source necessary to implement DurationControl in one place.

Extending an Existing View

What we have covered so far and what we have covered in Chapter 1 forms an excellent foundation for creating a custom view or extending an existing view. Also, in this chapter, we showed how to extend layout views. However, we haven't shown how to extend simpler pre-existing views like a TextView. Knowing what you do now, this should be a walk in the park. The steps to extend an existing view like a TextView would be as follows:

1. Extend from TextView. TextView will take care of measuring, drawing, etc.

2. In the constructor, read any custom attributes you may have defined in attrs.xml.

3. Implement any view state that you want to manage yourself in addition to TextView or just delegate that to the TextView.

We will leave this effort for you as an exercise to test your mastery of the topic.

Implementation Detail of DurationControl

If you are confidant with everything we have covered so far in this chapter, you can tie up the loose ends yourself, and you don't need to read this section where we show you all the relevant code files in one place. Some of these files have already been presented in their entirety; for these files, we simply refer back to their earlier listings. For some files, we have reproduced them below so that the entire source codes for these files are in one place. We start the source code of the primary class DurationControl.java.

DurationControl.java

The class DurationControl presented in Listing 2-19 carries the lion's share of the burden of implementation.

Listing 2-19. DurationControl.java

```java
public class DurationControl extends LinearLayout
implements    android.view.View.OnClickListener
{
    private static final String tag = "DurationControl";
    private Calendar fromDate = null;
    private Calendar toDate = null;

    // 1: days, 2: weeks
    private static int ENUM_DAYS = 1;
    private static int ENUM_WEEKS = 1;
    private int durationUnits = 1;

    // public interface
    public long getDuration() {
        if (validate() == false)
            return -1;
        long fromMillis = fromDate.getTimeInMillis();
        long toMillis = toDate.getTimeInMillis();
        long diff = toMillis - fromMillis;
        long day = 24 * 60 * 60 * 1000;
        long diffInDays = diff / day;
        long diffInWeeks = diff / (day * 7);
        if (durationUnits == ENUM_WEEKS) {
            return diffInDays;
        }
        return diffInWeeks;
    }

    public boolean validate() {
        if (fromDate == null || toDate == null) {
            return false;
        }
```

```java
        if (toDate.after(fromDate)) {
            return true;
        }
        return false;
    }

    public DurationControl(Context context) {
        super(context);
        initialize(context);
    }

    public DurationControl(Context context, AttributeSet attrs, int defStyle) {
        super(context, attrs, defStyle);
        TypedArray t = context.obtainStyledAttributes(attrs,
                R.styleable.DurationComponent, 0, 0);
        durationUnits = t.getInt(R.styleable.DurationComponent_durationUnits,
                durationUnits);
        t.recycle();
        initialize(context);
    }

    public DurationControl(Context context, AttributeSet attrs) {
        this(context, attrs, 0);
    }

    private void initialize(Context context) {
        LayoutInflater lif = (LayoutInflater) context
                .getSystemService(Context.LAYOUT_INFLATER_SERVICE);
        lif.inflate(R.layout.duration_view_layout, this);
        Button b = (Button) this.findViewById(R.id.fromButton);
        b.setOnClickListener(this);
        b = (Button) this.findViewById(R.id.toButton);
        b.setOnClickListener(this);
        this.setSaveEnabled(true);
    }

    private FragmentManager getFragmentManager() {
        Context c = getContext();
        if (c instanceof Activity) {
            return ((Activity) c).getFragmentManager();
        }
        throw new RuntimeException("Activity context expected instead");
    }
    public void onClick(View v) {
        Button b = (Button) v;
        if (b.getId() == R.id.fromButton) {
            DialogFragment newFragment = new DatePickerFragment(this,
                    R.id.fromButton);
            newFragment.show(getFragmentManager(),
                    "com.androidbook.tags.datePicker");
            return;
        }
```

```
        // Otherwise
        DialogFragment newFragment = new DatePickerFragment(this, R.id.toButton);
        newFragment.show(getFragmentManager(),
                "com.androidbook.tags.datePicker");
        return;
    }// eof-onclick

    public void onDateSet(int buttonId, int year, int month, int day) {
        Calendar c = getDate(year, month, day);
        if (buttonId == R.id.fromButton) {
            setFromDate(c);
            return;
        }
        setToDate(c);
    }

    private void setFromDate(Calendar c) {
        if (c == null)
            return;
        this.fromDate = c;
        TextView tc = (TextView) findViewById(R.id.fromDate);
        tc.setText(getDateString(c));
    }

    private void setToDate(Calendar c) {
        if (c == null)
            return;
        this.toDate = c;
        TextView tc = (TextView) findViewById(R.id.toDate);
        tc.setText(getDateString(c));
    }

    private Calendar getDate(int year, int month, int day) {
        Calendar c = Calendar.getInstance();
        c.set(year, month, day);
        return c;
    }

    public static String getDateString(Calendar c) {
        if (c == null)
            return "null";
        SimpleDateFormat df = new SimpleDateFormat("MM/dd/yyyy");
        df.setLenient(false);
        String s = df.format(c.getTime());
        return s;
    }

    @Override
    protected void dispatchSaveInstanceState(SparseArray<Parcelable> container) {
        // Don't call this so that children won't be explicitly saved
        // super.dispatchSaveInstanceState(container);
        // Call your self onsavedinstancestate
```

```java
        super.dispatchFreezeSelfOnly(container);
        Log.d(tag, "in dispatchSaveInstanceState");
}


@Override
protected void dispatchRestoreInstanceState(
        SparseArray<Parcelable> container) {
    // Don't call this so that children won't be explicitly saved
    // .super.dispatchRestoreInstanceState(container);
    super.dispatchThawSelfOnly(container);
    Log.d(tag, "in dispatchRestoreInstanceState");
}


@Override
protected void onRestoreInstanceState(Parcelable state) {
    Log.d(tag, "in onRestoreInstanceState");
    if (!(state instanceof SavedState)) {
        super.onRestoreInstanceState(state);
        return;
    }
    // it is our state
    SavedState ss = (SavedState) state;
    // Peel it and give the child to the super class
    super.onRestoreInstanceState(ss.getSuperState());
    // this.fromDate = ss.fromDate;
    // this.toDate= ss.toDate;
    this.setFromDate(ss.fromDate);
    this.setToDate(ss.toDate);
}


@Override
protected Parcelable onSaveInstanceState() {
    Log.d(tag, "in onSaveInstanceState");
    Parcelable superState = super.onSaveInstanceState();
    SavedState ss = new SavedState(superState);
    ss.fromDate = this.fromDate;
    ss.toDate = this.toDate;
    return ss;
}


/*
 * ************************************************************
 * Saved State inner static class
 * ************************************************************
 */
public static class SavedState extends BaseSavedState {
    //null values are allowed
    private Calendar fromDate;
    private Calendar toDate;
```

```java
SavedState(Parcelable superState) {
    super(superState);
}

@Override
public void writeToParcel(Parcel out, int flags) {
    super.writeToParcel(out, flags);

    if (fromDate != null) {
        out.writeLong(fromDate.getTimeInMillis());
    } else {
        out.writeLong(-1L);
    }
    if (fromDate != null) {
        out.writeLong(toDate.getTimeInMillis());
    } else {
        out.writeLong(-1L);
    }
}

@Override
public String toString() {
    StringBuffer sb = new StringBuffer("fromDate:"
            + DurationControl.getDateString(fromDate));
    sb.append("fromDate:" + DurationControl.getDateString(toDate));
    return sb.toString();
}

@SuppressWarnings("hiding")
public static final Parcelable.Creator<SavedState> CREATOR
    = new Parcelable.Creator<SavedState>() {
    public SavedState createFromParcel(Parcel in) {
        return new SavedState(in);
    }

    public SavedState[] newArray(int size) {
        return new SavedState[size];
    }
};

// Read back the values
private SavedState(Parcel in) {
    super(in);

    // Read the from date
    long lFromDate = in.readLong();
    if (lFromDate == -1) {
        fromDate = null;
    } else {
        fromDate = Calendar.getInstance();
        fromDate.setTimeInMillis(lFromDate);
    }
```

```
            // Read the from date
            long lToDate = in.readLong();
            if (lFromDate == -1) {
                toDate = null;
            } else {
                toDate = Calendar.getInstance();
                toDate.setTimeInMillis(lToDate);
            }
        }
    }// eof-state-class
}// eof-class
```

We have discussed and debated all aspects of this code earlier in this chapter. We did, however, add a new method to this code called validate(). This allows the activity to see if all the views in that activity are in a good state. It is something you can architect on your own, but is laid out here as a suggestion.

/layout/duration_view_layout.xml

This is the custom layout file for the control DurationControl to go with the code in Listing 2-19. A custom layout file, this is loaded in the constructor of Listing 2-19. The full layout XML file is already given in Listing 2-2.

DatePickerFragment.java

This is the dialog fragment class that we used to show the date picker dialog. The source for this class is shown in Listing 2-7.

Main Activity XML file

This is the file where we placed the DurationControl in a linear activity layout. This file is given in Listing 2-4.

/values/attrs.xml

This is where we defined custom attributes. This file is given in Listing 2-17.

We have also included a link that will enable you to download the entire project, which you can use to build in eclipse in the References.

References

Most of the sources cited in Chapter 1's References are valid for this chapter as well. So, we list here only references that are unique to this chapter.

- Our research log on compound components: `http://androidbook.com/item/4338`.

- Complete code snippets for this chapter: `http://androidbook.com/item/4341`.

- Android SDK documentation on custom components including compound components: `http://developer.android.com/guide/topics/ui/custom-components.html`.

- An excellent and succinct article on saving state from Charles Harley: `http://www.charlesharley.com/2012/programming/views-saving-instance-state-in-android/`.

- Download the test project dedicated for this chapter at `www.androidbook.com/expertandroid/projects`. The name of the ZIP file is `ExpertAndroid_Ch02_CompoundControls.zip`.

Summary

In this chapter, we covered how to create compound components by aggregating existing components. We showed how to extend an existing view group like linear layout to have custom children and how it can be dedicated to a specific behavior. We showed how to integrate this approach with fragment dialogs. Importantly, we showed how to restore callback pointers for fragment dialogs. We also showed the subtle differences in view state management for compound controls.

Review Questions

The following questions should help consolidate what you have learned in this chapter.

1. What classes do you extend to create compound controls?

2. What is `merge` node in XML layouts?

3. How do you load layout XML files in the constructor of a compound control?

4. How do you use fragment dialogs from custom compound controls?

5. How do you reestablish callback views for fragment dialogs?

6. How do you manage state for a custom compound control?

7. What is `dispatchFreezeSelfOnly` and why do you care?

8. How do you define and use custom attributes for a compound control?

Chapter 3

Principles and Practice of Custom Layouts

In the previous two chapters, we covered how to create and work with custom views and compound controls. We are now on the third leg of this view-customization journey: creating and working with custom layouts. The material in these first three chapters is clearly related. This material relies on the same fundamental architecture of views that is covered in Chapter 1. However, each chapter conveys a different aspect of the view architecture.

Contrasting Custom Layouts

Let us take a moment to compare and contrast the three approaches to customizing controls in the Android UI framework: custom views, compound controls, and custom layouts. This comparison will help us to focus on the material that is special for custom layouts: extending from ViewGroup, measuring child views, and laying out child views.

Custom Views

When we are designing custom views, the primary focus is onMeasure() and onDraw(). A custom view has no children. So methods like onLayout() won't apply, as onLayout() is meant for children. The base layout() method of the view takes care of this. Also, onMeasure() is quite simple, as you are dealing with just one view. Your focus primarily shifts to onDraw() and how you use the canvas.

Of course, the way you define and read custom attributes is very similar in all three approaches. Because custom views have no children, layout parameters do not play a role in custom views but do play a significant role in custom layouts. In custom views, we also worry about saving the state of the view using the BaseSavedState pattern. In summary, when you are customizing a view, you have to worry about the following items:

- Extending the View
- Overriding onMeasure()
- Overriding onDraw()
- Saving state using the BaseSavedState pattern
- Working with custom attributes
- Understanding and applying requestLayout and invalidate

In contrast, you can ignore the following details when creating custom views:

- Overriding onLayout()
- Implementating and using LayoutParams

Compound Controls

In regard to compound controls, the primary focus is on how to use existing layouts like linear layout and relative layout to compose a consolidated component with a specific behavior.

Because we are using an existing layout, we don't need to measure, layout, or draw. Our primary focus in compound controls is on saving the view state using the BaseSavedState pattern for the compound control itself and its children. Of course, we could use custom attributes as well. So for compound controls, you need to worry about:

- Extend an existing layout
- Saving state using the BaseSavedState pattern
- Taking control of saving state for its child views
- Working with custom attributes

While you can ignore:

- Overriding onMeasure()
- Overriding onDraw()
- Overriding onLayout()
- Worrying about requestLayout() and invalidate()
- Implementing and using LayoutParams

Custom Layouts

Now you can contrast the above two approaches with the following steps required to implement custom layouts (the third approach):

1. Inherit from ViewGroup
2. Override onMeasure()
3. Override onLayout()
4. Implement custom LayoutParams with any additional layout attributes
5. Override layout parameters construction methods in the custom layout class

We explain each of these steps, along with providing an annotated sample code. First, we present the custom layout we are planning to write, as an example to illustrate all of the indicated steps.

Planning a Simple Flow Layout

To document the creation of a custom layout like a linear layout, we use flow layout as an example. To demonstrate flow layout, we take a set of buttons and lay them out horizontally, then wrap them around to the next line when we run out of space horizontally. Figure 3-1 shows the flow layout we are going to design, laid out in an activity.

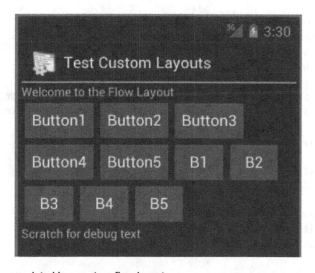

Figure 3-1. *A set of buttons encapsulated in a custom flow layout*

In Figure 3-1, the whole activity is in a linear layout. The flow layout is in the middle, between the text view that says "Welcome to the Flow Layout," and the text view at the bottom says "Scratch for debug text." You can see that the flow layout has taken a number of buttons of varying sizes and wrapped them around.

By the end of this chapter, you will have a clear idea of how to do this really well, and also will have the foundation for writing your own custom layouts. Custom layouts are a bit tricky, but they are practical for simplifying UI designs. Our intention here is to empower you with all you need to approach custom layouts with confidence.

Now that you have a mental picture of the FlowLayout, we get started exploring each of the steps required to implement it.

Deriving from the ViewGroup Class

Just as in the built-in LinearLayout, FlowLayout extends the ViewGroup. Listing 3-1 shows how FlowLayout extends a ViewGroup. This listing also shows a) how the FlowLayout uses constructors to read its specific custom attributes and b) initializes the super class ViewGroup appropriately.

Listing 3-1. FlowLayout Extending from a ViewGroup

```
public class FlowLayout
extends ViewGroup
{
    private int hspace=10;
    private int vspace=10;
    public FlowLayout(Context context) {
        super(context);
        initialize(context);
    }
    public FlowLayout(Context context, AttributeSet attrs, int defStyle) {
        super(context, attrs, defStyle);
        TypedArray t = context.obtainStyledAttributes(attrs,
                    R.styleable.FlowLayout, 0, 0);
        hspace = t.getDimensionPixelSize(R.styleable.FlowLayout_hspace, hspace);
        vspace = t.getDimensionPixelSize(R.styleable.FlowLayout_vspace, vspace);
        t.recycle();
        initialize(context);
    }
    public FlowLayout(Context context, AttributeSet attrs) {
        this(context, attrs, 0);
    }
    private void initialize(Context context) {
        //Do any common initializations you may have
        //It is empty in our implementation
    }
```

This code in Listing 3-1 is quite like any other extension of custom views as discussed in Chapters 1 and 2: extend a base class (View, or an existing layout like a LinearLayout, or here the ViewGroup). In all cases, you can have custom attributes; we define the custom attributes in attrs.xml and read them in constructors. In case of FlowLayout, the custom attributes are "hspace" (horizontal spacing) and "vspace" (vertical spacing) for child views and new lines as we wrap the child views. Let's look now at the attrs.xml that goes with the constructor code in Listing 3-1.

Defining custom attributes in Attrs.xml for the FlowLayout

Listing 3-2 shows the `attrs.xml` for our custom `FlowLayout`. This file needs to be in the "/res/values" subdirectory.

Listing 3-2. Defining Custom Attributes for FlowLayout

```
<resources>
<declare-styleable name="FlowLayout">
    <attr name="hspace" format="dimension"/>
    <attr name="vspace" format="dimension" />
</declare-styleable>
<declare-styleable name="FlowLayout_Layout">
    <attr name="layout_space" format="dimension"/>
</declare-styleable>
</resources>
```

The styleable `FlowLayout` in Listing 3-2 defines two custom attributes: `hspace` and `vspace`. The styleable `FlowLayout_Layout` custom attributes are defined for the `LayoutParams` object that needs to be defined by the `FlowLayout` as an inner class. (We cover this shortly.) These later custom layout parameters are stored in each child view on behalf of the parent layout class, like the `FlowLayout`, to allow the children to override any parent attributes when necessary.

By convention, we call styleables that belong to the main layout by the name of the layout—in this case, "FlowLayout." Also by convention, we call the styleables that belong to the `LayoutParams` with the layout name followed by "`layout`." In Listing 3-2, this name is "FlowLayout_layout."

You will see later in the chapter how both types of attributes are given values in layout files (future Listing 3-8). You have already seen in Listing 3-1 how `FlowLayout` styleables are read. Later you will see how to read the `FlowLayout_layout` styleables (future Listing 3-5).

Working with onMeasure()

Here are the key aspects of `onMeasure()`when you are working with a custom layout such as `FlowLayout`.

When you are extending a `ViewGroup`, you need to measure the children first and add those measures to return as the measurement of the `ViewGroup`. In Chapter 1, we said that a view has a method called "measure()" that is intended to be called by the parents of views as part of the parents' `onMeasure()`. In the case of `FlowLayout`, `FlowLayout` is the parent. The buttons in Figure 3-1 are the child views. So the `FlowLayout` needs to call each of the child `Button` control's `measure()` method in its `onMeasure()`.

There is a catch, however. You will be eager to use `child.measure()`. But don't. You need instead to use `ViewGroup.measureChild()`, and then add those measures to get your total size. This is because the `measureChild()` is a smart method that takes into account the measure spec of the `ViewGroup` (AT_MOST, UNSPECIFIED, EXACT) and properly asks the children with a different measure spec, if required. If you call `child.measure()`, then you have to do this logic yourself. We have included at the end of this chapter the source code `ViewGroup.measureChild()` to help you understand this. (We thought including that lengthy code here would distract you from the main focus of this section.)

Once you have the total size of FlowLayout, which is the sum of all its children, you call the prefabricated method resolveSize() to figure out the final measured size of the flow layout. Let us explain resolveSize() a bit further. Let's say you have lot of children. The total measured size of the children could exceed the suggested size for the flow layout by the parent of the flow layout. When the measure spec of the flow layout is UNSPECIFIED, it is okay to return the larger size. But if the measure spec is AT_MOST, then you need to return the suggested size and not exceed it. The measure spec may also say EXACT. In this case also, you cannot exceed the suggested exact size. All this logic is addressed by the built-in method resolveSize(). This resolveSize() takes into account the measure spec variation and clips the possibly larger measured size to the appropriate size that is in line with the size specified in the measure spec of onMeasure().

Once this measure pass is completed, you need to override onLayout() where you need to position the child views. This exercise is identical to measuring because you need to know the size of each view so that you can place the views one after the other, allowing enough space between each view both vertically and horizontally. So why measure twice? If you can also remember the origin of each child during the measure pass, then you can just use that origin and the dimension of each view in onLayout(). To store the origin of each view, you can use the layout parameters object, which is held with each view on behalf of the parent FlowLayout.

That concludes the theory of how onMeasure() should be implemented for FLowLayout. Before we jump into the implementation of onMeasure(), we want to present a pictorial representation (Figure 3-2) of the suggested size, measured size of the flow layout, and measured size of the children and how they related to each other. We also explain the measuring algorithm, using Figure 3-2.

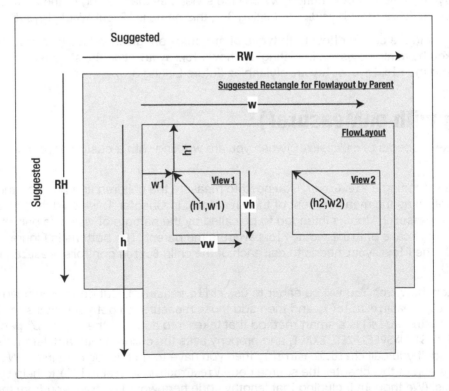

Figure 3-2. Measuring a compound control: DurationControl

Let's take a quick tour of Figure 3-2. The values RW and RH stand for "real width" and "real height." This is the suggested width and height from the parent of the FlowLayout. We receive these values from the measurespec passed to the onMeasure() method. Of course, RH and RW are valid only for AT_MOST and EXACT. In case of UNSPECIFIED, a child like FlowLayout can return its maximum with no heed to the passed-in size.

At the next level, w and h are the measured width and height of the FlowLayout, determined by combining the measured width (vw = view width) and the measured height (vh = view height) of the child views.As we go through each of the child views of FlowLayout, we will increment h and w accordingly.

In the logic, we rely on the origins of the child views. In Figure 3-2, we used the point (h1,w1) as the origin point for the current view. We then calculate the origin point of the next view by calculating (h2,w2). As we calculate this (h2,w2), we take into account how much space is available horizontally and vertically. Once we measure the current view at hand and record its origin, we move to the next view and set (h2,w2) back to (h1,w1) as the new origin, and repeat this process until we exhaust all the views. (See Listing 3-3 for actual source code that performs this logic.)

In Figure 3-2, it is not difficult to see, as we go through each view, when to increment w and when to increment h (the currently needed total width and height). The width is incremented as we go to the right; height is incremented when we detect a new line. A new line is when the current origin width (w1) is added to the current child width (VW), and together they exceed the available real width (RW).

Given this pictorial representation of the logic (Figure 3-2), Listing 3-3 shows how we have implemented the onMeasure() for FlowLayout.

Listing 3-3. Implementing onMeasure()

```
//This is very basic
//doesn't take into account padding
//You can easily modify it to account for padding
@Override
protected void onMeasure(int widthMeasureSpec, int heightMeasureSpec)
{
  //********************
  //Initialize
  //********************
  int rw = MeasureSpec.getSize(widthMeasureSpec);
  int rh = MeasureSpec.getSize(heightMeasureSpec);
  int h = 0; //current height
  int w = 0; //current width
  int h1 = 0, w1=0; //Current point to hook the child to

  //********************
  //Loop through children
  //********************
  int numOfChildren = this.getChildCount();
  for (int i=0; i < numOfChildren; i++ )
  {
    //********************
    //Front of the loop
    //********************
```

```java
    View child = this.getChildAt(i);
    this.measureChild(child,widthMeasureSpec, heightMeasureSpec);
    int vw = child.getMeasuredWidth();
    int vh = child.getMeasuredHeight();

    if (w1 + vw > rw)
    {
        //new line: max of current width and current width position
        //when multiple lines are in play w could be maxed out
        //or in uneven sizes is the max of the right side lines
        //all lines don't have to have the same width
        //some may be larger than others
        w = Math.max(w,w1);
        //reposition the point on the next line
        w1 = 0; //start of the line
        h1 = h1 + vh; //add view height to the current heigh
    }
    //*******************
    //Middle of the loop
    //*******************
    int w2 = 0, h2 = 0; //new point for the next view
    w2 = w1 + vw;
    h2 = h1;
    //latest height: current point + height of the view
    //however if the previous height is larger use that one
    h = Math.max(h,h1 + vh);

    //*******************
    //Save the current origin coords for the view
    //in its layout
    //*******************
    LayoutParams lp = (LayoutParams)child.getLayoutParams();
    lp.x = w1;
    lp.y = h1;

    //*******************
    //Restart the loop
    //*******************
    w1=w2;
    h1=h2;
}
//*******************
//End of for
//*******************
w = Math.max(w1,w);
//h = h;
setMeasuredDimension(
        resolveSize(w, widthMeasureSpec),
        resolveSize(h,heightMeasureSpec));
};
```

As we have indicated in the explanation of onMeasure(), the points (h1,w1) represent the origin for each child view. To assist the layout phase, the onMeasure() code in Listing 3-3 deposits this origin in the layout parameters object held by that child view. Every child view of a ViewGroup is guaranteed to have a LayoutParams object. A custom layout like the FlowLayout can specialize this base LayoutParms object to have additional parameters like the origin, in this case. In Listing 3-3, we retrieve this layout parameters object LayoutParams and set the origin for that view. We have highlighted the code in Listing 3-3 to show the setting of this view origin.

Also, to keep the logic in Listing 3-3 obvious and focused, we haven't used the spacing layout parameters that we have defined in attrs.xml of Listing 3-2. But you could read this spacing parameter using the code below by placing it anywhere in the onMeasure() method of Listing 3-2. See Listing 3-5 for the FlowLayout.LayoutParams inner class definition.

```
LayoutParams lp = (LayoutParams)child.getLayoutParams();
int spacing = lp.spacing;
//Adjust your widths based on this spacing.
```

Before we move on to describing onLayout(), let's summarize a few facts about onMeasure():

1. Each child is measured independently of its siblings in a view group.

2. You have to alter the measurespec passed to the FlowLayout before measuring the children. This is evident when you consider EXACT coming into FlowLayout becomes AT_MOST when applied to children; otherwise, each child will take all the space given to the FlowLayout. This alteration is done by the ViewGroup.measureChild(). So unless you have a reason not to, you should call this method to measure children.

3. It is perfectly okay to add all the children's measurements. No need to worry about the total size being too large (exceeding the suggested height or width) because the resolveSize() will clip the final reported size for the FlowLayout.

4. FlowLayout is not playing favorites and distributing the available space by itself. It relies on well-behaved children to claim space on a first come, first served basis. It is possible that a misbehaving view could take most of the space!

5. A layout like FlowLayout first forms a full picture of all its children in a best-case scenario, and could be larger than what is suggested. It is the resolveSize() that cuts its size down as appropriate. So when you are envisioning your layout, imagine its full picture and not a constrained one by the input size.

Now let's talk about onLayout.

Implementing onLayout()

In Chapter 1, we covered the measure pass and layout pass. A measure pass is used to measure children. It does not concern itself with the placement of each child. Rather, this is done in the layout pass. Layout pass is defined in the onLayout() method.

In the case of our FlowLayout's onMeasure() we have stored the layout origins for each view, the implementation of onLayout() becomes really simple. Go through each child and retrieve its LayoutParams object. From that object, get the x and y positions. Use these x and y positions and the measured width and height of the children, and call layout() on the children. This is what you see in Listing 3-4.

Listing 3-4. Implementing onLayout()

```
@Override
protected void onLayout(boolean arg0, int arg1, int arg2, int arg3, int arg4)
{
  //Call layout() on children
  int numOfChildren = this.getChildCount();
  for (int i=0; i < numOfChildren; i++ )
  {
    View child = this.getChildAt(i);
    LayoutParams lp = (LayoutParams)child.getLayoutParams();
    child.layout(lp.x,
          lp.y,
          lp.x + child.getMeasuredWidth(),
          lp.y + child.getMeasuredHeight());
  }
}
```

Defining Custom LayoutParams

As we have indicated, LayoutParams is an object holding a number of parameters that are specific to a layout like FlowLayout. The reason they are separate from other local variables of FlowLayout is that these LayoutParams are created and held by child views. However, it is FlowLayout that defines what these are, how to read them, and how to interpret them.

Listing 3-5 shows how we define layout parameters for our class FlowLayout. The LayoutParams class defines a variable called spacing to indicate how much a view wants to be spaced compare to its sibling views. This is similar to the "hspace" in Listing 3-1. The difference is this: hspace defines spacing for all views, whereas spacing in the LayoutParams is specific to each view. So spacing in Listing 3-5 has an opportunity to override the layout level setting of hspace.

Listing 3-5. Defining Custom FlowLayout LayoutParams Class

```
//**********************************************************
//Custom Layout Definition
//**********************************************************
public static class LayoutParams extends ViewGroup.MarginLayoutParams {
    public int spacing = -1;
    public int x =0;
    public int y =0;

    public LayoutParams(Context c, AttributeSet attrs) {
        super(c, attrs);
        TypedArray a =
                c.obtainStyledAttributes(attrs, R.styleable.FlowLayout_Layout);
```

```
        spacing = a.getDimensionPixelSize(R.styleable.FlowLayout_Layout_layout_space, 0);
        a.recycle();
    }
    public LayoutParams(int width, int height) {
        super(width, height);
        spacing = 0;
    }
    public LayoutParams(ViewGroup.LayoutParams p) {
        super(p);
    }
    public LayoutParams(MarginLayoutParams source) {
        super(source);
    }
}//eof-layout-param
```

Lisitng 3-5 shows how to read the spacing variable from XML layout files. The approach is very similar to how we have used custom attributes in Chapters 1 and 2: define the variable names in `attrs.xml` (see Listing 3-2) and then read it through typed attributes in the constructor.

In addition to the layout parameters, we have assigned an additional responsibility for `FlowLayout`'s `LayoutParams` class. See the x and y public members on the layout parameters class. We have used these public variables to store the origin of a child view during the measure pass and reuse it in the layout pass.

Overriding Custom LayoutParams Construction

Child views, like a `Textview` or a `Buttonview`, can be embedded in any parent layout like a `LinearLayout` or a `FlowLayout`. How does a child view know how to construct and hold a `LayoutParams` object that is relevant to the parent layout? This cannot be hard-coded into the view because the view doesn't know at the compile time what its parent is.

To solve this dilemma, Android SDK has provided a number of standard methods on the `ViewGroup` (parent of all layouts) that need to be overridden. As a view is placed into a view group, these standard methods are called to construct the derived `LayoutParams` and associate it to the view. These `ViewGroup` standard methods that construct the derived `FlowLayout.LayoutParams` are indicated in Listing 3-6.

Listing 3-6. Overriding LayoutParams Creation

```
//*******************************************************
//Layout Param Support
//*******************************************************
@Override
public LayoutParams generateLayoutParams(AttributeSet attrs) {
    return new FlowLayout.LayoutParams(getContext(), attrs);
}
@Override
protected LayoutParams generateDefaultLayoutParams() {
    return new LayoutParams(LayoutParams.WRAP_CONTENT, LayoutParams.WRAP_CONTENT);
}
```

```
@Override
protected LayoutParams generateLayoutParams(ViewGroup.LayoutParams p) {
    return new LayoutParams(p);
}
// Override to allow type-checking of LayoutParams.
@Override
protected boolean checkLayoutParams(ViewGroup.LayoutParams p) {
    return p instanceof FlowLayout.LayoutParams;
}
```

The first method is called to instantiate the derived layout's layout parameter class. If we don't override this, then the base view group will instantiate its implementation, the MarginLayoutParams. And that guy or gal will not have the x and y in it, nor will it read the custom "spacing" variable.

The rest of the methods are appropriately called at various times. Listing 3-6 is the standard set of methods that can be copied and pasted for your custom latouts as we have done here for the FlowLayout.

Source Code for FlowLayout

Listing 3-7 shows the entire source code for FlowLayout; here you can see all the steps we have covered so far for a custom layout in one place: (a) extending view group, (b) reading custom attributes, (c) onMeasure(), (d) onLayout, (e) implement FlowLayout.LayoutParams, and (f) implement support methods for custom layout parameters. To be able to compile and run this file, you will also need the attrs.xml file shown in Listing 3-2, placed in the /res/values subdirectory.

Listing 3-7. Complete Source Code for FlowLayout

```
public class FlowLayout
extends ViewGroup
{
    private int hspace=10;
    private int vspace=10;
    public FlowLayout(Context context) {
        super(context);
        initialize(context);
    }

    public FlowLayout(Context context, AttributeSet attrs, int defStyle) {
        super(context, attrs, defStyle);
        TypedArray t = context.obtainStyledAttributes(attrs,
                R.styleable.FlowLayout, 0, 0);
        hspace = t.getDimensionPixelSize(R.styleable.FlowLayout_hspace,
                hspace);
        vspace = t.getDimensionPixelSize(R.styleable.FlowLayout_vspace,
                vspace);
        t.recycle();
        initialize(context);
    }
```

```java
public FlowLayout(Context context, AttributeSet attrs) {
    this(context, attrs, 0);
}

private void initialize(Context context) {
}

//This is very basic
//doesn't take into account padding
//You can easily modify it to account for padding
@Override
protected void onMeasure(int widthMeasureSpec, int heightMeasureSpec)
{
    //*******************
    //Initialize
    //*******************
    int rw = MeasureSpec.getSize(widthMeasureSpec);
    int rh = MeasureSpec.getSize(heightMeasureSpec);
    int h = 0; //current height
    int w = 0; //current width
    int h1 = 0, w1=0; //Current point to hook the child to

    //*******************
    //Loop through children
    //*******************
    int numOfChildren = this.getChildCount();
    for (int i=0; i < numOfChildren; i++ )
    {
        //*******************
        //Front of the loop
        //*******************
        View child = this.getChildAt(i);
        this.measureChild(child,widthMeasureSpec, heightMeasureSpec);
        int vw = child.getMeasuredWidth();
        int vh = child.getMeasuredHeight();

        if (w1 + vw > rw)
        {
            //new line: max of current width and current width position
            //when multiple lines are in play w could be maxed out
            //or in uneven sizes is the max of the right side lines
            //all lines don't have to have the same width
            //some may be larger than others
            w = Math.max(w,w1);
            //reposition the point on the next line
            w1 = 0; //start of the line

            h1 = h1 + vh; //add view height to the current height
        }
```

```
              //********************
              //Middle of the loop
              //********************
              int w2 = 0, h2 = 0; //new point for the next view
              w2 = w1 + vw;
              h2 = h1;
              //latest height: current point + height of the view
              //however if the previous height is larger use that one
              h = Math.max(h,h1 + vh);

              //********************
              //Save the current coords for the view
              //in its layout
              //********************
              LayoutParams lp = (LayoutParams)child.getLayoutParams();
              lp.x = w1;
              lp.y = h1;

              //********************
              //Restart the loop
              //********************
              w1=w2;
              h1=h2;
         }
     //********************
     //End of for
     //********************
        w = Math.max(w1,w);
        //h = h;
        setMeasuredDimension(
               resolveSize(w, widthMeasureSpec),
               resolveSize(h,heightMeasureSpec));
    };
    @Override
    protected void onLayout(boolean arg0, int arg1, int arg2, int arg3, int arg4)
    {
        //Call layout() on children
        int numOfChildren = this.getChildCount();
        for (int i=0; i < numOfChildren; i++ )
        {
           View child = this.getChildAt(i);
           LayoutParams lp = (LayoutParams)child.getLayoutParams();
           child.layout(lp.x,
                  lp.y,
                  lp.x + child.getMeasuredWidth(),
                  lp.y + child.getMeasuredHeight());
        }
    }
```

```java
//*********************************************************
//Layout Param Support
//*********************************************************
@Override
public LayoutParams generateLayoutParams(AttributeSet attrs) {
    return new FlowLayout.LayoutParams(getContext(), attrs);
}
@Override
protected LayoutParams generateDefaultLayoutParams() {
    return new LayoutParams(LayoutParams.WRAP_CONTENT, LayoutParams.WRAP_CONTENT);
}
@Override
protected LayoutParams generateLayoutParams(ViewGroup.LayoutParams p) {
    return new LayoutParams(p);
}
// Override to allow type-checking of LayoutParams.
@Override
protected boolean checkLayoutParams(ViewGroup.LayoutParams p) {
    return p instanceof FlowLayout.LayoutParams;
}
//*********************************************************
//Custom Layout Definition
//*********************************************************
public static class LayoutParams extends ViewGroup.MarginLayoutParams {
    public int spacing = -1;
    public int x =0;
    public int y =0;

    public LayoutParams(Context c, AttributeSet attrs) {
        super(c, attrs);
        TypedArray a =
                c.obtainStyledAttributes(attrs, R.styleable.FlowLayout_Layout);

        spacing = a.getDimensionPixelSize(R.styleable.FlowLayout_Layout_layout_space, 0);
        a.recycle();
    }
    public LayoutParams(int width, int height) {
        super(width, height);
        spacing = 0;
    }

    public LayoutParams(ViewGroup.LayoutParams p) {
        super(p);
    }
    public LayoutParams(MarginLayoutParams source) {
        super(source);
    }
}//eof-layout-params
}// eof-class
```

FlowLayout in Action

You may be eager now to learn how to use FlowLayout in an activity layout file to see the view as shown in Figure 1-1. Here is the layout file in Listing 3-8 that produces Figure 1-1:

Listing 3-8. Using FlowLayout for an Activity

```xml
<?xml version="1.0" encoding="utf-8"?>
<LinearLayout xmlns:android="http://schemas.android.com/apk/res/android"
    xmlns:cl="http://schemas.android.com/apk/res/com.androidbook.customLayouts"
    android:orientation="vertical"
    android:layout_width="fill_parent"
    android:layout_height="match_parent"
    >
<TextView
    android:id="@+id/text2"
    android:layout_width="fill_parent"
    android:layout_height="wrap_content"
    android:text="Welcome to the Compound Controls"
    />
<com.androidbook.customLayouts.FlowLayout
    android:id="@+id/durationControlId"
    android:layout_width="fill_parent"
    android:layout_height="wrap_content"
    cl:hspace="10dp"
    cl:vspace="10dp">
    <Button android:text="Button1"
        android:layout_width="wrap_content"
        android:layout_height="wrap_content"
        cl:layout_space="20dp"
    />
    <Button android:text="Button2"
        android:layout_width="wrap_content"
        android:layout_height="wrap_content"
    />
    <Button android:text="Button3"
        android:layout_width="wrap_content"
        android:layout_height="wrap_content"
    />
    <Button android:text="Button4"
        android:layout_width="wrap_content"
        android:layout_height="wrap_content"
    />
    <Button android:text="Button5"
        android:layout_width="wrap_content"
        android:layout_height="wrap_content"
    />
    <Button android:text="B1"
        android:layout_width="wrap_content"
        android:layout_height="wrap_content"
    />
```

```
    <Button android:text="B2"
        android:layout_width="wrap_content"
        android:layout_height="wrap_content"
     />
    <Button android:text="B3"
        android:layout_width="wrap_content"
        android:layout_height="wrap_content"
     />
    <Button android:text="B4"
        android:layout_width="wrap_content"
        android:layout_height="wrap_content"
     />
    <Button android:text="B5"
        android:layout_width="wrap_content"
        android:layout_height="wrap_content"
     />
</com.androidbook.customLayouts.FlowLayout>

<TextView
    android:id="@+id/text1"
     android:layout_width="fill_parent"
     android:layout_height="wrap_content"
     android:text="Scratch for debug text"
     />
</LinearLayout>
```

Notice especially how we have indicated the custom attributes using our own custom name space "cl" (Custom Layouts).

Understanding ViewGroup.getChildMeasureSpec

When covering onMeasure(), we have indicated to use ViewGroup.measureChild()and not use child.measure() directly. This becomes really clear when you see the implementation of ViewGroup.getChildMeasureSpec()(triggered by ViewGroup.measureChild()) in Listing 3-9. The code in Listing 3-9 is taken directly from the Android source code for the ViewGroup class.

Key thing to notice in Listing 3-9 is how the FlowLayout's (or ViewGroup's) measure spec is looked at more closely, and if necessary, a different measure spec is passed to the children to measure the children's size.

Listing 3-9. Figuring Out the Right Child Measure Spec

```
public static int getChildMeasureSpec(int spec, int padding, int childDimension)
{
    int specMode = MeasureSpec.getMode(spec);
    int specSize = MeasureSpec.getSize(spec);

    int size = Math.max(0, specSize - padding);
```

```
int resultSize = 0;
int resultMode = 0;

switch (specMode) {
// Parent has imposed an exact size on us
case MeasureSpec.EXACTLY:
    if (childDimension >= 0) {
        resultSize = childDimension;
        resultMode = MeasureSpec.EXACTLY;
    } else if (childDimension == LayoutParams.MATCH_PARENT) {
        // Child wants to be our size. So be it.
        resultSize = size;
        resultMode = MeasureSpec.EXACTLY;
    } else if (childDimension == LayoutParams.WRAP_CONTENT) {
        // Child wants to determine its own size. It can't be
        // bigger than us.
        resultSize = size;
        resultMode = MeasureSpec.AT_MOST;
    }
    break;

// Parent has imposed a maximum size on us
case MeasureSpec.AT_MOST:
    if (childDimension >= 0) {
        // Child wants a specific size... so be it
        resultSize = childDimension;
        resultMode = MeasureSpec.EXACTLY;
    } else if (childDimension == LayoutParams.MATCH_PARENT) {
        // Child wants to be our size, but our size is not fixed.
        // Constrain child to not be bigger than us.
        resultSize = size;
        resultMode = MeasureSpec.AT_MOST;
    } else if (childDimension == LayoutParams.WRAP_CONTENT) {
        // Child wants to determine its own size. It can't be
        // bigger than us.
        resultSize = size;
        resultMode = MeasureSpec.AT_MOST;
    }
    break;

// Parent asked to see how big we want to be
case MeasureSpec.UNSPECIFIED:
    if (childDimension >= 0) {
        // Child wants a specific size... let him have it
        resultSize = childDimension;
        resultMode = MeasureSpec.EXACTLY;
    } else if (childDimension == LayoutParams.MATCH_PARENT) {
        // Child wants to be our size... find out how big it should
        // be
        resultSize = 0;
        resultMode = MeasureSpec.UNSPECIFIED;
```

```
        } else if (childDimension == LayoutParams.WRAP_CONTENT) {
            // Child wants to determine its own size.... find out how
            // big it should be
            resultSize = 0;
            resultMode = MeasureSpec.UNSPECIFIED;
        }
        break;
    }
    return MeasureSpec.makeMeasureSpec(resultSize, resultMode);
}
```

References

Most of the references listed in Chapters 1 and 2 are valid for this chapter as well. So, we add only few references here that are unique to this chapter.

- Our research log on compound components: `http://androidbook.com/item/4349`

- Complete code snippets for this chapter: `http://androidbook.com/item/4359`

- Romain Guy on custom layouts: `http://www.parleys.com/#st=5&id=2191&sl=3`

- Android SDK documentation on custom components, including custom layouts: `http://developer.android.com/guide/topics/ui/custom-components.html`

- To download the test project dedicated for this chapter: `www.androidbook.com/expertandroid/projects`. The name of the ZIP file is `ExpertAndroid_ch03_CustomLayouts.zip`.

Summary

In Chapter 1, we showed the basic architecture of views and how to customize an open-ended view object and how to use a canvas directly. In Chapter 2, we talked about composing user-level controls by extending existing layouts. In this chapter, we covered how to create custom layouts by directely extending the view group. Of the three methods, we feel that you will have most opportunity to use custom layouts. For example, the need for a flow layout is essential, but it is not in the native SDK. To cite an example, we are working on a word game for which we needed to lay out the letters of the word in a flow layout. In the same game we wanted to present a set of menu icons as a spinning table. You can see this game in Google Play titled *Unscramble Expert*. Or, you may want to create a roller deck of images, such as a photo album. These are all examples of custom layouts. With that in mind, we have covered onMeasure() and onLayout() thoroughly here so as to help you with your own custom layouts.

Review Questions

The following detailed set of questions should consolidate what you have learned in this chapter:

1. What classes do you extend to create custom layouts?

2. Can you use custom attributes for the custom layout?

3. What are LayoutParams?

4. Who implements the LayoutParams class?

5. Who has methods to construct a LayoutParams class?

6. Why do views hold LayoutParams on behalf of a parent layout?

7. Why should you use resolveSize()?

8. Why should you use ViewGroup.measureChild() and not child.measure()?

9. What would be wrong if a layout passes its measure spec as is to each of its children?

10. What happens if the total measured size of the children exceeds the suggested size of the parent layout?

11. How do you define and read layout parameters from attrs.xml?

JSON for On-Device Persistence

A key aspect of mobile applications or games is the need for persistence on the device. Android provides a number of very good options for persistence, including relational storage. However, all the provided mechanisms that use the relational storage take a sizable amount of development time. This chapter provides a shortcut for a number of simple to medium persistence needs. The approach uses GSON/JSON technology to store object trees directly in non-SQL storage, such as the shared preferences and internal file storage.

JSON stands for JavaScript Object Notation. GSON is a Java library from one of Google Projects that uses JSON structure to serialize and deserialize Java objects to strings.

You will be surprised to learn how GSON can propel your mobile app productivity. Especially, those apps requiring modest to medium persistence can benefit from GSON. In this approach, you will represent the persistent state of your app as a JSON string. You will then use the magical GSON Java library to convert your application objects to JSON and persist the resulting JSON string, either in a shared preference or in an internal file on the device.

This approach is suitable for writing moderate to medium-size apps really quickly. Using this approach, it is not unreasonable to release a new app every couple of weeks, whereasdeveloping such apps would probably take a month or two. In fact, you may get a two- to three-times the advantage on some apps. Even when you consider complex apps, you may gain significant advantage from this approach, as you can prototype the idea and test it in a limited release.

To help you understand this JSON-based approach to app storage, we cover the following in this chapter:

1. Using GSON to convert Java objects to JSON strings and back

2. Storing and retrieving JSON strings using shared preferences

3. Storing and retrieving JSON strings from Android internal file storage

In covering these topics, we answer the following key questions: (1) What are the limitations of using shared preferences as data storage for simple apps and games? (2) Is there an official word not to use shared preferences for more than simple key/value pairs? (3) Is there a maximum limit to the amount of data that can be stored using this scheme? (4) Should I explore other data storage options? (5) What is meant by Android internal storage and external storage? (6) Should I use shared preferences or internal files? (7) Should I use files on an external storage card instead? (8) When would I need to use SQL storage? and (8) Could I write my app in such a way that I could migrate to SQL storage for later releases?

We start with a quick review of the data storage options available in Android for managing persistent state.

Data Storage Options in Android

There are five ways to store data in Android: (1) shared preferences, (2) internal files, (3) external files, (4) SQLite, and (5) network storage in the cloud. Let's review each.

Shared preferences are internal to the application and device. This data is not available to other applications. The user cannot directly manipulate this data by mounting onto a USB port. The data is removed automatically when the application is removed. Shared preferences are structured key/value pair data and follow a few other semantics imposed by Android for using the stored data as preferences. Shared preferences are maintained as XML files.

Internal files are unstructured private files that an application can create and store data in. Like shared preferences, internal files follow the life cycle of the application. When the application is uninstalled, the internal files created by the application are also removed.

External files are stored on the SD card. These become public files that other apps incuding the user could see outside the context of your application. External files are typically used for data that is primarily created by the user and is meaningful outside of the app that creates it—for example, audio files, video files, word documents, etc. External files are also suitable when the amount of data is large, say 10MB or more.

SQLite is a relational database. For structured data, like the data that you are planning to use JSON for, SQLite is preferred. However, it is lot of work to go between Java objects and a relational database. Even in the simplest case of using wonderfully crafted o/r mapping tools or libraries, it is still lot of work. However, SQLite is an excellent option for tuning and refactoring your application for subsqent releases. This refactoring will make your application respond much faster and use much less power. The database also is private to the application and not available to outside apps unless you wrap the database in a content-provider framework. (Refer to our companion book *Pro Android 4* for detailed coverage on content providers.)

Network storage allows your application to choose to save persistent data in the cloud. Network storage cannot be a complete option for lot of apps, however, as you likely will need the app to work when disconnected from the Internet. There may be suppplemental opportunities to use parse.com or a similar BaaS (backend as a service) platform to do a hybrid approach, whereby some data is stored in the cloud and is synched when needed with the device.

Our research has led us to recommend using either shared preferences or internal files as the storage mechanism for your objects after converting them to JSON using GSON. These storage options have two advantages. First, they are private; second, they are removed when the application is removed. Their disadvantage is that they are limited in size; if the files become too large (10s of megabytes or have images or videos), you can migrate to SQLite in a follow-up release once your app takes off.

General Approach to Using JSON for Persistence

JSON is a string format to represent JavaScript objects as strings. You can take a set of JavaScript objects and convert them to JSON strings. These strings can then be transported across a network and be read back as JavaScript objects. As Java objects are similar to JavaScript objects, you can use the same JSON string format to convert Java objects to strings. The resulting JSON strings can then be converted back to Java objects.

Because JSON has emerged as the leading format for transporting objects across networks, lot of tools have emerged around JSON to make the process easy. In our case, we use the JSON strings, not to transport but to persist them to the disk and read them back.In this approach, we use the Google tool GSON to convert the Java objects to JSON strings and back. The JSON strings can then be stored in internal files or in shared preferences, as noted above.

Working with GSON

GSON is a Java library (a single jar file) that you can use to convert Java objects to JSON and back. (You can see links to the home page, user guide, and the API in the References at the end of this chapter.) Let's look quickly at the features and limitations of GSON while serializing and deserializing Java objects to JSON.

Features of GSON

Most types of Java objects can be converted to JSON strings using GSON. With GSON, you can have objects inside objects in a nested structure. If you mirror your Java objects with a focus on their storage structure, you can serialize most, if not all, of them as JSON strings. So you want your Java objects to represent primarily data and not full-blown behavior that may interfere with serializing them with GSON.

As long as your member collections use Java generics, GSON can serialize your collections successfully. You will see an example of this shortly. When you use Java generics, you specify the type of the collections. This is what helps GSON to instantiate the right type of objects when deserializing. (You can refer to the GSON user guide for more features and limitations.)

GSON will also escape the quote characters and any other character that is special for JSON. GSON, by default, escapes the HTML and XML characters. In our research, we found this behavior very satisfying, as it allows you to serialize any Java object—even its members contain arbitrary strings with any type of characters.

Adding the GSON Jar to Your Application

To start using GSON in your Android code, you will need to add the GSON jar file to your Eclipse/ ADT project. Here are the steps you need to add the GSON jar file:

1. Go to GSON home page: http://code.google.com/p/google-gson/.

2. download the GSON jar file.

3. Create a subdirectory under the root of your Eclipse project called "libs" (a sibling of src).

4. Copy the GSON jar to that lib directory.

5. Go go "project properties."

6. Go to the "Java Build Path" option in project properties.

7. Go to "Library" tab.

8. Add the GSON jar as an external jar.

9. Go to the "order/export" tab.

10. Choose the GSON jar to be exported as well.

These steps will make the GSON jar available for compiling your code and also for deploying it with the GSON jar on to the emulator or device. The steps required to add an external jar may vary slightly with the release of the Eclipse/ADT you are using.

You may be able to link the external GSON jar without copying to your APK project, as indicated here. In that case, you will be able to compile and link successfully. However, when you run an application on the device or the emulator, you will have a "Run time class not found" exception. So follow the steps indicated above to add the GSON jar to your Eclipse/ADT project.

Planning Java Objects for GSON

You can model your persistence structure as a set of interconnected Java objects. Then you can take the root Java object and convert it to JSON, using GSON. We show you a couple of Java objects that are representative; using these examples, you can then model your storage objects in a similar manner.

We start with the root object, and we call it the MainObject. Listing 4-1 is the source code for this root MainObject.

Listing 4-1. Sample Structure for a Root Object to Store Application State

```
public class MainObject
{
    public int intValue = 5;
    public String stringValue = "st<ri>\"ng\"Value<node1>test</node2>";
    public String[] stringArray;
    public ArrayList<ChildObject> childList = new ArrayList<ChildObject>();
...
}
```

Notice that we have modeled a number of storage types in the MainObject Listing 4-1. We have plain integers, strings, arrays, and embedded collections of child objects. In the string value, we even have stored nested XML nodes. These nested XML nodes will allow us to test the escape characteristics of both GSON and Android shared preferences.

In Listing 4-1, also notice how we have used a generic `ArrayList` collection to hold a collection of child objects. Each child object has its own internal structure. The class definition for the child object is shown in Listing 4-2.

Listing 4-2. Sample Structure for Child Objects to Store as JSON

```
public class ChildObject {
    public String name;
    public int age;
    public boolean likesVeggies = false;
    public ChildObject(String inName, int inAge)   {
        name = inName;
        age = inAge;
    }
}
```

Although we have represented the member variables of `ChildObject` as public, GSON does allow them as private members as long as you provide get/set methods matching their names.

Although these objects in Listings 4-1 and 4-2 are there for primarily modeling the storage needs, you can add basic behavior to these classes and provide nice ways to initialize and store data in a structured manner. You can see this in Listing 4-3, where we have expanded the `MainObject` to add some behavior.

Listing 4-3. Objects Displaying Behavior

```
public class MainObject
{
    public int intValue = 5;
    public String strinValue = "st<ri>\"ng\"Value<node1>test</node2>";
    public String[] stringArray;
    public ArrayList<ChildObject> childList = new ArrayList<ChildObject>();

    public void addChild(ChildObject co)   {
        childList.add(co);
    }

    public void populateStringArray()   {
        stringArray = new String[2];
        stringArray[0] = "first";
        stringArray[1] = "second";
    }
    //This method is used to create a sample MainObject
    public static MainObject createTestMainObject()   {
        MainObject mo = new MainObject();
        mo.populateStringArray();
        mo.addChild(new ChildObject("Eve",30));
        mo.addChild(new ChildObject("Adam",28));
        return mo;
    }
```

```
//this method is used to verify two MainObject
//instances are the same.
public static String checkTestMainObject(MainObject mo)    {
    MainObject moCopy = createTestMainObject();
    if (!(mo.strinValue.equals(moCopy.strinValue)))
    {
        return "String values don't match:" + mo.strinValue;
    }
    if (mo.childList.size() != moCopy.childList.size())
    {
        return "array list size doesn't match";
    }
    //get first child
    ChildObject firstChild = mo.childList.get(0);
    ChildObject firstChildCopy = moCopy.childList.get(0);
    if (!firstChild.name.equals(firstChildCopy.name))
    {
        return "first child name doesnt match";
    }
    return "everything matches";
}

}
```

Converting Java Objects to JSON

Now that we have the object structure defined for our persistence needs, let us see how we can take an instance of a MainObject and convert it to JSON. We will also take the JSON string produced and turn it back into an instance MainObject. We will then compare this generated MainObject instance to see if it matches prototype MainObject. The code that does this is shown in Listing 4-4.

Listing 4-4. Using GSON to Serialize and Deserialize Java Objects

```
public void testJSON()
{
    MainObject mo = MainObject.createTestMainObject();
    Gson gson = new Gson();

    //Convert to string
    String jsonString = gson.toJson(mo);

    //Convert it back to object
    MainObject mo1 = gson.fromJson(jsonString, MainObject.class);
    String compareResult = MainObject.checkTestMainObject(mo1);
    Log.i("sometag",compareResult);
}
```

Incredibly simple.

All that is left now is how to store and retrieve this resulting JSON string in a persistent place. We have two options: shared preferences and internal file storage. We cover shared preferences first.

Using Shared Preferences for JSON Persistence

In Android, shared preferences are used to meet two primary needs. Android SDK uses the shared preferences mechanism to create the UI necessary to automatically create preference screens for applications. Android SDK also exposes the shared preferences directly, without the UI component. In this later mode, a shared preference is merely a storage/retrieval mechanism for key/value pairs. Android SDK offers a number of classes and methods to work directly with these key/value pairs. (You can read more about shared preference in our companion *Pro Android* series of books from Apress.)

At its heart, a shared preference is an XML file that holds key/value pairs in a persistent manner. The XML file is an implementation detail; Android may choose a different representation in the future, should it decide to do so. You can have as many shared preferences (XML files) as you like. Each shared preference can have as many key/value pairs as you wish.

These shared preference XML files are private to your application. They are removed when your application is uninstalled. To get a reference to a shared preference, you will need a context object. `Activity` is an example of a context object in Android. Once you have a context object, you call the method `getSharedPreferences()` with a filename to get access to a shared preference object. You can then use that object to save and retrieve key/value pairs.

If you have access to an `Activity`, you can just call `getPreferences()` instead. This method merely calls the former `getShaerdPreferences()` with the activity name as the name of the XML file.

Getting Access to an Application Context

Each activity in your application can have its own shared preference file. But what we are interested in here is the persistence needs of an entire application and not just a specific activity. So we can't use the `getPreferences()` method on the `Activity` class. For all you know, you may not even have an activity in your application.

So we need a context that is applicable at the whole application level. To do this, you need to override the `Application` class and create an instance of your application. This is shown in Listing 4-5.

Listing 4-5. Gathering Application Context

```
public class MyApplication extends Application
{
   public final static String tag="MyApplication";
   public static Context s_applicationContext = null;

   @Override
   public void onConfigurationChanged(Configuration newConfig) {
      super.onConfigurationChanged(newConfig);
      Log.d(tag,"configuration changed");
   }

   @Override
   public void onCreate() {
      super.onCreate();
```

```
        s_applicationContext = getApplicationContext();
        Log.d(tag,"oncreate");
    }
    @Override
    public void onLowMemory() {
        super.onLowMemory();
        Log.d(tag,"onLowMemory");
    }
    @Override
    public void onTerminate() {
        super.onTerminate();
        Log.d(tag,"onTerminate");
    }
}
```

Key lines in Listing 4-5 are highlighted in bold type. In this listing, we get the application context and store it in a public static variable so that the application context is globally available in the application.

Once you have your application MyApplication, as shown in Listing 4-5, you need to adjust your manifest file to register MyApplication, as shown in Listing 4-6.

Listing 4-6. Registering Application Object in the Manifest File

```
<application android:name="com.androidbook.testjson.MyApplication"
...
</application>
```

This declaration in Listing 4-6 will result in the invocation of onCreate() method of MyApplication as shown in Listing 4-5

Saving and Restoring Strings Using Shared Preferences

Armed with the static global application context in MyApplication, you can use the code in Listing 4-7 to save and restore strings from shared preferences.

Listing 4-7. Saving and Restoring Strings Using Shared Preferences

```
//Use an XML file called myprefs.xml to represent shared preferences
//for this example.
private SharedPreferences getSharedPreferences()
{
  SharedPreferences sp
  = MyApplication
        .s_applicationContext
            .getSharedPreferences("myprefs", Context.MODE_PRIVATE);
  return sp;
}
```

```
public void testEscapeCharactersInPreferences()
{
  //Use a string that is a bit more complicated
  //to see how escape characters work
  String testString = "<node1>blabhhh</node1>";

  //get shared preferences
  SharedPreferences sp = getSharedPreferences();

  //Prepare the shared preferences for save
  SharedPreferences.Editor spe = sp.edit();

  //add a key/value pair
  spe.putString("test", testString);

  //Commit the changes to persistence
  spe.commit();

  //Retrieve what is stored
  String savedString = sp.getString("test", null);
  if (savedString == null)
  {
     Log.d(tag,"no saved string");
     return;
  }

  //Compare the two strings
  Log.d(tag,savedString);
  if (testString.equals(savedString))
  {
     Log.d(tag,"Saved the string properly. Match");
     return;
  }
  //they dont match
  Log.d(tag,"They don't match");
  return;
}
```

Let's review the code in Listing 4-7. We have first used the static global context to use myprefs.xml as the shared preferences file for testing of storing strings. We have also indicated that the myprefs.xml be created and maintained in a private mode. The other possible modes are shown in Listing 4-8.

Listing 4-8. Mode Bits for Shared Preferences

```
MODE_PRIVATE (value of 0 and default)
MODE_WORLD_READABLE
MODE_WORLD_WRITEABLE
MODE_MULTI_PROCESS
```

In the test method shown in Listing 4-7, we used a string that contains XML characters, knowing that the shared preferences are stored in XML nodes. We wanted to see if the shared preferences mechanism is smart enough to escape those characters.

You may wonder at this point when the shared preference file `myprefs.xml` is created, because we are not explicitly asking any file to be created. The documentation suggests that the underlying XML file for a shared preference is created when we try to save the first key/value pair using the code segment shown in Listing 4-9. (This listing is extracted from the earlier Listing 4-7.)

Listing 4-9. Using an Editor to Save and Commit Preferences

```
SharedPreferences.Editor spe = esp.edit();
spe.put...();
spe.commit();
```

From the code in Listing 4-9, you can see that `SharedPreferences` is a bit of an odd animal. We don't use the `SharedPreferences` object directly to save values. Instead, we use its inner class `SharedPreferences.Editor` to do the save. It is just a pattern that you have to get used to. You may choose to add a number of key/value pairs to a shared preference during the lifetime of a project. In the end, a `commit()` will write it out to the persistence store, which will save multiple writes to the file.

A curious question at this point is, Where is this `myprefs.xml` stored on the device? This file is stored in the path on your device, shown in Listing 4-10.

Listing 4-10. Shared Preferences File Path

```
/data/data/YOUR_PACKAGE_NAME/shared_prefs/myprefs.xml
```

In eclipse/ADT, you use the file manager tool to see the files on your emulator or the device, and you pull the `myprefs.xml` file to your local drive and view it. Listing 4-11 shows the `myprefs.xml` file created by the code in Listing 4-7. See how XML characters in the string values are escaped by Android preferences.

Listing 4-11. Contents of a Shared Preference XML File

```
<?xml version='1.0' encoding='utf-8' standalone='yes' ?>
<map>
<string name="test">&lt;node1&gt;blabhhh&lt;/ndoe1&gt;</string>
</map>
```

Saving/Restoring Objects Using GSON in Shared Preferences

So you now have all the information you need to save and restore Java objects from shared preferencs. Listing 4-12 shows how this is done. In this example, we create the `MainObject` and convert it to JSON using GSON. We then use shared preferences to store it. We use the file name `myprefs.xml` as earlier, and we use the key for our `MainObject` JSON string as `json`. Once we store the object successfully, we retrieve the JSON string and convert it back to the `MainObject`. We then compare it to the original object to see if they match.

Listing 4-12. Storing/Retrieving Objects from Shared Preferences

```
public void storeJSON()
{
    MainObject mo = MainObject.createTestMainObject();
    //
    Gson gson = new Gson();
    String jsonString = gson.toJson(mo);
    Log.i(tag, jsonString);
    MainObject mo1 = gson.fromJson(jsonString, MainObject.class);
    Log.i(tag, jsonString);

    SharedPreferences sp = getSharedPreferences();
    SharedPreferences.Editor spe = sp.edit();
    spe.putString("json", jsonString);
    spe.commit();
}

public void retrieveJSON()
{
    SharedPreferences sp = getSharedPreferences();
    String jsonString = sp.getString("json", null);
    if (jsonString == null)
    {
        Log.i(tag,"Not able to read the preference");
        return;
    }
    Gson gson = new Gson();
    MainObject mo = gson.fromJson(jsonString, MainObject.class);
    Log.i(tag,"Object successfully retrieved");
    String compareResult = MainObject.checkTestMainObject(mo);
    if (compareResult != null)
    {
        //there is an error
        Log.i(tag,compareResult);
        return;
    }
    //compareReesult is null
    Log.i(tag,"Retrieved object matches");
    return;
}
```

You may want to see how the myprefs.xml looks after executing the code in Listing 4-12, as this will give you an opportunity to see how GSON is escaping strings. Here is that file in Listing 4-13.

Listing 4-13. Demostrating Escape Characters in Shared Preferences

```
<?xml version='1.0' encoding='utf-8' standalone='yes' ?>
<map>
<string name="test">&lt;node1&gt;blabhhh&lt;/ndoe1&gt;</string>
<string name="json">{&quot;childList&quot;:[{&quot;name&quot;:&quot;Adam&quot;,&quot;likes
Veggies&quot;:false,
```

```
&quot;age&quot;:30},{&quot;name&quot;:&quot;Eve&quot;,&quot;likesVeggies&quot;:false,
&quot;age&quot;:28}],&quot;stringArray&quot;:[&quot;first&quot;,&quot;second&quot;],
&quot;strinValue&quot;:&quot;st\u003cri\u003e\&quot;ng\&quot;Value\u003cnode1\u003etest\u003c/node2\
u003e
&quot;,&quot;intValue&quot;:5}</string>
</map>
```

Notice in Listing 4-13 how the escaping works between GSON and Android preferences. Both have escape sequences. So don't worry about the string values in objects containing special characters. They are automatically handled well both by GSON and by Android preferences.

As a last point in covering shared preferences, we provide an answer to the question, Is there a limit to the amount of data that can be stored in a shared preference? The answer is that it is pretty large, theoretically at least. In essence, the amount of internal storage available on the device provides the upper limit. Importantly, Android has not imposed any arbitrary limit on the size of a shared preference file. However, as all applications share the same storage device, you want to be prudent about how much you use. Probably anything less than 10MB should be reasonable.

Using Internal Storage for JSON

Ultimately, shared preferences are stored as key/value pairs in an XML file. Android handles shared preferences in a particular way, as demonstrated in the section earlier on shared preferences. For example, the fact that the shared preferences are files is not directly exposed to programmers. Also, the key/value pairs are stored as node/value pairs inside an XML document. Instead, you may want full control of the file where the JSON is stored. In that case, you can use the internal storage option provided by Android. These internal files, much like the shared preference XML files, are also stored on the device specifically for your app and are private by default.

Storing and Retrieving from Internal Storage

Storing and retrieving JSON in internal files is straight forward. Android SDK has an API to open and close internal files. Android SDK also decides where these files reside. As a programmer, you have control of the filenames. You also have control over when to read/write to them. You use standard Java I/O libraries to read from the file stream and to write to the file stream.

The code snipplets in Listings 4-14 and 4-15 demonstrate how to do the following:

1. Open an internal file for writing

2. Convert objects to JSON and write to the file

3. Open the same internal file for reading

4. Read the JSON string from the file

5. Convert the JSON string to objects

6. Compare the source and target objects to ensure they are same

Listing 4-14. Storing/Retrieving Objects from Internal File Storage

```java
public void saveJSONToPrivateStorage()
{
    String json = createJSON();
    saveToInternalFile(json);
    String retrievedString = this.readFromInternalFile();

    //Create the object from retrievedString
    Gson gson = new Gson();
    MainObject mo = gson.fromJson(retrievedString, MainObject.class);
    //makesure it is the same object
    MainObject srcObject = MainObject.createTestMainObject();
    String compareResult = mo.checkTestMainObject(srcObject);
    Log.i(tag,compareResult);
}
private String createJSON()
{
    MainObject mo = MainObject.createTestMainObject();
    Gson gson = new Gson();
    String jsonString = gson.toJson(mo);
    return jsonString;
}
private String readFromInternalFile()
{
    FileInputStream fis = null;
    try {
        Context appContext = MyApplication.s_applicationContext;
        fis = appContext.openFileInput("datastore-json.txt");
        String jsonString = readStreamAsString(fis);
        return jsonString;
    }
    catch(IOException x)
    {
        Log.d(tag,"Cannot create or write to file");
        return null;
    }
    finally
    {
        closeStreamSilently(fis);
    }
}
private void saveToInternalFile(String ins)
{

    FileOutputStream fos = null;
    try {
        Context appContext = MyApplication.s_applicationContext;
        fos = appContext.openFileOutput("datastore-json.txt"
                            ,Context.MODE_PRIVATE);
        fos.write(ins.getBytes());
    }
    catch(IOException x)
```

```
    {
        Log.d(tag,"Cannot create or write to file");
    }
    finally
    {
        closeStreamSilently(fos);
    }
}
```

Nothing complicated at all. The code in Listing 4-14 uses a couple of file utility methods. You could probably craft these methods to your liking. But here are those methods in Listing 4-15, if you want to see a quick implementation for them.

Listing 4-15. Supporing File Utility Methods

```
private void copy(InputStream reader, OutputStream writer)
throws IOException
{
  byte byteArray[] = new byte[4092];
    while(true)   {
        int numOfBytesRead = reader.read(byteArray,0,4092);
        if (numOfBytesRead == -1)        {
            break;
        }
        // else
        writer.write(byteArray,0,numOfBytesRead);
    }
    return;
}
private String readStreamAsString(InputStream is)
throws FileNotFoundException, IOException
 {
    ByteArrayOutputStream baos = null;
    try    {
        baos = new ByteArrayOutputStream();
        copy(is,baos);
        return baos.toString();
    }
    finally    {
        if (baos != null)
            closeStreamSilently(baos);
    }
 }
private void closeStreamSilently(OutputStream os)
{
    if (os == null) return;
    //os is not null
    try {os.close();} catch(IOException x)    {
        throw new RuntimeException(
            "This shouldn't happen. exception closing a file",x);
    }
}
```

```
private void closeStreamSilently(InputStream os)
{
    if (os == null) return;
    //os is not null
    try {os.close();} catch(IOException x)    {
        throw new RuntimeException(
            "This shouldn't happen. exception closing a file",x);
    }
}
```

In Listing 4-14, we have used the file name datastore-json.txt. You can find this file on your device at the location as shown in Listing 4-16.

Listing 4-16. File Location for Android Internal Files

```
data/data/<your-pkg-name>/files/datastore-json.txt
```

You can use the file manager in the Eclipse/ ADT to take a look at the contents of this file once you have executee the code in Listing 4-14. The contents of this file will look like the text shown in Listing 4-17.

Listing 4-17. JSON String in an Internal Storgage File

```
{"childList":[{"name":"Adam","likesVeggies":false,"age":30},
{"name":"Eve","likesVeggies":false,"age":28}],"stringArray":["first","second"],
"strinValue":"st\u003cri\u003e\"ng\"Value\u003cnode1\u003etest\u003c/node2\u003e",
"intValue":5}
```

You can use multiple files to store multiple Java root objects to break down the granularity of saves. This would help with some level of optimization.

Storing JSON on External Storage

Android SDK provides APIs to control directories and files on the external SD card. As we have indicated in the earlier section "Data Storage Options," these external files are public. Should you choose to store JSON strings in these external files, you could follow a similar pattern of internal files as documented in the previous section. However, there are good arguments for the external storage option for most cases.

Because typically the data you would represent as JSON is specific to your application, it doesn't make sense to have this available as external storage, which is typically used for music files, video files, or files that are in a common format understandable by other applications.Because external storage such as an SD card can be in various states (available, not mounted, full, etc.), it is harder to program this card for simple apps when the data is small enough that it can be managed by the simpler means of internal files.

So we don't foresee the application state as being maintained on external storage. Maybe a hybrid approach is meaningful if the application requires music and photos, and those can go on the external storage while you keep the core state data in JSON and internal files. Should you choose to use external storage, refer to the Android SDK docs for a number of APIs to manage external storage correctly.

Using SQLite for Structured Storage

Nothing as easy and sweet as GSON could exist without a kink. This JSON approach will be expensive if you are writing the file every time something changes. For sure, there is a breakeven point where you will want to migrate your code to SQLite and use granular updates.

If so, you can structure your code so that you can swap the persistence layer with alternatives such as SQLite without significantly altering your code. To do this, break your app into a persistence service layer and the remainder. You will need to be disciplined enough to use the service layer as a stateless set of services for which you can use a different implementation later. And remember the interfaces and service interface firewalls. In the References, we have included a link to an article by one of the co-authors that he wrote in 2006 about extreme prototyping. You could borrow the same principles to construct a service layer that can be swapped.

References

We found the following links helpful in our research for this chapter.

- Android SDK documentation on various data storage options: http://developer.android.com/guide/topics/data/data-storage.html

- Our research log on GSON: http://androidbook.com/item/4439. You will find here various links to GSON, such as home page, user guide, and APIs. You will also find basic GSON code snippets.

- Complete code snippets for this chapter are at: http://androidbook.com/item/4440. You will also find here some of the early research material for this chapter. There are also links to every API used in this chapter. You can use this link as a background when you follow this approach for managing your application state.

- GSON home page: http://code.google.com/p/google-gson/

- GSON user guide: https://sites.google.com/site/gson/gson-user-guide

- Reshaping IT project delivery through extreme prototyping: http://onjava.com/lpt/a/6797.This article shows a mechanism to isolate the service layer, allowing multiple implementations that can be perfected over time.

Download the test project dedicated for this chapter at: www.androidbook.com/expertandroid/projects. The name of the ZIP file is ExpertAndroid_ch04_TestGSON.zip.

Summary

GSON is useful for quickly deploying your apps to the marketplace. It is a good way to test market strengths. It is also helpful in releasing a whole lot of simple apps really fast, with minimal work on persistence. In pursuit of that goal, we covered in this chapter how to use GSON to store your objects in shared preferences or internal files. In the process, we also discussed the other data storage options of Android in regard to their suitability for storing JSON.

Review Questions

The following set of questions should consolidate what you learned in this chapter:

1. What are the five different storage options for Android applications?

2. How would you use JSON for persisting Android application state?

3. What are the pros and cons of using JSON for persistence?

4. What is GSON?

5. Can you save nested objects using GSON?

6. Can you save nested collections of objects using GSON?

7. How are characters in strings escaped in GSON?

8. How do you add external jar files like the GSON jar to the Android APK file?

9. What are shared preferences?

10. What is the difference between getSharedPreferences and getPreferences?

11. How do you get a context independent of an activity?

12. Where are shared preference files stored?

13. How do you save JSON to a shared preference file?

14. What does the saved preference file look like?

15. How do you read JSON from shared preferences back as Java objects?

16. How do escape characters work in Android preferences?

17. What is internal storage?

18. How do you save to internal storage?

19. How do you restore objects from internal storage?

20. Should you use external storage like the SD card?

21. What are the useful references while working with this approach?

22. How do you code in such a way that you can migrate in the future to SQLite?

Chapter 5

Programming for Multiple Devices

One of the wonderful things about Android is that there are so many devices that run it. From phones to tablets, to televisions to cameras to treadmills, Android is hugely popular as the software platform for all kinds of electronic devices. This can also be a huge challenge for the application developer. The differences between devices can be numerous, from different sizes of screens to different screen densities, from different hardware features to different versions of Android. Dealing with all these differences gracefully is possible, and perhaps easier than you would imagine.

As Android has evolved, so have the options available to the developer. This chapter will explore device differences and how to deal with them, so that an application can run on as many devices as you want.

Different Screen Densities

The first concept you need to fully understand is that of *screen density*. There are many terms that swirl around in this space, and there are common misunderstandings. To start, Table 5-1 lists some of the terms and their true meaning.

Table 5-1. Density Terms and Their Meanings

Term	Definition	Meaning
pixel	A point of color in an image	A pixel can be a physical thing on a screen, or can be the points that make up a digital image (on file or in memory)
Px	Android screen pixel	A tiny physical spot on a video screen that displays a color. You could also refer to this as an absolute pixel. The term px is used with dimensions in Android.
PPI	pixels per inch	The actual number of physical display pixels per inch of display
DPI	dots per inch	DPI started out as a printing concept but is sometimes used to describe video displays. However, a video pixel is usually made up of multiple colored dots, so DPI gets confusing in terms of video displays. Avoid using this term.
Dp	density-independent pixel	It might be best to call this a virtual pixel since it does not exist in the physical world. But Android uses these as units of measurement for graphic objects in applications. One dp is approximately the same size as a 160 PPI pixel.
Sp	scale-independent pixel	Very similar to a dp, but used for fonts only.

All About Pixels

Screens are physical objects, with the surface made of physical pixels. Exactly how the pixels get created can differ with the screen technology; for example, some use multiple dots of different colors to produce one pixel. When a screen has many pixels packed into 1 inch of its surface, we say that the pixel density is high. The exact value is the screen's PPI. For example, the Google Nexus 10 tablet has a PPI of 300. This means 1 inch is 300 pixels wide. Put another way, a Google Nexus 10 pixel is 1/300th of an inch wide. The original Motorola Xoom tablet has a PPI of 149, or 149 physical pixels per inch. Yet both tablets are about the same overall physical size. The Nexus 10 has a higher pixel density (PPI) than the Xoom. That means the Nexus 10 can display more detail in a 1-inch square of its screen than can the Xoom.

> **Note** A common misconception is that larger screens have higher screen densities (PPIs). This is simply not true, as was explained with the comparison of the Google Nexus 10 and the Motorola Xoom tablets.

Graphic images such as bitmaps, icons, glyphs, and so on are made up of pixels, too, but arranged in rows and columns of colors. The number of rows represents the height of the image, and the number of columns represents the width. But an image's dimensions are not expressed in terms of inches; their dimensions are just width and height.

If you decided to map a 96x96 bitmap graphic 1 image pixel to 1 screen pixel onto the screen of a Nexus 10 tablet, it would take up 96 screen pixels in width and 96 screen pixels in height, or approximately 0.32 inches by 0.32 inches of the screen. That same bitmap displayed in the same way on a Xoom tablet would also take up 96 pixels in each dimension, but that would be 0.64 inches by 0.64 inches. This may not seem like a big difference (only 0.32 inches extra per side), but it is. The bitmap would appear to be four times larger on the Xoom! And that's a problem because you'd like to have some consistency for how your application looks across devices that are the same overall size.

Mapping Views to Densities

A button in a tablet app should look about the same regardless of who the manufacturer is of the tablet. If you created a version of your graphic file for the Xoom that was one-fourth the size of the 96x96 image (i.e., 48x48), then it would appear to be the same size when displayed on the Xoom as the 96x96 as displayed on the Nexus 10. Or, if someone dynamically scaled the graphic to one-fourth the size for the Xoom, that could work, too. Hold on to that thought because you'll get back to it a little later.

It gets even more complicated though, because real screens come in many different PPI values. The Android team did not want developers to have to deal with the math of converting graphics to every single density size so it would look right on different screen densities. Nor would it make sense to create unique graphic files for each PPI possible across all the available devices. So they decided on four density-size buckets, called ldpi, mdpi, hdpi, and xhdpi (for low, medium, high, and extra-high) and these correspond to PPIs of 120, 160, 240, and 320, respectively. Manufacturers of devices choose which of these buckets their device falls into, and then configure Android for that device to tell applications that it is one of these dpi values.

The true PPI of a device may be different from the stated density size (i.e., the bucket size), but that's okay. Of the two tablets mentioned above, neither is exactly the same as one of these values. The Xoom is classified as an mdpi device, since 149 is closest to 160. The Google Nexus 10 tablet is classified as an xhdpi device, since 300 is closest to 320. As a developer, you don't need to know or care about the actual PPI of the device; you will be dealing with just the screen density-size bucket PPI value of the device.

The possible solutions mentioned above—to do scaling of graphics to fit the actual PPI of the device, and creating multiple versions of graphics for different screen densities—are both used with Android. The manufacturers deal with the adjustments between the stated screen density and the true PPI of the device, and the developer is responsible for creating versions of each graphic file, one for each of the density-size buckets the application supports. This means you only have to worry about four PPI values when creating your graphic files for your application. And in fact, Android can even take care of the scaling between buckets, if you prefer.

Density Scaling Factors

As it turns out, the scaling factors between the bucket sizes are nice and easy values. If we say that mdpi is 1.0, then ldpi is 0.75 of that, hdpi is 1.5 of that, and xhdpi is 2.0 of that. If you want a graphic that is 200x200 to appear to the user to be the same size across devices, you could make a 75x75 version for ldpi devices, 100x100 for mdpi, 150x150 for hdpi, and 200x200 for xhdpi. The best practice is to create your original artwork in as high a density as possible—or even better, use a vector graphics package—then generate the graphics for the Android density buckets from there. The reason for this is that you want as much detail as you can have at each size. Starting with a smaller size and scaling the graphic up to a larger size will result in pixelation or blocking—that is, the effect of seeing blocks instead of smooth curves and gradients in the image.

Another approach is to provide just a 100x100 file for mdpi and Android will scale it accordingly for the other densities. If you choose this approach, however, the graphic that is auto-scaled from mdpi to xhdpi may not look as sharp as you'd like.

Technically, there is another density on the very high end: xxhdpi. This corresponds to a density of approximately 480 PPI and a scaling factor of 3.0. Google says not to worry about providing graphics files for this density, but as devices appear on the market with this density, don't be surprised if that will affect you. You may need to provide the additional graphics files after all, which will increase the overall size of your application, and may have other ramifications for performance and application limitations.

There is one other screen density-size bucket defined by the Android team, and that is tvdpi. With a comparable PPI of approximately 213, it sits between mdpi and hdpi, and it is intended for use with Google TV applications. The recommendation is not to worry about this density bucket for smartphone or tablet apps. But if you do want to create graphics for this density, you take that 100x100 graphic for mdpi and make a 133x133 version for tvdpi.

Resource Directories

Within the application files of an Android application, there are separate directories for the graphic files (also known as drawables) for ldpi, mdpi, hdpi, xhdpi, and xxhdpi. For example, the ldpi drawable files are located in the drawable-ldpi directory under the res directory. Based on the screen density setting of the device on which the application runs (i.e., ldpi, mdpi, hdpi, xhdpi, or xxhdpi), Android will select the appropriate graphic file from the appropriate directory. If Android cannot locate the named drawable in the corresponding resource directory for the device's screen density-size bucket, it will either look for the drawable file in the default drawable directory (/res/drawable) or it will select one from another drawable directory and scale it appropriately. Android decides the best choice of which other drawable directory will be used by choosing which one will produce the best results when scaled.

If you create a new Android project and look at the initial drawable directories, you should see the default icon files called ic_launcher.png (or something like that). Notice that the filenames are the same across each directory. This is important; you will specify the image in your layout files using the filename, so the filename must be the same across the different densities—otherwise Android won't be able to find it. As mentioned before, you don't actually need to provide every graphic file for every directory. Android will select one and scale it as necessary for the device the application is running on.

Specifying Dimensions Using dp

You've learned that different screen densities are simplified into five density-size buckets, and that developers are expected to provide different versions of graphic files to be used for devices that fall into those buckets. But what about the specifications of graphic elements in an Android application's UI? How does Android know which graphic to use? And how do you lay out a UI simply?

This is where density-independent pixels come into play. Using the short-form "dp," you should specify your graphic element sizes using density-independent pixel sizes. A density-independent pixel is approximately equivalent to the size of a physical pixel on a 160 PPI screen. By specifying a drawable size with "dp," Android will determine the actual number of physical pixels to use to draw the drawable onto the device the application is running on. If the device is classified as a mdpi device, the number of physical pixels used will be about the same as the number of dps. If the device is xhdpi, then the number of physical pixels used will be about twice the number of dps. This means that the graphic will be approximately the same size on either device, and the layout instruction will have used the same number of dps. For example, if you specify an ImageView in your UI with:

```
android:layout_width="96dp"    android:layout_height="96dp"
```

then that image will be about 96x96 pixels when on a mdpi screen and use the mdpi drawable file. It will be 72x72 pixels on a ldpi screen and use the ldpi drawable file, 144x144 on hdpi and use the hdpi drawable file, and 192x192 on xhdpi and use the xhdpi drawable file. That is, 72 is 0.75 times 96; 144 is 1.5 times 96; and 192 is 2 times 96.

A device that is really 216 PPI, such as the Google Nexus 7 tablet, is likely in the hdpi (240 PPI) bucket, as is the Nexus 7. Under the covers, adjustments are taking place. If your app specifies 480x480dp for a square graphic, that will work out to a distance of approximately 3 inches per side. (Remember that a dp is approximately the same as a 160 PPI pixel, and 480 divided by 160 pixels per inch is 3.) In the case of the Google Nexus 7, the graphic would not be 2 inches per side (480 divided by 240), nor would it be 2.222 inches per side (480 divided by 216). Android is making adjustments so that the graphic results in 3 inches per side, or around 648 physical Google Nexus 7 pixels per side. However, because there are adjustments going on here, the graphic may also not be *exactly* 3 inches per side. If you thought a graphic was going to appear as one absolute size on the screen, it could be a little bit different in reality.

Another misconception about Android is that you can determine the actual exact PPI of the screen. Unfortunately, there (so far) have not been reliable API calls that return this information. The documentation says to use DisplayMetrics (see the References at the end of the chapter for more details) and the properties xdpi and ydpi. However, in some cases the data retrieved is not even close to the truth. Do not attempt to draw stuff to an Android screen where you require the drawn image to have precise dimensions—unless you tie your application to a single device where you know exactly what you're dealing with in terms of the screen and how the scaling and adjustments get made. But that severely limits your application.

Different Screen Sizes

Your application will most likely be laid out differently depending on the overall size of the screen it will be displayed on, regardless of the actual number of physical pixel resolution of the screen. If you are targeting 10-inch tablets, you will almost certainly have the same arrangement of buttons, labels, input fields, images, etc., and it won't really matter whether the tablet is low density (ldpi) or extra-high (xhdpi). The density will affect which graphic image file is used for that ImageView on the screen, but not how big it should appear to the user or where on the screen it should be.

Screen Size Buckets

It's worth repeating that device screen sizes do not correspond to their screen densities. Screen densities have everything to do with the appearance of graphic files to be displayed on the screens, and the ability to show detail, but it's quite possible to have a large screen with a low density and a small screen with a high density. Table 5-2 shows the known combinations of devices as of May 1, 2013, in terms of their size and density.

Table 5-2. Known Device Sizes and Densities (as of May 1, 2013)

	ldpi	mdpi	tvdpi	hdpi	xhdpi	xxhdpi
small	9.8%					
normal	0.1%	16.1%		37.3%	24.9%	1.3%
large	0.6%	2.9%	1.0%	0.4%	0.7%	
xlarge	0.2%	4.5%		0.1%	0.1%	

As you can see in Table 5-2, some devices do seem to prove the claim that size and density go together, with some small screens being ldpi and some extra-large screens being xhdpi. But the majority of tablets (large and xlarge screens) are mdpi density, and most phones (normal screens) are hdpi or xhdpi density. And that proves once again that screen size does not correlate to screen density.

Screen sizes have to do with how much stuff you can display at one time to the user. The bigger the screen, the more stuff that can be displayed. Here again the manufacturers have made lots of screen sizes to choose from, and it would be nearly impossible for an application to deal with each possible exact screen size individually. Therefore, the Android team chose four screen-size buckets from which to choose: small, normal, large, and xlarge. The first two are generally phones and the latter two are generally tablets. The large size was originally intended for the 7-inch tablets and the xlarge size for the 10-inch tablets.

It turns out that TVs fall into the large category even though they are clearly larger than 10 inches. The reason for this is that TVs are viewed from a distance, so objects on the screen must take up more physical pixels to be seen properly. If the TV were considered xlarge, items might be too small to be readable by the viewer. Of course, some TVs are huge, so these buckets aren't necessarily the best way to figure out how to lay out your screens. You'll see shortly there is another way.

Revisiting Layouts

Layouts are typically how you specify where everything goes in the user interface of your application. They are expressed as XML files containing tags for buttons, labels, input fields, images, fragments, and other user interface objects. These view objects are arranged inside of layout tags.

If the display is a tablet, a common layout pattern is the master/detail, where a list on one side of the screen allows the user to make a selection and the detailed information about that selection can appear at the same time on the screen on the other side. Many e-mail applications work like this on a tablet. But on a smaller screen such as for a phone, there just isn't enough room to display the list and the details at the same time. So the list is displayed by itself, and if the user clicks on an item in the list, a detail activity is displayed overlaid on top of the list activity. The user then hits the Back key to get back to the list of items. See Figure 5-1.

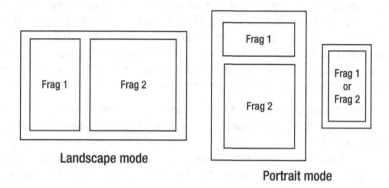

Landscape mode

Portrait mode

Figure 5-1. Tablet vs. phone screen layout

In Figure 5-1, the layouts on the left and in the center represent tablets with fragments laid out on them. The layout on the right represents a smartphone screen that is, by its nature, smaller. The smartphone uses fragments, but only one fragment is visible at a time. Imagine, if you will, that this is the same application on all three devices. The layout for the tablet landscape mode is different from the layout for the tablet portrait mode, and different again for the smartphone portrait mode. From a functional point of view, what happens with the list in Frag. 1 is the same for all three. That is, an adapter will pull data into a list and display it with a scroll bar on the right. When the user clicks on an item in the list, detail for that list item will get displayed in Frag. 2 (which may or may not be visible at the same time as the list in Frag. 1). You want to reuse as much as you can of Frag. 1, and the code behind it, while accommodating different layouts because of different devices. Now let's cover how to manage different layouts for different devices.

Handling Screen Sizes with Layouts

The layouts for the application's activities will differ depending on the screen size. They are also going to be different depending on whether or not the device is being held in landscape mode or in portrait mode. As your app displays the UI, Android is going to find the appropriate layout based on the device's screen size and the orientation of the device at the time the activity is created. And within the layout files will be the layout and control definitions.

As before with the different directories under /res for the graphic files of different densities, Android has different directories under /res for different layouts. In this case, there can be quite a few different directories. Not only could you have different layouts for size and orientation (the most common ones), but you could also have different layouts by country, language, night mode, and many other conditions. At the time that Android needs to locate a named layout resource file, it will select the best one based on the available layout resource files with the same name, and then use the other qualifiers on your layout directory names to compare to the device's attributes and current configuration.

The simplest way to specify a layout directory is something like this:

```
/res/layout-normal-land
```

This represents a landscape layout on a normal-size screen. You could create alternate layout directories for small, large, and xlarge screens, and port (portrait) mode as well. You will find a default /res/layout directory in your application project; that is where Android will look if it can't find anything better to use. You can also store layout files in the default directory to be included in other layout files in other directories. This allows you to create parts of a layout and use them anywhere in your application while only having to maintain them once.

What you shouldn't do is create layout directories based on the device's screen density (PPI). For layouts, you really don't care what the density is. You do care about how much screen real estate you've got to deal with. And here again, Android would prefer to work with density-independent pixel (dp) specifications of screen dimensions. The screen size (usually expressed in inches) is not as relevant as the dimensions of the screen in dps. Table 5-3 shows how the different screen-size buckets relate to the dp dimensions.

Table 5-3. *Screen-size bucket specs in dps*

Screen-size bucket name	Should be at least this (in dp)
small	426 x 320
normal	470 x 320
large	640 x 480
xlarge	960 x 720

The screen dimensions are expressed in terms of height and width, where the height is more than the width. This is regardless of how the device would normally be used (i.e., in landscape vs. portrait mode). And now we can cover the other way to specify a layout directory.

The Android team figured out that the screen-size buckets were not sufficient. Starting in Android 3.2, they added some additional qualifiers for layout resource directories based on dp width and dp height. Since most user interfaces will scroll vertically and be natural to the user, it is rare to see the height qualifier used with a layout resource directory. Therefore, width is the qualifier you will be most interested in. And here the Android team went with two options: smallest width, and current width. *Smallest width* is a system value that represents the shorter of the two dimensions of the screen size, regardless of the orientation of the device. *Current width* is the width of the device in the orientation as of right now. The qualifier in the layout resource directory name will be -sw<N>dp or -w<N>dp, respectively, where <N> is the minimum size of the width you want to specify. For example, use /res/layout-sw600dp or /res/layout-w720dp to specify a shortest width of 600 density-independent pixels or more, or a current width of 720 dp or more.

It is possible to have more than one layout directory with a -w<N>dp qualifier in your application, with the largest one being chosen depending on the orientation of the device. For example, if your application is running on a 10-inch tablet, and you have both a -w600dp and a -w1000dp layout resource directory, when the 10-inch tablet is in portrait mode, the -w600dp layout would be chosen; when the tablet is in landscape mode, the -w1000dp layout would be chosen.

This does not work the same if you use the -sw<N>dp qualifier. The device either has a smallest width of <N> or greater, or it does not. The layout file selection wouldn't change depending on orientation. Therefore, if you are using the -sw<N>dp qualifier and you want a different layout for portrait vs. landscape, you'll need to add -land and/or -port as another qualifier so the expected layout file will be selected for your application.

Depending on which version of ADT you are running, Google may provide /res/values-sw600dp and /res/values-sw720dp-land resource directories by default when you create a new Android project. For layouts, however, the default is just the default layout resource directory. Looking inside the default layout XML file, you will find some margin specifications that refer to dimensions that are stored under those default values resources directories. The dimensions files are called dimens.xml. Inside these files you will find <dimen> tags to override the dimensions in the layout XML file. This is another technique to tailor the layout to different devices and orientations without having to create lots of different layout XML files. At runtime, the values for the layout will come from different values resources files based on the device's current configuration.

Different Qualifiers Beyond Screens

We've covered qualifiers having to do with drawables and layouts, but Android has lots of other qualifiers that you can take advantage of to deliver the best user experience in your application. While there are many qualifiers having to do with keys and keyboards, night vs. day, and so on, let's briefly cover language. You might not think that language would have an effect on your layouts, but then you probably have not seen your user interface with its buttons and labels translated into another language. The translated words that fill up buttons, and take up space in labels, could dramatically alter the way your user interface looks. Buttons could be much wider or narrower; the same is true of labels. This could force you to create alternate layouts for other languages.

Different Hardware Features

Android devices can have lots of different hardware features. Some have a gyroscope, GPS, light sensor, magnetometer, cameras, Bluetooth and so on, while other devices have few additional hardware features. Because it wouldn't make sense for your application to be installed onto a device that does not have the hardware your application needs to function properly, Android provides a mechanism so you can declare what hardware your application requires. In this way, Google Play will filter out your application from users on devices that do not have that hardware. If your application requires a front-facing camera, for example, a user with a device that does not have a front-facing camera will not see your application in Google Play.

Using <uses-feature> Tags

Your application's AndroidManifest.xml file should contain <uses-feature> tags for each hardware feature your application uses. The syntax of the tag is as follows:

```
<uses-feature android:name="name.of.feature" android:required="true" android:glEsVersion="#" />
```

where `name.of.feature` would be replaced with the appropriate string name of the feature, such as `android.hardware.camera.front`. This tag would be inside of `<manifest>` and before `<application>`. The required attribute would be either true or false, so it is possible to specify that your application could use a hardware feature if it exists, but it is not required. If `android:required` is set to `false`, your application would in fact be visible in Google Play to users with devices that do not support that hardware feature. This also means that your application needs to be graceful when that hardware feature is not present. Within your application, you could do the following:

```
boolean hasFrontCamera =
    getPackageManager()
        .hasSystemFeature(PackageManager.FEATURE_CAMERA_FRONT);
```

then take appropriate steps to function properly when `hasFrontCamera` is `false`.

The last attribute (`android:glEsVersion`) is optionally used when your application requires an advanced version of the OpenGL library. All Androids support version 1.1, so you do not need to specify this attribute if that's all you need or if your application does not use OpenGL. If you need version 2.0, then set the value to "0x00020000"; for version 2.1, set the value to "0x00020001." The higher 16 bits represent the major version number, the lower 16 bits are for the minor version number.

Let's not forget that access to a camera on a device also requires a permission (`android.permission.CAMERA`), and that the user must grant permission when installing your application. So how does `<uses-permission>` work with `<uses-feature>`? There must be `<uses-permission>` tags in the manifest file for anything your application uses that requires permission. The `<uses-permission>` tag does not have a required attribute; there's no way to make the permission optional. For `<uses-permission>` tags related to hardware features, Android will then implicitly assume a corresponding `<uses-feature>` tag with required set to true. The exception to this rule is for Bluetooth; see the online reference documentation for `<uses-feature>` for more details on that.

It is best practice to always specify all `<uses-feature>` tags that your application needs. But you *must* specify a `<uses-feature>` tag (with `android:required` set to `false`) if your application does *not* require that feature. Otherwise, the `<uses-permission>` will end up causing your application to be hidden from devices that do not have the hardware feature.

When your application needs permission for a hardware feature but that feature is not required, at installation time the user will still see that the permission is being requested even though the feature is not present on that device. You may want to put something in your application's description on Google Play to explain this to users so they don't get confused.

Using <compatible-screens> and <supports-screens> Tags

It's worth pointing out that screen sizes are a kind of hardware feature, but the tag that gets used is either `<compatible-screens>` or `<supports-screens>`. Using one of these tag types allows you to specify which types of device screens your application can run on. In the first case, within `<compatible-screens>` you would provide separate `<screen>` tags listing the combinations of screen bucket size and screen bucket density that will work for your application. Google Play will use these combinations to hide your application from devices that don't have one of the listed combinations.

If you don't list a specific combination, Google Play will not show your application to a user with a device like that. For example:

```
<compatible-screens>
    <screen android:screenSize="normal" android:screenDensity="mdpi" />
    <screen android:screenSize="normal" android:screenDensity="hdpi" />
</compatible-screens>
```

would result in your application being visible only to users with a normal screen size and medium to high pixel density. It also means that when the new xxhdpi screens appear in the wild, your application will not be visible to them. That might be a good thing or a bad thing depending on your point of view.

> **Note**   `<compatible-screens>` is *only* used by Google Play and associated services. It is never used *on* or *by* a device.

By contrast, the following example:

```
<supports-screens android:smallScreens="false"
                   android:normalScreens="false"
                   android:largeScreens="true"
                   android:xlargeScreens="true"
                   android:requiresSmallestWidthDp="600" />
```

says that your application works on large or xlarge screen devices that have their smallest side at least 600dp long. However, this tag is really telling Google Play the smallest screen size that is supported. Any screen size larger than the first one with an attribute value of true will also see this application in Google Play. If you had set the normalScreens attribute value to true, and the largeScreens and xlargeScreens attribute values to false, your application could still be visible in Google Play for devices with large and xlarge screens. Android assumes that it's okay to resize your application onto a larger screen; if you don't want resizing to take place, specify the `android:resizeable` attribute to false. If you *really* want to control exactly which devices can receive your application, stick with `<compatible-screens>`.

Different Versions of Android

In this final section, we cover how to deal with all of the different versions of Android that exist "in the wild." Being a popular operating system on so many different devices is a blessing and a curse. Most manufacturers and carriers do not quickly upgrade the Android operating system (OS) for all their devices when that new OS is released by Google. Some never get an upgrade. Others get one upgrade after many months, and then never get another. The result is many devices in the wild running Froyo (2.2), Gingerbread (2.3), Ice Cream Sandwich (4.0), and Jelly Bean (4.1, 4.2, and 4.3). There are yet other devices running Donut (1.6), Éclair (2.1), and Honeycomb (3.x), but they are few now.

Each new version of Android has come with new features, and some classes and/or methods get deprecated so they should no longer be used. Some features even change their meaning from one version to the next (e.g., pointer IDs and pointer indexes in MotionEvent since Froyo). And in some cases, major concepts of Android programming get back-ported to the old versions in compatibility libraries. What's a developer to do?

The <uses-sdk> Tag

For starters, the <uses-sdk> tag in the manifest file can and should be used to specify compatibility with versions of Android. Its syntax is:

```
<uses-sdk android:minSdkVersion="integer"
          android:targetSdkVersion="integer"
          android:maxSdkVersion="integer" />
```

where minSdkVersion tells Google Play what the oldest version is that will run the application, and maxSdkVersion tells Google Play what the newest version is that will run the application. The integer value is an API level that corresponds to the more common Android OS version. For example, Android Froyo version 2.2 has an SdkVersion number of 8. The maxSdkVersion value has no bearing on the device itself, so if the application is installed on the device, and the device then receives an OS update past the maxSdkVersion, the application will still exist on the device and the user will still be allowed to run it. The Android team says that future versions of Android are backward compatible, and that the new OS will take care of making the application work, as long as best practices were followed by the developer.

Android's built-in compatibility behaviors kick in if the version of the OS is newer than the targetSdkVersion. If the device's version of the OS matches the targetSdkVersion, then it is assumed the application has been thoroughly tested and no special handling by the OS is required.

In theory, therefore, you could create separate APKs of your application, one for each version of Android, and set the <uses-sdk> tag accordingly. You are even allowed to upload multiple APKs for a single application listing in Google Play, so it would look to the users like it's a single application when in fact it could be quite a few. However, *don't do this*. You've already seen that an OS update on a device will result in the application APK being mismatched with the OS. And if you start testing each of your application APKs against the next higher version of the OS, you'll go crazy. You'll also find that most of your application is the same between versions of Android anyway. So you might as well take a different approach.

You'll still want to use the <uses-sdk> tag to specify the minimum and the target SDK versions. Setting max isn't as important, and in fact is discouraged by Google. Based on the features and Android APIs that your application requires, you want to pick the lowest version of Android that will work for you and your users. That's what you will use for the minSdkVersion attribute value. Then you want to specify targetSdkVersion for the version you expect will be most popular, or that makes your life the easiest. This again could be based on the APIs available in that version of Android. It is just fine to pick a minSdkVersion that is missing something that your application could use, as long as your application can still function without that thing. You will accommodate the missing item in code, as you'll soon see.

One of the simplest ways to deal with Android versions in code is to ask the device what version it is running, and to act accordingly. The `Build.VERSION.SDK_INT` static int holds what the API level is of the device, as an integer value. So it's very simple to use:

```
if (Build.VERSION.SDK_INT >= 14) { ...
```

Then you do things that you could only do on Android 4.0 and above. To see the definitive list of values, check out the documentation on `Build.VERSION_CODES`.

You could also employ Java reflection to see if a class or class method exists, and if so, you could use it, and if not, then you don't. You might also use this method if your application is dependent on some manufacturer-specific APIs that won't exist across every device of some version of Android. For an example of using reflection in this way, see the section in Chapter 8 (Advanced Debugging) on "StrictMode with Old Android Versions."

The Compatibility Libraries

When Android introduced fragments in Honeycomb, it represented a major new concept for how to structure an Android application. Instead of creating new versions of the previous releases of the Android OS, the Android team created a compatibility library that contains code for Fragments, Loaders, and several others to be used with the older OSs. There are now several versions of the library, with additional features added along the way. By including the Android-support library in your application and targeting an Android API level of 11 or higher, you can fairly easily use Fragments and other modern features while simultaneously supporting the older releases of Android.

> **Note**   If you experience problems building your applications with a high targetSDK, Google recommends that you try setting the targetSDK to the same release as your minSDK.

The library jar files are located in the Android SDK under `extras/support/android`. However, the simplest way to include the library is to right-click on your project name in Eclipse, select the Android Tools menu, and then the menu item Add Support Library. This sets everything up for you. And now for the caveats . . .

In order for the compatibility library to function for both the old versions of Android that don't support the new features and the newer versions of Android that do, you'll have to change a few things in your code. The first main one is to use a `FragmentActivity` instead of just an `Activity`; to use the `FragmentActivity.getSupportFragmentManager()` method instead of `FragmentActivity.getFragmentManager()`; and to use `FragmentActivity.getSupportLoaderManager()` instead of `FragmentActivity.getLoaderManager()`. Unlike before, where you were checking the version of Android to execute different code for one release of Android or another, you just use the compatibility library classes for all releases of Android, and under the covers everything works out for whatever release of Android your application is running on.

Another big difference between writing an application for Honeycomb or later and writing an application with the compatibility library is that the `ActionBar` is *not* supported in the compatibility library. There was a shift in thinking with Honeycomb from using menus on applications to using the `ActionBar`.

When your application runs on a release of Android that has `ActionBar`, you want it used properly. When your application is running on an older release, you'll end up with an Options menu. What you will need to do is code for the Options menu, but call a special compatibility library utility method for each menu item you want on the `ActionBar`. At runtime, the correct behavior occurs. Listing 5-1 shows what the menu XML file might look like, followed by the Java code to properly instantiate either the `ActionBar` or the Options menu.

Listing 5-1. XML and Java for a Compatibility Menu and ActionBar

```
<!-- This file is /res/menu/options.xml -->
<menu xmlns:android="http://schemas.android.com/apk/res/android">
    <item android:id="@+id/menu_item1"
        android:title="Item1"
        android:icon="@android:drawable/ic_media_previous"
        android:orderInCategory="0" />

    <item android:id="@+id/menu_item2"
        android:title="Item2"
        android:icon="@android:drawable/ic_media_next"
        android:orderInCategory="1" />

    <item android:id="@+id/menu_item3"
        android:title="Item3"
        android:icon="@android:drawable/ic_menu_compass"
        android:orderInCategory="1" />
</menu>

@Override
public boolean onCreateOptionsMenu(Menu menu) {
    MenuInflater inflater = getMenuInflater();
    inflater.inflate(R.menu.options, menu);

    MenuItemCompat.setShowAsAction(menu.findItem(R.id.menu_item1),
            MenuItemCompat.SHOW_AS_ACTION_ALWAYS);
    MenuItemCompat.setShowAsAction(menu.findItem(R.id.menu_item2),
            MenuItemCompat.SHOW_AS_ACTION_ALWAYS);
    MenuItemCompat.setShowAsAction(menu.findItem(R.id.menu_item3),
            MenuItemCompat.SHOW_AS_ACTION_NEVER);

    return true;
}
```

This listing takes some shortcuts, like hard-coding the text of the menu items in the XML file, which you would not normally do. And we borrow from the Android icons rather than creating our own. But it makes this easier to demonstrate. The menu looks pretty standard. The change comes in the `onCreateOptionsMenu()` code within the `Activity`. Once the menu has been created, whether or not you're on pre-Honeycomb Android or newer Android, you use the `MenuItemCompat.setShowAsAction()` method and specify how that item should appear on the `ActionBar`. The compatibility library treats this method as a no-op for the older releases of Android that don't have an `ActionBar`, so there's no need to do anything special. For the releases of Android that do support `ActionBar`, this method call will set up the `ActionBar` instead of the Options menu.

> **Note**   The code in Listing 5-1 is included in the downloadable zip file from our website. Please see the References at the end of the chapter for more information.

There are very many classes and methods in the compatibility libraries that we cannot cover in this chapter. To see everything that is available, go to the online Android Reference documentation, and start a search for android.support. As you type that into the search field, you will then see the choices of packages that are in the compatibility libraries. If you are curious, you can also download the source code to the compatibility libraries through the Android SDK Manager, which will install it with the jar files in the Android SDK directory under extras/android/support. Most source is under extras/android/support/v4/src/java/android/support/v4/app.

References

Here are some helpful references to topics you may wish to explore further:

- http://www.androidbook.com/expertandroid/projects: From our website you can download ExpertAndroid_Ch05_Multiple.zip, which contains Android applications to demonstrate some of the concepts included in this chapter.

- http://developer.android.com/guide/practices/screens_support.html: Developer documentation for supporting multiple screens. Discusses density and screen sizes but may still be old and incomplete.

- http://developer.android.com/about/dashboards/index.html: Dashboards of device metrics in the wild. Table 5-2 came from this page.

- http://developer.android.com/guide/topics/manifest/uses-feature-element.html: Developer documentation for the <uses-feature> tag for AndroidManifest.xml. Includes a list of the standard features available. Note that a device manufacturer could have its own features in addition to these. See also the list of features under PackageManager.

- http://developer.android.com/training/basics/supporting-devices/platforms.html: Developer documentation for supporting different versions of Android.

Summary

Here is what has been covered in this chapter:

- Screen density and the differences between physical pixels and density-independent pixels

- How screen density is related to images in terms of size and quality

- Descriptions of screen sizes and the four buckets

- Explanation of how screen sizes are related to layouts

- Layout resource qualifiers added in Android 3.2 (-sw<N>dp and –w<N>dp)

- The language qualifier and how that could also affect layouts

- How to specify hardware features that your application might need or use, including screens

- A few ways to handle dealing with different versions of Android, including the compatibility library

Review Questions

Here are some questions you can ask yourself to solidify your understanding of this topic:

1. True or false? The more pixels on a device's display, the bigger the display is.

2. True or false? An image file that is 160x160 pixels will always appear 1-inch square on a display.

3. What density bucket would a device with a PPI of 206 be in?

4. To make an image that is 120x240 on an hdpi display look the same size on an ldpi display, what should its dimensions be?

5. What kinds of files would you find in a drawables resource directory?

6. What are the differences between physical pixels and density-independent pixels?

7. Why are there four screen sizes: small, normal, large, and xlarge? Why use these and not actual screen dimensions?

8. What are some of the qualifiers that can be used for a layout resource directory? Describe their relevance to layouts.

9. When should you use the <uses-feature> tag in the AndroidManifest.xml file? Why?

10. How would you ensure that your application could be seen in Google Play for devices that use a normal screen, but not on devices that use a large or xlarge screen?

11. What are three attributes of the <uses-sdk> tag?

12. True or false? All Android applications for Gingerbread devices must now be built using the compatibility library.

13. Under what circumstances would you *not* need to use the compatibility library?

14. Does the compatibility library provide an ActionBar for pre-Honeycomb releases of Android?

Chapter 6

Advanced Form Processing

Form processing is a common need in writing computer applications, including mobile apps. In Android, you can address this need by designing activities, dialogs, or fragments that behave like forms that have a number of data entry fields.

Out of the box, the Android SDK has the basic mechanisms to control the behavior of each field based on its type. Android SDK also allows you to set error icons and messages on each field programmatically when you detect if that field is in error. These basic mechanisms serve well when you have one or two fields on the form. Based on our experience, though, this field-by-field validation gets to be repetitive and unwieldy for even as fews as three or four fields.

So we asked the question, "Are there any form processing libraries for Android?" In our research we found a handful of libraries in the open-source Android community. We will give you some references to one of the solutions at the end of this chapter. Although you can download and use one of these libraries, we felt it necessary to explain the general principles of advanced form processing in this chapter. In addition, we also show you how to develop a simple yet an effective form processing framework.

The general steps for solving this form processing problem are quite simple. Knowing these steps will allow you to tailor the solution for a number of situations you may run into that the open-source libraries are not addressing.With that in mind, we will cover the following in this chapter:

1. A simple application that requires form processing in order to address challenges of field-by-field validation

2. A general-purpose design to deal with form and field validations

3. Annotated source code that you can use to further customize the presented form processing framework

When you use the approach we document in this chapter, form processing becomes simple. You can then focus on the primary behavior of the application and not get lost in the minutia of granular field level validations.

Planning Form-Based Application

To demonstrate the concepts and code for field validations, we create a simple form that allows a user to sign up for a service. This signup form has the usual fields, such as user ID, e-mail address, and password, as shown in Figure 6-1. The password field is repeated to ensure accuracy.

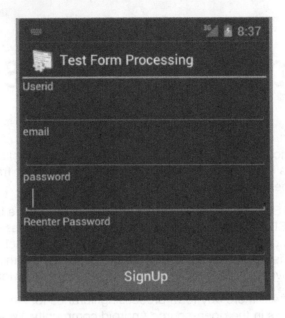

Figure 6-1. A sample signup form

All of the fields in Figure 6-1 are needed to complete the signup. If the user is to click the signup button without filling in some of the fields, you need to highlight them and tell the user to fill those fields before submitting the form.

Figure 6-2 shows what the screen would look like if the user is to click the Signup button without filling in the fields.

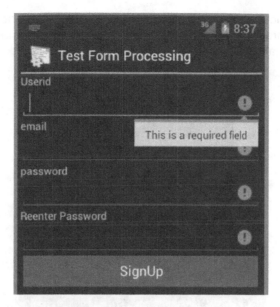

Figure 6-2. Required field validation on form submit

In Figure 6-2, notice that all the fields that are required, but not filled in, are highlighted. Also, for the first field that is required, but left empty, there is an error message indicating that the field is required. Figure 6-3 shows this form when some of the fields are filled in and the user submits the form by clicking the Signup button.

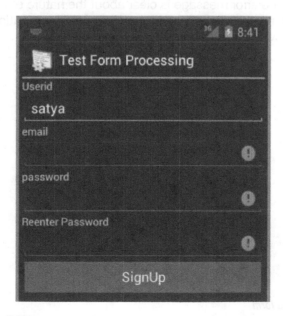

Figure 6-3. Partially filled-in form fields

In Figure 6-3, notice that once the user starts entering information into one of the fields, the error indicator disappears for that field. Figure 6-4 shows another variation of this form when the password fields don't match.

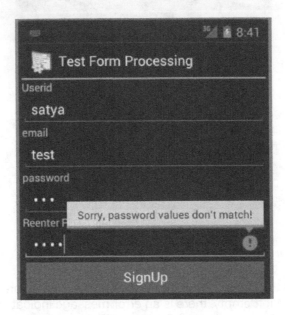

Figure 6-4. Multi-field validation

In Figure 6-4, observe how the error message is clear about the nature of the error. When the user fills in all the fields successfully and clicks the Signup button, the application will move forward and might display a success activity like the one shown in Figure 6-5.

Figure 6-5. Successfully submitted form

So far, we have stated the requirements for a reasonably well-behaved form-based application. We now move to design an elegant field validation framework that can meet these form-processing requirements. We will start with the general principles.

General Steps for Form Validation

There is no built-in framework in Android that completely implements the behavior indicated in our representative application. Android, however, does have the basic features needed to put together a very nice form-validation framework.

The general steps to formulate a good form-processing framework are as follows:

1.   When you create the layout file for your form activity, use `inputType` attribute on the controls (or fields) that make up the form. There are a number of default input types, such as plain text, email, or a decimal number. Specifying the right input type automatically controls the user input that can be entered into that field on every key stroke. This feature is out of the box in the Android SDK.

2.   Then you write validators that can check the behavior that is specific to that field when the form is submitted. These specific validators are attached to each field. They are not in the core framework, so you need to design them. We will show you an implementation for this.

3.   Once you have the validators for each field, you attach the validators through code (as we do in this chapter) to the corresponding fields. You can also attach the validators to their fields through metadata-driven Java annotations. We have provided a URL to a framework that does precisely this; see the References at the end of this chapter.

4.   Once the validators are attached to all the fields, you gather the fields into an abstraction called a `Form` or a `FieldSet`, so that you can validate the entire field set just once when the form is submitted. Again, this step is not core Android, but it will be part of the form-validation framework.

Most frameworks you encounter in the Android community use a similar approach or a slight variation on it. In the rest of the chapter, we will show you how to adapt these general procedures to implement your form-validation framework.

Designing a BaseActivity

Our sample form-validation framework uses an inheritance-based solution that includes three levels of activity.

```
BaseActivity extends Activity
   FormActivity extends BaseActivity
      SignupFormTestActivity extends FormActivity
```

In this activity hierarchy, the SignupFormActivity is shown in Figure 6-1. The FormActivity abstracts the field set and allows methods for field validation. The BaseActivity encapsulates very common methods. Let'slook at the code and analyze the design of the BaseActivity first. The code for this activity is shown in Listing 6-1.

Listing 6-1. BaseActivity to Encapsulate Often Used Functions

```
/*
 * Provides many utility methods that are used by inherited classes.
 * The utility methods include such things as toasts, alerts, log messages,
 * and navigating to other activities.
 * Also includes the ability to turn on/off progress dialogs.
 */
public abstract class BaseActivity extends Activity
{
    //Uses the tag from derived classes
    private static String tag=null;

    //To turn/off progress dialogs
    private ProgressDialog pd = null;

    //Transfer the tag from derived classes
    public BaseActivity(String inTag)    {
        tag = inTag;
    }

    //Just a way to log a message
    public void reportBack(String message)    {
        reportBack(tag,message);
    }
    public void reportBack(String tag, String message)    {
        Log.d(tag,message);
    }

    //report a transient message and log it
    public void reportTransient(String message)    {
        reportTransient(tag,message);
    }
    //Report it using a toast
    public void reportTransient(String tag, String message)
    {
        String s = tag + ":" + message;
        Toast mToast = Toast.makeText(this, s, Toast.LENGTH_SHORT);
        mToast.show();
        reportBack(tag,message);
        Log.d(tag,message);
    }

    //we often need to do string validations
    public boolean invalidString(String s)    {
        return StringUtils.invalidString(s);
    }
```

```java
    public boolean validString(String s)    {
        return StringUtils.validString(s);
    }
    //we often need to transfer to other activities
    public void gotoActivity(Class activityClassReference)
    {
        Intent i = new Intent(this,activityClassReference);
        startActivity(i);
    }


    //On callbacks turn on/off progress bars
    public void turnOnProgressDialog(String title, String message){
        pd = ProgressDialog.show(this,title,message);
    }
    public void turnOffProgressDialog()    {
        pd.cancel();
    }


    //Sometimes you need an explicit alert
    public void alert(String title, String message)
    {
        AlertDialog alertDialog = new AlertDialog.Builder(this).create();
        alertDialog.setTitle(title);
        alertDialog.setMessage(message);
        alertDialog.setButton(DialogInterface.BUTTON_POSITIVE,
                    "OK",
                    new DialogInterface.OnClickListener() {
            public void onClick(DialogInterface dialog, int which) {
            }
        });
        alertDialog.show();
    }
}//eof-class
```

The BaseActivity in Listing 6-1 is pretty much self-documented through inline comments in the code. We have found this approach of encapsulating the most common functions in the base class very useful for the inherited classes. In fact, if you notice, in the same Listing 6-1, we have even taken some pains to redefine some methods from an otherwise static class called StringUtils to make the most common methods easy to invoke. For completeness of the BaseActivity, here is the code for StringUtils, shown in Listing 6-2.

Listing 6-2. Oten Used String-based Methods

```java
public class StringUtils {
    public static boolean invalidString(String s)    {
        return !validString(s);
    }
    public static boolean validString(String s)    {
        if (s == null)        {
            return false;
        }
```

```
        if (s.trim().equalsIgnoreCase("")) {
            return false;
        }
        return true;
    }
}
```

> **Note**   Note that you can download the entire project from our site. This URL is given at the end of this chapter.

Now that we have a BaseActivity, let's get into the FormActivity class that is the gateway to the form-validation framework.

Design and Implementation of the FormActivity

Extending from the BaseActivity class, a FormActivity provides its sub-classes, other form-based activities, a streamlined and less error-prone approach to collect and validate fields. The responsibilities of this base class (FromActivity) are:

1. Provide an ability for derived form-based classes to add fields that can be validated

2. Provide a method to run validation on all of the fields when the form is submitted

3. As part of the validation, make the fields responsible for setting themselves up with appropriate errors

We will talk about each of these responsibilities after we look at the source code for the FormActivity, shown in Listing 6-3.

Listing 6-3. FormActivity Encapsulating Field Validation

```
public abstract class FormActivity
extends BaseActivity
{
    public FormActivity(String inTag) {
        super(inTag);
    }

    //Provide an opportunity to add fields
    //to this form. This is called a hook method
    protected abstract void initializeFormFields();
```

```java
//See how the above hook method is called
//whenever the content view is set on this activity
//containing the layout fields.
@Override
public void setContentView(int viewid) {
    super.setContentView(viewid);
    initializeFormFields();
}

//A set of fields or validators to call validation on
private ArrayList<IValidator> ruleSet = new ArrayList<IValidator>();

//Add a field which is also a validator
public void addValidator(IValidator v)     {
    ruleSet.add(v);
}

//Validate the every field in the form
//Call this method when a form is submitted.
public boolean validateForm()
{
    boolean finalResult = true;
    for(IValidator v: ruleSet)
    {
        boolean result = v.validate();
        if (result == false)
        {
            finalResult = false;
        }
        //if true go around
        //if all true it should stay true
    }
    return finalResult;
}
}//eof-class
```

Key portions of Listing 6-3 are highlighted. Let's consider first how this FormActivity class allows the derived classes to add fields. The FormActivity has an abstract method called initializeFormFields(). This method needs to be implemented by derived classes to initialize and add the fields that need validation.

To make sure the method initializeFormFields() is called, the FormActivity reverts to the trick of overriding the setContentView() of the Activity class. The method setContentView() is usually called by derived classes to set the layout or the primary screen for the activity. So this is as good a place as any to go ahead and collect the fields in that view that need to be validated. Recognizing this, the FormActivity automatically calls the initializeFormFields() as part of the overridden setContentView().

> **Note**   If for some reason this approach of overriding setContentView() doesn't work for you, then you can call the initializeFormFields() function directly from your activity creation callback. That way, there is no magic to this call; it just needs to be called at the beginning of the activity creation.

The approach of forcing the derived classes to stick to a prescribed protocol is called the template/hook pattern. The hook method here is the initializeFormField(). The template method that triggers the hook at a particular time is the setContentView(). In this pattern, the derived classes merely implement isolated units of action (such as initializeFormFields). The template method will define the protocol when to call those actions in what order and when and how many times, and so on.

You will shortly see how the derived classes implement the initializeFormField() where they will call the addValidator() method. The addValidator() method relies on the following classes to work:

```
IValueValidator //Represents how to validate any string
IValidator //Represents a validatable entity that can self report errors
Field //extends a Validator and also allows
```

Listing 6-4 shows the definition for the IValueValidator interface.

Listing 6-4. IValueValidator: A Contract for ValueValidating Classes

```
/*
 * An interface for such value validators as RegExValidator
 */
public interface IValueValidator
{
    //Given a string to see if it is valid
    boolean validateValue(String value);

    //what should be the error message when the field is wrong
    String getErrorMessage();
}
```

So, a value validator is responsible for validating a string value, and if it is not valid, it determines what is wrong with it. The intention of this interface is that an object like a Field can have a number of value validators attached to it. One validator may be checking that the value must be 10 characters. Another validator could be checking that all the characters are digits. A Field then can go through each of the value validators by passing its value and evaluating it against the set of validators.

The class Field implements a slightly different interface, called an IValidator. Let's cover that before we look at the implementation for the Field, as shown in Listing 6-5.

Listing 6-5. IValidator: A Contract for Self-Reporting Entities such as Fields

```
public interface IValidator {
        public boolean validate();
}
```

An IValidator is similar to an IValueValidator. However, unlike the IvalueValidator, an IValidator is expected to not only validate but also to reflect the implications of validating that entity, such as changing the state of the validated entity. For example, when a Field is validated and if the Field is wrong, the Field will display an error message and also show an icon (see Figure 6-1). You will see this relationship when you examine the implementation of the Field class, without delay, which is now presented in Listing 6-6.

Listing 6-6. Field: A Concrete Class that Represents the Validation Behavior of a Control

```java
public class Field
implements IValidator
{
    //The underlying control this field is representing
    private TextView control;
    //Because whether required or not is so essential
    //give it a special status.
    private boolean required = true;

    //A list of value validators to be attached
    private ArrayList<IValueValidator> valueValidatorList
            = new ArrayList<IValueValidator>();

    public Field(TextView tv) {
        this(tv, true);
    }
    public Field(TextView tv, boolean inRequired) {
        control = tv;
        required = inRequired;
    }

    //Validate if it is a required field first.
    //Also run through all the value validators.
    //Stop on the first validator that fails.
    //Show the error message from the failed validator.
    //Use the android setError to show the errors.
    @Override
    public boolean validate()
    {
        String value = getValue();
        if (StringUtils.invalidString(value))
        {
            //invalid string
            if (required)
            {
                warnRequiredField();
                return false;
            }
        }
```

```
        for(IValueValidator validator: valueValidatorList)
        {
            boolean result = validator.validateValue(getValue());
            if (result == true) continue;
            if (result == false)
            {
                //this validator failed
                String errorMessage = validator.getErrorMessage();
                setErrorMessage(errorMessage);
                return false;
            }
        }//eof-for
        //All validators passed
        return true;
    }//eof-validate

    private void warnRequiredField() {
        setErrorMessage("This is a required field");
    }
    public void setErrorMessage(String message)    {
        control.setError(message);
    }
    public String getValue() {
        return this.control.getText().toString();
    }
}//eof-class
```

Now, we can talk about the implementation detail of the key component of the form-validation framework. The `Field` is both a validator by itself and also has a collection of value validators. A `Field` implements the contract of the `IValidator` because it not only wants to validate itself but also to display any clues or hints required to correct the field.

Whether a given field is required or not in a form is so basic and essential that we have implemented that functionality directly as hard-coded into the `Field` definition. The rest of the validations on a field can be encapsulated into a number of value validators.

So, here is how a `Field` works. The derived classes initialize a `Field` with its underlying edit fields. The derived class then attaches a series of value validators to further validate the field. The `Field` is then added to the `FormAcvity` to become part of a field set that gets validated when the form is validated. Here is the pseudocode for how you use a `Field` object, as shown in Listing 6-7.

Listing 6-7. Pseudocode for Creating and Registering Field Objects

```
//Say emailEditText is a required form field
EditText emailEditText;

//Create a Field object that wraps the emailEditText
//By default the field becomes a required field
Field emailField = new Field(emailEditText);

//Add further validators. Here are some sample validators
emailField.addValidator(new StrictEmailValidator());
emailField.addValidator(new MaxLenghtValidator());
```

```
//Add this field to the form field set
addValidator(emailField);

...add other fields similarly if you have them
addValidator(field2);
..etc
```

The pseudocode in Listing 6-7 shows how to work with individual fields. Sometimes you also have to do cross-field validation. For example, in Figure 6-1, if the two password fields must match to pass the form validation, any one field validation cannot satisfy this requirement. So Listing 6-8 shows how to create a composite field that can do this sort of multi-field validation.

Listing 6-8. PasswordRule: An Example of Multi-field Validation

```java
/*
 * A class simulating multi-field validation
 */
public class PasswordFieldRule implements IValidator
{
    private TextView password1;
    private TextView password2;

    public PasswordFieldRule(TextView p1, TextView p2)
    {
        password1 = p1;
        password2 = p2;
    }
    @Override
    public boolean validate()
    {
        String p1 = password1.getText().toString();
        String p2 = password2.getText().toString();
        if (p1.equals(p2))
        {
            return true;
        }
        //They are not the same
        password2.setError("Sorry, password values don't match!");
        return false;
    }
}//eof-class
```

The class `PasswordFieldRule` can be added to the form as if it were another field. Listing 6-9 is an example of a value valdiator that is based on general-purpose regular expressions.

Listing 6-9. A Regular Expression Value Validator

```java
/*
 * A general purpose regular expression value validator
 */
public class RegExValueValidator
implements IValueValidator
```

```
{
    private String regExPattern;
    private String error;
    private String hint;
    RegExValueValidator(String inRegExPattern,
            String errorMessage, String inHint)
    {
        regExPattern = inRegExPattern;
        error = errorMessage;
        hint = inHint;
    }
    @Override
    public boolean validateValue(String value) {
        if (value.matches(regExPattern) == true)
        {
            return true;
        }
        return false;
    }
    @Override
    public String getErrorMessage() {
        return error + ". " + hint;
    }
}
```

We have by now explained all the classes needed to finally implement the SignupTestFormActivity that will implement the behavior required by the sample application.

Implementing the SignupActivityTestForm

Listing 6-10 shows the source code that brings together all the details of this chapter covered so far and demonstrates how simple it is now to do field validations.

Listing 6-10. SignupActivityTestForm: Putting It All Together

```
/*
 * A test form to demonstrate field validation
 */
public class SignupActivityTestForm
extends FormActivity
{
    private static String tag = "SignupActivity";

    //Form Fields
    EditText userid;
    EditText password1;
    EditText password2;
    EditText email;
```

```java
public SignupActivityTestForm()     {
    super(tag);
}
/** Called when the activity is first created. */
public void onCreate(Bundle savedInstanceState) {
    super.onCreate(savedInstanceState);
    setContentView(R.layout.signup);
}
//from FormActivity
@Override
protected void initializeFormFields()
{
    this.reportBack("form initialized");
    //Keep local variables
    userid = (EditText)findViewById(R.id.userid);
    password1 = (EditText)findViewById(R.id.password1);
    password2 = (EditText)findViewById(R.id.password2);
    email = (EditText)findViewById(R.id.email);

    //Setup the validators
    addValidator(new Field(userid));
    addValidator(new Field(password1));
    addValidator(new Field(password2));
    addValidator(new Field(email));
    addValidator(new PasswordFieldRule(password1,password2));
}

public void signupButtonClick(View v)
{
    if (validateForm() == false)
    {
        reportTransient("Make sure all fields have valid values");
        return;
    }
    //everything is good
    String userid = getUserId();
    String password = getPassword1();
    String email = getUserEmail();
    reportTransient("Going to sign up now");
    signup(userid, email, password);
}
private void signup(String userid, String email, String password)
{
    gotoActivity(WelcomeActivity.class);
}

//Utility methods
private String getUserId()     {
    return getStringValue(R.id.userid);
}
private String getUserEmail()     {
    return getStringValue(R.id.email);
}
```

```java
    private String getPassword1()     {
        return getStringValue(R.id.password1);
    }
    private String getStringValue(int controlId)
    {
        TextView tv = (TextView)findViewById(controlId);
        if (tv == null)
        {
            throw new RuntimeException("Sorry Can't find the control id");
        }
        //view available
        return tv.getText().toString();
    }
}//eof-class
```

Along with the source for the signup form activity, let's look at the corresponding layout file, as shown in Listing 6-11, so that you can recognize the fields you are trying to validate.

Listing 6-11. Layout File to Support Fields Required by SignupActivityTestForm

```xml
<?xml version="1.0" encoding="utf-8"?>
<LinearLayout xmlns:android="http://schemas.android.com/apk/res/android"
    android:layout_width="fill_parent"
    android:layout_height="fill_parent"
    android:orientation="vertical" >
    <!-- Userid  -->
    <TextView android:layout_width="fill_parent"
        android:layout_height="wrap_content" android:text="Userid" />
    <EditText android:id="@+id/userid"
        android:layout_width="fill_parent" android:layout_height="wrap_content"/>
    <!-- email -->
    <TextView android:layout_width="fill_parent"
        android:layout_height="wrap_content" android:text="email" />
    <EditText android:id="@+id/email" android:layout_width="fill_parent"
        android:layout_height="wrap_content" android:inputType="textEmailAddress"/>
    <!-- password1 -->
    <TextView android:layout_width="fill_parent" android:layout_height="wrap_content"
        android:text="password" />
    <EditText android:id="@+id/password1" android:layout_width="fill_parent"
        android:layout_height="wrap_content" android:inputType="textPassword"/>
    <!-- password2 -->
    <TextView android:layout_width="fill_parent" android:layout_height="wrap_content"
        android:text="Reenter Password" />
    <EditText android:id="@+id/password2" android:layout_width="fill_parent"
        android:layout_height="wrap_content" android:inputType="textPassword"
        />
    <!-- form submit button -->
    <Button android:id="@+id/SignupButton" android:layout_width="fill_parent"
        android:layout_height="wrap_content" android:onClick="signupButtonClick"
        android:text="SignUp" />
</LinearLayout>
```

Now let's analyze section by section the behavior of the `SignupActivityTestForm` in Listing 6-10. We start with the `initializeFormFields()` method. Here, we first gather all of the controls representing our fields. Then, we register all the fields into the form as required fields. In addition, we create a `PasswordRule` that takes the `password1` and `password2` fields as inputs.

When the Signup button (see Figure 6-1 and Listing 6-11) is clicked, it calls the function `signupButtonClick()`. This method in turn calls the `validateForm()` method defined by the base class `FormActivity`. (See Listing 6-3 for the implementation of this method.) If the fields are not valid, they automatically set their error indicators and messages. User focus is taken to the first field that is in error.

If the entire form is valid, then the control goes to the `signupSuccessful()` method. This method merely calls the `gotoActivity()` as defined by the `BaseActivity` to invoke the `WelcomeActivity`, which is shown in Figure 6-5.

> **Note** Note that we have not given the source code for the WelcomeActivity. You can use the download for this chapter (see References) if you want to see this simplest of all activities that can be done with Android.

In a real-world scenario, the signup may involve server side calls requiring you to provide progress dialogs. These provisions are available in the `BaseActivity` when you need them. (See the `BaseActivity` Listing 6-1.)

Also notice in the layout file (Listing 6-11) that is used for the `SignupActivityTestForm`, we have used the `android:inputType` attribute to describe the nature of the input fields. This is a key provision in Android that restricts what can be typed into a text field. We have provided a URL, in the References for this chapter, where you can find all the possible `inputTypes`. Some of these input types are:

```
text
textCapCharacters
textCapWords
textMultiLine
textUri
textEmailSubject
textEmailAddress
textPersonName
textPostalAddress
textWebEditText
number
numberSigned
numberDecimal
numberPassword
phone
datetime
date
time
```

Finally, as a note, you can download the sample program from the URL specified at the end of this chapter to test the behavior for yourself.

Improvements to Creating Form-Based Activities

Creating form-based activities is tedious and repetitive. We have outlined here how you can simplify that work. You can further tailor and optimize this framework for your needs, as well. For example, you may want to use Java metadata annotations to register the fields. In this chapter, we have used Java code instead to make the framework transparent to you. Or you may want to allow both approaches. In this chapter we also used the inheritance approach by prescribing the respective activities as extending each other. This may impose limitations, as `multiple inheritance` is not available in Java for other than interfaces. You may want to convert the approach to one based on delegation so as to ease this constraint. It is also possible that your forms are in an Android `Fragment` and not in an activity. In that case, you need to tailor your framework to adjust for fragments, as opposed to activities.

If you have lot of activities that are form based, you may want to use a simple code-generation framework to create the activity class and the xml layout file, and register the fields for validation. Then you can alter the code using the generated code as the starting point. Here is a quick example of such an intention. Say, you want to an activity like the one we have shown in this chapter. All you have to say is:

```
<form>
  <email>
  <userid>
  <password1>
  <password2>
  <signup type="button">
</form>
```

Now the code generator can create all the artifacts: the activity class, the layout xml file, the necessary methods to create the fields, and so on. In fact, we encourage you to refine this solution for your specific needs.

References

We found the following links helpful in our research for this chapter.

- Android SDK documentation on TextView:
  `http://developer.android.com/reference/android/widget/TextView.html`.
  You can use this URL to understand how the setError() method works.

- Here is the URL that lists all of the input types:
  `http://developer.android.com/reference/android/widget/TextView.html#attr_android:inputType`. Or you can also use Eclipse to prompt the available input types.

- Research log for this chapter is available at: `http://androidbook.com/item/4491`. You will find here links to other approaches and what is happening around the web in this space.

- An early article on this work is published at: `http://androidbook.com/item/4494`. You will also find here quick references to the key source code that is in this chapter.

- Java annotations based library for form validation is available at: `https://github.com/ragunathjawahar/android-saripaar`.

- As you are creating Android forms, you may want to style them for pleasing disposition. We have a substantial amount of fundamental research on styles and themes for Android. You can find this research at: `http://androidbook.com/item/3864`.

- Download the test project dedicated for this chapter at `www.androidbook.com/expertandroid/projects`. The name of the ZIP file is `ExpertAndroid_ch06_TestForms.zip`.

Summary

Form-based activities are common when writing mobile applications as well. This chapter presents a flexible framework for validating form fields. Developers can further enhance this framework to suit their specific needs.

Review Questions

The following questions should help you consolidate what you learned in this chapter:

1. What is a good way to write form-based activities in Android?

2. What base Android SDK features are available to aid field validations in the Android SDK?

3. How do you use regular expressions to validate form fields?

4. What is an `android:inputType` attribute and how many input types are available?

5. How can you abstract progress dialogs in base classes?

6. How can you abstract alerts in base classes?

Chapter 7

Using the Telephony APIs

Many Android devices are smartphones, but so far, we haven't talked about how to program applications that use phone features. In this chapter, we will show you how to send and receive Short Message Service (SMS) messages. We will also touch on several other interesting aspects of the telephony APIs in Android, including the Session Initiation Protocol (SIP) functionality. SIP is an IETF standard for implementing Voice over Internet Protocol (VoIP) by which the user can make telephone-like calls over the Internet. SIP can also handle video.

Working with SMS

SMS stands for Short Message Service, but it's commonly called *text messaging*. The Android SDK supports sending and receiving text messages. By using an SMS manager, you can send and receive messages of any length. If the message is larger than the character limit for a single message, the SMS manager provides a way to send a longer message in chunks. The SMS manager also gives status updates on the success or failure of sending messages. We'll start by discussing how to send SMS messages with the SDK.

Sending SMS Messages

To send a text message from your application, you need to add the android.permission.SEND_SMS permission to your manifest file and then use the android.telephony.SmsManager class. See Listing 7-1 for the first piece of Java code for this example, which does the message sending.

Listing 7-1. Sending SMS (Text) Messages

```
public class TelephonyDemo extends Activity
{
    protected static final String TAG = "TelephonyDemo";
    protected static final String SENT_ACTION =
        "com.androidbook.telephony.SMS_SENT_ACTION";
    protected static final String DELIVERED_ACTION =
        "com.androidbook.telephony.SMS_DELIVERED_ACTION";
```

```
@Override
protected void onCreate(Bundle savedInstanceState) {
    super.onCreate(savedInstanceState);
    setContentView(R.layout.main);
}

public void doSend(View view) {
    EditText addrTxt =
            (EditText)findViewById(R.id.addrEditText);

    EditText msgTxt =
            (EditText)findViewById(R.id.msgEditText);

    try {
        sendSmsMessage(
                addrTxt.getText().toString(),
            msgTxt.getText().toString());
    } catch (Exception e) {
        Toast.makeText(this, "Failed to send SMS",
                Toast.LENGTH_LONG).show();
        e.printStackTrace();
    }
}

private void sendSmsMessage(String address, String message)
        throws Exception
{
    SmsManager smsMgr = SmsManager.getDefault();
    // Split the message up into manageable chunks if needed
    ArrayList<String> messages = smsMgr.divideMessage(message);

    if(messages.size() > 1) {
        int count = messages.size();

        // Will need to send with multipart,
        // so prepare the pending intents
        ArrayList<PendingIntent> sentPIs =
            new ArrayList<PendingIntent>(count);

        ArrayList<PendingIntent> deliveredPIs =
            new ArrayList<PendingIntent>(count);

        for(int i = 0; i<count; i++) {
            sentPIs.add(PendingIntent.getBroadcast(
                TelephonyDemo.this, 0,
                new Intent(SENT_ACTION), 0));
            deliveredPIs.add(PendingIntent.getBroadcast(
                TelephonyDemo.this, 0,
                new Intent(DELIVERED_ACTION), 0));
        }
```

```
            smsMgr.sendMultipartTextMessage(address, null,
                    messages, sentPIs, deliveredPIs);
            Toast.makeText(this, "Multipart SMS Sent",
                    Toast.LENGTH_LONG).show();
        }
        else {
            smsMgr.sendTextMessage(address, null, message,
                    PendingIntent.getBroadcast(
                        TelephonyDemo.this, 0,
                        new Intent(SENT_ACTION), 0),
                    PendingIntent.getBroadcast(
                        TelephonyDemo.this, 0,
                        new Intent(DELIVERED_ACTION), 0)
                    );
            Toast.makeText(this, "SMS Sent",
                    Toast.LENGTH_LONG).show();
        }
    }
}
```

> **Note**   We will give you a URL at the end of the chapter that you can use to download projects in this chapter. This will allow you to import these projects directly into your Eclipse.

The code to send SMS message(s) is called from the button click in the UI. The address and text message are passed to sendSmsMessage(). You would want to do some edit checking in your real application. SmsManager has a method called divideMessage() to split a message string into chunks that will fit within the SMS specification. If there is more than one chunk, you want to use the sendMultipartTextMessage() method; otherwise, you want to use sendTextMessage(). In either case, you want to know if the send was successful or not. That is where the PendingIntents come in.

By including a PendingIntent for the sent status and the delivered status of each chunk (or the entire message if it fits within one SMS message), your application can be notified of failures and, in some cases, success. The SmsManager can broadcast intents back to your application to let it know what happened to the SMS message you sent. These intents are handled by a BroadcastReceiver whose source code is provided in Listing 7-2.

Listing 7-2. Receiving SMS Status Intents

```
public class MyBReceiver extends BroadcastReceiver {

    @Override
    public void onReceive(Context context, Intent intent) {
        String action = intent.getAction();
        Log.d(TelephonyDemo.TAG, "Got action of " + action);
        if(TelephonyDemo.SENT_ACTION.compareTo(action) == 0) {
            Log.d(TelephonyDemo.TAG, "SMS sent intent received.");
            switch(getResultCode()) {
            case Activity.RESULT_OK:
```

```
            Log.d(TelephonyDemo.TAG, "SMS sent OK.");
            break;
        case SmsManager.RESULT_ERROR_RADIO_OFF:
            Log.d(TelephonyDemo.TAG,
                "*** SMS not sent. Radio is off.");
            break;
        case SmsManager.RESULT_ERROR_NO_SERVICE:
            Log.d(TelephonyDemo.TAG,
                "*** SMS not sent. No SMS service.");
            break;
        case SmsManager.RESULT_ERROR_NULL_PDU:
            Log.d(TelephonyDemo.TAG,
                "*** SMS not sent. PDU was null.");
            break;
        case SmsManager.RESULT_ERROR_GENERIC_FAILURE:
            Log.d(TelephonyDemo.TAG,
                    "*** SMS not sent. Unknown failure.");
            break;
        default:
            Log.d(TelephonyDemo.TAG, "*** Unknown sent code: "
                    + getResultCode());
            break;
        }
    }
    if(TelephonyDemo.DELIVERED_ACTION.compareTo(action) == 0) {
        Log.d(TelephonyDemo.TAG, "SMS delivered intent received.");
        switch(getResultCode()) {
        case Activity.RESULT_OK:
            Log.d(TelephonyDemo.TAG, "SMS delivered.");
            break;
        case Activity.RESULT_CANCELED:
            Log.d(TelephonyDemo.TAG, "*** SMS not delivered.");
            break;
        default:
            Log.d(TelephonyDemo.TAG, "*** Unknown delivery code: "
                    + getResultCode());
            break;
        }
    }
  }
}
```

The BroadcastReceiver will get triggered when a message (or part of a message) is attempted to be sent to the SMS server of the carrier. You will notice that there are two actions that could be returned to this application: the sent status and the delivered status. It is important to realize that the sent status is much more reliable than the delivered status. In our experience, and also judging by the Android examples, receipt of a delivered status is not guaranteed. That is, you may or may not receive any indication of the delivered status of the SMS message. But it can't hurt to include code like that in Listing 7-2 for indicating the delivered status in case your application is notified that delivery failed. However, don't rely on receipt of a positive delivered status to know for sure that the SMS message was delivered, or you could end up resending needlessly.

In many demonstration applications, the BroadcastReceiver is registered in onResume() and unregistered in onPause(). However, since you probably want to receive broadcasts even if your activity goes into the background, you will want to handle the broadcasts using a registered BroadcastReceiver of your own. Listing 7-3 shows what the AndroidManifest.xml section would look like to register your BroadcastReceiver.

Listing 7-3. AndroidManifest.xml for MyBReceiver

```
<receiver android:name="MyBReceiver">
  <intent-filter>
    <action
      android:name="com.androidbook.telephony.SMS_SENT_ACTION" />
  </intent-filter>
  <intent-filter>
    <action
      android:name="com.androidbook.telephony.SMS_DELIVERED_ACTION" />
  </intent-filter>
</receiver>
```

The example in Listing 7-1 demonstrates sending SMS text messages using the Android SDK. The user interface has two EditText fields: one to capture the SMS recipient's destination address (the phone number) and another to hold the text message. The user interface also has a button to send the SMS message, as shown in Figure 7-1.

Figure 7-1. The UI for the SMS example

When testing this application, you can send a text message to the same device. Watch LogCat for the messages that indicate what the application is doing. The interesting part of the sample is the sendSmsMessage() method. The method uses the SmsManager class's sendTextMessage() method to send the SMS message. Here's the signature of SmsManager.sendTextMessage():

```
sendTextMessage(String destinationAddress, String smscAddress,
    String textMsg, PendingIntent sentIntent,
    PendingIntent deliveryIntent);
```

In this example, you populate only the destination address and the text-message parameters. You can, however, customize the method so it doesn't use the default SMS center (the address of the server on the cellular network that will dispatch the SMS message). As shown above, there is another method for sending multipart messages, and that is `sendMultipartTextMessage()`. There is one other method of SmsManager for sending a data message, using a byte array instead of a string message. This method also allows for specifying an alternate port number on the SMS server.

There are two main steps for sending an SMS message: sending and delivering. As each step is completed, if provided by your application, a pending intent is broadcast. You can put whatever you want into the pending intent, such as the action, but the result code passed to your `BroadcastReceiver` will be specific to SMS sending or delivery. Also, you may get extra data related to radio errors or status reports depending on the implementation of the SMS system.

Without pending intents, your code can't tell if the text message was sent successfully or not. While testing, though, you can tell. If you launch this sample application in an emulator and launch *another* instance of an emulator (either from the command line or from the Eclipse Window ➤ Android SDK and AVD Manager screen), you can use the port number of the other emulator as the destination address. The port number is the number that appears in the emulator window title bar—it's usually something like 5554. After clicking the Send Text Message button, you should see a notification appear in the other emulator indicating that your text message has been received on the other side.

Sending SMS messages is only half the story. Now, we'll show you how to monitor incoming SMS messages.

Monitoring Incoming SMS Messages

You use the same application that you just created to send SMS messages, and you add a `BroadcastReceiver` to listen for the action `android.provider.Telephony.SMS_RECEIVED`. This action is broadcast by Android when an SMS message is received by the device.

When you register your receiver, your application will be notified whenever an SMS message is received. The first step in monitoring incoming SMS messages is to request permission to receive them. To do that, you add the `android.permission.RECEIVE_SMS` permission to the manifest file. To implement the receiver, you write a class that extends `android.content.BroadcastReceiver` and then register the receiver in the manifest file. Listing 7-4 includes both the `AndroidManifest.xml` file and your receiver class. Notice that both permissions are present in the manifest file because you still need to send permission for the activity you created above.

Listing 7-4. Monitoring SMS Messages

```
<!-- This file is AndroidManifest.xml -->
<manifest xmlns:android="http://schemas.android.com/apk/res/android"
    package="com.androidbook.telephony" android:versionCode="1"
    android:versionName="1.0">
    <uses-permission android:name="android.permission.RECEIVE_SMS"/>
    <uses-permission android:name="android.permission.SEND_SMS"/>
[ ... ]
        <receiver android:name="MySMSMonitor">
          <intent-filter>
            <action
                android:name="android.provider.Telephony.SMS_RECEIVED"/>
          </intent-filter>
        </receiver>
[ ... ]
</manifest>
```

```java
// This file is MySMSMonitor.java
import android.content.BroadcastReceiver;
import android.content.Context;
import android.content.Intent;
import android.telephony.SmsMessage;
import android.util.Log;

public class MySMSMonitor extends BroadcastReceiver
{
    private static final String ACTION =
                "android.provider.Telephony.SMS_RECEIVED";
    @Override
    public void onReceive(Context context, Intent intent)
    {
        if(intent!=null && intent.getAction()!=null &&
            ACTION.compareToIgnoreCase(intent.getAction())==0)
        {
            Object[] pduArray= (Object[]) intent.getExtras().get("pdus");
            SmsMessage[] messages = new SmsMessage[pduArray.length];
            for (int i = 0; i<pduArray.length; i++) {
                messages[i] = SmsMessage.createFromPdu(
                                    (byte[])pduArray [i]);
                Log.d("MySMSMonitor", "From: " +
                        messages[i].getOriginatingAddress());
                Log.d("MySMSMonitor", "Msg: " +
                        messages[i].getMessageBody());
            }
            Log.d("MySMSMonitor","SMS Message Received.");
        }
    }
}
```

The top portion of Listing 7-4 is the manifest definition for the BroadcastReceiver to intercept SMS messages. The SMS monitor class is MySMSMonitor. The class implements the abstract onReceive() method, which is called by the system when an SMS message arrives. One way to test the application is to use the Emulator Control view in Eclipse. Run the application in the emulator, and go to Window ➤ Show View ➤ Other ➤ Android ➤ Emulator Control. The user interface allows you to send data to the emulator to emulate receiving an SMS message or phone call. As shown in Figure 7-2, you can send an SMS message to the emulator by populating the "Incoming number" field and selecting the SMS radio button. Next, type some text in the Message field, and click the Send button. Doing this sends an SMS message to the emulator and invokes your BroadcastReceiver's onReceive() method.

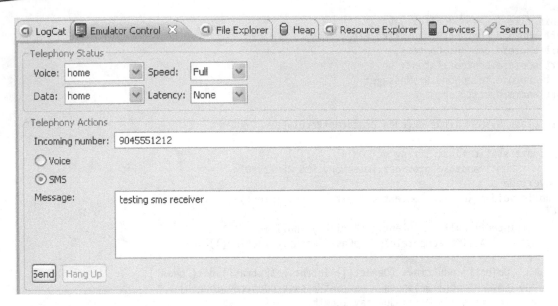

Figure 7-2. Using the Emulator Control UI to send SMS messages to the emulator

The onReceive() method will have the broadcast intent, which will contain the SmsMessage in the bundle property. You can extract the SmsMessage by calling intent.getExtras().get("pdus"). This call returns an array of objects defined in Protocol Description Unit (PDU) mode—an industry-standard way of representing an SMS message. You can then convert the PDUs to Android SmsMessage objects, as shown in Listing 7-4. As you can see, you get the PDUs as an object array from the intent. You then construct an array of SmsMessage objects equal to the size of the PDU array. Finally, you iterate over the PDU array and create SmsMessage objects from the PDUs by calling SmsMessage.createFromPdu().

What you do after reading the incoming message must be quick. A broadcast receiver gets high priority in the system, but its task must be finished quickly, and it does not get put into the foreground for the user to see. Therefore, your options are limited. You should not do any direct UI work. Issuing a notification is fine, as is starting a service to continue work there. Once the onReceive() method completes, the hosting process of the onReceive() method could get killed at any time. Starting a service is okay, but binding to one is not, since that would require your process to exist for a while, which might not happen.

Now, let's continue our discussion about SMS by looking at how you can work with various SMS folders.

Working with SMS Folders

Accessing the SMS inbox is another common requirement. To get started, you add read SMS permission (android.permission.READ_SMS) to the manifest file. Adding this permission gives you the ability to read from the SMS inbox.

To read SMS messages, you execute a query on the SMS inbox, as shown in Listing 7-5.

Listing 7-5. Displaying the Messages from the SMS Inbox

```xml
<?xml version="1.0" encoding="utf-8"?>
<!-- This file is /res/layout/sms_inbox.xml -->
<LinearLayout xmlns:android="http://schemas.android.com/apk/res/android"
    android:orientation="vertical"
    android:layout_width="fill_parent"
    android:layout_height="fill_parent" >

  <TextView android:id="@+id/row"
    android:layout_width="fill_parent"
    android:layout_height="fill_parent"/>

</LinearLayout>
```

```java
// This file is SMSInboxDemo.java
import android.app.ListActivity;
import android.database.Cursor;
import android.net.Uri;
import android.os.Bundle;
import android.widget.ListAdapter;
import android.widget.SimpleCursorAdapter;

public class SMSInboxDemo extends ListActivity {

    private ListAdapter adapter;
    private static final Uri SMS_INBOX =
            Uri.parse("content://sms/inbox");

    @Override
    public void onCreate(Bundle bundle) {
        super.onCreate(bundle);
        Cursor c = getContentResolver()
                .query(SMS_INBOX, null, null, null, null);
        startManagingCursor(c);
        String[] columns = new String[] { "body" };
        int[]      names = new int[]    { R.id.row };
        adapter = new SimpleCursorAdapter(this, R.layout.sms_inbox,
                c, columns, names);

        setListAdapter(adapter);
    }
}
```

The code in Listing 7-5 opens the SMS inbox and creates a list in which each item contains the body portion of an SMS message. The layout portion of Listing 7-5 contains a simple TextView that will hold the body of each message in a list item. To get the list of SMS messages, you create a URI pointing to the SMS inbox (content://sms/inbox) and then execute a simple query. You then filter on the body of the SMS message and set the list adapter of the ListActivity. After executing the code from Listing 7-5, you'll see a list of SMS messages in the inbox. Make sure you generate a few SMS messages using the Emulator Control before running the code on the emulator.

Because you can access the SMS inbox, you would expect to be able to access other SMS-related folders, such as the sent or draft folder. The only difference between accessing the inbox and accessing the other folders is the URI you specify. For example, you can access the sent folder by executing a query against `content://sms/sent`. Following is the complete list of SMS folders and the URI for each folder:

- *All*: `content://sms/all`

- *Inbox*: `content://sms/inbox`

- *Sent*: `content://sms/sent`

- *Draft*: `content://sms/draft`

- *Outbox*: `content://sms/outbox`

- *Failed*: `content://sms/failed`

- *Queued*: `content://sms/queued`

- *Undelivered*: `content://sms/undelivered`

- *Conversations*: `content://sms/conversations`

Android combines MMS and SMS, and allows you to access content providers for both at the same time, using an AUTHORITY of `mms-sms`. Therefore, you can access a URI such as this:

`content://mms-sms/conversations`

Sending E-mail

Now that you've seen how to send SMS messages in Android, you might assume that you can access similar APIs to send e-mail. Unfortunately, Android does not provide APIs for you to send e-mail. The general consensus is that users don't want an application to start sending e-mail on their behalf without their knowing about it. Instead, to send e-mail, you have to go through a registered e-mail application. For example, you could use `ACTION_SEND` to launch the e-mail application, as shown in Listing 7-6.

Listing 7-6. Launching the E-mail Application via an Intent

```
Intent emailIntent=new Intent(Intent.ACTION_SEND);

String subject = "Hi!";
String body = "hello from android....";

String[] recipients = new String[]{"aaa@bbb.com"};
emailIntent.putExtra(Intent.EXTRA_EMAIL, recipients);

emailIntent.putExtra(Intent.EXTRA_SUBJECT, subject);
emailIntent.putExtra(Intent.EXTRA_TEXT, body);
emailIntent.setType("message/rfc822");

startActivity(emailIntent);
```

This code launches the default e-mail application and allows the user to decide whether to send the e-mail or not. Other "extras" that you can add to an e-mail intent include EXTRA_CC and EXTRA_BCC.

Let's assume you want to send an e-mail attachment with your message. To do this, you use something like the following, where the Uri is a reference to the file you want as the attachment:

```
emailIntent.putExtra(Intent.EXTRA_STREAM,
    Uri.fromFile(new File(myFileName)));
```

Next, let's talk about the telephony manager.

Working with the Telephony Manager

The telephony APIs also include the telephony manager (android.telephony.TelephonyManager), which you can use to obtain information about the telephony services on the device, get subscriber information, and register for telephony state changes. A common telephony use case requires that an application execute business logic on incoming phone calls. For example, a music player might pause itself for an incoming call and resume when the call has been completed.

The easiest way to listen for phone state changes is to implement a broadcast receiver on android.intent.action.PHONE_STATE. You can do this in the same way as you listened for incoming SMS messages, detailed above. The other way is to use the TelephonyManager. In this section, we show you how to register for telephony state changes and how to detect incoming phone calls. Listing 7-7 shows the details.

Listing 7-7. Using the Telephony Manager

```
<?xml version="1.0" encoding="utf-8"?>
<!-- This file is res/layout/main.xml -->
<LinearLayout xmlns:android="http://schemas.android.com/apk/res/android"
    android:orientation="vertical"
    android:layout_width="fill_parent"
    android:layout_height="fill_parent"
    >
<Button
    android:id="@+id/callBtn"
    android:layout_width="wrap_content"
    android:layout_height="wrap_content"
    android:text="Place Call"
    android:onClick="doClick"
    />
<Button
    android:id="@+id/quitBtn"
    android:layout_width="wrap_content"
    android:layout_height="wrap_content"
    android:text="Quit"
    android:onClick="doClick"
    />
</LinearLayout>

// This file is PhoneCallActivity.java
package com.androidbook.phonecall.demo;
```

```java
import android.app.Activity;
import android.content.Context;
import android.content.Intent;
import android.net.Uri;
import android.os.Bundle;
import android.telephony.PhoneStateListener;
import android.telephony.TelephonyManager;
import android.util.Log;
import android.view.View;

public class PhoneCallActivity extends Activity {
    private static final String TAG = "PhoneCallDemo";
    private TelephonyManager teleMgr = null;
    private MyPhoneStateListener myListener = null;

    @Override
    protected void onCreate(Bundle savedInstanceState)
    {
        super.onCreate(savedInstanceState);
        setContentView(R.layout.main);

        teleMgr =
            (TelephonyManager)getSystemService(Context.TELEPHONY_SERVICE);
        myListener = new MyPhoneStateListener();
        teleMgr.listen(myListener, PhoneStateListener.LISTEN_CALL_STATE);

        String myIMEI = teleMgr.getDeviceId();
        Log.d(TAG, "device IMEI is " + myIMEI);

        if (teleMgr.getSimState() == TelephonyManager.SIM_STATE_READY) {
            String country = teleMgr.getSimCountryIso();
            Log.d(TAG, "SIM country ISO is " + country);
        }
    }

    // Only unregister the listener if this app is going away.
    // Otherwise, when the user tries to make or receive a phone
    // call, this app will get paused and we don't want to stop
    // listening when we're put into the background.
    @Override
    public void onDestroy() {
        super.onDestroy();
        Log.d(TAG, "In onDestroy");
        teleMgr.listen(myListener, PhoneStateListener.LISTEN_NONE);
    }

    public void doClick(View target) {
        switch(target.getId()) {
        case R.id.callBtn:
            Intent intent = new Intent(Intent.ACTION_VIEW,
                Uri.parse("tel:5551212"));
            startActivity(intent);
```

```
                break;
        case R.id.quitBtn:
            finish();
            break;
        default:
            break;
        }
    }

    public class MyPhoneStateListener extends PhoneStateListener
    {
        @Override
        public void onCallStateChanged(int state, String incomingNumber){
            super.onCallStateChanged(state, incomingNumber);

            switch(state)
            {
                case TelephonyManager.CALL_STATE_IDLE:
                    Log.d(TAG, "call state idle...incoming number ["+
                        incomingNumber+"]");
                    break;
                case TelephonyManager.CALL_STATE_RINGING:
                    Log.d(TAG, "call state ringing...incoming number ["+
                        incomingNumber+"]");
                    break;
                case TelephonyManager.CALL_STATE_OFFHOOK:
                    Log.d(TAG, "call state offhook...incoming number ["+
                        incomingNumber+"]");
                    break;
                default:
                    Log.d(TAG, "call state ["+state+"]");
                    break;
            }
        }
    }
}
```

When working with the telephony manager, be sure to add the android.permission.READ_PHONE_STATE permission to your manifest file so you can access phone state information. As shown in Listing 7-7, you get notified about phone state changes by implementing a PhoneStateListener and calling the listen() method of the TelephonyManager. When a phone call arrives, or the phone state changes, the system will call your PhoneStateListener's onCallStateChanged() method with the new state. As you will see when you try this out, the incoming phone number is only available when the state is CALL_STATE_RINGING. You write a message to LogCat in this example, but your application could implement custom business logic in its place, such as pausing the playback of audio or video.

> **Note** If your application needs to change audio volume levels owing to phone calls (or notifications or alarms), you should investigate Android's Audio Focus feature set. Audio Focus is not covered in this book.

To emulate incoming phone calls, you can use Eclipse's Emulator Control UI—the same one you used to send SMS messages (see Figure 7-2)—but choose Voice instead of SMS.

Notice that we tell the TelephonyManager to stop sending us updates in onDestroy(). It is always important to turn off messages when your activity goes away. Otherwise, the TelephonyManager could keep a reference to your object and prevent it from being cleaned up later. However, when the activity goes into the background, you still want to receive updates.

This example deals with only one of the phone states that are available for listening. Check out the documentation on PhoneStateListener for others, including for example LISTEN_MESSAGE_WAITING_INDICATOR. When dealing with phone state changes, you might also need to get the subscriber's (user's) phone number. TelephonyManager.getLine1Number() will return that for you.

You may be wondering if it's possible to answer a phone via code. Unfortunately, at this time the Android SDK does not provide a way to do this, even though the documentation implies that you can fire off an intent with an action of ACTION_ANSWER. In practice, this approach does not yet work, although you may want to check to see if this has been fixed since the time of this writing. There appear to be some hacks out there that work on some devices but not all. An Internet search for ACTION_ANSWER should find them.

Similarly, you may want to place an outbound phone call via code. Here, you will find things easier. The simplest way to make an outbound call is to invoke the Dialer application via an intent with code such as the following:

```
Intent intent = new Intent(Intent.ACTION_CALL, Uri.parse("tel:5551212"));
startActivity(intent);
```

Note that for this to actually dial, your application will need the android.permission.CALL_PHONE permission. Otherwise, when your application attempts to invoke the Dialer application, you will get a SecurityException. To do dialing without this permission, change the action of the intent to Intent.ACTION_VIEW, which will cause the Dialer application to appear with your desired number to dial, but the user will need to press the Send button to initiate the call.

Your other option for detecting changes in the phone's state is to register a broadcast receiver for phone state changes (android.intent.action.PHONE_STATE), similar to how you received SMS messages in the example at the beginning of this chapter. This can be done in code, or you can specify a <receiver> tag in your manifest file.

Session Initiation Protocol (SIP)

Android 2.3 (Gingerbread) introduced new features to support SIP in the android.net.sip package. SIP is an Internet Engineering Task Force (IETF) standard for orchestrating the sending of voice and video over a network connection to link people together in calls. This technology is sometimes called Voice over IP (VoIP), but note that there is more than one way to do VoIP.

Skype, for instance, uses a proprietary protocol to do their VoIP, and it notincompatible with SIP. SIP is also not the same as Google Voice. Google Voice does not (as of this writing) support SIP directly, although there are ways to integrate Google Voice with a SIP provider in order to tie things together. Google Voice sets up a new telephone number for you that you can then use to connect with other phones such as your home, work, or mobile phone. Some SIP providers will generate a telephone number that can be used with Google Voice, but in this case Google Voice does not really know that the number is for a SIP account. A search of the Internet will reveal quite a few SIP providers, many with reasonable calling rates and some that are free.

It is important to note that the SIP standard does not address passing audio and video data over a network. SIP is only involved in setting up, and tearing down, the direct connections between devices to allow audio and video data to flow. Client computer programs use SIP, as well as audio and video codecs and other libraries, to set up the calls between users. Other standards often involved with SIP calls include the Real-time Transport Protocol (RTP), Real-time Streaming Protocol (RTSP), and Session Description Protocol (SDP). Android 3.1 brought direct support in Android for RTP, in the android.net.rtp package. RTSP has been supported by the MediaPlayer for some time, although not all RTSP servers are compatible with Android's MediaPlayer. SDP is an application-level protocol for describing multimedia sessions, so you'll see message content in SDP format.

Users can make SIP calls from desktop computers without incurring long-distance phone charges. The computer program can just as easily be running on a mobile device such as an Android smartphone or tablet. SIP computer programs are often called "soft phones." The real advantage of a soft phone on a mobile device is when the device is connecting to the Internet using Wi-Fi, so that the user is not using any wireless minutes but is still able to make or receive a call. On the receiving end, a soft phone must have registered its location and capabilities with a SIP provider so that the provider's SIP server can respond to invite requests to set up the direct connection. If the receiver's soft phone is not available, the SIP server can direct the inbound request to a voicemail account, for example.

Google provides a demonstration application for SIP, called SipDemo. Let's explore that application now, so you understand how it works. Certain aspects are not obvious if you are new to SIP. If you'd like to experiment with SipDemo, you're probably going to need a physical Android device that supports SIP. This is because the Android emulators, as of this writing, do not support SIP (or Wi-Fi, for that matter). There are some attempts on the Internet to make SIP work in the emulator, and by the time you read this some may be easy to implement and be robust.

To play with SipDemo you need to get a SIP account from a SIP provider. You need to have your SIP ID, SIP domain name (or proxy), and your SIP password. These are thenplugged into the SipDemo application's preferences screen to be used by the application. Lastly, you need a Wi-Fi connection from your device to the Internet. However, if you don't want to actually experiment with SipDemo on a device, you should still be able to understand the rest of this section. The SipDemo looks as shown in Figure 7-3.

Figure 7-3. The SipDemo application with the menu showing

To load SipDemo as a new project into Eclipse, use the New Android Project wizard, click the Android Sample Project option, choose Android 2.3 or higher in the Build Target section, then choose SipDemo. Click Finish and Eclipse will create the new project for you. You can run this project with no changes to it, but as mentioned before, it won't do anything unless the device supports SIP, Wi-Fi is enabled, you've got a SIP account somewhere, you've used the Menu button to edit your SIP info, and you use the Menu button to initiate a call. You will need some other SIP account to call so as to test the application. Pressing the big microphone image on the screen allows you to talk to the other side. This demo application can also receive an incoming call. Now let's talk about the inner workings of the android.net.sip package.

The android.net.sip package has four basic classes: SipManager, SipProfile, SipSession, and SipAudioCall. SipManager is at the core of this package; it provides access to the rest of the SIP functionality. You invoke the static newInstance() method of SipManager to get a SipManager object. With a SipManager object, you can then get a SipSession for most SIP activity, or you can get a SipAudioCall for an audio-only call. This means Google has provided features in the android.net.sip package beyond what standard SIP provides—namely, the ability to set up an audio call.

SipProfile is used to define the SIP accounts that will be talking to each other. This does not point directly to an end user's device but, rather, to the SIP account at a SIP provider. The servers assist in the rest of the details to set up actual connections.

A SipSession is where the magic happens. Setting up a session includes your SipProfile so that your application can make itself known to your SIP provider's server. You also pass a SipSession. Listener instance that is going to be notified when things are happening. Once you've set up a SipSession object, your application is ready to make calls to another SipProfile or to receive incoming calls. The listener has a bunch of callbacks so your application can properly deal with the changing states of the session.

As of Honeycomb, the easiest thing to do is to use SipAudioCall. The logic is all there to hook up the microphone and the speaker to the data streams so that you can carry on a conversation with the other side. There are lots of methods on SipAudioCall for managing mute, hold, and so on. All of the audio pieces are also handled for you.

For anything more than that, you have work to do. The SipSession class has the makeCall() method for placing an outbound call. The main parameter is the session description (as a string). This is where things require more work. Building a session description requires formating according to the Session Description Protocol (SDP) mentioned earlier. Understanding a received session description means parsing it according to SDP. The standards documentation for SDP is at: http://tools.ietf.org/html/rfc4566. Unfortunately, the Android SDK does not provide any support for SDP. Thanks to some very kind people, however, there are a couple of free SIP applications for Android that have built this capability. They are sipdroid (http://code.google.com/p/sipdroid/) and csipsimple (http://code.google.com/p/csipsimple/).

We haven't even started considering the codecs for managing video streams between SIP clients, although sipdroid has this capability. Other aspects of SIP that are very appealing are the ability to set up conference calls among more than two people. These topics are beyond the scope of this book, but we hope you can appreciate what SIP can do for you.

Note that SIP applications will need, at minimum, the android.permission.USE_SIP and android.permission.INTERNET permissions in order to function properly. If you use SipAudioCall, you will also need the android.permission.RECORD_AUDIO permission. And assuming you're using Wi-Fi, you should add android.permission.ACCESS_WIFI_STATE and android.permission.WAKE_LOCK. It is also a good idea to add the following tag to your AndroidManifest.xml file, as a child of <manifest>, so that your application will be installable only on devices that have hardware support for SIP:

```
<uses-feature android:name="android.hardware.sip.voip" />
```

References

Here are some helpful references to topics you may wish to explore further.

- www.androidbook.com/expertandroid/projects. Look here for a list of downloadable projects related to this book. For this chapter, look for a zip file called ExpertAndroid_ch07_Telephony.zip. This zip file contains all projects from this chapter, listed in separate root directories. There is also a README.TXT file that describes exactly how to import projects into Eclipse from one of these zip files.

- http://en.wikipedia.org/wiki/Session_Initiation_Protocol. The Wikipedia page for SIP.

- http://tools.ietf.org/html/rfc3261. This is the official IETF standard for Session Initiation Protocol (SIP).

- http://tools.ietf.org/html/rfc4566. This is the official IETF standard for Session Description Protocol (SDP).

- http://www.ietf.org/rfc/rfc3551.txt. This is the official IETF standard for Real-time Transport Protocol (RTP). See also the android.net.rtp package.

- http://code.google.com/p/sipdroid/, http://code.google.com/p/csipsimple/. Two open source applications for Android that implement SIP clients.

Summary

This chapter discussed the Android telephony APIs. In particular:

1. You learned how to send and receive an SMS message.

2. You learned about SMS folders and reading SMS messages.

3. We covered the sending of e-mail from an application.

4. You learned about the TelephonyManager and how to detect an incoming call.

5. You saw how SIP can be used to create a VoIP client program.

Review Questions

You can use the following questions as a way to consolidate your understanding of this chapter.

1. Can an SMS message contain more than 140 characters?

2. True or false? You get an SmsManager instance by calling Context. getSystemService(MESSAGE_SERVICE).

3. Where is the ADT feature that allows you to send a test SMS message to an emulator?

4. Can an application send an e-mail without the user's knowing?

5. Can an application send an SMS message without the user's knowing?

6. Can an application make a phone call without the user's knowing?

7. Is SIP the same as Skype?

8. What are the four main classes of the android.net.sip package?

9. Which SIP class defines the SIP accounts that will be talking to each other?

10. What tag do you put into the AndroidManifest.xml file to ensure a SIP app will be seen only by devices that support SIP?

11. What permissions are needed in order to make SIP work properly?

Chapter 8

Advanced Debugging and Analysis

At this point in your Android learning, you've probably got a few applications under your belt, and you may have encountered some unexpected behavior from them. This chapter takes some time to explore the advanced ways you can debug an application, so you can look inside the application and find out what's going on. The chapter also covers how to analyze your application to make sure it's performing as well as it can, and helps you ensure that it isn't doing something it shouldn't be doing.

What you will explore here are various tools and capabilities, many within Eclipse and with the Android Developer Tools (ADT) plug-in for Eclipse. You'll learn where to find these tools and how they work. In the process, you'll use some sample applications that have been deliberately written poorly to demonstrate how these tools find problems.

The Eclipse Debug perspective is the standard one that comes with Eclipse, and it isn't specific to Android programming. However, you will soon learn what can be done with it. The Android Dalvik Debug Monitor Server (DDMS) perspective has quite a few very useful features to help you debug your applications. These include Devices view (for seeing what you're connected to), Emulator Control (for sending telephone calls, SMS messages, and GPS coordinates), File Explorer (for viewing/ transferring files on the device), Network Statistics (for viewing traffic to and from a device), Threads, Heap, Allocation Tracker (for seeing inside your application), systrace (for seeing inside your Android device), and OpenGL tracer. You'll also learn about Traceview, which makes it much easier to analyze a dump file from an application.

This chapter also dives into the Hierarchy View perspective so you can traverse the actual view structure of a running application. Finally, you cover the `StrictMode` class, which can be used to trap policy violations to catch design errors that can cause poor user experiences.

Enabling Advanced Debugging

When you test in an emulator, the Eclipse Android Developer Tools (ADT) plug-ins take care of setting everything up for you so you can use all the tools you're about to see.

You need to know two things about debugging applications on a real device. First, the application must be set to be debuggable. This involves adding android:debuggable="true" to the <application> tag in the AndroidManifest.xml file. Fortunately, ADT sets this properly so you don't have to. When you're creating debug builds for the emulator or deploying directly from Eclipse to a device, this attribute is set to true by ADT. When you export your application to create a production version of it, ADT automatically sets debuggable to false. Note that if you set it yourself in AndroidManifest.xml, it stays set no matter what.

The second thing to know is that the device must be put into USB Debug mode. To find this setting for Android versions up to Gingerbread, go to the device's Settings screen, choose Application, and then choose Development. Make sure Enable USB Debugging is selected.

On newer versions of Android (Ice Cream Sandwich and later), go to Settings, choose Developer options, and enable USB debugging. If you don't see Developer options, you'll have to do a simple trick to unhide them. From the list of Settings, choose About phone, then scroll down until you see the Build number. Quickly tap this repeatedly—seven times ought to do it—and you'll be rewarded with a message saying you are now a developer, and the menu option will appear back in Settings.

> **Easter Egg Note** For more fun if you're running Jelly Bean, find the Android version entry under About phone and quickly tap that multiple times until you get a big smiling jelly bean. Press and hold the jelly bean until you see a field of floating beans. Touch and fling these beans. Press the Back button to quit this.

The Debug Perspective

Although LogCat is very useful for watching log messages, you definitely want more control and more information about your application as it runs. Debugging in Eclipse is fairly easy and is described in detail in many places on the Internet. As such, this chapter doesn't go into great detail about Eclipse, but these are some of the useful features you get:

- Setting breakpoints in your code so execution stops there when the application runs
- Inspecting variables
- Stepping over and into lines of code
- Attaching the debugger to an application that's already running
- Disconnecting from an application you were attached to
- Viewing stack traces
- Viewing a list of threads
- Viewing LogCat

Figure 8-1 shows a sample screen layout of what you can do with the Debug perspective.

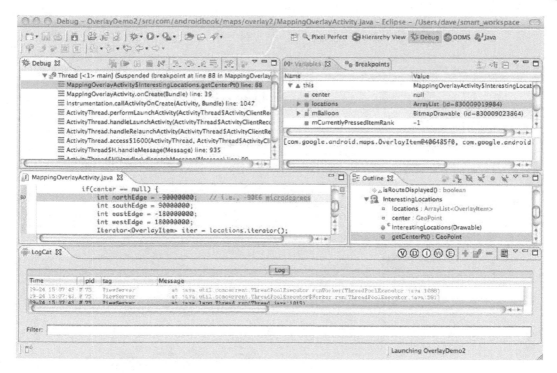

Figure 8-1. *The Debug perspective*

You can start debugging an application from the Java perspective (where you write the code) by right-clicking the project and selecting Debug As ➤ Android Application; this launches the application. You can also choose Debug from the Run menu, Debug from the toolbar, or use the keyboard shortcut F11. You may need to switch to the Debug perspective to do the debugging.

The DDMS Perspective

DDMS stands for Dalvik Debug Monitor Server. This perspective gives you insight into the applications that are running on the emulator or device, allowing you to watch threads and memory, as well as gather statistics as the applications run. Figure 8-2 shows how it might look on your workstation. Note that when this section uses the term *device*, it means device or emulator.

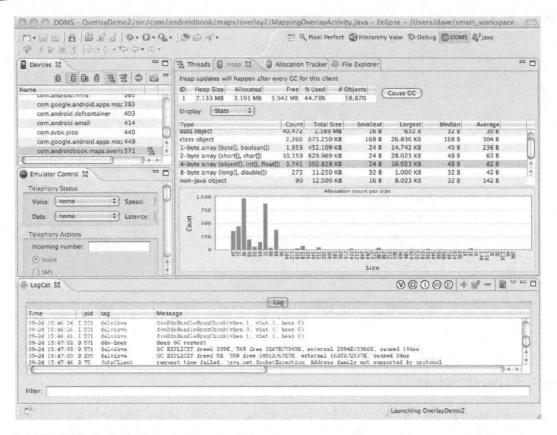

Figure 8-2. The DDMS perspective

Alternatively, you can navigate to the Android SDK directory, and under the tools, find the monitor program. Launching this produces the same DDMS window as you would see inside Eclipse.

In the upper-left corner of Figure 8-2, notice the Devices view. This shows you all devices connected to your workstation (you can have more than one device or emulator connected simultaneously) and, if you expand the view, all applications that are available for debugging. In Figure 8-2, you're viewing an emulator, so the stock applications appear available for debugging. On a real device, you may see only a few applications, if any. Don't forget that if you're debugging a production application on a real device, you may need to tweak the `AndroidManifest.xml` file to set `android:debuggable` to `true`.

Within the Devices view are buttons to start debugging an application, update the heap, dump a Heap and CPU Profiling Agent (HPROF) file, cause a garbage collection (GC), update the threads list, start method profiling, stop the process, take a picture of the device's screen, analyze the view hierarchy, and generate a system trace or capture an OpenGL trace. The buttons are shown in Figure 8-3. Let's go into more detail about each of these, from left to right. With the exception of the camera and systrace buttons, all of these buttons act on whatever application has been selected in the Devices view list. If you don't see any applications listed, you may need to click the + sign next to the device name. Or you may need to set your application to debuggable, as described above.

Figure 8-3. The DDMS advanced debugging buttons

The Debug Button

The little green bug button starts debugging on the selected application. Clicking it takes you to the Debug perspective, just described. What's nice about this option is that you can attach the debugger to a running application. You can get an application to a state where you want debugging to begin, select it, and click this button. Then, as you continue to exercise the application, the breakpoints will cause execution to stop, and you can inspect variables and step through the code.

Debugging an Android application is no different from debugging any other application in Eclipse. As mentioned earlier, you can set breakpoints, inspect variables, and step through and into code. This chapter won't go into those details, but there are plenty of resources on the Internet to learn more about debugging in Eclipse.

The Heap Buttons

The next three buttons are used to analyze the memory heap of a running process. You want your apps to use as little memory as feasible and not to allocate memory too frequently. Similar to using the Debug button, you select the application you want to inspect and then click the Update Heap button (the first of these three). You should pick only applications that you're actively debugging. In the Heap view tab to the right in Figure 8-2 , you can click the Cause GC button to collect information about memory in the heap. The summary results are displayed, with detailed results below. Then, for each type and size of allocated memory, you can see additional details about how memory is being used.

Some of the things you will look for in this view include:

- *High counts of large objects*: you will probably have a few objects in the several KB size range; this is normal. If you see lots of large objects, this could mean your code is recreating some large object over and over again; that's probably a problem. Select each line in the Stats list, and view the graphs below. If you see a tall bar far to the right of the graph, that indicates a lot of large objects.

- *Some really large objects*: in general, a mobile application should avoid creating these as memory is a precious resource. The column labeled Largest will tell you what your largest object is, and coming up you'll see how to go find out where it came from.

- *Really high counts of any size of object*: the best way to avoid garbage collection pauses of your application is to not create a lot of garbage in the first place. If your application is creating MBs of objects within seconds, your users will experience GC pauses that will interfere with the user experience. Use either the Count column or the graphs to identify any types of objects with really high occurrences.

The Dump HPROF File button does just that: it gives you an HPROF file. If you have installed the Eclipse Memory Analyzer (MAT) plug-in, this file is processed and results are displayed. This can be a powerful way to look for memory leaks. By default, an HPROF file is opened in Eclipse, but won't be very helpful without the MAT plug-in. See the References at the end of this chapter for more information on this plug-in. Depending on the power of your workstation, this operation can take up to a minute or more, so be patient if it appears that nothing is happening. There is a Preferences setting for this under Android ➤ DDMS, where you can opt to save to a file instead.

The MAT will report on memory usage of the objects in your application. For any problems you may have seen in the Heap above, this tool can dig deeper to identify where the problem objects are coming from. For example, from the Overview tab of the MAT view, if you click on the Top Consumers link, you'll see the objects taking up the most heap. If instead you clicked on Leak Suspects, you'll see objects that could be leaking memory. This report can even reveal the object reference name to help locate the code where the memory is allocated.

The Threads Buttons

The Update Threads button populates the Threads tab to the right with the current set of threads from the selected application. This is a great way to watch as threads are created and destroyed, and to get some idea of what's happening at the thread level in your application. Below the list of threads, you can see where a thread is by following what looks like a stack trace (objects, source-code file reference, and line number).

For example, the stock Google Maps app uses a lot of threads, and you can watch them come and go by selecting the app in the Devices view, then click the Update Threads button. In the Threads view to the right, you'll see many threads as Maps talks to the various Google Maps services. Double-clicking one of the thread entries displays the detail information in the list below.

The next button, Start Method Profiling, allows you to collect information about the methods in your application, including number of calls and timing information. You click this button, interact with your application, and then click the button again (it toggles between Start and Stop Method Profiling). When you click Stop Method Profiling, Eclipse switches to the Traceview view, which is covered in the next section of this chapter. As with the HPROF dump, bringing up the Traceview view can take a minute or more, depending on the power of your workstation, so be patient if Eclipse doesn't seem to be doing anything.

The Stop Button

The Stop button (which looks like a stop sign) allows you to stop the selected process. This is a hard application stop—it isn't like clicking the Back button, which only affects an activity. In this case, the entire application goes away.

The Camera Button

The button that looks like a camera captures the current state of the device screen, regardless of which application is selected in the Device view. You can then refresh the image, rotate it, save it, or copy it. The Save option only uses the PNG format, but if you click the Copy button, you can then paste into some other tool (for example, Paint) and save in whatever formats that tool uses.

The Dump View Hierarchy Button

This button (officially called Dump View Hierarchy for UI Automator) acts on the selected application to capture the current screen and all of the views that are on it, whether visible or not. Once captured, the View Hierarchy view is shown, which will resemble Figure 8-4.

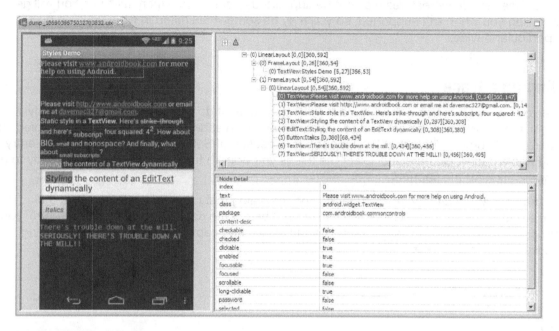

Figure 8-4. The View Hierarchy view

The purpose of this feature is to provide the information you need to create automated UI testing using the UI Automator. The window in the upper right shows the hierarchy of all views from the screenshot on the left. Remember that everything on the screen is a View object, including the text and the buttons. For the selected Layout or View, the details are shown in the lower right window.

This tool is similar but different from the View Hierarchy perspective discussed later in this chapter. This view simply shows you the views and their hierarchy. The tool described later gives you much more information about the rendering of the views.

The Systrace Button

The systrace button launches a dialog so you can set the parameters for capturing a system trace (systrace) from a device. A systrace tracks method calls of many system processes as well as your programs. It is used to identify issues at a very low level that could be causing user experience problems, such as delays in responsiveness. It allows you to select the processes that could be involved in a problem and easily compare method call timings to see what is impacting what, even across process boundaries—for example, when services are used. The output of a systrace is an HTML file that you can then load into a browser (Chrome preferred) to do the analysis.

In this specific case, the emulator cannot be used to get a systrace, and you must have a physical device. The device must be running Android 4.1 or above, and it must be capable of capturing system traces. The Google Nexus devices are enabled, as is the Samsung Galaxy S3. To see if your device is capable, check its file system to see if the /sys/kernel/debug directory exists. If it does exist, then you're probably good to go. There are some features of systrace that require root access on the device, and other features may not be supported by the device manufacturer. You will get errors telling you what isn't supported, so you may be somewhat limited in what you can do with your particular device.

Setting up a trace

Before you can begin a trace, there are a few things you must do on the device to get it ready. To begin, the device must be connected to your workstation and have USB Debugging enabled, as was explained above. Within the Developer options section of Settings, you will also find an entry called Enable traces. Go here and select the things you want to trace. Click OK and get ready to run your application for the capture.

Now, turn your attention to your workstation and the dialog that pops up when you click the Systrace button, as shown in Figure 8-5. Either right before the capture or right after (or both), you will probably want to run the ps command on the device and capture the output. The following works well from your workstation:

```
adb shell ps > c:\temp\ps.txt
```

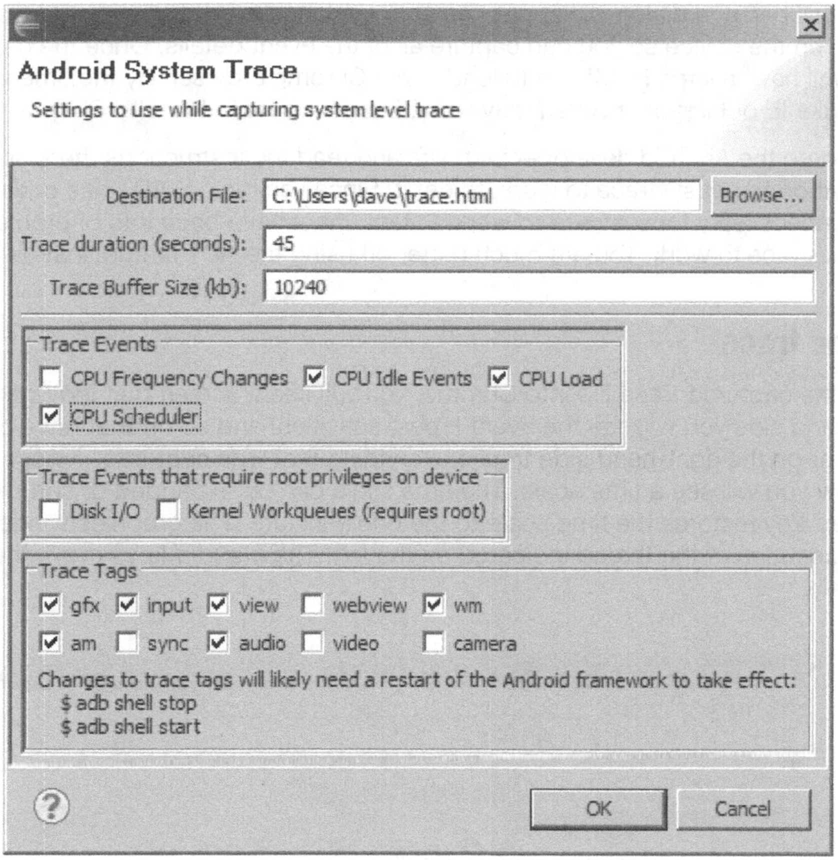

Figure 8-5. The Systrace dialog

Use whatever output filename is appropriate for your platform. This will capture the list of active processes that will be useful when analyzing the trace information.

The first two fields are self-explanatory. The Trace Buffer Size (kb) field needs to be pretty big in order to capture all the data. In this example, the buffer is set to 10MB, which seems to work pretty well. You can choose larger sizes if you find that your capture is truncated.

The first four Trace Event choices are obviously related to CPU activity, which you will want to see. Not all devices will support all of these events. If you get an error message related to one of these event types, just deselect it on this dialog and try again. For the Trace Events that require root, you will need to restart your adbd with the command adb root. This only works, of course, if you have rooted your device and installed an insecure boot.img.

The Trace Tags match the choices on the device under Settings ➤ Developer options ➤ Enable traces. Most of the labels are self-explanatory with the exception of am (Activity Manager) and wm (Window Manager). You do not need to choose all of the tags in the dialog that you enabled on the device, but for any you do choose in the dialog you must have selected the corresponding Enable traces settings option on the device. You do not need to perform the adb shell commands as instructed, unless for some reason you don't get a valid trace.html file as output. When you click

OK, the tracing will begin, a dialog will appear on your workstation, and you should start exercising your application on the device so you can capture all of the event details. Once the capture is complete, you will have a large HTML file to load into a Chrome browser. By the time you read this, other browsers like IE or Firefox or Safari may work, but your best bet is with Chrome.

If you ventured onto the Android developer web site and read the instructions there about downloading python to get systrace to work, forget it. Since version 21, ADT has code in it that makes python unnecessary for systrace to work. In fact, there have been lots of problems in getting python-based systrace to work. You are much better off using the ADT feature instead.

Analyzing the trace

Once you load the captured trace file into Chrome, you will see a screen that looks like Figure 8-6. Down the left-hand side you will see the event types, activities, and so on that have been captured. Use the scroll bar on the right-hand side to see everything that was captured. Across the top of the graphics window you will see a time scale. The time scale can be expanded or shrunk using the *w* and *s* keys. The *z* key restores the time scale to the original state. The graphics window displays lines for each execution of the thread indicated on the left. The *a* and *d* keys move the lines left and right, respectively.

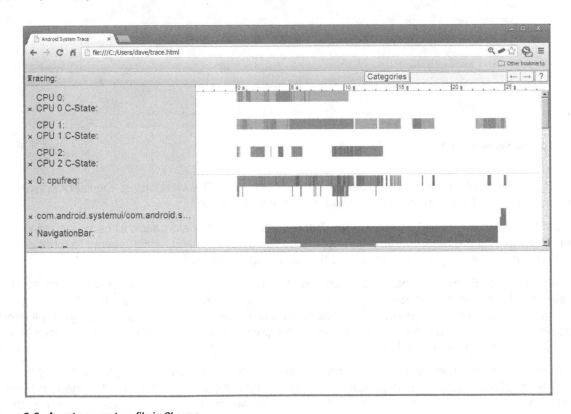

Figure 8-6. A systrace capture file in Chrome

As you've no doubt discovered, there's too much to look at all at the same time. You need some guideposts. Fortunately, you can click on the time scale to add vertical lines that extend down through all of the rows. This allows you to focus on a particular time slice and compare threads. You can have more than two vertical lines if you like; you can click a line again to remove it; and you can click and drag a line to move it. You can also click on an *x* on the far left-hand side to eliminate a row that you decide you don't care about. The data is still in the systrace file, so you can always reload it if you want it back.

Zoom in on the lines in the graphics window until you see some width. Now click on a line. You will see some details about the timing of that event in the lower portion of the window. Click on another line and you'll see the details for it. Now click and drag a box around a cluster of lines. As you drag, you will see the time slice duration of the box, and when you let go, the events within that box will be summarized in the lower portion of the window. This is a very powerful way to see everything that is going on with the device.

A couple of the key rows to look at are SurfaceFlinger and its secondary thread, surfaceflinger. If everything is going well on the device, SurfaceFlinger will look very regular, with very short lines evenly spaced apart. This ensures that the user experience is snappy and responsive. In fact, all applications should be exhibiting this kind of behavior—that is, processing within your application should be short and regular. Any time your application is processing an event (a user click, receiving a broadcast), it should be quickly doing whatever it can do and making sure the main thread isn't blocked. If you see a break in the SurfaceFlinger lines, it means something else is tying up the device's resources and potentially causing jerky behavior in the user's experience. With this systrace tool, you can track down exactly where the bad stuff occurs, and presumably do something about it to resolve the issue.

A full explanation of the underlying architecture of Android is beyond the scope of this chapter, but you might be interested in knowing what some of the items are in the list of event sources. VSYNC is Vertical Sync, which Android uses to manage the display buffers. Binders are how data is passed between processes, including to the graphics server.

The Start OpenGL Trace Button/Tracer for OpenGL ES

This button launches a dialog to allow you to capture OpenGL frames for analysis. Or, at least it's supposed to. There have been problems with getting to the OpenGL tracing feature using this method. You may have better success using the Tracer for OpenGL ES perspective instead. Use the Window menu to find and launch this perspective. Then use the Start Trace button here (which looks the same as the Start OpenGL Trace button on the DDMS screen) to get the dialog window that will look like Figure 8-7.

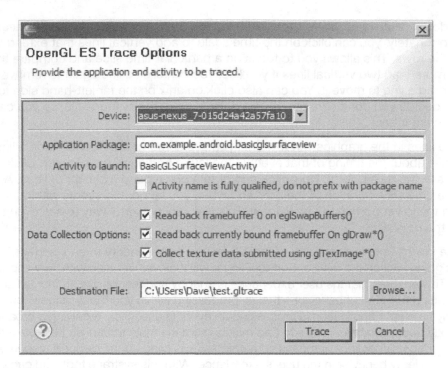

Figure 8-7. An OpenGL trace dialog

The device will likely be defaulted for you. For the Application Package, enter the name of the activity's package that you want to be tracing. For the Activity to launch, enter the name of the activity. If you get an error on the activity name, try prepending the activity name with a period (.). Choose the collection options and provide a filename—typically one that ends with .gltrace. Press the Trace button when ready. A new dialog window will appear that shows the progress of the frame captures. Press the Stop Tracing button when you've collected what you want.

The perspective then changes to show the results of the frame captures. You can use this screen to see how well OpenGL is working. If needed, click the Open a saved OpenGL Trace File button to load the file that you specified in the previous dialog. Use the frame slider to select a frame, then review the OpenGL ES calls. The drawing commands will be highlighted in blue.

The Devices View Menu

Finally, a menu includes all of the button features; in addition, there is a Reset adb menu item. Adb is the Android Debug Bridge, a server process that runs on your workstation to talk to emulators on your workstation or devices connected to it. The Reset adb option restarts the adb server in case things get out of sync and you can no longer see a device or emulator. This should (in effect) refresh the list of devices in the view. The other way you can reset the adb server is to use the following pair of commands in a tools window:

```
adb kill-server
adb start-server
```

Allocation Tracker

Figure 8-8 shows the Allocation Tracker tab. This lets you begin tracking individual memory allocations. After you click Start Tracking, you exercise your application and then click Get Allocations. The list of memory allocations in that time period is displayed, and you can click a specific allocation to see where it came from (class, method, source-code file reference, and line number). The Stop Tracking button is there so you can reset and start over.

Threads	Heap	Allocation Tracker ⊠	Network Statistics	File Explorer	Emulator Control		

Stop Tracking   Get Allocations   Filter: com.example   ☐ Inc. trace

Alloc Order ▼	Allocation Size	Allocated Class	Thread Id	Allocated in	Allocated in
445	52	android.graphics.Paint	1	com.example.android.notepad.NoteEditor$LinedEditText	onDraw
289	52	android.graphics.Paint	1	com.example.android.notepad.NoteEditor$LinedEditText	onDraw
266	52	android.graphics.Paint	1	com.example.android.notepad.NoteEditor$LinedEditText	onDraw
264	52	android.graphics.Paint	1	com.example.android.notepad.NoteEditor$LinedEditText	onDraw
262	52	android.graphics.Paint	1	com.example.android.notepad.NoteEditor$LinedEditText	onDraw
260	52	android.graphics.Paint	1	com.example.android.notepad.NoteEditor$LinedEditText	onDraw
258	52	android.graphics.Paint	1	com.example.android.notepad.NoteEditor$LinedEditText	onDraw
256	52	android.graphics.Paint	1	com.example.android.notepad.NoteEditor$LinedEditText	onDraw

Class	Method	File	Line	Native	
com.example.android.notepad.NoteEditor$LinedEditText	onDraw	NoteEditor.java	98	false	
android.view.View	draw	View.java	7000	false	
android.view.ViewGroup	drawChild	ViewGroup.java	1646	false	
android.view.ViewGroup	dispatchDraw	ViewGroup.java	1373	false	
android.view.View	draw	View.java	6900	false	
android.widget.FrameLayout	draw	FrameLayout.java	357	false	
android.view.ViewGroup	drawChild	ViewGroup.java	1646	false	
android.view.ViewGroup	dispatchDraw	ViewGroup.java	1373	false	
android.view.ViewGroup	drawChild	ViewGroup.java	1644	false	
android.view.ViewGroup	dispatchDraw	ViewGroup.java	1373	false	
android.view.View	draw	View.java	6900	false	
android.widget.FrameLayout	draw	FrameLayout.java	357	false	
com.android.internal.policy.impl.PhoneWindow$DecorView	draw	PhoneWindow.java	1908	false	

Figure 8-8. The Allocation Tracker view

The columns of the allocation list can be clicked to sort by that column. This makes it easy to look for large allocations, for example. There's also a Filter field that makes it easy to restrict the displayed rows to only those that contain the text typed into this field. By typing in the beginning of the package name of your application, the list will shrink to show you allocations made from your code. You can then sort by the Allocated in columns, and look for many occurrences of the same class of object being allocated over and over again. In the example shown, the recurring instantiations of the Paint class is probably a problem. We explore this in more detail shortly.

Traceview

You saw earlier how you can collect statistics about the execution of methods in your application. Using DDMS, you can perform method profiling, after which the Traceview window is shown with the results. Figure 8-9 shows what this looks like.

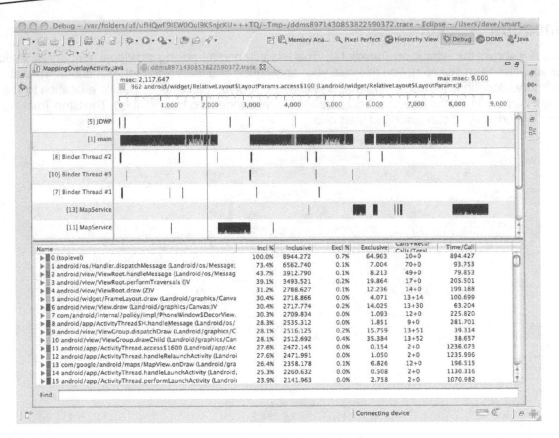

Figure 8-9. Traceview

Using the technique shown earlier to launch this view, you get the results for all methods in the application that executed while DDMS was capturing method call information. The more you exercise the application while capturing methods, the more information you'll get in this view. One approach is to capture methods for a specific application operation so you can zero in on what is happening just for that duration. If you have a large application with a lot of functionality, this approach could take a long time. In that case, you may want to test for a much longer time, although then you'll have a lot of data to work through, which could hide some problems that are not so serious.

As you can see from Figure 8-9, activity from each thread of the application is shown graphically to let you know which threads are doing work and when. If you place your mouse over each bar on a thread line, you'll see information above about which method call was made, along with the CPU timing.

Notice that the results of the analysis indicate what's being called, how often, and how much time is spent in each method. The breakdown is by thread, with color coding. The columns here can be clicked for sorting results by that value.

One good way to look for problems is to sort by Incl Cpu Time % in descending order (i.e., largest value at the top). This will indicate where the time is spent in your application, from most to least. But each value is inclusive of the time spent in methods called from within each method. By looking at the first several dozen rows with this sort order, you can usually spot if some unexpected method is using up too much overall time. You should have some idea of what the application should have been doing while you were capturing method calls, and if time was being spent where it shouldn't be, you can then go investigate that.

Another thing to watch for with this sort order is a large value in the Excl Cpu Time % near the top. This value represents the time spent just in the code of the method, excluding the time spent in method calls from this method. This is a truer measure of how much time is spent in this particular method, so a high value indicates that the method is doing a lot of work. You need to judge whether or not that method *should be doing* a lot of work. If the time spent in that method seems high, go take a look and figure out why. You can, of course, sort by this column straight away, and see if the methods using the most CPU time are ones you would expect.

You can click on a row for a method call, and it will display the parent calls into this method, the child calls to methods from this method, plus the timings for each. You can click on either a parent or child method to switch the view to that method. Of course, clicking on a child method will then show the current method in the list of the child's parents. Or clicking on a parent method will then show the current method in the list of the parent's children. In this way you can traverse up and down the application method call tree to see where time is being spent.

You can also get more specific tracing information for your Android application by using the android.os.Debug class, which provides a start-tracing method (Debug.startMethodTracing("basename")) and a stop-tracing method (Debug.stopMethodTracing()). Android creates a trace file on the device's SD card with the file name basename.trace, although you can specify a full pathname and the file will go there instead. You put the start and stop code around what you want to trace, thus limiting how much data is collected into the trace file. You can then copy the trace file to your workstation and view the tracer output using the traceview tool included in the Android SDK tools directory, with the trace filename as the only argument to traceview.

> **Note**   when capturing methods into trace files, there is some additional overhead that affects the timing of the application methods. The timing should not be considered absolutely accurate but, rather, relative. Without tracing on, everything would go faster; but the parts that go the fastest would very likely be fastest whether or not tracing is on. With tracing on, the slowest parts would still be slowest relative to everything else.

Putting Your Debugging Skills to the Test

Now that you've learned about debugging tools, here is a test to see if you can debug an application with known problems in it. From the book's website (www.androidbook.com/expertandroid/projects), download the sample program for Chapter 8 called NoteBad, using the file called ExpertAndroid_ Ch08_Debugging.zip. This is the Android sample application NotePad, but with some tweaks that should get fixed before this goes to production. Import this project into Eclipse, then run it on either a real device or in an emulator. Use the Menu button and the Add Note menu choice to create some notes in the app. The Back button saves the current note and returns the user to the list of notes. You may or may not notice some sluggishness of this application; no matter, you're about to use the tools to find the causes of performance issues.

Click on the Start Method Profiling button to begin capturing method calls. Now exercise the app by editing one of the notes you created. Click on the Stop Method Profiling button, wait a while, and view the Traceview view that comes up. Double-click the .trace tab if need be to get it to fill the window. Now look at the method calls in the list. See anything unusual? Like a sharp drop in the time spent in the method calls from NoteEditor$LinedEditText.onDraw to TextView.onDraw? Did you notice that the Excl Cpu Time % for NoteEditor$LinedEditText.onDraw is significantly larger than anything around it? This method definitely needs to be looked at.

If you click on the NoteEditor$LinedEditText.onDraw line in the list, it will expand to show the parents and children. Under Children is self, which is taking up most of the time. This means the code within the onDraw method is doing quite a lot of processing, not within methods that onDraw is calling. Open up the NoteEditor.java file and navigate to the onDraw method. Do you see the inner for loop that is causing a serious delay? If you remove this little meaningless loop and try again, you'll find that the time spent in this method goes down significantly.

Now use the Allocation Tracker view to capture some allocation events for the application while you edit another of the notes you already created. Once you click on the Get Allocations button, you'll see quite a few rows show up in the list. To restrict the list to just allocations from your code, type com.androidbook into the Filter field. As you type, you'll see the list shrink to only rows that contain com.androidbook. I hope you see quite a few allocations of a Paint object. That's odd! Why would you allocate a Paint object over and over again?

Clicking on one of the allocation rows, you get a trace below showing where this allocation comes from. Double-clicking the top row for the onDraw method in NoteEditor.java, Eclipse takes you directly to the code. The onDraw method is called many times per second, and it makes no sense to allocate a new Paint object every time. If you scroll up a little in NoteEditor.java, you'll see where the real Paint object allocation should be. Within the onDraw method you should be referencing the existing object, not creating a new one every time. Go ahead and refactor the code to reference mPaint instead of creating a new one within onDraw. Now when you rerun the application, you might even notice a marked improvement in application performance.

The Hierarchy View Perspective

In the Hierarchy View perspective, you connect to a running instance of your application in an emulator (not on a real device). You can then explore the views of the application, their structure, and their properties. You start by selecting which application you want. When it's selected and read, the view hierarchy is displayed in various ways, as shown in Figure 8-10.

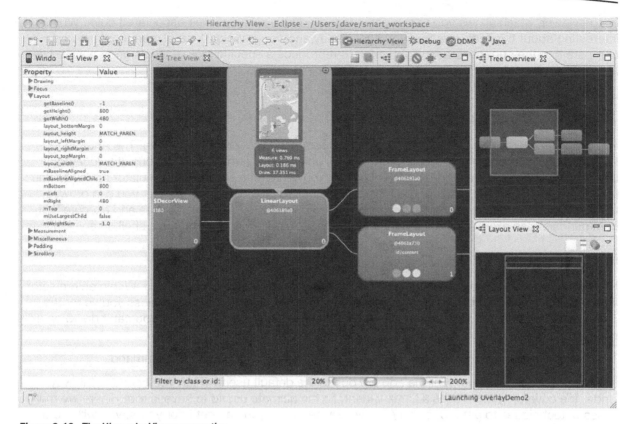

Figure 8-10. *The Hierarchy View perspective*

You can navigate around the structure, checking properties and making sure you don't have more views than you need. For example, if you have many nested layouts, you can probably replace them with a single RelativeLayout.

When you try this yourself, you probably will notice the three colored balls in the views in the center window. These correspond (left to right) to a rating of that view's performance in terms of measuring, laying out, and drawing the view (which includes enclosed views). The colors are relative, so a red ball doesn't necessarily mean something is wrong, but it certainly means you should investigate.

Also notice the selected view and the information above it. Not only does it include a capture of the image of that view, but it also shows the absolute times for measuring, laying out, and drawing that view. These are valuable numbers for determining if you truly need to dig into that view and make improvements. Besides collapsing layouts as mentioned previously, you can alter how views are initialized and how much work is done for drawing. If your code is creating lots of objects, you may be able to reuse objects instead, to avoid that overhead. Use background threads, Loaders, AsyncTasks, or other techniques to do work that can take a long time.

Pixel Perfect View

Similar to the Hierarchy View and the Camera button in the Devices view, you can take the current screen image and bring it up in the Pixel Perfect view. This Eclipse plug-in gives you a zoomed-in image viewer, which allows you to see down to individual pixels and their associated color. What's interesting about this feature is that you can overlay another graphic (like a screen mockup) and compare it to the current screen. If you need to reproduce a specific look, this is a great way to see how well you're doing.

The adb Command

You can use several other debugging tools from a command line (or tools window). The Android Debug Bridge (adb) command allows you to install, update, and remove applications. It is located under platform-tools in the Android SDK directory. You can start a shell on the emulator or device and from there run the subset of Linux commands that Android provides. For example, you can browse the file system, list processes, read the log, and even connect to SQLite databases and execute SQL commands. As an example, the following command (in a tools window) creates a shell on an emulator:

```
adb -e shell
```

Notice the -e to specify an emulator. You use -d if you are connecting to a device. Within an emulator shell, you have elevated Linux privileges, whereas on a real device you don't (unless you've rooted it). This means you can poke around in SQLite databases within the emulator, but you can't do so on a real device, even if it's your application!

Typing adb with no arguments shows all the available capabilities of the adb command.

The restrictions of a normal shell via adb are due to the default userid when you connect this way. Under the covers, Android uses a Linux variant, so the ultimate userid to have is root. There are many cases of techniques to get root on an Android device, and if you can get it for yours, you will find a lot of possibilities open up. For example, with root access to an Android device, you will be able to inspect any and all SQLite databases on your device. Because the techniques for acquiring root are different for each device, and in fact keep changing because the manufacturers try to eliminate the ability to acquire root, this book will not go into any details on how to root your device. Be advised that attempting to acquire root could break your device, rendering it unusable.

The Emulator Console

Another powerful debugging technique is to run the Emulator Console, which obviously only works with the emulator. To get started once the emulator is up and running, type the following in a tools window:

```
telnet localhost port#
```

where port# is where the emulator is listening. The port number is typically displayed in the emulator window title and is often a value such as 5554. After the emulator console has launched, you can type commands to simulate GPS events, SMS messages, and even battery and network status changes. See the References at the end of this chapter for a link to the Emulator Console commands and their usage.

StrictMode

Android 2.3 introduced a new debugging feature called StrictMode, and according to Google, this feature was used to make hundreds of improvements to the Google applications available for Android. So what does it do? It reports violations of policies related to threads and the virtual machine. If a policy violation is detected, you get an alert, which includes a stack trace to show where your application was when the violation occurred. You can force a crash with the alert, or you can log the alert and let your application carry on.

StrictMode Policies

Two types of policies are currently available with StrictMode. The first policy relates to threads and is intended mostly to run against the main thread (also known as the UI thread). It is not good practice to do disk reads and writes from the main thread, nor is it good practice to perform network accesses from the main thread. Google has added StrictMode hooks into the disk and network code; if you enable StrictMode for one of your threads, and that thread performs disk or network access, you can be alerted. You get to choose which aspects of the ThreadPolicy you want to alert on, and you can choose the alert method.

Some of the violations you can look for include custom slow calls, disk reads, disk writes, and network accesses. For alerts, you can choose to write to LogCat, display a dialog, flash the screen, write to the DropBox log file, or crash the application. The most common choices are to write to LogCat and to crash the application. Listing 8-1 shows a sample of what it takes to set up StrictMode for thread policies.

Listing 8-1. Setting StrictMode's ThreadPolicy

```
StrictMode.setThreadPolicy(new StrictMode.ThreadPolicy.Builder()
    .detectDiskReads()
    .detectDiskWrites()
    .detectNetwork()
    .penaltyLog()
    .build());
```

Note that the Builder class makes it easy to set up StrictMode. The Builder methods that define the policy all return a reference to the Builder object, so these methods can be chained together as shown in Listing 8-1. The last method call, build(),returns a ThreadPolicy object that is the argument expected by the setThreadPolicy() method of StrictMode. Note that setThreadPolicy() is a static method, so you don't need to instantiate a StrictMode object.

Internally, setThreadPolicy() uses the current thread for the policy, so subsequent thread actions are evaluated against the ThreadPolicy and alerted as necessary. In this sample code, the policy is defined to alert on disk reads, disk writes, and network accesses with messages to LogCat. Instead of the specific detect methods, you can use the detectAll() method. You can also use different or additional penalty methods. For instance, you can use penaltyDeath()to cause the application to crash after it has written StrictMode alert messages to LogCat (as a result of the penaltyLog() method call).

Because you enable StrictMode on a thread, once you've enabled it, you don't need to keep enabling it. Therefore, you can enable StrictMode at the beginning of your main activity's onCreate() method, which runs on the main thread, and it is then enabled for everything that happens on that main thread. Depending on what sorts of violations you want to look for, the first activity may happen soon enough to enable StrictMode. You can also enable it in your application by extending the Application class and adding StrictMode setup to the application's onCreate() method. Anything that runs on a thread can conceivably set up StrictMode, but you certainly don't need to call the setup code from everywhere; once is enough.

Similar to ThreadPolicy, StrictMode has a VmPolicy. VmPolicy can check for several different kinds of memory leaks. A VmPolicy is created via a similar Builder class, as shown in Listing 8-2. One difference between a VmPolicy and a ThreadPolicy is that a VmPolicy can't alert via a dialog.

Listing 8-2. Setting StrictMode's VmPolicy

```
StrictMode.setVmPolicy(new StrictMode.VmPolicy.Builder()
    .detectActivityLeaks()
    .detectLeakedClosableObjects()
    .detectLeakedRegistrationObjects()
    .detectLeakedSqlLiteObjects()
    .penaltyLog()
    .penaltyDeath()
    .build());
```

Turning off StrictMode

Because the setup happens on a thread, StrictMode finds violations even as control flows from object to object to object. When a violation occurs, you may be surprised to realize that the code is running on the main thread, but the stack trace is there to help you follow along to uncover how it happened. You can then take steps to resolve the issue by moving that code to its own background thread. Or you may decide that it's okay to leave things the way they are. It's up to you. Of course, you probably want to turn off StrictMode when your application goes to production; you don't want your code crashing on users because of an alert.

There are a couple of ways to turn off StrictMode for a production application. The most straightforward way is to remove the calls, but that makes it more difficult to continue to do development on the application. You can always define an application-level boolean and test it before calling the StrictMode code. Setting the value of the boolean to false just before you release your application to the world effectively disables StrictMode.

A more elegant method is to take advantage of the application's debug mode, as defined in AndroidManifest.xml. One of the attributes for the <application> tag in this file is android:debuggable. As mentioned earlier, you set this value to true when you want to debug an application; doing so results in the ApplicationInfo object getting a flag set, which you can then read in code. Listing 8-3 shows how you might use this to your advantage, so that when the application is in debug mode, StrictMode is active (and when the application is not in debug mode, StrictMode is not active).

Listing 8-3. Setting StrictMode Only for Debugging

```
// Return if this application is not in debug mode
ApplicationInfo appInfo = context.getApplicationInfo();
int appFlags = appInfo.flags;
if ((appFlags & ApplicationInfo.FLAG_DEBUGGABLE) != 0) {
    // Do StrictMode setup here
}
```

Remember that ADT sets this attribute to `true` when launching a development version of an application in the emulator or on a device, which therefore enables `StrictMode` in the previous code. When you're exporting your application to create a production version, ADT sets the attribute to `false`.

StrictMode Exercise

As an exercise, go into Eclipse and make a copy of one of the applications you've developed so far. You have to pick a build target of 2.3 or later so it finds the `StrictMode` class. In the `onCreate()` method of an activity that launches first, add code like that in Listings 8-1, 8-2, and 8-3; run the program on Android 2.3 or later in the emulator. You may see the occasional violation messages in LogCat as you use your application.

References

Here are some helpful references to topics you may wish to explore further:

- `http://developer.android.com/guide/developing/tools/index.html`: Developer documentation for the Android debugging tools described here.

- `http://developer.android.com/guide/developing/devices/emulator.html#console`: Syntax and usage for the Emulator Console commands. This allows you to use a command-line interface to simulate events for an application running in the emulator.

- `www.eclipse.org/mat/`: The Eclipse project called Memory Analyzer (MAT). You can use this plug-in to read HPROF files as collected by that DDMS feature. Onoc on the MAT main page, look for the Download link. The MAT can be downloaded as a stand-alone tool to be used with a saved HPROF file. Or you will see an Update Site link that you can use with Eclipse's Install New Software dialog to get the plugin. With the plug-in installed, change the Android ➤ DDMS preferences to open HPROFs in Eclipse.

Summary

Here is what has been covered in this chapter:

- How to set up Eclipse and your device for debugging.

- The Debug perspective, which lets you stop an application to inspect variable values and also step through code, line by line.

- The DDMS perspective, which has quite a few tools for investigating threads, memory, and method calls, as well as taking snapshots of the screen and generating events to send to the emulator.

- Resetting the adb server from DDMS and from the command line.

- Traceview, which shows the methods that are called while an application is running, as well as statistics to help you identify problem methods that need attention for a better user experience.

- The Hierarchy view, which exposes the view structure of a running application and includes metrics to help you tune and troubleshoot the application.

- The adb command, which you can use to log in to a device and look around.

- The Emulator Console, which is a great way to talk to an emulator from a command line. Imagine the scripting possibilities.

- StrictMode, a special class for verifying that your application is not doing nonrecommended things, like disk or network I/O, from the main thread.

Review Questions

Here are some questions you can ask yourself to solidify your understanding of this topic:

1. True or false? If you want to debug an application, you must explicitly set the android:debuggable attribute to true in the <application> tag of the AndroidManifest.xml file.

2. Name four things you can do with your application while using the Eclipse Debug perspective.

3. Is it possible to connect more than one device and/or emulator to Eclipse at the same time? If so, where do you select which application you want to work with?

4. Which DDMS feature do you use to get statistics for an application's current memory allocations?

5. How do you determine how many threads are running in your application?

6. How do you find out the number of times a particular method is called in your application, and what the time of execution is within that method?

7. Where do you go to capture a picture of a device's screen?

8. What Eclipse perspective is used to analyze the structure of an application's views?

9. What do the three colored balls mean in this perspective? Does yellow mean you have a big problem? Does red?

10. If you see a yellow or red ball and want to know how bad the situation is, what should you do to see the actual numeric metric values?

11. If you want to look at method profiles, but you don't want to see all the methods for the entire application, what do you do?

12. How do you create a Linux shell inside a running emulator?

13. Can you also do this on a real device? If so, are there any limitations to what you can do on a real device?

14. How do you figure out the port number of an emulator so you can connect to it using the Emulator Console?

15. What two main things does StrictMode check for?

Chapter 9

Programming 3D Graphics with OpenGL

In this chapter, you will learn all about the OpenGL ES 3D graphics API on the Android platform. OpenGL ES is a version of OpenGL that is optimized for embedded systems (ES) and other low-powered devices such as mobile phones.

The Android platform supports OpenGL ES 1.0 and OpenGL ES 2.0. The OpenGL ES 2.0 is available from API level 8, corresponding to Android SDK release 2.2. ES 2.0 is significantly different from ES 1.0 and is not backward compatible.

ES 1.0 does not rely on the programmability of the GPU (graphics card or the graphics processing unit). The mechanics of drawing is pretty fixed (on the GPU) in this model. Your client code sets the vertices and the necessary transformation matrices and calls the GPU to do the rest. The GPU follows a pre-laid protocol to draw the geometry (vertices) and color the surfaces (fragments).

ES 2.0 is a model where "C"-like programs written in GLSL (OpenGL Shading Language) are compiled, linked, and run on the GPU to affect OpenGL drawings. These GLSL programs written on the GPU allow you more flexibility on how your vertices are positioned and how fragments are colored.

We will cover both ES 1.0 and 2.0 in this chapter. The future belongs to the programmable GPU, so expect more and more mobile devices supporting ES 2.0. Keep in mind that it is pretty hard to find documentation on how to run the ES 2.0 OpenGL programs on the emulator. We used a real device to test the ES 2.0 samples in this chapter.

You can read about the history, scope, and definition for OpenGL ES at

```
http://www.khronos.org/opengles/
```

Fundamentals of OpenGL

This section will help you understand the concepts behind OpenGL and the OpenGL ES API. We explain all the key concepts and APIs, but first we cover these APIs in the context of the fixed-function OpenGL ES 1.0. The knowledge you gain here is applicable to ES 2.0 as well.

OpenGL follows a client server model. The client is the one that requests something be drawn, and the server is the one that receives, interprets, and draws the data. Typically a GPU acts like a server. Unlike typical"C" APIs, however, OpenGL APIs are "stateful." This means that one API affects the behavior of a subsequent API. For example, the first API could set up the vertices. A subsequent API could set up the colors. And a third API could issue a draw command based on the information provided by the first and the second APIs. Then the GPU uses all this information gathered so far to draw.

Key Concepts in OpenGL

As you go through the OpenGL APIs in this chapter, or other OpenGL literature, the following OpenGL key concepts will prove to be invaluable. So get a chair, sit back, and casually scan these OpenGL concepts and terms. Knowing these ideas upfront is the quickest way to understand any OpenGL material, including our detailed coverage in this chapter.

Vertex

In OpenGL, complex figures are drawn by connecting points that are defined in a three-dimensional space. These points are also called vertices. Each vertex is defined in three dimensions: x, y, and z, usually represented as floats. You then instruct OpenGL how to connect these points, whether using lines (two points) or triangles (using three points), and so on. These basic shapes are sometimes refered to as "basic geometry."

Fragment

When two points are joined together, the line that joins those two points needs to be drawn as a set of discontinuous fragments. Each fragment can be a pixel wide. Similarly, when three points define a triangular surface, that surface can be seen as a collection of fragments where each fragment can be a pixel or more wide. Such fragments (set of, including one, pixels) can then have such characteristics as color, depth (how far or near from a viewing angle), and so on. While a vertex exists in 3D space, a fragment exists on a flattened virtual space like your screen (a 2D space). However, before a fragment becomes a pixel, the fragment goes through a series of tests to evaluate if it should become a pixel. For example, based on the depth of a fragment and whether another near fragment is sitting on top of it, you may choose to ignore the farther fragment. This is what is called a "depth test." Refer to OpenGL literature to find out about a number of other tests, such as the scissor test, alpha test, stencil test, dithering, and so on.

Pixel

Although a fragment doesn't become a pixel until later along the graphics pipeline, many times a pixel is synonymous with a fragment. For example, the logic that colors a fragment is sometimes refered to as a "pixel shader" or a "fragment shader." We will cover what a "shader" means a little later.

GLUT

OpenGL is a set of core APIs that primarily deal with taking a three-dimensional set of points and rendering them to a fictitious screen surface. Whether that screen surface is in memory, a large screen, a small screen, or a printer is not core OpenGL. Those details are left for the OS and the respective windowing system.

The way OpenGL interacts with a windowing system depends on the operating system. OpenGL does not provide APIs to interact with screens, mouse, menus, or buttons. Each OS does this in its own fashion. GLUT is a common "C" library to hide these details. Each OS then provides an implementation of the GLUT API to enable this interaction.

So GLUT is an API that allows you to write executable (of course, you will need to compile and link) "C" programs that can run on multiple platforms without recoding for each OS or environment. If you are using the Android Java SDK, you don't deal with GLUT but you do work with Android-specific Java classes that provide this interaction.

GLEW

OpenGL allows additional APIs as extensions to its core. GLEW is a common portable API to discover and manage these extension APIs from GPU vendors. In this chapter. we are not covering extension APIs so there is no occasion to talk about this, another portable "C" API that manages these extensions.

EGL

OpenGL APIs require two things to work: a rendering context and surface buffers. The APIs need a place to manage the state of OpenGL like a working memory; this is the rendering context. OpenGL also needs a surface to draw on. Various OpenGL buffers are attached to this drawing surface; these are called *surface buffers*. Example buffers are a color buffer, stencil buffer, and depth buffer. (We will explain stencil and depth a bit later in this key concepts section.)

Setting up and managing these two aspects is the responsibility of the underlying OS. In OpenGL ES, there is a standard called EGL that deals with these integration APIs. Unlike GLUT and GLEW (which are convenience APIs), EGL is an essential API for an OpenGL ES implementation. So Android does expose the EGL APIs to control the OpenGL, rendering context and the frame buffers and binding to the displays that are available. At the same time, Android also encapsulates the EGL behavior and provides a much simpler mechanism to interact with OpenGL through a class called GLSurfaceView. We will cover and use this class later in the chapter.

The OpenGL ES 2.0 programming guide has excellent coverage of EGL. If you are not doing system-level programming on Android, you won't need this level of detail, however.

Color Buffer

Each pixel on a screen has a color value. Depending on the hardware, the amount of space required to hold this value could vary. For instance, it could be a 24-bit value, 8 bits for each color channel (R,G,B). For example, my laptop has a 1280 × 1024 screen. This means that there are 1280 x 1024 pixels. A color buffer then needs to hold 24 bits for each of these pixels in a buffer; this is called the "color buffer." A color buffer, therefore, holds color values for *all* pixels. A given pixel doesn't have a color buffer of its own, but the whole display frame has a color buffer. If you are displaying stereo images, then you may have two color buffers: a left one and a right one. If you are using double buffering you may have an additional two more, front and back.

Depth Buffer

Structurally, a depth buffer is very much like a color buffer. A depth buffer holds the depth values of each pixel for all the pixels in a scene. A depth value is how far or near a pixel (more accurately, a fragment) is on the *z* axis. You can use this buffer to perform a depth test and tell OpenGL not to draw hidden surfaces. For example, to hide the hidden surfaces of an object like a cube, you can use the sequence of APIs shown in Listing 9-1.

Listing 9-1. How to Hide Hidden Surfaces Using Depth

```
// Enable depth test
glEnable(GL_DEPTH_TEST);
// Accept fragment Or Draw a pixel if it closer to the camera than the former one
glDepthFunc(GL_LESS);
```

Stencil Buffer

Much like color and depth buffers, a stencil buffer is related to pixels. A stencil buffer can hold an arbitrary set of bits for all the pixels in the scene. There are a couple of APIs in OpenGL that allow you to control whether a fragment (pixel) should be drawn or not, based on these bits (stencil bits) of information. You can then use this facility to simulate the way we use stencils in the real world—to paint over a cut-out shape—so that your drawing or painting is constrained. If a stencil buffer is specified and active, it can impact what you see on the screen. One example often given is the dashboard of a car that allows you to see only through the windshield. The dashboard is represented by a stencil that frames a border around your view.

Frame Buffer

A frame buffer is a collection of all the pixel buffers, such as the color, depth, and stencil buffers.

Renderscript

Renderscript is a "C" or "C"-like programming language available since Android 3.0 for high-performance computations. The aim of renderscript is to be portable across various physical processors. Renderscript also provides parallelism between multiple processors. Android provides an interfacing API to programs written in renderscript through Java so as to compile and run these scripts on physical processors. Renderscript is expected to be used for image processing, mathematical modeling, and computations. Although it was tied to graphics processing in Android 3.0, starting with Android 4.0 this facility has become a general-purpose computation facility. As far as learning OpenGL is concerned, you can ignore Renderscript until you have a need for demanding transformations or computations.

Renderscript has lot of built-in functions for math, including a lot of matrix manipulations. Renderscript, as stated earlier, provides an EJB like (but far simpler and more direct) Java interface for clients. Ease of use while providing portable high-performance computation is the motivation underlying Renderscript. OpenCL is a similar effort from Khronos to bring parallel high-performance computing to GPUs. CUDA (Compute Unified Device Architecture) is another term you will hear in this space, introduced by Nvidia to take advantage of their highly parallel GPUs for computer-intensive tasks, be they graphics related or otherwise.

GLSL and Shaders

In OpenGL ES 2.0, you see references to vertex shaders and fragment shaders. In both instances, a shader is a program written in "C"-like shading language called GLSL. A vertex shader is a program that is invoked to transform each vertex into its final position on the screen; a vertex shader is invoked once for each vertex. A fragment shader is a program that is invoked for each pixel (more accurately, each fragment) as it gets rendered. (See Fragment above.)

GLSL was introduced with OpenGL version 2.0. OpenGL ES 1.x, which is based on OpenGL 1.3, is a fixed-function pipeline and has no programmability, and hence did not need any language like GLSL. OpenGL ES 2.0, on the other hand, is based on the programmable pipeline of OpenGL 2.0, and hence it requires its own version of GLSL. The GLSL ES for OpenGL ES 2.0 is based on 1.2 version of the GLSL (designed for OpenGL 2.0).

Meanwhile OpenGL has evolved all the way to version 4.0, and its version of GLSL has also been upgraded. So if you are reading the liteature on GLSL, pay attention to the version number of the spec for GLSL you are using.

Programs written in GLSL ES 1.x typically indicate their version number as the first line in their source file. Here is an example: #version 100.Although it is uncommon at the time of this writing, if you are usign OpenGL ES 3.0, the corresponding version for GLSL ES is 3.0, which is indicated as: #version 300. If you read the spec (the URL is specified in the references section of this document) for GLSL ES that goes with ES 2.0, you will see that the spec states the version number as 1.00 and revision as 17. So it appears you will ignore the revision and just use the main version number, without the decimals. If you don't specify the version number, it is taken as 1.00.

Object Coordinates

In 3D drawing, you create objects and place them at a certain point in a three-dimensional scene. Object coordinates specify the size and position of this object by specifying the vertices of this object. You can model this object in such a way that you are relative to the origin of (0,0,0). You can then apply a number of transformations on this object to either scale it or rotate it, and then even place it relative to another object that you have already drawn or are planning to draw.

These transformations that you apply on a given object are called *model transforms*. When you are drawing multiple objects, it is likely that each object you draw could go through its own model transformation; otherwise, it becomes tedious to define the vertices for all your objects in one swoop.

The scale and position of object coordinates can be as you imagine suitable to your modeling. This is similar to drawing various charts on a graph paper. You choose the scale and accordingly scale the coordinates. (Choosing the scale is later explained in this chapter.) So while you are designing object coordinates, you pick a relative scale that is suitable for that object. For example, if you are drawing an object from the real world, like a car, you can choose its real dimensions and then later choose your scene to be big enough. In the end, though, all these dimensions will be appropriately scaled down or clipped to the size of the window you are going to use.

World Coordinates

When you draw multiple objects as indicated in the previous definition, you are placing the objects in a conceptual world that has its own center and dimensions. In other words, there is a scene you are imagining. These scene coordinates are called world coordinates. Lots of times programmers may choose to use the same dimensions and center for both object and world coordinates. This is what we have done in this chapter.

Another way to look at object and world coordinates is as follows: when you apply a model transformation on an object, you arrive at placing the object in world coordinates.

Model Coordinates

An object that you are drawing can be seen as a model. Or, sometime you can see the entire world you are trying to depict as a model. As a result, some authors refer to object coordinates as model coordinates; they also refer to world coordinates as model coordinates.

There is a line of thought that world coordinates are not really recognized by OpenGL, as there is no specific transformation other than the "model" transformation that takes place on each individual object. For instance, you have in OpenGL a model matrix, a view matrix, and a projection matrix. So the model matrix addresses the needs of the object, model, and world coordinates.

Camera and Eye Coordinates

Your conceptual world (say, a large cube) could be as big or as small as you imagine it, with its own idea of where the center is. For visualizing this world, you need an observer that looks at this world. If this observer is too far from the imaginary center, then the world looks small, and if the observer is close, then the world looks bigger. Placement and orientation (up, down, slanted) of the "eye" affects how the model coordinates are transformed as they become the final screen coordinates. The transformed coordinates of the world as seen by the eye are called eye coordinates.

Of course, you won't start specifying something in eye coordinates. Instead, you start with the object coordinates and apply the model transform to arrive at the world coordinates. You then apply a "view" transform (as indicated by the position and orientation of the eye) to arrive at the device/screen coordinates.

Frustum and Device Coordinates

When you imagine your world, you have to define the boundaries for your world by defining a box. This box can be a long rectangular tube (rectangular prism) or a truncated pyramid (with an eye like projection; see Figure 9-1) called a frustum. This limited boxed-in area decides what is seen and what is not.

So we take the eye coordinates and apply a projection matrix to project the vertices to the front of the frustum. These projected coordinates need to be scaled or adjusted by the size of the window before they get an (x, y) coordinate on the screen.

View Port and Window/Screen Coordinates

A frustum defines the mechanism for projecting a 3D space into a 2D space. The conceptual box that a frustum is then needs to be tied to a fixed window size where the scene is displayed. This window size definition is called, appropriately, a view port. The projected coordinates are transformed to the screen coordinates internally by OpenGL and do not require an explicit matrix.

MVP or Model View Projection Matrix

If you start with your original coordinates for a vertex, that vertex is transformed through three different matrices before arriving at the screen coordinates. These three matrices individually are:

```
Model Matrix       //Get to the world coordinates
View Matrix        //Apply the eye
Projection Matrix //Apply the frustum
```

Instead of individually multiplying the vertex coordinates with each of these matrices, you can arrive at a single multiplication matrix (called the model view projection matrix, or MVP) by applying the formula in Listing 9-2:

Listing 9-2. Calculating a Model View Matrix

```
MVP matrix = Projection Matrix * View Matrix  * Model Matrix
```

In this equation (Listing 9-2), the model matrix itself may have been a result of multiplying multiple individual model matrices like scale, rotate, and translate. This is common if you take an object and rotate it via a rotation matrix, and translate it via a translation matrix, and then scale it via a scaling matrix.

Once you have this MVP matrix, you can translate any vertex to its final position by applying the matrix multiplication:

```
Final vertex = MVP Matrix *  Initial Vertex
```

Vertex Attributes

A vertex is a position. We can also associate a color with a vertex. These characteristics of a vertex are called attributes of that vertex. So, position is an attribute. Color is an attribute. On a given texture image, where a vertex is pinned at, that can be another vertex attribute. The idea of vertex attributes is not limited to these well-accepted OpenGL attributes.In ES 2.0, you can represent any number of arbitrary attributes for a vertex. For each attribute, you can send an array of that attribute's values for all the vertices in an attribute buffer. For example, color values for all vertices can be specified in a color attribute array. Positions for all vertices can be specified in a postion attribute array. You will see examples of this in this chapter as we go through a couple of ES 2.0 sample programs.

Winding of Vertices

If you were to draw a triangle using three vertices in OpenGL, that triangle is considered to have a front face and a back face. How do you know which is the front face and which is the back face? Here is how this is determined: Imagine a right-hand screw at the center of that triangle. If you were to turn that screw in the same direction as the order of the vertices, you will see whether the RHS screw will come away from the surface or go into the surface. The surface that the screw is coming away from is the front, and the surface that the screw is proceeding into (even as it recedes) is the back. So a counterclockwise winding will indicate the front face. Keep in mind that the order of vertices makes a difference. However, it really doesn't matter which vertex you start from as long as the traversal of those vertices is as you desire: counterclockwise or clockwise. If the screw is coming out of the object, then you are specifying your vertices correctly and your vertices consistently form the outside surface.

Anti-aliasing

Pixels on a computer screen are arranged in a grid. A given pixel cannot be partially colored: it's either all or nothing for that pixel. You can draw horizontal lines or vertical lines without any jagged edges, but the moment you draw a diagonal, you will see a jagged diagonal because you can't divide and paint half a pixel. As you come down the diagonal, you will leave one pixel on and one pixel off, like a staircase. Anti-aliasing, therefore, is an algorithm to paint additional pixels with a suitable shading color so that your eye will blend the colors to get the impression of a smooth line. These anti-aliasing algorithms need to calculate how many adjacent pixels there are and what shade to use.

Blending

One of the outputs of a fragment processor or shader is color. Without blending, colors will become (assuming there is no culling or other effects to ignore the pixel for drawing) the colors of the framebuffer and you will see them on the screen. But if blending is in effect, there may already be colors in the color buffer that need to be blended with this new set of colors. One of the common uses of blending is to provide a degree of transparency. OpenGL allows a number of blending functions to control the blending behavior.

Dithering

Blotches on a digital image arise from differences in the color depth of the image and the monitors on which the image is displayed. Color depth is the number of bits allocated per pixel to represent its color. If it is a 24-bit color, then 8 bits represent the 256 shades of each of the R, G, and B. When these shades are approximated owing to a lack of depth, you may see a single color replacing a number of approximated colors, producing images with blotches. Dithering is a technique to blend available shades (color pallette) to approximate an original shade by employing a number of adjacent pixels that provide the blending. For example, If you take 500 red pixels and 500 yellow pixels and mix them, from far enough away you will see a new color that is neither red nor yellow.

Fog

The fog effect in OpenGL is the process of adjusting a pixel color based on its distance from the observer.

Color Sum

After texturing is complete in the OpenGL pipeline, a secondary color can be specified to be added to the textured color. This secondary color may have been produced by lighting effects that are in place or are explicitly specified (as long as the lighting is turned off). Fog is applied after the color sum.

Fragment Testing

The output of fragment processing is to figure out the target pixels and their color characteristics. However, before these pixels are written to the frame buffer to become part of the screen, they undergo number of tests. Is the pixel position in the frame buffer currently owned by this OpenGL context? Or is that controlled by some other application?. If the depth testing is on, is this pixel behind another pixel? Is there a stencil active that may block this pixel from showing? These are called fragment tests. If the pixels don't pass the test, they won't be written to the frame buffer.

Although there are lot more terms you will see as you read the OpenGL literature, knowing these terms will greatly help your understanding of what is presented in the rest of this chapter.

Essential Drawing with OpenGL ES 1.0

The primary focus of this chapter is OpenGL ES 2.0. However, understanding the basics of OpenGL ES 1.0 is useful for a good grasp of OpenGL ES 2.0. So first we cover the basics of OpenGL drawing using ES 1.0.

In OpenGL, you draw in 3D space. You start out by specifying a series of vertices. A vertex has three values: *x, y*, and *z*. Vertices are then joined together to form a shape. You can join these vertices into a variety of shapes called *primitive shapes* (also called *primitive geometry*), which could be points, lines, and triangles. Note that in OpenGL, primitive shapes also include rectangles and polygons. As you work with OpenGL and OpenGL ES, you will continue to see differences whereby the latter has fewer features than the former.

OpenGL ES 1.0 offers two primary methods for drawing:

- glVertexPointer
- glDrawElements

You use glVertexPointer to specify a series of vertices, and you use glDrawElements to draw them using one of the primitive shapes mentioned earlier.

glVertexPointer and Specifying Drawing Vertices

The glVertexPointer method is responsible for specifying an array of points to be drawn. Each point is specified in three dimensions, so each point will have three values: x, y, and z. Listing 9-3 shows how to specify the three points in an array.

Listing 9-3. *Vertex Coordinates Example for an OpenGL Triangle*

```
float[] coords = {
    -0.5f, -0.5f, 0,      //p1: (x1,y1,z1)
     0.5f, -0.5f, 0,      //p2: (x1,y1,z1)
     0.0f,  0.5f, 0       //p3: (x1,y1,z1)
};
```

The structure in Listing 9-3 is a contiguous set of floats kept in a Java-based float array. You might be wondering what units are used for the coordinates in points p1, p2, and p3. The short answer is this: as you model your 3D space, these coordinate units can be anything you'd like. Subsequently, you will need to specify something called a *bounding volume* (or *bounding box*) that quantifies these coordinates in a relative fashion.

For example, you can specify the bounding box as a cube with 5-inch sides or a cube with 2-inch sides. These coordinates are the *world coordinates* because you are conceptualizing your world independent of the physical device's limitations. (We will explain these coordinates more in the subsection "Understanding OpenGL Camera and Coordinates." For now, assume that you are using a cube that is 2 units across all its sides and centered at ($x = 0$, $y = 0$, $z = 0$). In other words, the center is at the center of the cube and the sides of the cube are one unit apart from the center.

> **Note**   The terms *bounding volume*, *bounding box*, *viewing volume*, *viewing box*, and *frustum* all refer to the same concept: the pyramid-shaped 3D volume that determines what is visible onscreen. You'll learn more in the "glFrustum and the Viewing Volume" subsection under "Understanding OpenGL Camera and Coordinates."

You can also assume that the origin is at the center of the visual display. The z axis will be negative going into the display (away from you) and positive coming out of the display (toward you); x will go positive as you move right and negative as you move left. However, these coordinates will also depend on the direction from which you are viewing the scene.

To draw the points in Listing 9-3, you need to pass them to OpenGL ES through the glVertexPointer method. For efficiency reasons, however, glVertexPointer takes a native buffer that is language-agnostic rather than an array of Java floats. For this, you need to convert the Java-based array of floats to an acceptable "C"-like native buffer. You'll need to use the java.nio classes to convert the float array into the native buffer. Listing 9-4 shows an example of using nio buffers.

Listing 9-4. Creating NIO Float Buffers

```
jva.nio.ByteBuffer vbb = java.nio.ByteBuffer.allocateDirect(3 * 3 * 4);
vbb.order(ByteOrder.nativeOrder());
java.nio.FloatBuffer mFVertexBuffer = vbb.asFloatBuffer();
```

In Listing 9-4, the byte buffer is a buffer of memory ordered into bytes. Each point has three floats because of the three axes, and each float is 4 bytes. So together you get 3 x 4 bytes for each point. Plus, a triangle has three points. So you need 3 x 3 x 4 bytes to hold all three float points of a triangle.

Once you have the points gathered into a native buffer, you can call glVertexPointer, as shown in Listing 9-5.

Listing 9-5. glVertexPointer API Definition

```
glVertexPointer(
        3,                  // Are we using (x,y) or (x,y,z) in each point
        GL10.GL_FLOAT,      // each value is a float value in the buffer
        0,                  // Between two points in the buffer there is no space
        mFVertexBuffer);    // pointer to the start of the buffer
```

The first argument tells OpenGL ES how many dimensions there are in a point or a vertex. In this case, we specified 3 for *x, y,* and *z.* You could also specify 2 for just *x* and *y.* In that case, *z* would be zero. Note that this first argument is not the number of points in the buffer but, rather, the number of dimensions used. So if you pass 20 points to draw a number of triangles, you will not pass 20 as the first argument; you would pass 2 or 3, depending on the number of dimensions used.

The second argument indicates that the coordinates need to be interpreted as floats. The third argument, called a stride, points to the number of bytes separating each point. In this case, it is zero because one point immediately follows the other. Sometimes you can add color attributes as part of the buffer after each point. If you want to do so, you'd use a stride to skip those as part of the vertex specification. The last argument is the pointer to the buffer containing the points.

Now that you know how to set up the array of points to be drawn, let's see how to draw this array of points using the glDrawElements method.

glDrawElements

Once you specify the series of points through glVertexPointer, you use the glDrawElements method to draw those points with one of the primitive shapes that OpenGL ES allows. Note that OpenGL is a state machine; it remembers the values set by one method when it invokes the next method in a cumulative manner. So you don't need to explicitly pass the points set by glVertexPointer to glDrawElements. glDrawElements will implicitly use those points. Listing 9-6 shows an example of this method with possible arguments.

Listing 9-6. Example of glDrawElements

```
glDrawElements(
        GL10.GL_TRIANGLES,      // type of shape
        3,                      // Number of indices
        GL10.GL_UNSIGNED_SHORT, // How big each index is
        mIndexBuffer);          // buffer containing the 3 indices
```

The first argument indicates the type of geometric shape to draw: GL_TRIANGLE_STRIP signifies a triangle strip. Other possible options for this argument are points only (GL_POINTS), line strips (GL_LINE_STRIP), lines only (GL_LINES), line loops (GL_LINE_LOOP), triangles only (GL_TRIANGLES), and triangle fans (GL_TRIANGLE_FAN).

The concept of a STRIP in GL_LINE_STRIP and GL_TRIANGLE_STRIP is to add new points while making use of the old ones. By doing so, you can avoid specifying all the points for each new object. For example, if you specify four points in an array, you can use strips to draw the first triangle out of (1,2,3) and the second one out of (2,3,4). Each new point will add a new triangle. (Refer to the OpenGL red book for more details.) You can also vary these parameters to see how the triangles are drawn as you add new points.

The idea of a FAN in GL_TRIANGLE_FAN applies to triangles where the first point is used as a starting point for all subsequent triangles. So you're essentially making a fan- or circle-like object with the first vertex in the middle. Suppose you have six points in your array: (1,2,3,4,5,6). With a FAN, the triangles will be drawn at (1,2,3), (1,3,4), (1,4,5), and (1,5,6). Every new point adds an extra triangle, similar to the process of extending a fan or unfolding a pack of cards.

The rest of the arguments of glDrawElements involve the method's ability to let you reuse point specification. For example, a square contains four points. Each square can be drawn as a combination of two triangles. If you want to draw two triangles to make up the square, do you have to specify six points? No. You can specify only four points and refer to them six times to draw two triangles. This process is called *indexing into the point buffer*.

Here is an example:

```
Points: (p1, p2, p3, p4)
Draw indices (p1, p2, p3,    p2,p3,p4)
```

Notice how the first triangle comprises p1, p2, p3 and the second one comprises p2, p3, p4. With this knowledge, the second argument of glDrawElements identifies how many indices there are in the index buffer.

The third argument to glDrawElements (see Listing 9-6) points to the type of values in the index array, whether they are unsigned shorts (GL_UNSIGNED_SHORT) or unsigned bytes (GL_UNSIGNED_BYTE).

The last argument of glDrawElements points to the index buffer. To fill up the index buffer, you need to do something similar to what you did with the vertex buffer. Start with a Java array and use the java.nio package to convert that array into a native buffer.

Listing 9-7 shows some sample code that converts a short array of {0,1,2} into a native buffer suitable to be passed to glDrawElements.

Listing 9-7. Converting Java Array to NIO Buffers

```
//Figure out how you want to arrange your points
short[] myIndecesArray = {0,1,2};
//get a short buffer
java.nio.ShortBuffer mIndexBuffer;
//Allocate 2 bytes each for each index value
ByteBuffer ibb = ByteBuffer.allocateDirect(3 * 2);
ibb.order(ByteOrder.nativeOrder());
mIndexBuffer = ibb.asShortBuffer();
//stuff the index array into the nio buffer
for (int i=0;i<3;i++) {
   mIndexBuffer.put(myIndecesArray[i]);
}
```

Now that you've seen mIndexBuffer at work in Listing 9-7, you can revisit Listing 9-6 and see how the index buffer pointer In that listing is created and manipulated.

> **Note**   Rather than create any new points, the index buffer merely indexes into the array of points that are already indicated through the glVertexPointer.

Next we look at two commonly used OpenGL ES methods: glClear and glColor.

glClear

You use the glClear method to erase the drawing surface. Using this method, you can reset the color, depth, and the type of stencils used. (Refer to the earlier key concepts section to understand these three buffers.) You specify which bufer to reset by the constant that you pass in: GL_COLOR_BUFFER_BIT, GL_DEPTH_BUFFER_BIT, or GL_STENCIL_BUFFER_BIT.

For example, you can use code in Listing 9-8 to clear just the color buffer:

Listing 9-8. Clearing the Color Buffer

```
//Clear the surface of any color
gl.glClear(gl.GL_COLOR_BUFFER_BIT);
```

glColor

You use glColor to set the default color for the subsequent drawing that takes place. In the code segment of Listing 9-9, the method glColor4f sets the color to red:

Listing 9-9. Setting Color

```
//Set the current color
glColor4f(1.0f, 0, 0, 0.5f);
```

The basic method name is glColor. The 4f refers to the four arguments that the method takes, each of which is a float. The four arguments are components of red, green, blue, and alpha (color gradient/opacity). The starting values for each are (1,1,1,1): "1" means full color; "0" means no color. In this case, the color has been set to red with half a gradient (specified by the last alpha argument).

Although we have covered the basic drawing APIs (specifying vertices, specifying indecies, drawing geometric primitives, clearing and assigning colors), we still need to address a few things regarding the coordinates of the points that you specify in 3D space. The next subsection explains how OpenGL models a real-world scene through the viewing perspective of an observer looking through a camera. This next subsection should also make clear what was mentioned in the earlier key concepts section about various coordinates.

Understanding OpenGL Camera and Coordinates

So far we have a triangle object (Listing 9-3) that we have modeled to be drawn in our own imaginary coordinate space. As you draw in 3D space, you ultimately must project the 3D view onto a 2D screen—much like capturing a 3D scene using a camera in the real world.

The part of your drawing that becomes visible depends on the location of the camera, the direction of the camera lens, the orientation of the camera (such as upside down or tilted), the zoom level, and the size of the capturing "film."

These aspects of projecting a 3D picture onto a 2D screen are controlled by three methods in OpenGL:

- gluLookAt controls the direction of the camera.
- glFrustum controls the viewing volume, zoom, or distance (from and to) you care about.
- glViewport controls the size of the screen or the size of the camera's film.

gluLookAt and the Camera Symbolism

Imagine you are taking photographs of a landscape. You arrive at a meadow with a camera; the scene that lies before you is equivalent to the drawing scene in OpenGL. You can make these drawings big, like mountains, or small, like flowers—as long as they are proportional to one another. The coordinates you use for these drawings, as we hinted earlier, are called *world coordinates*. Under these coordinates, for example, you can establish a line to be four units long on the *x* axis by setting your end points of that line as (0,0,0) to (4,0,0).

As you prepare to take a photograph, you find a spot to place your tripod. Then you place the camera on the tripod. The location of your camera—not the tripod, but the camera itself—becomes the origin of your camera in the world. So you need to take a piece of paper and write down this location, which is called the *eye point*.

If you don't specify an eye point, the camera is located at (0,0,0), which is the exact center of your screen. Usually you want to step away from the origin so that you can see the (*x,y*) plane that is sitting at the origin of *z* = 0. For argument's sake, suppose you position the camera at (0,0,5). This would move the camera off your screen toward you by five units.

You can refer to Figure 9-1 to visualize how the camera is placed.

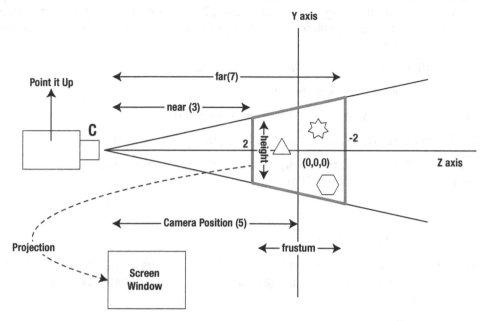

Figure 9-1. *OpenGL viewing concepts using a camera analogy*

Looking at Figure 9-1, you might wonder why the axes in the figure are *y* and *z* and not *x* and *y*. This is because we use the convention that the OpenGL camera looks toward the the depth—the *z* axis if your normal plane of scene is the *xy* plane. This convention works fine because we usually associate the *z* axis as the axis of depth.

Once you place the camera, you start looking ahead or forward to see which portion of the scene you want to capture. You position the camera in the direction you are looking. This far-off point that you are looking at is called a *view point* or a *look-at point*. The point specification is really a specification of the direction. If you specify your view point as (0,0,0), then the camera is looking along the *z* axis toward the origin from a distance of five units, assuming the camera is positioned at (0,0,5). You can see this in Figure 9-1, where the camera is looking down the *z* axis.

Imagine further that there is a rectangular building at the origin. You want to look at it, not in a portrait fashion but in a landscape fashion. What do you have to do? You obviously can leave the camera in the same location and still point it toward the origin, but now you need to turn the camera by 90 degrees (similar to tilting your head to see sideways). This is the *orientation* of the camera, as the camera is fixed at a given eye point and looking at a specific look-at point or direction. This orientation is called the *up vector*.

The up vector merely identifies the orientation of the camera (up, down, left, right, or at an angle). This orientation of the camera is also specified using a look-at point. Imagine a line from the origin—not the camera origin, but the world-coordinate origin—to this look-at point. Whatever angle this line subtends in three dimensions at the origin is the orientation of camera.

For example, an up vector for a camera might look like (0,1,0) or even (0,15,0), both of which would have the same effect. The point (0,1,0) is a point away from the origin along the *y* axis going up. This means you position the camera upright. If you use (0,−1,0), you would position the camera upside down. In both cases, the camera is still at the same point (0,0,5) and looking at the same origin (0,0,0).

We can now summarize the three camera-related coordinates:

- (0,0,5): Eye point (location of the camera)

- (0,0,0): Look-at point (direction the camera is pointing)

- (0,1,0): Up vector (whether the camera is up, down, or slanted)

You will use the gluLookAt method to specify these three points—the eye point, the look-at point, and the up vector—as shown in Listing 9-10:

Listing 9-10. Setting up the Camera

```
gluLookAt(gl, 0,0,5,    0,0,0,    0,1,0);
```

The arguments are: (1) the first set of coordinates belongs to the eye point, (2) the second set of coordinates belongs to the look-at point, and (3) the third set of coordinates belongs to the up vector with respect to the origin.

Let's discuss the viewing volume now.

glFrustum and the Viewing Volume

You might have noticed that none of the points describing the camera position using gluLookAt deals with size. They all deal only with positioning, direction, and orientation. How can you tell the camera where to focus? How far away is the subject you are trying to capture? How wide and how tall is the subject area? You use the OpenGL method glFrustum to specify the area of the scene that you are interested in.

If you were to imagine yourself sitting at a play in an auditorium, then the stage is your viewing volume. You really don't need to know what happens outside of that stage. However, you do care about the dimensions of this stage because you want to observe all that goes on upon/within that stage.

Think of the scene area as bounded by a box, also called the *frustum* or *viewing volume* (this is the area marked by the bold border in the middle of Figure 9-1). Anything inside the box is captured, and anything outside the box is clipped and ignored. So how do you specify this viewing box? You first decide on the *near point*, or the distance between the camera and the beginning of the box. Then you can choose a *far point*, which is the distance between the camera and the end of the box. The distance between the near and far points along the *z* axis is the depth of the box. If you specify a near point of 50 and a far point of 200, then you will capture everything between those points and your box depth will be 150. You will also need to specify the left side of the box, the right side of the box, the top of the box, and the bottom of the box. The dimensions you use here are relative to the objects that you model. For example, the triangle dimensions in Listing 9-3 will be relative to this viewing volume.

In OpenGL, you can imagine this box in one of two ways. One is called a *perspective projection*, which involves the frustum we've been talking about. This view, which simulates a camera-like function, involves a pyramidal structure in which the far plane serves as the base and the camera serves as the apex. The near plane cuts off the top of the pyramid, forming the frustum between the near plane and the far plane.

The other way to imagine the box involves thinking of it as a rectangular prism (a cube that is longer in one dimension). This second scenario is called an *orthographic projection* and is suited for geometric drawings that need to preserve sizes despite their distance from the camera. Listing 9-11 shows how to specify the frustum for our example.

Listing 9-11. Specifying a Frustum through glFrustum

```
//calculate aspect ratio first
//w - width of the window/view
//h - height of the window/view
float ratio = (float) w / h;

//indicate that we want a perspective projection
glMatrixMode(GL10.GL_PROJECTION);

//Specify the frustum: the viewing volume
gl.glFrustumf(
    -ratio,     // Left side of the viewing box
    ratio,      // right side of the viewing box
    1,          // top of the viewing box
    -1,         // bottom of the viewing box
    3,          // how far is the front of the box from the camera
    7);         // how far is the back of the box from the camera
```

Because we set the top to 1 and bottom to -1 in the preceding code (Listing 9-11), we have set the front height of the box to 2 units. We specify the sizes for the left and right sides of the frustum by using proportional numbers, taking into account the window's aspect ratio. This is why this code uses the window height and width to figure out the proportion. The code also assumes the area of action to be between 3 and 7 units along the z axis. Anything drawn outside these coordinates, relative to the camera, won't be visible.

Because we set the camera at (0,0,5) and pointing toward (0,0,0), three units from the camera toward the origin will be (0,0,2) and seven units from the camera will be (0,0,–2). This leaves the origin plane right in the middle of your 3D box.

So now we've identified the size of the viewing volume. There's one more important API and it maps these sizes to the screen: glViewport.

glViewport and Screen Size

glViewport is responsible for specifying the rectangular area on the screen onto which the viewing volume will be projected. This method takes four arguments to specify the rectangular box: the x and y coordinates of the lower-left corner, followed by the width and height. Listing 9-12 is an example of specifying a view as the target for this projection.

Listing 9-12. Defining a ViewPort through glViewPort

```
glViewport(0,        // lower left "x" of the rectangle on the screen
           0,        // lower left "y" of the rectangle on the screen
           width,    // width of the rectangle on the screen
           height);  // height of the rectangle on the screen
```

If your window or view size is 100 pixels in height and the frustum height is 10 units, then every logical unit of 1 in the world coordinates translates to 10 pixels in screen coordinates.

So far we have covered key introductory concepts in OpenGL irrespective of the platform on which OpenGL is implemented. Understanding these OpenGL fundamentals is essential for learning how to write OpenGL code on the Android platform as well. With these prerequisites behind us, we now discuss what is needed in Android to call the OpenGL ES APIs that we have covered so far and try our hand at drawing the triangle as envisioned by Listing 9-3.

Interfacing OpenGL ES with Android

OpenGL ES, as indicated, is a standard that is supported by a number of platforms. At the core, as you have seen, it's a "C"-like API that addresses all of the OpenGL drawing chores. However, each platform and OS is different in the way it implements OpenGL contexts, displays, screen buffers, and the like. These OS-specific aspects are left to each operating system to implement. A standard called EGL is used to implement these specifics. Although Android exposes the EGL API directly if necessary, it also defines an object-oriented abstraction to hide the repetitive cadence of EGL.

Using GLSurfaceView and Related Classes

Starting with 1.5 of the SDK, the common usage pattern for using OpenGL is quite simplified. (Refer to the first edition of this book to see the Android 1.0 approach.) The key class and interface that implement this interaction are GLSurfaceView and Renderer. (So you don't work with EGL directly unless you want to go after a specific behavior.)

Here are the typical steps to draw using these classes:

1. Implement the GLSurfaceView.Renderer interface.

2. Set up key OpenGL parameters that control the general behavior of OpenGL, and provide the camera settings needed for your drawing in the implementation of this renderer. (You do this in onCreateSurface and onSurfaceChanged callbacks of the renderer interface)

3. Provide drawing code in the onDrawFrame method of the renderer implementation.

4. Construct a GLSurfaceView, to which you can pass your implemented renderer.

5. Set the renderer implemented in steps 1 to 3 in the GLSurfaceView.

6. Indicate whether you want animation or not to the GLSurfaceView.

7. Set the GLSurfaceView in an activity as the content view. You can also use this view wherever you can use a regular view. But keep in mind that all drawing in a GLSurfaceView takes place in a dedicated secondary thread. This is in contrast to regular views, which are painted by the main thread of your application.

Let's start with how to implement the renderer interface.

Implementing the Renderer

The signature of the renderer interface is shown in Listing 9-13.

Listing 9-13. The Renderer Interface

```
public static interface GLSurfaceView.Renderer
{
    void onDrawFrame(GL10 gl);
    void onSurfaceChanged(GL10 gl, int width, int height);
    void onSurfaceCreated(GL10 gl, EGLConfig config);
}
```

The main drawing happens in the onDrawFrame() method. Whenever a new surface is created for this view, the onSurfaceCreated() method is called. We can call a number of OpenGL APIs in this method that are considered setting up the OpenGL context and other global-level OpenGL parameters. See Listing 9-14 (where we define an abstract renderer) for the type of methods that get called from this method.

Similarly, when a surface changes, such as the width and height of the window, the onSurfaceChanged() method is called. We can set up our viewing volume here.

In the onDrawFrame() method, we set up the camera and draw needed vertices. If we are drawing multiple objects in a scene or planning to use the same setup to draw multiple examples, it helps to have an abstract class that does all of the following in respective methods:

1. Set up global OpenGL behavior (onSurfaceCreated)

2. Set up view port (onSurfaceChanged)

3. Set up camera (onDrawFrame)

Then we can have the onDrawFrame delegate the actual drawing (specifying vertices, model transformations, and drawing) to a derived class through an overridden method like "draw()." This is what you see in Listing 9-14, where we have given the source code for the abstract renderer class.

Listing 9-14. The AbstractRenderer //filename: AbstractRenderer.java

```
//...Not all imports listed: See the full file in the download
//Or you can autogenerate the rest
import javax.microedition.khronos.egl.EGLConfig;
import javax.microedition.khronos.opengles.GL10;
import android.opengl.GLU;
```

```java
public abstract class AbstractRenderer
implements android.opengl.GLSurfaceView.Renderer
{
    public void onSurfaceCreated(GL10 gl, EGLConfig eglConfig) {
        gl.glDisable(GL10.GL_DITHER);
        gl.glHint(GL10.GL_PERSPECTIVE_CORRECTION_HINT,
                GL10.GL_FASTEST);
        gl.glClearColor(.5f, .5f, .5f, 1);
        gl.glShadeModel(GL10.GL_SMOOTH);
        gl.glEnable(GL10.GL_DEPTH_TEST);
    }

    public void onSurfaceChanged(GL10 gl, int w, int h) {
        gl.glViewport(0, 0, w, h);
        float ratio = (float) w / h;

        //The following three methods used in succession
        //sets up the projection matrix.

        //Indicate we are going to target the projection matrix
        gl.glMatrixMode(GL10.GL_PROJECTION);
        // Set that matrix to the identity matrix
        gl.glLoadIdentity();
        //This multiplies the previous matrix with the projection matrix
        gl.glFrustumf(-ratio, ratio, -1, 1, 3, 7);
    }

    public void onDrawFrame(GL10 gl)
    {
        gl.glDisable(GL10.GL_DITHER);
        gl.glClear(GL10.GL_COLOR_BUFFER_BIT | GL10.GL_DEPTH_BUFFER_BIT);

        //See how similarly we are working with and setting the model/view matrix
        gl.glMatrixMode(GL10.GL_MODELVIEW);
        gl.glLoadIdentity();
        GLU.gluLookAt(gl, 0, 0, -5, 0f, 0f, 0f, 0f, 1.0f, 0.0f);
        gl.glEnableClientState(GL10.GL_VERTEX_ARRAY);
        draw(gl);
    }
    protected abstract void draw(GL10 gl);
}
```

Having this abstract class is very useful, as it allows us to focus on just the drawing methods. We use this class to create a SimpleTriangleRenderer class; Listing 9-15 shows the source code.

Listing 9-15. SimpleTriangleRenderer

```java
//filename: SimpleTriangleRenderer.java
public class SimpleTriangleRenderer extends AbstractRenderer
{
    //Number of points or vertices we want to use
    private final static int VERTS = 3;
```

```
//A raw native buffer to hold the point coordinates
private FloatBuffer mFVertexBuffer;

//A raw native buffer to hold indices
//allowing a reuse of points.
private ShortBuffer mIndexBuffer;

public SimpleTriangleRenderer(Context context)
{
    ByteBuffer vbb = ByteBuffer.allocateDirect(VERTS * 3 * 4);
    vbb.order(ByteOrder.nativeOrder());
    mFVertexBuffer = vbb.asFloatBuffer();

    ByteBuffer ibb = ByteBuffer.allocateDirect(VERTS * 2);
    ibb.order(ByteOrder.nativeOrder());
    mIndexBuffer = ibb.asShortBuffer();

    float[] coords = {
            -0.5f, -0.5f, 0, // (x1,y1,z1)
             0.5f, -0.5f, 0,
             0.0f,  0.5f, 0
    };
    for (int i = 0; i < VERTS; i++) {
        for(int j = 0; j < 3; j++) {
            mFVertexBuffer.put(coords[i*3+j]);
        }
    }
    short[] myIndecesArray = {0,1,2};
    for (int i=0;i<3;i++)
    {
        mIndexBuffer.put(myIndecesArray[i]);
    }
    mFVertexBuffer.position(0);
    mIndexBuffer.position(0);
}

//overridden method: more accurately implemented method
protected void draw(GL10 gl)
{
    gl.glColor4f(1.0f, 0, 0, 0.5f);
    gl.glVertexPointer(3, GL10.GL_FLOAT, 0, mFVertexBuffer);
    gl.glDrawElements(GL10.GL_TRIANGLES, VERTS,
            GL10.GL_UNSIGNED_SHORT, mIndexBuffer);
}
}
```

Although there seems to be a lot of code here, most of it is used to define the vertices and then translate them to NIO buffers from Java buffers. Otherwise, the draw method is just three lines: set the color, set the vertices, and draw.

> **Note**   Although we are allocating memory for `nio` buffers, we never release them in our code. So who releases these buffers? How does this memory affect OpenGL?
>
> According to our research, the `java.nio` package allocates memory space outside of the Java heap that can be directly used by such systems as OpenGL, File I/O, etc. The `nio` buffers are actually Java objects that eventually point to the native buffer. These `nio` objects are garbage collected. When they are garbage collected, they go ahead and delete the native memory. Java programs don't have to do anything special to free the memory.
>
> However, the `gc` won't get fired unless memory is needed in the Java heap. This means you can run out of native memory and `gc` may not realize it. The Internet offers many examples on this subject where an out-of-memory exception will trigger a `gc` and then it's possible to inquire if memory is now available owing to `gc` having been invoked.
>
> Under ordinary circumstances you can allocate the native buffers and not worry about releasing allocated memory explicitly because that is done by the `gc`.

Now that you have a sample renderer, let's see how you can supply this renderer to a `GLSurfaceView` and have it show up in an activity.

Using GLSurfaceView from an Activity

Listing 9-16 shows a typical activity that uses a `GLSurfaceView` along with a suitable renderer.

Listing 9-16. A Simple OpenGLTestHarness Activity

```java
public class OpenGLTestHarnessActivity extends Activity {
    private GLSurfaceView mTestHarness;
    @Override
    protected void onCreate(Bundle savedInstanceState) {
        super.onCreate(savedInstanceState);
        mTestHarness = new GLSurfaceView(this);
        mTestHarness.setEGLConfigChooser(false);
        mTestHarness.setRenderer(new SimpleTriangleRenderer(this));
        mTestHarness.setRenderMode(GLSurfaceView.RENDERMODE_WHEN_DIRTY);
        //mTestHarness.setRenderMode(GLSurfaceView.RENDERMODE_CONTINUOUSLY);
        setContentView(mTestHarness);
    }
    @Override
    protected void onResume()    {
        super.onResume();
        mTestHarness.onResume(); //Important
    }
```

```
    @Override
    protected void onPause() {
        super.onPause();
        mTestHarness.onPause(); //Important
    }
}
```

Let's examine the key elements of this source code. Here is the code that instantiates the GLSurfaceView:

```
mTestHarness = new GLSurfaceView(this);
```

We then tell the view that we don't need a special EGL config chooser, and the default will work by doing the following:

```
mTestHarness.setEGLConfigChooser(false);
```

Then we set our renderer as follows:

```
mTestHarness.setRenderer(new SimpleTriangleRenderer(this));
```

Next, we use one of these two methods to allow for animation or not:

```
mTestHarness.setRenderMode(GLSurfaceView.RENDERMODE_WHEN_DIRTY);
//mTestHarness.setRenderMode(GLSurfaceView.RENDERMODE_CONTINUOUSLY);
```

If we choose the first line, the drawing is going to be called only once or, more accurately, whenever it needs to be drawn. If we choose the second option, our drawing code will be called repeatedly so that we can animate our drawings.

> **Note** According to Android SDK documentation, your activity should tell the GLSurfaceView to pause and resume as the activity gets paused and resumed. This is to inform the GL drawing thread to pause and resume as well. Either way, you have to do this every time you use a GLSurfaceView in one of your activities.

That's all there is to interfacing with OpenGL on Android.

Previous editions of this book, at this point in the chapter, have given code for a driver program to invoke this activity. It was not an immensely useful addition to an understanding of OpenGL. So we have removed all that code and leave that as an exercise for the reader, as the reader should be able to create a simple test program to invoke the activity of Listing 9-16. We have the sample program available for download, which includes the complete source code. Once you download, compile, and run the program, pick the menu option "Simple Triangle" and you will see the triangle like the one in Figure 9-2.

Figure 9-2. A simple OpenGL triangle

Changing Camera Settings

To understand the OpenGL coordinates better, let's experiment with the camera-related methods and see how they affect the triangle that we drew in Figure 9-2. Remember that these are the points of our triangle: (-0.5,-0.5,0   0.5,-0.5,0   0,0.5,0). With these points, the following three camera-related methods as used in AbstractRenderer (Listing 9-14) yielded the triangle as it appears in Figure 9-2:

```
//Look at the screen (origin) from 5 units away from the front of the screen
GLU.gluLookAt(gl, 0,0,-5,    0,0,0,    0,1,0);

//Set the height to 2 units and depth to 4 units
gl.glFrustumf(-ratio, ratio, -1, 1, 3, 7);

//normal window stuff
gl.glViewport(0, 0, w, h);
```

Now suppose you change the camera's up vector toward the negative *y* direction, like this:

```
GLU.gluLookAt(gl, 0,0,5,    0,0,0,    0,-1,0);
```

If you do this, you'll see an upside-down triangle (Figure 9-3). If you want to make this change, you can find the method to change in the AbstractRenderer.java file (Listing 9-14).

Figure 9-3. A triangle with the camera upside down

Now let's see what happens if we change the frustum (also called the viewing volume or box). The following code increases the viewing box's height and width by a factor of 4 (see Figure 9-1 to understand these dimensions). If you recall, the first four arguments of glFrustum points to the front rectangle of the viewing box. By multiplying each value by 4, we have scaled the viewing box four times, like so:

```
gl.glFrustumf(-ratio * 4, ratio * 4, -1 * 4, 1 *4, 3, 7);
```

With this code, the triangle we see shrinks because the triangle stays at the same units while our viewing box has grown (Figure 9-4). This method call appears in the AbstractRenderer.java class (see Listing 9-14).

Figure 9-4. A triangle with a viewing box that is four times bigger

Using Indices to Add Another Triangle

We conclude these simple triangle examples by inheriting from the AbstractRenderer class and creating another triangle simply by adding an additional point and using indices. Conceptually, we define the four points as (-1,-1,   1,-1,   0,1,   1,1). And we ask OpenGL to draw these as (0,1,2   0,2,3). Listing 9-17 shows the code that does this (notice that we changed the dimensions of the triangle).

Listing 9-17. The SimpleTriangleRenderer2 Class

```
//filename: SimpleTriangleRenderer2.java
public class SimpleTriangleRenderer2 extends AbstractRenderer
{
        float[] coords = {
                -1.0f, -1.0f, 0, // (x1,y1,z1)
                1.0f, -1.0f, 0,
                0.0f,  1.0f, 0,
                1.0f,  1.0f, 0
        };
        ......other code modifications to match coords variable
        ..use listing 9-15 as an example
        short[] myIndecesArray = {0,1,2,    0,2,3};
}
```

After we add this code, we can run the program again and choose the menu option "Two Triangles" to see the two triangles drawn out (see Figure 9-5).

Figure 9-5. Two triangles with four points

Animating the Simple OpenGL Triangle

We can easily accommodate OpenGL animation by changing the rendering mode on the GLSurfaceView object. Listing 9-18 shows the sample code.

Listing 9-18. Specifying Continuous-Rendering Mode

```
//get a GLSurfaceView
GLSurfaceView openGLView;

//Set the mode to continuous draw mode
openGLView.setRenderMode(GLSurfaceView.RENDERMODE_CONTINUOUSLY);
```

Note that we're showing how to change the rendering mode here because we had specified RENDERMODE_WHEN_DIRTY in the previous section (see Listing 9-16). As mentioned, RENDERMODE_CONTINUOUSLY is the default setting, so animation is enabled by default.

Once the rendering mode is continuous, it is up to the renderer's onDraw method to do what's necessary to affect animation. To demonstrate this, let's use the triangle drawn in the previous example (see Listing 9-15 and Figure 9-2) and rotate it in a circular fashion.

AnimatedSimpleTriangleRenderer

The AnimatedSimpleTriangleRenderer class is very similar to the SimpleTriangleRenderer (see Listing 9-15), except for what happens in the onDraw method. In this method, we set a new rotation angle every four seconds. As the image gets drawn repeatedly, we see the triangle spinning slowly. Listing 9-19 contains the complete implementation of the AnimatedSimpleTriangleRenderer class.

Listing 9-19. AnimatedSimpleTriangleRenderer Source Code

```java
//filename: AnimatedSimpleTriangleRenderer.java
public class AnimatedSimpleTriangleRenderer extends AbstractRenderer
{
    .....Same code here as in the SimpleTriangleRenderer method
  //overridden method
   protected void draw(GL10 gl)
   {
      long time = SystemClock.uptimeMillis() % 4000L;
      float angle = 0.090f * ((int) time);

      gl.glRotatef(angle, 0, 0, 1.0f);

      gl.glColor4f(1.0f, 0, 0, 0.5f);
      gl.glVertexPointer(3, GL10.GL_FLOAT, 0, mFVertexBuffer);
      gl.glDrawElements(GL10.GL_TRIANGLES, VERTS,
              GL10.GL_UNSIGNED_SHORT, mIndexBuffer);
   }
}
```

In Listing 9-19, the method glRotate() is deceptively simple and doesn't invite eagerly an underlying question. However, we ask: We know that rotation is a transformation and hence involves a matrix, but which matrix? As indicated earlier, there are three matrices: model view, projection, and texture. The documentation says that the rotation call updates the current model view matrix. Where did we set the current model view matrix? What is its previous value? Well, it turns out that we are a bit lucky for this to have worked. If you see the abstract renderer of Listing 9-14 you realize that we have set the target matrix to be model view through a call to glMatrixMode(). In the same abstract renderer code, we have then applied the eye coordinate transformations on the model view matrix. This means the rotation applies to the *entire* scene, not just to the triangular object.

So the implication is this: if your intention is to place objects multiple times and rotate the object first before rotating the scene, then the eye coordinate transform should be applied after the model transforms. We now leave this as an exercise, in order to reshape your abstract class to accommodate this objective.

To see the animated triangle that is implemented in Listing 9-19, you can use the sample program provided in this chapter. You can see a reference to the zip file for this program in the references section. In the sample program, choose the menu option "Animated Triangle" to see the triangle implemented by Listing 9-19 and originally shown in Figure 9-2 spinning.

Braving OpenGL: Shapes and Textures

In this section, we present three things: using shapes to simplify vertex specification, using textures (attaching images to surfaces), and drawing multiple figures in a scene. These fundamentals should take you a bit closer to starting to create workable 3D figures and scenes. Although the subsections that follow also focus on ES 1.0, the information is equally applicable to ES 2.0. In fact, it is easier to explain these concepts first in the context of 1.0, and then point out the flexible approach taken in ES 2.0.

Working with Shapes

The method of explicitly specifying vertices to draw can be tedious. For example, if you want to draw a polygon of 20 sides, then you need to specify 20 vertices, with each vertex requiring up to three values. That's a total of 60 values. It's tedious.

A Regular Polygon as a Shape

A better approach to drawing figures like triangles or squares is to define an abstract polygon by defining some aspects of it, such as the origin and radius, and then have that polygon give you the vertex array and the index array. Say, you call this class RegularPolygon. Then you can use this clas as shown in Listing 9-20 to render various regular polygons.

Listing 9-20. Using a RegularPolygon Object

```
//A polygon with 4 sides and a radious of 0.5
//and located at (x,y,z) of (0,0,0)
 RegularPolygon square = new RegularPolygon(0,0,0,0.5f,4);

//Let the polygon return the vertices
 mFVertexBuffer = square.getVertexBuffer();

//Let the polygon return the triangles
 mIndexBuffer = square.getIndexBuffer();

//you will need this for glDrawElements
 numOfIndices = square.getNumberOfIndices();

//set the buffers to the start
 this.mFVertexBuffer.position(0);
 this.mIndexBuffer.position(0);

//set the vertex pointer
 gl.glVertexPointer(3, GL10.GL_FLOAT, 0, mFVertexBuffer);

//draw it with the given number of Indices
 gl.glDrawElements(GL10.GL_TRIANGLES, numOfIndices,
         GL10.GL_UNSIGNED_SHORT, mIndexBuffer);
```

Notice how you have obtained the necessary vertices and indices from the shape square. It is even further possible that RegularPolygon could be deriving from a basic shape that defines an interface for a "shape" contract. Listing 9-21 shows an example of the shape interface.

Listing 9-21. Shape Interface

```
public interface Shape
{
    FloatBuffer    getVertexBuffer();
    ShortBuffer    getIndexBuffer();
    int            getNumberofIndices();
    //You could even go further with
    //getTextureBuffer(), getTextureImage() etc.
}
```

Implementing the RegularPolygon Shape

As indicated, this RegularPolygon has the responsibility of returning what is needed to draw using OpenGL vertices. For a regular polygon, there are a number of ways of doing this. Owing to space limitations, we are not going to present the entire source code for some of these classes here. You can see the source code for those classes that are mentioned but not included in this chapter in the download sample for this chapter (see References). More important than code, here's the approach and logic used to arrive at these vertices.

In our approach, we have defined the regular polygon using the number of sides and the distance from the center of the regular polygon to one of its vertices. We called this distance the *radius*, because the vertices of a regular polygon fall on the perimeter of a circle whose center is also the center of the regular polygon. So the radius of such a circle and the number of sides will tell us the polygon we want. By specifying the coordinates of the center, we also know where to draw the polygon in our geometry.

We start with the assumption that the radius is one unit. We figure out the angles for each line connecting the center to each vertex of the polygon. We keep these angles in an array. For each angle, we calculate the *x*-axis projection and call this the "x multiplier array." (We use "multiplier array" because we started out with a unit of radius.) When we know the real radius, we multiply these values with the real radius to get the real *x* coordinate. These real *x* coordinates are then stored in an array called "x array." We do the same for the *y*-axis projections. Although the logic as stated here is quite simple, the code is lengthy and pretty detailed, and it reads like math. Instead, we recommend downloading the zip file and looking at the code.

Animating Regular Polygons

Now that we have shown the basic idea of drawing a shape generically through RegularPoygon, let's get a bit sophisticated. Let's see if we can use an animation whereby we start with a triangle and end with a circle by using a polygon whose sides increase every four seconds or so. To do this simply in the draw method, instantiate a polygon with increasing size count and tell the renderer to draw continuously. Here is this class in Listing 9-22.

Listing 9-22. PolygonRenderer

```java
public class PolygonRenderer extends AbstractRenderer
{
    //Number of points or vertices we want to use
    private final static int VERTS = 4;
    //A raw native buffer to hold the point coordinates
    private FloatBuffer mFVertexBuffer;
    //A raw native buffer to hold indices
    //allowing a reuse of points.
    private ShortBuffer mIndexBuffer;

    private int numOfIndices = 0;
    private long prevtime = SystemClock.uptimeMillis();
    private int sides = 3;

    public PolygonRenderer(Context context)      {
        prepareBuffers(sides);
    }

    //Parameterized polygon whose sides vary
    //with each animation time.
    private void prepareBuffers(int sides)     {
        RegularPolygon t = new RegularPolygon(0,0,0,1,sides);
        this.mFVertexBuffer = t.getVertexBuffer();
        this.mIndexBuffer = t.getIndexBuffer();
        this.numOfIndices = t.getNumberOfIndices();
        this.mFVertexBuffer.position(0);
        this.mIndexBuffer.position(0);
    }
    //overridden method
    protected void draw(GL10 gl)     {
        long curtime = SystemClock.uptimeMillis();
        if ((curtime - prevtime) > 2000)        {
            prevtime = curtime;
            sides += 1;
            if (sides > 20)        {
                sides = 3;
            }
            this.prepareBuffers(sides);
        }

        gl.glColor4f(1.0f, 0, 0, 0.5f);
        gl.glVertexPointer(3, GL10.GL_FLOAT, 0, mFVertexBuffer);
        gl.glDrawElements(GL10.GL_TRIANGLES, this.numOfIndices,
                GL10.GL_UNSIGNED_SHORT, mIndexBuffer);
    }
}
```

If you run the sample program and choose the menu item "Polygons," you'll see a set of transforming polygons whose sides continue to increase. It is instructive to see the progress of the polygons over time. Figure 9-6 shows a hexagon toward the beginning of the cycle.

Figure 9-6. *Hexagon at the beginning of the polygon drawing cycle*

Figure 9-7 shows it toward the end of the cycle.

Figure 9-7. *A circle being drawn as a regular polygon*

You can extend this idea of abstract shapes to more complex shapes, and even to a scene graph where it consists of a number of other objects that are defined through some type of XML and then renders them in OpenGL, using those instantiated objects.

Let's now move on to textures to see how to integrate the idea of sticking wallpapers to the surfaces we have drawn so far, such as squares and polygons.

Working with Textures

Textures are another core topic in OpenGL. OpenGL textures have a number of nuances. We cover the fundamentals of textures in this chapter, so that you can get started with OpenGL textures. The fundamentals of textures are similar in ES 1.x and 2.0, though they do differ slightly in implementation. We cover the ES 1.0 textures in this section, and then cover the ES 2.0 textures in the ES 2.0 section.

Understanding Textures

An OpenGL texture is a bitmap that you paste onto a surface in OpenGL. (In this chapter, we cover only 2D surface textures.) For example, you can take the image of a postage stamp and stick it onto a square so that the square looks like a postage stamp. Or you can take the bitmap of a brick and paste it onto a rectangle and repeat the brick image so that the rectangle looks like a wall of bricks.

The process of attaching a texture bitmap to an OpenGL surface is similar to that of pasting a piece of wallpaper (in the shape of a square) onto the side of a regularly or irregularly shaped object. The shape of the surface doesn't matter as long as you choose a paper that is large enough to cover it. However, to place the paper so that the image is correctly lined up, you have to take each vertex of the OpenGL shape (each surface) and exactly mark it on the wallpaper so that the wallpaper and the object's shape are in lockstep. If the OpenGL surface shape is odd looking and has a number of vertices, each vertex needs to be marked on your paper (texture) as well.

Another way of looking at this is to envision that you lay the flat OpenGL object on the ground face up and put the wallpaper on top of it, then rotate the paper until the image is aligned in the right direction. Now you poke holes in the paper at each vertex of the shape. You remove the paper and see where the holes are and note their coordinates on the paper, assuming the paper is calibrated. These coordinates are called the *texture coordinates*.

Normalized Texture Coordinates

An unstated detail here is the size of the object and the paper. OpenGL uses a normalized approach to resolve this. OpenGL assumes that the paper is always a 1 × 1 square with its origin at (0,0) and the top right corner at (1,1). Then OpenGL wants you to shrink your object surface so that it fits within these 1 × 1 boundaries. So the burden is on the programmer to figure out the vertices of the object surface in a 1 × 1 square. When you want the texture image to take the entire space of the object surface, you make sure that the object vertices all lie within the (0,0) to (1,1) of the texture coordinates. You can, however, specify the texture coordinate of a particular vertex to be greater than 1, either in the *x* direction or the *y* direction. In this case, you need to tell OpenGL how to map the space that is outside of (0,0) and (1,1). This is called the *wrapping mode*.

In one wrapping mode, you can tell OpenGL to repeat the texture image every time it crosses the boundary of 0 to 1. So, if you say 1.4 as your vertex's texture coordinate, then your texel (the corresponding pixel in the texture image) will be the 40th percentile from the beginning. If your vertex is at 2.4, then your texel that gets painted at this vertex will be the 40th percentile texel again from the beginning (from 0). So you will have painted in the given direction the texture image twice and then a 4/10ths of it by the time you get to the vertex that is at 2.4. This is a very roundabout way of saying that you repeat the image until you run out of space. This is further explained when we talk about wrapping modes in the context of the specific APIs.

Abstracting Common Texture Handling

Once you understand this mapping between texture coordinates and vertex coordinates, and can figure out the coordinates for the texture map, the rest is simple enough. (Nothing in OpenGL can be boldly stated as "quite simple!") Subsequent work involves loading the texture bitmap into memory and giving it a texture ID so that you can refer to this texture in subsequent APIs. This texture ID is sometimes also referred to as "texture name." Then, to allow for multiple textures loaded at the same time, you have a mechanism to set the current texture by specifying the ID.

Once the texture is loaded and available, during the drawing pipeline, you specify the texture coordinates along with the vertex coordinates. Then you draw. Because the process of loading textures is fairly common, we have abstracted this process through an abstract class called `SingleAbstractTextureRenderer` that inherits from `AbstractRenderer` (see Listing 9-14). This means that we continue to use the previous abstractions through the base class of `AbstractRenderer` and provide additional abstraction of textures through the `SingleAbstractTextureRenderer`.

Listing 9-23 shows the source code that abstracts all the setup code for a single texture. Following the source code, we explain pretty much every function, line by line.

Listing 9-23. Abstracting Single Texturing Support

```
public abstract class AbstractSingleTexturedRenderer
extends AbstractRenderer
{
    int mTextureID;        // var to hold ID/Name of the single texture
    int mImageResourceId;  // Image that becomes the texture
    Context mContext;      // In case we need the activity context

    public AbstractSingleTexturedRenderer(Context ctx,
                                          int imageResourceId) {
        mImageResourceId = imageResourceId;
        mContext = ctx;
    }

    public void onSurfaceCreated(GL10 gl, EGLConfig eglConfig) {
        super.onSurfaceCreated(gl, eglConfig);
        gl.glEnable(GL10.GL_TEXTURE_2D);
        prepareTexture(gl);
    }
```

```java
private void prepareTexture(GL10 gl)
{
    int[] textures = new int[1];
    gl.glGenTextures(1, textures, 0);
    mTextureID = textures[0];

    gl.glBindTexture(GL10.GL_TEXTURE_2D, mTextureID);

    gl.glTexParameterf(GL10.GL_TEXTURE_2D, GL10.GL_TEXTURE_MIN_FILTER,
            GL10.GL_NEAREST);
    gl.glTexParameterf(GL10.GL_TEXTURE_2D, GL10.GL_TEXTURE_MAG_FILTER,
            GL10.GL_LINEAR);
    gl.glTexParameterf(GL10.GL_TEXTURE_2D, GL10.GL_TEXTURE_WRAP_S,
            GL10.GL_CLAMP_TO_EDGE);
    gl.glTexParameterf(GL10.GL_TEXTURE_2D, GL10.GL_TEXTURE_WRAP_T,
            GL10.GL_CLAMP_TO_EDGE);

    gl.glTexEnvf(GL10.GL_TEXTURE_ENV, GL10.GL_TEXTURE_ENV_MODE,
            GL10.GL_REPLACE);

    InputStream is = mContext.getResources()
            .openRawResource(this.mImageResourceId);
    Bitmap bitmap;
    try {
        bitmap = BitmapFactory.decodeStream(is);
    } finally {
        try {
            is.close();
        } catch(IOException e) {
            // Ignore.
        }
    }
    GLUtils.texImage2D(GL10.GL_TEXTURE_2D, 0, bitmap, 0);
    bitmap.recycle();
}

public void onDrawFrame(GL10 gl)
{
    gl.glDisable(GL10.GL_DITHER);
    gl.glClear(GL10.GL_COLOR_BUFFER_BIT | GL10.GL_DEPTH_BUFFER_BIT);
    gl.glMatrixMode(GL10.GL_MODELVIEW);
    gl.glLoadIdentity();
    GLU.gluLookAt(gl, 0, 0, -5, 0f, 0f, 0f, 0f, 1.0f, 0.0f);

    gl.glEnableClientState(GL10.GL_VERTEX_ARRAY);
    gl.glEnableClientState(GL10.GL_TEXTURE_COORD_ARRAY);
    gl.glActiveTexture(GL10.GL_TEXTURE0);
    gl.glBindTexture(GL10.GL_TEXTURE_2D, mTextureID);

    draw(gl);
}
}
```

In this code, the single texture (a bitmap) is loaded and prepared in the onSurfaceCreated method. The code for onDrawFrame, just like the AbstractRenderer, sets up the dimensions of your drawing space so that your coordinates make sense. Depending on your situation, you may want to change this code to figure out your own optimal viewing volume. Note how the constructor takes a texture bitmap, which it prepares for later use. Depending on how many textures you have, you can craft your abstract classes accordingly.

We now explain the key segments and APIs from Listing 9-23.

Generating a Texture Name: glGenTextures

The OpenGL method glGenTextures is responsible for generating (more like reserving) unique IDs for textures so that those textures can be referenced later. Notice the code in Listing 9-24.

Listing 9-24. Generating a Texture Name

```
int[] textures = new int[1];
gl.glGenTextures(1, textures, 0);
mTextureID = textures[0];
```

For glGenTextures, the first argument is the number of textures we want and the second argument is the array for the API to write the texture integer IDs (names) that are returned. The third argument is the offset in the array to write to by the API.

During this ID or name allocation no bitmap has been loaded. We need this ID upfront because we need to direct OpenGL to set some parameters to control the behavior of this texture, including the subsequent loading of the bitmap. In a sense, this is like creating a texture object in order to start defining its properties.

Setting up Texture Target: glBindTexture

OpenGl can apply multiple types of textures. These are: GL_TEXTURE_1D, GL_TEXTURE_2D, GL_TEXTURE_3D or GL_TEXTURE_CUBE_MAP. When you call texture APIs, each API takes as its first argument which type of texture you are referring to out of these four. For this reason, these are called *texture targets*. Now consider this code in Listing 9-25.

Listing 9-25. Binding a Texture Target to a Texture Name

```
glBindTexture(GL10.GL_TEXTURE_2D, mTextureID);
```

The first argument of this method is the texture target. The second argument is the name or ID of the texture. You know from code Listing 9-23 that mTextureID is the name we have gotten by allocating it after calling the glGenTextures.

So what does this binding mean? OpenGL is annoyingly stateful. There are a number of APIs in OpenGL that operate on textures that merely indicate they want to operate on the current 2D texture. So when a subsequent API specifies an operation on target GL_TEXTURE_2D, this binding says that let that API affect the texture object indicated by the texture ID: mTextureID. In other words, you are saying your current 2D texture refers to the texture bound to mTextureID. if you were to generate/allocate five texture names, and if you were to bind texture named "3" to the 2D texture, then all the subsequent APIs referring to the 2D texture point of the texture object "3." That's quite a circuit, but there you go.

Controlling the Texture behavior: glTexParameter

Once the texture of your interest (through its name) is bound to the 2D texture, you can control its behavior by setting a number of texture parameters. See the code in Listing 9-26.

Listing 9-26. Setting up Texture Behavior

```
gl.glTexParameterf(GL10.GL_TEXTURE_2D, GL10.GL_TEXTURE_MIN_FILTER,
            GL10.GL_NEAREST);
gl.glTexParameterf(GL10.GL_TEXTURE_2D, GL10.GL_TEXTURE_MAG_FILTER,
            GL10.GL_LINEAR);
gl.glTexParameterf(GL10.GL_TEXTURE_2D, GL10.GL_TEXTURE_WRAP_S,
            GL10.GL_CLAMP_TO_EDGE);
gl.glTexParameterf(GL10.GL_TEXTURE_2D, GL10.GL_TEXTURE_WRAP_T,
            GL10.GL_CLAMP_TO_EDGE);
```

These methods are indicating, for the current 2D texture (based on binding), the behavior of the texture when it is applied.

Filtering Parameters: You may only have an icon like small bitmap as your texture and the surface of the OpenGL object may be the size of your tablet window. Then a single texel may map to multiple pixels, resulting in magnification. This is essentially enlarging or magnifying the texture image. We have specified extrapolating the values linearly. In this case, we take four texels around this pixel and get their average value. When the texture is larger, then we need to shrink (act of minifioation) the texture to fit the surface. In our case, we have indicated using the texel that is nearest to the pixel coordinate.

Wrapping Parameters: GL_REPEAT is an option for the texture image to be repeated on the surface in either direction (s, or t – same as x, y). With GL_REPEAT, when the texture coordinate is larger than 1—say, 1.3—just use the 0.3 as your new coordinate, ignoring the integer value. The result is that you end up redrawing the figure in that direction. You can apply this in both directions, resulting in copying the texture in multiple directions. In contrast, when you clamp with the option GL_CLAMP, when the texture coordinate is 1.3, it will set it to 1. Essentially, you repeat the last texel that is at coordinate 1 for the rest of the picture. So the result of a GL_CLAMP is to draw the picture just once and color the rest of the area based on the edge of the picture.

Controlling the Texture Blending Behavior: glTexEnv

Texture parameters, discussed in the previous section controlled the destination color for each pixel based on the pixel and texture coordinates. So you have a destination color that you want to go with. With the API glTexEnv, you can indicate how you want to react to the original color attributes of the pixel that are already there. For an example, take a look at the code in Listing 9-27.

Listing 9-27. How to Blend the Texture

```
gl.glTexEnvf(GL10.GL_TEXTURE_ENV, GL10.GL_TEXTURE_ENV_MODE,
            GL10.GL_REPLACE);
```

The first argument is always GL_TEXTURE_ENV for OpenGL ES. There appears to be more possible values in main OpenGL (filter control, point sprites). The second argument is set to environment mode when the goal is to control the blending behavior. For texture environment mode, the possible options are specified in the third argument: GL_REPLACE, GL_DECAL, GL_MODULATE, and GL_BLEND.

```
GL_REPLACE: Use the texel color as the pixel color
GL_DECAL: Blend the texel color with the pixel color controlled by the alpha value of the texel
GL_MODULATE: Multiply the texel color with the pixel color (especially to retain lighting effects)
```

GL_BLEND: Blending could be in effect with or without textures. Blending takes the foreground colors and blends them based on a function you specify with the background (using depth) colors, and the resulting color will be the final color. Now in the context of a texture, you use the texel color as your foreground color and use the pixel as the background color, and you blend them using the blend function that is in play. Using GL_BLEND well is an advanced topic.

Loading the Bitmap as a Texture: GLUtils.texImage2D

Let's look at the code that loads the bitmap image, as shown in Listing 9-28.

Listing 9-28. Loading the Texture Image

```
InputStream is = mContext.getResources()
                .openRawResource(this.mImageResourceId);
Bitmap bitmap;
try { bitmap = BitmapFactory.decodeStream(is);} finally {
        try { is.close();}catch(IOException e) {// Ignore.}}
GLUtils.texImage2D(GL10.GL_TEXTURE_2D, 0, bitmap, 0);
bitmap.recycle();
```

First you load the bitmap using BitmapFactory and a raw bitmap resource stream. Then you use that bitmap object as the texture bitmap to use for the current 2D texture (which is already bound to the texture name you generated). Yes! It is important to call bitmap.recycle() as the protocol of the bitmap class demands.

Internally GLUtils.texImage2D calls the OpenGL ES method glTexImage2D. The corresponding arguments to this method are (1) texture target, (2) level, (3) bitmap pointer, and (4) border. "Target" refers to the 2D target we have been using so far. The level is related to another texture idea called *mip/mapping*. Mip/mapping allows multiple images to be used for texturing when minifying or magnifying is required. In our case, we have only one level image that is represented as base level of 0. The bitmap pointer argument refers to the bitmap image stored in the client memory. The border specifies the width of the border, but for ES the documentation says this should be 0.

Setting the Texture Unit: glActiveTexture

When a surface is textured, OpenGL allows multiple texture units to be in effect. All the APIs we have used so far work on the active texture unit. By default, the texture unit is the base structure unit. When we called glEnable (GL_TEXTURE_2D), we have enabled the base texture unit with texture 2D as its target (this API and its counter part glDisable works on the current active texture unit). When multiple texture units are enabled, then the final color of the pixel is a combination of all the textures.

Let's examine the code that we have used for setting the active texture, Listing 9-29.

Listing 9-29. Activating the Texture Unit

```
gl.glActiveTexture(GL10.GL_TEXTURE0);
gl.glBindTexture(GL10.GL_TEXTURE_2D, mTextureID);
```

The base texture is always GL_TEXTURE0. As you can see, there is lot of binding going on with textures. You can find out how many texture units are supported by hardware. The hierarchy of this association is (a) texture unit, (b) texture target (1D or 2D, etc.), (c) texture name, and (d) the actual texture bitmap. No wonder texturing is daunting. (You can read up on most of these APIs from the OpenGL ES reference available at www.khronos.org/opengles/documentation/opengles1_0/html/index.html.)

Drawing Using Textures

Once the bitmap is loaded and set up as a texture, all you need are a set of vertex coordinates and a set of texture coordinates to draw textured figures. We demonstrate this idea by again employing shapes. We use a RegularPolygon that can generate the vertex and texture coordinations to draw a regular polygon along with the texture. Listing 9-30 shows the class that draws a textured square.

Listing 9-30. TexturedSquareRenderer

```
public class TexturedSquareRenderer extends AbstractSingleTexturedRenderer
{
   //Number of points or vertices we want to use
    private final static int VERTS = 4;

   //A raw native buffer to hold the point coordinates
    private FloatBuffer mFVertexBuffer;

   //A raw native buffer to hold the point coordinates
    private FloatBuffer mFTextureBuffer;

   //A raw native buffer to hold indices
   //allowing a reuse of points.
    private ShortBuffer mIndexBuffer;

    private int numOfIndices = 0;

    private int sides = 4;

    public TexturedSquareRenderer(Context context)
    {
       super(context,com.androidbook.OpenGL.R.drawable.robot);
       prepareBuffers(sides);
    }

    private void prepareBuffers(int sides)
    {
       RegularPolygon t = new RegularPolygon(0,0,0,0.5f,sides);
       this.mFVertexBuffer = t.getVertexBuffer();
```

```
        this.mFTextureBuffer = t.getTextureBuffer();
        //These textured coordinates for a square will be:
        //0,0,    0,1,    1,1,    0,0

        this.mIndexBuffer = t.getIndexBuffer();
        this.numOfIndices = t.getNumberOfIndices();
        this.mFVertexBuffer.position(0);
        this.mIndexBuffer.position(0);
        this.mFTextureBuffer.position(0);

    }

    //overriden method
    protected void draw(GL10 gl)
    {
        prepareBuffers(sides);
        gl.glEnable(GL10.GL_TEXTURE_2D);
        gl.glVertexPointer(3, GL10.GL_FLOAT, 0, mFVertexBuffer);
        gl.glTexCoordPointer(2, GL10.GL_FLOAT, 0, mFTextureBuffer);
        gl.glDrawElements(GL10.GL_TRIANGLES, this.numOfIndices,
                GL10.GL_UNSIGNED_SHORT, mIndexBuffer);
    }
}
```

In Listing 9-30, most of the heavy lifting for textures is carried out by the abstract textured renderer class while the RegularPolygon calculates the texture mapping vertices. The only new texture-related method in Listing 9-30 is this:

```
gl.glTexCoordPointer(2, GL10.GL_FLOAT, 0, mFTextureBuffer);
```

This method is merely pointing to a set of float texture coordinate values contained in the buffer mTextureBuffer. The first argument value "2" refers to the number of floats per texture coordinate. Without having the code for the RegularPolygon, you may be wondering what the texture coordinates would be for a square.

When we cover ES 2.0 textures, we will actually texture a cube and you will be able to explicitly see the vertex coordinates and the corresponding texture coordinates. However, all is not lost. We should be able to indicate clearly even here what the texture coordinate array would be for our rectangle.

We know that the rectangle has four points. And we have used the indices to draw two triangles out of those four vertices forming a square. Each vertex point will have an equivalent texture point. So we know that there will be four texture points. Because texture coordinates always fall in the range (0,0) to (1,1) (assuming we don't want to repeat the image), the corresponding texture coordinates for the four vertex coordinates are:

(0,0) //left bottom

(0,1) //left top

(1,1) //right top

(1,0) //right bottom

There is one caveat, though! In a bitmap, the *y* coordinate grows downward, and in OpenGL, *y* is positive upward. So you may want to reverse the *y* coordinates to see your picture in proper orientation. Now these texture coordinates stay this way even if your vertex coordinates form a 10 x 10 square. The only time you want the texture coordinates to fall outside of (1,1) is if you want to repeat the pictcure (for example, taking a brick and repeating it on a large wall).

Now, if we run the sample program and choose the menu item "Textured Square," we will see the textured square drawn as shown in Figure 9-8.

Figure 9-8. A textured square

Drawing Multiple Figures

Every example in this chapter so far has involved drawing a simple figure following a standard pattern. The pattern is to set up the vertices, load the texture, set up the texture coordinates, and draw a single figure. What happens if you want to draw two figures? What if you want to draw a triangle using traditional means of specifying vertices and then a polygon using shapes such as the RegularPolygon? How do you specify combined vertices? Do you have to specify the vertices one time for both objects and then call the draw method?

As it turns out, between two draw() calls of the Android OpenGL renderer interface, OpenGL allows you to issue multiple glDraw methods. Between these multiple glDraw methods, you can set up fresh vertices and textures. All of these drawing methods then go to the screen once the draw() method completes.

There is another trick you can use to draw multiple figures with OpenGL. Consider the polygons we have created so far. These polygons have the capability to render themselves at any origin by taking the origin as an input. As it turns out, OpenGL can do this natively whereby it allows you to specify a RegularPolygon always at (0,0,0) and have the "translate" mechanism of OpenGL move it off of the origin to the desired position. You can do the same again with another polygon and translate it to a different position, thereby drawing two polygons at two different places on the screen.

Listing 9-31 demonstrates these ideas by drawing the textured polygon multiple times.

Listing 9-31. Textured Polygon Renderer

```
public class TexturedPolygonRenderer extends AbstractSingleTexturedRenderer
{
   //Number of points or vertices we want to use
   private final static int VERTS = 4;

   //A raw native buffer to hold the point coordinates
   private FloatBuffer mFVertexBuffer;

   //A raw native buffer to hold the point coordinates
   private FloatBuffer mFTextureBuffer;

   //A raw native buffer to hold indices
   //allowing a reuse of points.
   private ShortBuffer mIndexBuffer;

   private int numOfIndices = 0;

   private long prevtime = SystemClock.uptimeMillis();
   private int sides = 3;

   public TexturedPolygonRenderer(Context context)
   {
      super(context,com.androidbook.OpenGL.R.drawable.robot);
      prepareBuffers(sides);
   }

   private void prepareBuffers(int sides)
   {
   RegularPolygon t = new RegularPolygon(0,0,0,0.5f,sides);
   this.mFVertexBuffer = t.getVertexBuffer();
   this.mFTextureBuffer = t.getTextureBuffer();
   this.mIndexBuffer = t.getIndexBuffer();
   this.numOfIndices = t.getNumberOfIndices();
   this.mFVertexBuffer.position(0);
   this.mIndexBuffer.position(0);
   this.mFTextureBuffer.position(0);
   }

   //overridden method
   protected void draw(GL10 gl)
```

```java
{
    long curtime = SystemClock.uptimeMillis();
    if ((curtime - prevtime) > 2000)
    {
        prevtime = curtime;
        sides += 1;
        if (sides > 20)
        {
            sides = 3;
        }
        this.prepareBuffers(sides);
    }
    gl.glEnable(GL10.GL_TEXTURE_2D);

    //Draw once to the left
    gl.glVertexPointer(3, GL10.GL_FLOAT, 0, mFVertexBuffer);
    gl.glTexCoordPointer(2, GL10.GL_FLOAT, 0, mFTextureBuffer);

    gl.glPushMatrix();
    gl.glScalef(0.5f, 0.5f, 1.0f);
    gl.glTranslatef(0.5f,0, 0);
    gl.glDrawElements(GL10.GL_TRIANGLES, this.numOfIndices,
            GL10.GL_UNSIGNED_SHORT, mIndexBuffer);
    gl.glPopMatrix();

    //Draw again to the right
    gl.glPushMatrix();
    gl.glScalef(0.5f, 0.5f, 1.0f);
    gl.glTranslatef(-0.5f,0, 0);
    gl.glDrawElements(GL10.GL_TRIANGLES, this.numOfIndices,
            GL10.GL_UNSIGNED_SHORT, mIndexBuffer);
    gl.glPopMatrix();
}
}
```

This example demonstrates the following concepts:

■ Drawing using shapes.

■ Drawing multiple shapes using transformation matrices.

■ Providing textures.

■ Providing animation.

The main code in Listing 9-31that is responsible for drawing multiple times is in the method draw(). We have highlighted corresponding lines in that method. Note that inside one draw() invocation we have called glDrawElements twice. Each of these times we set up the drawing primitives independent of the other time.

One more point to clarify is the use of transformation matrices. Every time glDrawElements() is called, it uses a specific transformation matrix. If you were to change this to alter the position of the figure (or any other aspect of the figure), you would need to set it back to the original so that the next drawing could correctly draw. This is accomplished through the push-and-pop operations provided on the OpenGL matrices. The push and pop are required because the matrix operations are cumulative, so when you want to start over, you want to get back to the first state of the matrix. For this reason, a "push" operation allows you to save/remember a matrix at a given point and allows you to return to that point later through a "pop."

If we run the sample program and choose the menu item "Multiple Figures," we will see two sets of changing polygons drawn (as shown in Figure 9-9) at the beginning of the animation. (Note that we have set the render mode to continuous.)

Figure 9-9. A pair of textured polygons

Figure 9-10 shows the same exercise in the middle of the animation.

Figure 9-10. A pair of textured circles

This concludes another important concept in OpenGL. In summary, this section showed you how to accumulate a number of different figures or scenes and draw them in tandem so that the end result forms a fairly complex OpenGL scene.

Next, we consider the Android support for OpenGL ES 2.0.

OpenGL ES 2.0

Most devices now on the market have GPUs that can support OpenGL ES 2.0. Android has added support for OpenGL ES 2.0 since API level 8. However, you need a real device to test ES 2.0 programs. Although there are references on the Internet indicating that a few in the inner Google circle have demonstrated how to run ES 2.0 programs on an emulator, we are not able to find any information to tell you how to do this.

OpenGL ES 2.0 is a different animal from OpenGL ES 1.x. It is not backward compatible. To complicate matters for beginners, it is most different in its initialization and in learning how to draw the simplest of drawings. If you are good at OpenGL, it is not that hard to make the transition. Fear not. We have covered enough OpenGL basics so far, and we intend to make you very comfortable with ES 2.0 by the end of this chapter.

For programmable GPUs, OpenGL ES 2.0 introduced a language called GLSL (shading language) that gets executed on the GPU to draw the geometric figures indicated by vertices and to fill their surface fragments with color. These programs are called *shaders*. The shader that controls vertices is called a *vertex shader*. The program that controls the coloring of fragments (pixels) is called a *fragment shader*.

Experts and OpenGL literature primarily draw the distinction between the two versions of OpenGL ES as follows: ES 1.0 is a fixed-function OpenGL pipeline, whereas 2.0 is a programmable pipeline. Another way of saying this is that ES 1.0 is hard-wired in its behavior while ES 2.0 allows programmability in the pipeline. We would like to further clarify this difference by examining the ES 2.0 pipeline, as shown in Listing 9-32.

Listing 9-32. ES 2.0 Pipeline

Client Programming stage
    Setup OpenGL Environment
    Declare/Define vertices, textures etc in client memory
    Setup variables such as frustum, window etc that affect the graphics pipeline
Vertex Processing stage - Vertex Shader Program
    Apply Model transformations: scaling, positioning, rotation etc
    Apply View transformations: fixing the eye coordinates
    Apply Projection transformations: viewing volume or frustum
    Texture coordinates calculated/transformed
    Lighting impact on colors
    Also called T&L (Transformation and lighting stage)
Graphics Primitive assembly
    Gather enough vertices for a primitive: lines or triangles etc
    Pass them to the next stage where the following happens
      Figure out front/back faces
      Cull if needed
      (done not by a shader but like a fixed functionality pipeline)
Rasterization
    Convert geometric primitives to fragments (or pixels)
    Apply Anti-aliasing
Fragment processing - Fragment Shader Program
    Interpolate fragment attributes: color, texture etc
    Texture mapping
    Apply textures programmatically if needed
    Fog
    Color sum
 Per fragment operations
    Fragment testing: ownership, depth, etc
    Blending
    Dithering
Framebuffer transfer
    Pixels sent to the frame buffer for display

The two programmable stages in ES 2.0 are the vertex processing stage and the fragment processing stage. The very first stage in Listing 9-32, client programming stage, is not really an OpenGL graphics pipeline stage. We have included it here to tell you what happens prior to the first OpenGL stage, the vertex processing stage.

As you draw your figures, except for the two programmable stages, the rest of the work happens automatically (based on what is specified in the client program), as in a fixed pipeline. In comparison, in ES 1.0, all stages are fixed and strictly controlled by the client programming stage.

In the rest of the chapter, you will see what the shader programs look like, so that you have a sense of what is programmable! Although the stages in Listing 9-32 are self-explanatory, refer to the OpenGL key concepts section at the beginning of the chapter to review the meaning of the operations listed under each stage.

Because we have covered most of the introductory theory of OpenGL, we explore the ES 2.0 primarily through two working samples. We will draw a cube, texture it, and then control its spinning through a button.

Java Bindings for OpenGL ES 2.0

Java bindings for the ES 2.0 API on Android are available in the package android.opengl.GLES20. All the functions of this class are static and correspond to the respective "C" APIs in the Khronos spec. (The URL for Khronos can be found in the References.) GLSurfaceView and the corresponding renderer abstraction introduced here for OpenGL ES 1.0 are applicable to OpenGL ES 2.0 as well.

First, let's see how to figure out if the device or the emulator supports this version of OpenGL ES 2.0 by using the code in Listing 9-33.

Listing 9-33. Detecting OpenGL ES 2.0 Availability

```
private boolean detectOpenGLES20() {
        ActivityManager am =
            (ActivityManager) getSystemService(Context.ACTIVITY_SERVICE);
        ConfigurationInfo info = am.getDeviceConfigurationInfo();
        return (info.reqGlEsVersion >= 0x20000);
}
```

Once you have this function (detectOpenGLES20), you can start using the GLSurfaceView, as shown in Listing 9-34, in your activity.

Listing 9-34. Using GLSurfaceView for OpenGL ES 2.0

```
if (detectOpenGLES20())
{
        GLSurfaceView glview = new GLSurfaceView(this);
        glview.setEGLContextClientVersion(2);

        glview.setRenderer(new YourGLES20Renderer(this));
        glview.setRenderMode(GLSurfaceView.RENDERMODE_WHEN_DIRTY);
        setContentView(glview);
}
```

Notice how the GLSurfaceView is configured to use OpenGL ES 2.0 by setting the client version to 2. Then, the class YourGLESRenderer will be similar to the renderer classes introduced earlier in this chapter. However, in the body of the renderer class, you will be using the GLES20 APIs instead of the GL10 APIs.

To be able to use OpenGL ES 2.0 features in your activities, such as the one in Listing 9-34, you need to include the following <uses-feature> as a child of the application node (see Listing 9-35).

Listing 9-35. Using OpenGL ES 2.0 Feature

```
<application...>
......other nodes
 <uses-feature android:glEsVersion="0x00020000" />
 </application>
```

Rendering Steps

Rendering a figure in OpenGL ES 2.0 requires the following steps:

1. Write shader programs that run on the GPU to extract such things as drawing coordinates and model/view/projection matrices from the client memory, and impact the final positions for vertices and pixel colors. (See the pipeline where this happens.) There is no counterpart to this in OpenGL ES 1.0, as this functionality behaves in a fixed manner.

2. Compile the source code of shaders from step 1on the GPU.

3. Link the compiled units in step 2 into a program object that can be used at drawing time.

4. Retrieve address handlers from the program in step 3 so that data can be set into those pointers.

5. Define your vertex buffers.

6. Define your model view matrices (done through such things as setting the frustum, camera position, etc.; it's very similar to how it's done in OpenGL ES 1.1).

7. Pass the items from step 5 and 6 to the program through the handlers obtained in step 4.

8. Finally, draw. This will kick off the pipeline. Vertex shaders and fragment shaders are called. Note that the vertex shader program is called once for each vertex in your client memory. The fragment shader is called once for every pixel (or fragment). The outputs of the vertex shader become one of the inputs to the fragment shader.

We examine each of these steps through code snippets and then present a working renderer paralleling the SimpleTriangleRenderer that was presented as part of the OpenGL ES 1.0. Let's start with understanding shaders first.

Understanding Shaders

We have briefly introduced (in the key concepts section at the beginning of this chapter) GLSL, its versions, and the nature of vertex and fragment shaders. The inputs to a vertex shader are primarily arrays of raw vertex attributes and the necessary transformation matrices. The outputs of a vertex shader are the final positions of each vertex after going through the transformations or any other calculations you deem important. A vertex shader program is called once for each vertex.

The outputs of a vertex shader are fed to the fragment shader to color the pixels. For example, for three vertices of a triangle a vertex shader is called only three times. However, the surface of the triangle may have hundreds of fragments (pixels). The fragment shader is called many times, once for each of these fragments. The values passed to the fragment (such as color values) are interpolated to be meaningful for that particular (x,y) position of the fragment within that surface. For a triangular surface whose vertices sport different colors, the color passed for a given pixel is an interpolated color that is a blend of the three different vertex colors based on the relative distance of the pixels from each vertex.

These concepts become clearer when you see an example of each of the shader programs. Let us start with a vertex shader.

Vertex Shader

Listing 9-36 is an example of a vertex shader program segment.

Listing 9-36. A Simple Vertex Shader

```
uniform mat4 uMVPMatrix;
attribute vec4 aPosition;
void main() {
  gl_Position = uMVPMatrix * aPosition;
}
```

This program is written in the shading language GLSL. The first line indicates that the variable uMVPMatrix is an input variable to the program, and it is of type mat4 (a 4 x 4 matrix). It is also qualified as a uniform variable because this matrix variable applies to all the vertices and not to any specific vertex. Such variables are called *uniform variables*.

In contrast to a uniform variable, the variable aPosition is declared as a vertex attribute that deals with the position of the vertex (coordinates). It is identified as an attribute of the vertex and is specific to a vertex. The other attributes of a vertex include color, texture, etc. This aPosition variable is a four- point vector as well.

In fact, you can invent your own attributes for a vertex. Your vertex shader program then can access that attribute in a meaningful way either to alter the final position of the vertex or to pass something downstream (like color) based on that special attribute that you have invented. Because of this generic facility, in ES 2.0 you no longer have separate APIs to pass vertex positions and vertex colors and other vertex-level attributes. You just have one API, which takes the attribute as a variable, to pass all vertex-related data!

The program in Listing 9-36 is taking the coordinate position of the vertex and transforming it using a model view projection (MVP) matrix (which will have to be set by the calling program). The program does this by multiplying the coordinate position of the vertex with the MVP matrix. The result is the final vertex position identified by the reserved variable gl_Position of the vertex shader.

Once the positions of all the vertices are determined this way (vertex shader is invoked multiple times, once for each vertex in the vertex buffer), the fragments are calculated by the fixed pipeline and the fragment shader is called multple times for each fragment (or pixel).

Although gl_position is a reserved variable that is an input to the fragment shader, you can explicitly indicate any number of arbitrary variables that can be passed to the fragment shader. We will see an example of this later, when we pass color values and texture coordinates. There are also a few more reserved variables for a vertex shader that could be used by an advanced user; refer to the GLSL spec or one of the GLSL books to know more about these variables.

In summary, a vertex shader program is responsible for positioning the vertices. You may be eager to see how the client program uses the attribute variable aPosition to pass the vertex data! Listing 9-37 shows how.

Listing 9-37. Setting/Transferring Vertex Data to the Vertex Shader from a Client

```
GLES20.glVertexAttribPointer(positionHandle, 3, GLES20.GL_FLOAT, false,
                TRIANGLE_VERTICES_DATA_STRIDE_BYTES, mFVertexBuffer);
```

The vertex buffer is the last argument of this GLES 20 method. This looks very much like the glVertexPointer in OpenGL 1.0, except for the first argument, which is identified as positionHandle. This argument points to the aPosition input attribute variable from the vertex shader program in Listing 9-36. You get this handle using code similar to the one in Listing 9-38 below:

Listing 9-38. Binding to an Attribute Variable

```
positionHandle = GLES20.glGetAttribLocation(shaderProgram, "aPosition");
```

Essentially, in Listing 9-38, you are asking the shader program to give a handle to an input variable whose name is "aPosition." This handle can then be used in subsequent calls (Listing 9-53 draw method) that transfer data from the client space to the shader program space. When I say transfer data, I am merely indicating that this is the binding that allows passing one vertex at a time to the vertex shader as the vertex shader gets called.

Now in Listing 9-38, the variable shaderProgram needs to be constructed by passing the shader source code to the GPU for compilation and linking. Before we explain how that happens, let us cover a sample fragment shader.

Fragment Shader

Listing 9-39 is an example of a fragment shader.

Listing 9-39. Example of a Fragment Shader

```
void main() {
    gl_FragColor = vec4(1.0, 0.0, 0.0, 1.0);
}
```

In this program, gl_FragColor is a reserved variable defining the output color of a pixel or fragment. We take this reserved variable gl_FragColor and hard-code it to the color red to keep things simple. Instead of hard-coding it to red as in Listing 9-39, however, we can pass these color values all the way from the user program through the vertex shader to the fragment shader. Similar to the way you defined an attribute for the position of the vertex, you can define an attribute for the color of the vertex in the vertex shader. Then you can pass the color array for each vertex, targeting this color attribute in the vertex shader. The vertex shader will then need to declare an outgoing variable of type "varying" so that it can be used in the fragment shader. Here is an example of such a vertex shader in Listing 9-40.

Listing 9-40. A Vertex Shader with a Color Input

```
uniform mat4 uMVPMatrix;
attribute vec4 aPosition;
attribute vec4 aColor;

varying vec4 aFragmentColor;

void main() {
  gl_Position = uMVPMatrix * aPosition;
  aFragmentColor = aColor;
}
```

The type "varying" means to change the value of that variable as it flows down to the fragment shader by interpolating based on the (x,y) coordinate of the fragment for which the fragment shader is called. Here is the fragment shader code in Listing 9-41that can use this color input variable.

Listing 9-41. A Fragment Shader with a Color Input

```
varying vec4 aFragmentColor;
void main() {
    gl_FragColor = aFragmentColor;
}
```

Notice how the varying variable aFragmentColor is passed between the vertex shader and the fragment shader. For this to happen, the names have to match; otherwise you will see a compiler error when you try to compile the shader programs. Also, remember that a fragment shader is called for every fragment or pixel that is expected to be affected.

These shader programs are mandatory to start drawing in OpenGL ES 2.0. Now that you have seen the source code for a simple vertex shader and a simple fragment shader, let us see how this source code is compiled and linked into a program by the GPU.

Compiling Shaders into a Program

Once you have the shader program segments, as seen in Listings 9-40 and 9-41, you can use the code in Listing 9-42 to compile and load a shader program.

Listing 9-42. Compiling and Loading a Shader Program

```
//Call this function to load and compile a shader
private int loadShader(int shaderType, String source) {
    int shader = GLES20.glCreateShader(shaderType);
    if (shader == 0) {
      //throw an exception or return 0
      return 0;
    }
```

```
//associate shader source with the shader id
GLES20.glShaderSource(shader, source);

//Compile it
GLES20.glCompileShader(shader);

//Check compiled status
int[] compiled = new int[1];
GLES20.glGetShaderiv(shader, GLES20.GL_COMPILE_STATUS, compiled, 0);
if (compiled[0] == 0) {
    //if it is an error throw an exception or return 0
    return 0;
}
    return shader;
}
```

In this code segment, the shadertype is one of GLES20.GL_VERTEX_SHADER or GLES20.GL_FRAGMENT_SHADER. The variable source will need to point to a string containing the source, such as those shown in Listings 9-40 and 9-41. We will cover the error-checking function glGetShaderiv shortly.

Listing 9-43 shows how the function loadShader (from Listing 9-42) is utilized in constructing the program object.

Listing 9-43. Creating a Program and Getting Variable Handles

```
private int createProgram(String vertexSource, String fragmentSource) {
    int vertexShader = loadShader(GLES20.GL_VERTEX_SHADER, vertexSource);
    if (vertexShader == 0) {
        return 0; //or throw an exception
    }
    Log.d(TAG,"vertex shader created");
    int pixelShader = loadShader(GLES20.GL_FRAGMENT_SHADER, fragmentSource);
    if (pixelShader == 0) {
        return 0; //or throw an exception
    }
    Log.d(TAG,"fragment shader created");
    int program = GLES20.glCreateProgram();
    if (program == 0) { /* throw an exception or */ return 0;}

    GLES20.glAttachShader(program, vertexShader);
    checkGlError("glAttachShader");

    GLES20.glAttachShader(program, pixelShader);
    checkGlError("glAttachShader");

    GLES20.glLinkProgram(program);
    int[] linkStatus = new int[1];
    GLES20.glGetProgramiv(program, GLES20.GL_LINK_STATUS, linkStatus, 0);
    if (linkStatus[0] == GLES20.GL_TRUE) {
        return program;
    }
```

```
        //Report error
        Log.e(TAG, "Could not link program: ");
        Log.e(TAG, GLES20.glGetProgramInfoLog(program));
        GLES20.glDeleteProgram(program);
        //throw an exception or
        return 0
    }
}
```

The key steps are fairly clear. We load the vertex and shaders, then create a program object and attach the shaders to the program object and link the program object. If there are any errors, those errors are reported.

We do have a couple of functions to check status and report errors. One of them is checkGLError(), a utility function you can see used in Listing 9-43. Here is how that function is implemented, shown in Listing 9-44.

Listing 9-44. How to Check General OpenGL Errors

```
protected void checkGlError(String op) {
    int error;
    while ((error = GLES20.glGetError()) != GLES20.GL_NO_ERROR) {
        Log.e(TAG, op + ": glError " + error);
        throw new RuntimeException(op + ": glError " + error);
    }
}
```

Notice how this utility function uses GLES20.glGetError() in a loop until there are no more errors to be retrieved. According to the OpenGL documentation, calling a glGetError will reset the error flag to GL_NO_ERROR. However, the SDK advises that there could be multiple error flags out of which one of the flags is selected each time this method is called to be returned and reset. As a result, the recommendation from the SDK is to call this method until you exhaust all flags.

In addition to this function, we have also used the debug methods shown in Listing 9-45.

Listing 9-45. Debug Methods to Aid in Compiling and Linking Shaders

```
glGetShaderiv
glGetShaderInfoLog
glGetProgramiv
glGetProgramInfoLog
```

glGetShaderiv and glGetShaderInfoLog are used to see if the compile operation on shader source code is successful. See the Listing 9-43 to see how these two methods are used. For example, we first use glGetShaderiv to see if the GL_COMPILE_STATUS is GL_TRUE. If not, we use glShaderInfoLog to retrieve the exact error message that has caused the commpile status to go false. You can also use glGetShaderiv to get information about a shader, as shown in Listing 9-46.

Listing 9-46. Available Information about a Shader Source

```
GL_SHADER_TYPE
GL_COMPILE_STATUS
GL_DELETE_STATUS
GL_INFO_LOG_LENGTH
GL_SHADER_SOURCE_LENGTH
```

glGetProgamiv and glGetProgramInfoLog are used to see if the linking operation on a shader program is successful; see Listing 9-43 for how these methods are used. We first use glGetProgramiv to see if the GL_LINK_STATUS is GL_TRUE. If not, we use glProgramInfoLog to retrieve the exact error message that has caused the link status to go false. You can also use glGetProgramiv to get the information shown in Listing 9-47 about a shader program.

Listing 9-47. Available Information about a Linked Shader Program

```
GL_DELETE_STATUS,
GL_LINK_STATUS,
GL_VALIDATE_STATUS,
GL_INFO_LOG_LENGTH,
GL_ATTACHED_SHADERS,
GL_ACTIVE_ATTRIBUTES,
GL_ACTIVE_ATTRIBUTE_MAX_LENGTH,
GL_ACTIVE_UNIFORMS,
GL_ACTIVE_UNIFORM_MAX_LENGTH
```

Getting Access to the Shader Program Variables

Once the program is set up (compiled and linked), the program's handle (integer identifier) can be used to get handles for the input variables defined in the shaders. Listing 9-48 shows how.

Listing 9-48. Getting Vertex and Uniform Handles

```
int maPositionHandle =
    GLES20.glGetAttribLocation(mProgram, "aPosition");
int muMVPMatrixHandle =
    GLES20.glGetUniformLocation(mProgram, "uMVPMatrix");
```

A Simple ES 2.0 Triangle

We now have covered the basics necessary for you to put together a framework similar to the one we created for OpenGL 1.0. We now put together an abstract renderer that will encapsulate ES 2.0 initialization work (such as creating shaders, programs, etc.). This abstraction will allow us to focus on defining figures and drawing them in derived classes. Listing 9-49 shows the code for an ES20 abstract renderer.

Listing 9-49. ES20AbstractRenderer

```
//filename: ES20AbstractRenderer.java
/*
 * Responsibilities
 * ****************
 * 1. Load vertex and shader programs
 * 2. Provide model transformations
```

```
 * 3. provide default vertex/shader programs
 * 4. Provide default frustum and camera settings
 *
 * Abstract features
 * ******************
 * 1. allow derived shader programs
 * 2. allow derived draw
 * 3. allow derived figures
 * 4. allow derived frustum/viewing volume settings
 * 5. Act as a base class, if needed, for abstracting textures
 */
public abstract class ES20AbstractRenderer implements Renderer
{
    public static String TAG = "ES20AbstractRenderer";

    //Class level or global variables are usually
    //unhealthy. Try to minimize them!!

    //The target matrix that holds the end result
    //of all model transformations
    private float[] mCurrentModelMatrix = new float[16];

    //A matrix that is a result of setting the camera/eye
    private float[] mVMatrix = new float[16];

    //A matrix that is the result of setting the frustum
    private float[] mProjMatrix = new float[16];

    //A matrix that is a multiple of current model, view,
    //and projection matrices.
    private float[] mMVPMatrix = new float[16];

    //GLSL program object with both the shaders compiled,
    //linked, and attached.
    private int mProgram;

    //A handle for the uniform variable identifying the MVP matrix
    private int muMVPMatrixHandle;

    //An attribute handle in the vertex shader
    //for passing the vertex arrays.
    private int maPositionHandle;

    //Name of the default vertex shader
    //source code file in the asset directory.
    private static final String DEF_VERTEX_SHADER_FILENAME
            = "def_vertex_shader.txt";

    //Name of the default fragment shader
    //source code file in the asset directory.
    private static final String DEF_FRAGMENT_SHADER_FILENAME
            = "def_fragment_shader.txt";
```

```
/*
 * This class relies on virtual methods to specialize.
 * Doesn't use construction arguments for specialization.
 */
public ES20AbstractRenderer()    {
    initializeMatrices();
}

public void initializeMatrices()
{
    //Set the model matrix to identity
    //Subsequent scaling, rotation, etc will update this
    //in a stateful manner. So starting state matters.
    Matrix.setIdentityM(this.mCurrentModelMatrix, 0);

    //Although we use this matrix only once,
    //it is good to start with a known state.
    Matrix.setIdentityM(mMVPMatrix, 0);
}

//@Override the interface method of Renderer
//JDK 1.5 doesn't allow this override tag on ab
public void onSurfaceCreated(GL10 gl, EGLConfig eglConfig)    {
        prepareSurface(gl,eglConfig);
}
/**
 * 1. Create the GLSL program object by passing vertex
 * and shader code. Derived classes can supply their own shader programs.
 * 2. Get vertex position hanndle
 * 3. get the uniform mvp matrix handle
 */
public void prepareSurface(GL10 gl, EGLConfig eglConfig)
{
    Log.d(TAG,"preparing surface");
    mProgram = createProgram(
            this.getVertexShaderCodeString(),
            this.getFragmentShaderCodeString());
    if (mProgram == 0) {
        return;
    }
    Log.d(TAG,"Getting position handle:aPosition");
    maPositionHandle = getAttributeHandle("aPosition", "Getting Position Handle");

    Log.d(TAG,"Getting matrix handle:uMVPMatrix");
    muMVPMatrixHandle = getUniformHandle("uMVPMatrix",
                                        "Getting MVP uniform matrix handle");
}

  //Override this method to specify your
  //your own frustum or the dimensions of a viewing volume.
```

```java
protected FrustumDimensions getFrustumDimensions()    {
    //Get default dimensions in this base class
    return FrustumDimensions.getDefault();
}


//@Override the interface method of Renderer
//JDK 1.5 doesn't allow this override tag on absolute methods
//Based on width and height of the window set the
//viewport and the frustum.
public void onSurfaceChanged(GL10 gl, int w, int h)
{
    Log.d(TAG,"surface changed. Setting matrix frustum: projection matrix");
    GLES20.glViewport(0, 0, w, h);
    float ratio = (float) w / h;
    FrustumDimensions fd = this.getFrustumDimensions();
    Matrix.frustumM(mProjMatrix, 0, ratio * fd.bottom, ratio * fd.top,
            fd.bottom, fd.top, fd.near, fd.far);
}


//@Override the interface method of Renderer
//JDK 1.5 doesn't allow this override tag on absolute methods
//1. Set your camera. You can place this method while creating
//the surface or changing the surface. Or you can choose to
//vary it during the draw method.
//2. Do basic drawing methods like clear the pallet
//3. Use the shader program that is setup before
public void onDrawFrame(GL10 gl)
{
    Log.d(TAG,"set look at matrix: view matrix");
    Matrix.setLookAtM(mVMatrix, 0, 0, 0, -5, 0f, 0f, 0f, 0f, 1.0f, 0.0f);

    GLES20.glClearColor(0.0f, 0.0f, 1.0f, 1.0f);
    GLES20.glClear( GLES20.GL_DEPTH_BUFFER_BIT
                                    | GLES20.GL_COLOR_BUFFER_BIT);

    GLES20.glUseProgram(mProgram);
    checkGlError("glUseProgram");

    //Allow a derived class to set up drawing
    //for further down the chain.
    //the default doesn't do anything.
    preDraw(gl,this.maPositionHandle);

    //Real abstract method
    draw(gl,this.maPositionHandle);
}

/*
 * 1. Load vertex shader
 * 2. load fragment shader
 * 3. create program
 * 4. attach shaders
```

```java
 * 5. link program and return it
 * 6. returns 0 if the program cannot be created
 */
private int createProgram(String vertexSource, String fragmentSource)
{
    int vertexShader = loadShader(GLES20.GL_VERTEX_SHADER, vertexSource);
    if (vertexShader == 0) {    return 0;            }
    Log.d(TAG,"vertex shader created");

    int pixelShader = loadShader(GLES20.GL_FRAGMENT_SHADER, fragmentSource);
    if (pixelShader == 0) {         return 0;        }
    Log.d(TAG,"fragment shader created");

    int program = GLES20.glCreateProgram();
    if (program == 0) {
        checkGlError("Error Creating the program");
        return 0;
    }
    Log.d(TAG,"program created");
    GLES20.glAttachShader(program, vertexShader);
    checkGlError("glAttachShader");

    GLES20.glAttachShader(program, pixelShader);
    checkGlError("glAttachShader");

    GLES20.glLinkProgram(program);
    int[] linkStatus = new int[1];
    GLES20.glGetProgramiv(program, GLES20.GL_LINK_STATUS, linkStatus, 0);
    if (linkStatus[0] == GLES20.GL_TRUE) {
        Log.d(TAG,"Program successfully linked");
        return program;
    }

    Log.e(TAG, "Could not link program: ");
    Log.e(TAG, GLES20.glGetProgramInfoLog(program));
    GLES20.glDeleteProgram(program);
    return 0;
}
// Load a given type of shader and check for any errors
private int loadShader(int shaderType, String source)
{
    int shader = GLES20.glCreateShader(shaderType);
    if (shader == 0){
        checkGlError("Cannot create shader:"
                + getShaderTypeAsString(shaderType));
        return 0;
    }
    //Associaate shader id to source
    GLES20.glShaderSource(shader, source);
```

```java
        //Compile source
        GLES20.glCompileShader(shader);
        //Check if there is an error
        int[] compiled = new int[1];
        GLES20.glGetShaderiv(shader, GLES20.GL_COMPILE_STATUS, compiled, 0);

        //Return if there is no error
        if (compiled[0] == GLES20.GL_TRUE) {
            Log.d(TAG, getShaderTypeAsString(shaderType)
                    + " successfully compiled");
            return shader;
        }

        //report error if there is one and return 0
        Log.e(TAG, "Could not compile shader "
                + getShaderTypeAsString(shaderType));
        Log.e(TAG, GLES20.glGetShaderInfoLog(shader));
        GLES20.glDeleteShader(shader);
        return 0;
    }

    //Purely used for debugging purposes
    public String getShaderTypeAsString(int shaderType)    {
        if (shaderType == GLES20.GL_VERTEX_SHADER){
            return "Vertex Shader";
        }
        else if (shaderType == GLES20.GL_FRAGMENT_SHADER) {
            return "Fragment Shader";
        }
        else { return new String("Unknown Shader Type Value");}
    }
    //Use this method to check and log GL errors
    protected void checkGlError(String op) {
        int error;
        while ((error = GLES20.glGetError()) != GLES20.GL_NO_ERROR) {
            Log.e(TAG, op + ": glError " + error);
            throw new RuntimeException(op + ": glError " + error);
        }
    }

    /*
     * The following three methods update the mCurrentModelMatrix
     * with the given model transformation.
     * These are stateful accumulative methods.
     */
    public void translate(float x, float y, float z)
    {
        float[] tempModelMatrix = new float[16];
        Matrix.setIdentityM(tempModelMatrix, 0);
        Matrix.translateM(tempModelMatrix,0,x,y,z);
```

```java
        Matrix.multiplyMM(this.mCurrentModelMatrix, 0,
                tempModelMatrix, 0, this.mCurrentModelMatrix, 0);
}
public void rotate(float angle, float x, float y, float z)
{
    float[] tempModelMatrix = new float[16];
    Matrix.setIdentityM(tempModelMatrix, 0);
    Matrix.rotateM(tempModelMatrix,0,angle,x,y,z);
    Matrix.multiplyMM(this.mCurrentModelMatrix, 0,
            tempModelMatrix, 0, this.mCurrentModelMatrix, 0);
}
public void scale(float xFactor, float yFactor, float zFactor)
{
    float[] tempModelMatrix = new float[16];
    Matrix.setIdentityM(tempModelMatrix, 0);
    Matrix.scaleM(tempModelMatrix,0,xFactor,yFactor,zFactor);
    Matrix.multiplyMM(this.mCurrentModelMatrix, 0,
            tempModelMatrix, 0, this.mCurrentModelMatrix, 0);
}


/*
 * Calculaute the final model view matrix
 * 1. Order of matrix multiplication is important
 * 2. MVPmatrix = proj * view * model;
 * 3. Setup the MVP matrix in the vertex shader memory
 */
protected void setupMatrices()
{
    float[] tempModelMatrix = new float[16];
    Matrix.setIdentityM(tempModelMatrix, 0);

    //translate the model combo next
    Matrix.multiplyMM(mMVPMatrix, 0, //matrix and offset
            mCurrentModelMatrix, 0,
            tempModelMatrix, 0);

    //translate eye coordinates first
    Matrix.multiplyMM(mMVPMatrix, 0,
            this.mVMatrix, 0,
            mMVPMatrix, 0);

    //Project it: screen coordinates
    Matrix.multiplyMM(mMVPMatrix, 0,
            mProjMatrix, 0,
            mMVPMatrix, 0);

    //Set the vertex uniform handler representing the MVP matrix
    GLES20.glUniformMatrix4fv(muMVPMatrixHandle, //uniform handle
            1, //number of uniforms. 1 if it is not an array
            false, //transpose: must be false
```

```
            mMVPMatrix, //client matrix memory pointer
            0); //offset
}


//Override this method to continue the onDrawframe callback
//from the renderer.
protected abstract void draw(GL10 gl, int positionHandle);


//Override this to implement preDraw
//useful for derived classes to specialize pre-draws
protected void preDraw(GL10 gl, int positionHandle)    {
    //nothing to do for this class: No op
}


//Use this method if your intent is to return
//a default vertex shader.
public String getDefaultVertexShaderCodeString()    {
    return this.getStringFromAssetFile(DEF_VERTEX_SHADER_FILENAME);
}


//Use this method if your intent is to return
//a default fragment shader.
public String getDefaultFragmentShaderCodeString()    {
    return this.getStringFromAssetFile(DEF_FRAGMENT_SHADER_FILENAME);
}


//Override this method if you want to provide
//a different vertex shader program.
protected String getVertexShaderCodeString()
{
    String vertexShader =
        "uniform mat4 uMVPMatrix;\n" +
        "attribute vec4 aPosition;\n" +
        "void main() {\n" +
        "  gl_Position = uMVPMatrix * aPosition;\n" +
        "}\n";
    return vertexShader;
}


//Override this method if you want to provide
//a different vertex shader program.
//In a derived method call getStringFromAssetFile(filename)
//to read as string to be returned from here.
protected String getFragmentShaderCodeString()
{
    String fragmentShader =
        "void main() {\n" +
        "  gl_FragColor = vec4(0.5, 0.25, 0.5, 1.0);\n" +
        "}\n";
    return fragmentShader;
}
```

```java
//How to to read a text file from an asset
//directory. In this approach you will need to
//create your application object and provide a static
//variable to create the context.
//See MyApplication implementation to see how this works.
//Or see http://androidbook.com/item/4224
public String getStringFromAssetFile(String filename)
{
    Context ctx = MyApplication.m_appContext;
    if ( ctx == null) {
        throw new RuntimeException("Sorry your app context is null");
    }
    try        {
        AssetManager am = ctx.getAssets();
        InputStream is = am.open(filename);
        String s = convertStreamToString(is);
        is.close();
        return s;
    }
    catch (IOException x)        {
        throw new RuntimeException("Sorry not able to read filename:" + filename,x);
    }
}


//Converting a file stream to a string
//Optimize as you see fit. This may not be an efficient read
private String convertStreamToString(InputStream is)
throws IOException
{
    ByteArrayOutputStream baos = new ByteArrayOutputStream();
    int i = is.read();
    while (i != -1)        {
        baos.write(i);
        i = is.read();
    }
    return baos.toString();
}


//Use this if you need to use a program object
//directly. Make sure you call this after the
//surface is created and prepared in this base class.
//otherwise it will be null.
public int getGLSProgramObjectReference()        {
    return this.mProgram;
}
//Use this method to get a handle to any
//named attribute. It is a utility method.
//It uses the program object that is in effect.
//Ensure program object is valid before calling this.
public int getAttributeHandle(String GLSLAttributeName, String comment)
```

```
{
    String logComment = comment + ":" + GLSLAttributeName;
     Log.d(TAG,comment);
    int attributeHandle =
        GLES20.glGetAttribLocation(mProgram, GLSLAttributeName);
     checkGlError(logComment);
    if (attributeHandle == -1) {
        throw new RuntimeException(logComment);
    }
    return attributeHandle;
}
public int getUniformHandle(String GLSLUniformName, String comment)
{
    String logComment = comment + ":" + GLSLUniformName;
     Log.d(TAG,comment);
    int uniformHandle =
        GLES20.glGetUniformLocation(mProgram, GLSLUniformName);
     checkGlError(logComment);
    if (uniformHandle == -1) {
        throw new RuntimeException(logComment);
    }
    return uniformHandle;
}//eof-method
}//eof-class
```

Much of this code is an aggregation of the ideas introduced previously. OpenGL by its very nature is procedural and very "C" centric. In an OO language like Java, you could do better to mold it into a nice OO framework as you go along. In fact, this abstract class is an early demonstration of this desire.

The abstract class in Listing 9-49 also allows you to load vertex shader and fragment shader files from the asset directory of your project. By default, these two files are indicated as follows:

```
Project-root/assets/def_vertex_shader.txt
Project-root/assets/def_fragment_shader.txt
```

In this abstract class we have further relied on a utility class to define the frustum. In the method onSurfaceChanged in Listing 9-49, we have used this class frustum to supply the frustum dimensions and get the projection matrix. Listing 9-50 shows the class definition of FrustumDimensions.

Listing 9-50. Frustum Dimensions Utility Class

```
public class FrustumDimensions
{
    //These are usually set by figuring out the window ratio.
    public float left;
    public float right;
    public float bottom;
    public float top;
    public float near;
    public float far;
    public FrustumDimensions(float left, float right,
```

```
                   float bottom, float top,
                   float near, float far)      {
          this.left = left;
          this.right = right;
          this.bottom = bottom;
          this.top = top;
          this.near = near;
          this.far = far;
      }
      static public FrustumDimensions getDefault()      {
          return new FrustumDimensions(-1, 1, -1, 1, 3, 7);
      }
      static public FrustumDimensions getMedium()      {
          return new FrustumDimensions(-1, 1, -2, 2, 3, 15);
      }
}
```

Listing 9-51 shows the contents of the default vertex shader file.

Listing 9-51. Default Vertex Shader File

```
//assets/def_vertex_shader.txt
uniform mat4 uMVPMatrix;
attribute vec4 aPosition;
void main()
{
      gl_Position = uMVPMatrix * aPosition;
}
```

Listing 9-52 shows the contents of the default fragment shader file.

Listing 9-52. Default Fragment Shader File

```
//assets/def_fragment_shader.txt
void main()
{
      gl_FragColor = vec4(0.5, 0.25, 0.5, 1.0);
}
```

These very simple shaders can allow you to draw any geometry with a single color. You could use this for testing your basics. As you get more sophisticated, the derived classes can pass their own shaders. However, depending on the variables that you need to map, you may want to structure abstract classes a bit more flexibly than what is presented in this abstract design.

This base abstract class also provides the utility methods you would need to bind to any variable, whether it is an attribute variable or a uniform variable.

The function setupMatrices in Listing 9-49 for ES20AbstractRenderer could use some explanation. This function demonstrates how the matrix class is used to combine multiple matrices into a single matrix called mMVPMatrix by multiplying other matrices, starting with an identity matrix.

The variable mCurrentModelMatrix starts out as an identity matrix. Each of the model transformations accumulates its effects on this matrix. By the time the client calls the setup matrices, this matrix would have the final multiplication of all model transformations (translate, rotate, scale, etc.) on the object that is being drawn.

The variable mVMatrix is obtained by using the eye point or the look-at point of the camera. The projection matrix mProjMatrix is obtained by using the frustum specification on the matrix class. You can see both of these variables being set up in Listing 9-42. Both concepts—the eye point and the frustum—are identical to the concepts covered in OpenGL ES 1.0. The MVP matrix (mMVPMatrix in the code), then, is just a multiplication of these matrices in the right order. The order is important. You take the model matrix (mCurrentModelMatrix) and multiply it with the view matrix (mVMatrix). Then take the resultant matrix and multiply it with the projection (mProjMatrix) to get the final MVP matrix (mMVPMatrix).

Finally, the call glUniformMatrix4fv sets this (mMVPMatrix) model view projection variable in the vertex shader (Listing 9-49) so that the vertex shader can multiply each vertex position with this matrix to get the final position (see Listing 9-36).

Listing 9-53 shows the code for the ES20SimpleTriangleRenderer that extends the abstract renderer and the minimum necessary to define the points and draw a triangle.

Listing 9-53. ES20SimpleTriangleRenderer

```
public class ES20SimpleTriangleRenderer extends ES20AbstractRenderer
{
  //A raw native buffer to hold the point coordinates
  private FloatBuffer mFVertexBuffer;
  private static final int FLOAT_SIZE_BYTES = 4;
    private final float[] mTriangleVerticesData = {
            // X, Y, Z
            -1.0f, -0.5f, 0,
            1.0f, -0.5f, 0,
            0.0f,  1.11803399f, 0 };

    public ES20SimpleTriangleRenderer()
    {
        ByteBuffer vbb = ByteBuffer.allocateDirect(mTriangleVerticesData.length
                * FLOAT_SIZE_BYTES);
        vbb.order(ByteOrder.nativeOrder());
        mFVertexBuffer = vbb.asFloatBuffer();
        mFVertexBuffer.put(mTriangleVerticesData);
        mFVertexBuffer.position(0);
    }

    protected void draw(GL10 gl, int positionHandle)
    {
        GLES20.glVertexAttribPointer(positionHandle, 3, GLES20.GL_FLOAT, false,
                0, mFVertexBuffer);
        checkGlError("glVertexAttribPointer maPosition");
        GLES20.glEnableVertexAttribArray(positionHandle);
        checkGlError("glEnableVertexAttribArray maPositionHandle");
```

```
        this.setupMatrices();
        GLES20.glDrawArrays(GLES20.GL_TRIANGLES, 0, 3);
        checkGlError("glDrawArrays");
    }
}
```

This is a concrete renderer class. You can take this renderer and use the code in Listing 9-34 (where we have used a GLSurfaceView to draw in an activity with a renderer) to draw your chosen activity. If you want to see this in action, use the test program for this chapter and invoke the menu item "ES20 Triangle."

Spinning a Textured Cube

In the final section of this chapter, let's up the ante and do the following using ES 2.0:

- Venture into the 3D world with a cube

- Texture the cube

- Translocate the cube down from the center

- Rotate the cube

- Mix the GL views and regular views in an activity

- Use a button to control the rotation of the cube

To do all this, we take advantage of the ES20 abstract renderer of Listing 9-49 and extend it to add texture-related behavior. We can then use that texture-enabled abstract renderer to derive the final cube renderer.

Single Textured Abstract Renderer

Because we have covered textures extensively earlier in the chapter, we can easily extend the abstract renderer in Listing 9-49 with texture behavior. In this renderer, we leave the implementation of the "draw" method to the derived classes. The responsibilities of the textured renderer is to load the textures and set them up so that the derived classes focus on vertex coordinates and texture coordinates. Most of the texture-related work will be carried out in this abstract textured renderer.

Because we are assuming that there is a single texture that is applied to all surfaces, we call this textured abstract renderer ES20SingleTextureAbstractRenderer. Listing 9-54 is the annotated source code for this class.

Listing 9-54. ES20SingleTextureAbstractRenderer

```
//filename: ES20SingleTextureAbstractRenderer.java
public abstract class ES20SingleTextureAbstractRenderer
extends ES20AbstractRenderer
{
    public static String TAG = "ES20SingleTextureAbstractRenderer";
```

```java
//Handle to the texture attribute in the vertex shader
private int maTextureHandle;
//handle to the texture Sampler Uniform variable in the fragment shader
private int mu2DSamplerTexture;

//Client assigned name of the texture
int mTextureID;
//default texture ImageResourceId
int mDefTextureImageResourceId = R.raw.robot;

public ES20SingleTextureAbstractRenderer()   {
    super();
}
//give out the texture attribute handle
//if needed.
protected int getTextureHandle()   {
    return maTextureHandle;
}


//You can prepare and load your texture here
//so that you don't have to do this every time
//a surface just changed changing the height and width.
public void onSurfaceCreated(GL10 gl, EGLConfig eglConfig)
{
    //Give a chance to have the parent prepare the surface
    super.prepareSurface(gl,eglConfig);
    prepareSurfaceForTexture(gl,eglConfig);
}
public void prepareSurfaceForTexture(GL10 gl, EGLConfig eglConfig)
{
    //Get texture attribute handle
    Log.d(TAG,"Getting texture handle:aTextureCoordinate");
    maTextureHandle = getAttributeHandle("aTextureCoordinate",
            "Getting Texture handle");

    //Get uniform texture handle
    Log.d(TAG,"Getting texture 2D sampler handle");
    mu2DSamplerTexture = getUniformHandle("s_2DtextureSampler",
            "Getting 2D sampler for texture");

    this.prepareTexture();
}

@Override
protected void preDraw(GL10 gl, int positionHandle)
{
    //Call the parent's method first
     super.preDraw(gl, positionHandle);

    //texture support
    //Make texture unit 0 as the active texture unit
```

```
            //This is the default as well
            GLES20.glActiveTexture(GLES20.GL_TEXTURE0);

            //Make texture target 2D and texture name mTextureId
            //as the target texture for the active texture unit
            GLES20.glBindTexture(GLES20.GL_TEXTURE_2D, mTextureID);

            //Tell the texture sampler in GLSL that the texture to
            //sample belongs to the texture unit 0.
            //This is also the default
            GLES20.glUniform1i(mu2DSamplerTexture, 0);

    }
    //Get the texture name that is initialized
    //Make sure it is initialized before calling this
    //method.
    public int getTextureID()      {
        return mTextureID;
    }
    //Ultimately this code prepares the
    //texture ID mTextureID,
    //creates it, and binds it to the texture target 2D.
    public void prepareTexture()
    {
        //GLES20.glEnable(GLES20.GL_TEXTURE_2D);
        int[] textures = new int[1];
        GLES20.glGenTextures(1, textures, 0);

        mTextureID = textures[0];
        GLES20.glBindTexture(GLES20.GL_TEXTURE_2D, mTextureID);

        GLES20.glTexParameterf(GLES20.GL_TEXTURE_2D,
                GLES20.GL_TEXTURE_MIN_FILTER,
                GLES20.GL_NEAREST);
        GLES20.glTexParameterf(GLES20.GL_TEXTURE_2D,
                GLES20.GL_TEXTURE_MAG_FILTER,
                GLES20.GL_LINEAR);
        GLES20.glTexParameterf(GLES20.GL_TEXTURE_2D,
                GLES20.GL_TEXTURE_WRAP_S,
                GLES20.GL_REPEAT);
        GLES20.glTexParameterf(GLES20.GL_TEXTURE_2D,
                GLES20.GL_TEXTURE_WRAP_T,
                GLES20.GL_REPEAT);

        final BitmapFactory.Options options = new BitmapFactory.Options();
        options.inScaled = false;    // No pre-scaling

        int texturImageReourceId = getTextureImageResourceId();
        // Read in the resource
        final Bitmap bitmap = BitmapFactory.decodeResource(
                MyApplication.m_appContext.getResources(),
                texturImageReourceId, options);
```

```
        GLUtils.texImage2D(GLES20.GL_TEXTURE_2D, 0, bitmap, 0);
        bitmap.recycle();
    }

    //override this to give your own texture image resource id
    protected int getTextureImageResourceId()    {
        return this.mDefTextureImageResourceId;
    }
}//eof-main-class
```

The source code in Listing 9-54 is annotated with comments. The texture coverage earlier in the chapter should also help in clarifying what is happening in this class.

The abstraction in Listing 9-54 assumes a few contracts from the derived classes. For example, it assumes that there is a single 2D texture. It also assumes that the vertex processor has an attribute called aTextureCoordinate to pass texture coordinates to the vertex shader. This code further assumes that there is a texture uniform variable called s_2DTextureSampler in the fragment shader that is used to sample the texture image from the texture unit.

A texture sampler is a structure in the fragment shader that allows you to look at the texture coordinate and the texture unit and return a color to be applied to the pixel. Texture samplers were introduced in ES 2.0; they are not applicable to 1.0. This is one critical difference between 1.0 and 2.0 regarding textures.

To understand the connection between these variables, here's a vertex shader and a fragment shader that can work with this abstract class.

Vertex Shader with Texture Coordinates

Listing 9-55 shows the source code for a vertex shader that assumes two things. First, it assumes that the vertices are passed through an attribute variable called aPosition. Second, it assumes that the texture coordinates are passed through an attribute variable called aTextureCoordinate. Both of the abstract classes—ES20AbstractRenderer (Listing 9-49) and ES20SingleTextureAbstractRenderer (Listing 9-54)—assume the names of these variables to be as defined here. We leave it here as an exercise if you want to parametize these variable names through derived classes.

Listing 9-55. Vertex Shader with Texture Coordinates

```
//input: model view matrix
uniform mat4 uMVPMatrix;
//input: vertex points
attribute vec4   aPosition;
//input: vertex texture coordinates
attribute vec2   aTextureCoordinate;
//output: vertex texture coordinate
//will act as input to the fragment shader
varying vec2   v_TextureCoordinate;
void main()
```

```
{
    gl_Position = uMVPMatrix * aPosition;
    //Pass the texture coordinate as is to the fragment shader.
    v_TextureCoordinate = aTextureCoordinate;
}
```

This vertex shader, from a texturing perspective, does the least. It simply passes the texture coordinates through an output varying variable called a_TextureCoordinate. Because this is a varying variable, you can expect it to be interpolated when it Is passed to the fragment shader. Note that it is not the texture value (color value) that is varied and passed to the fragment shader but, rather, is the texture coordinate at a given fragment.

Fragment Coder with 2D Texture Sampling

Code for the fragment shader is shown in Listing 9-56. The variable name s_2DtextureSampler is what we used in our abstract class ES20SingleTextureAbstractRenderer (Listing 9-54). This fragment shader code gets called once per fragment. When it is called, it is passed a texture coordinate that is relevent to that fragment. The prebuilt GLSL function texture2D is used to sample the texture unit (indicated and bound to s_2DtextureSampler) at the texel coordinate that is passed from the vertex shader.

Listing 9-56. Fragment Shader that Uses Texture Coordinates

```
precision mediump float;
//Appears precision is mandatory for this version of GLSL
//if you are using samplers.

//Input from the vertex shader
//names have to match.
varying vec2 v_TextureCoordinate;

//A structure to sample the texture
//from the texture unit.
//A client needs to bind a texture unit to this
//variable.
uniform sampler2D s_2DtextureSampler;

void main()
{
    //texture2D is a prebuilt function in GLSL
    gl_FragColor = texture2D(s_2DtextureSampler, v_TextureCoordinate);
}
```

These two shaders (Listing 9-55 and Listing 9-56) are generic enough to be reused for any complex figure as long as you are planning to use a single texture. For derived classes, as if texturing details have melted away, you could focus on drawing and texturing images without paying attention to the mechanism of how that texture is applied to the surfaces of your model.

We will see in the next subsection how to texture the six surfaces of a cube with very little amount of work. If you want, you could do the same to a triangle or a square or a polygon, and not worry about the shaders. This is the beauty of abstraction.

Cube Renderer

Listing 9-57 is the code to draw a cube, texture it, and rotate it on command. Notice how simple this code is. In fact, most of the space in this class is taken by the definition of the 36 vertex points (two triangles each for each of the six surfaces) and 24 texture points.

Take a look at the code first. Following the code, we explain the crucial steps in this code.

Listing 9-57. A Controllable Spinning Cube

```
//filename: ES20ControlledAnimatedTexturedCubeRenderer.java
public class ES20ControlledAnimatedTexturedCubeRenderer
extends ES20SingleTextureAbstractRenderer
{
    //A raw native buffer to hold the point coordinates for the cube.
    private FloatBuffer mFVertexBuffer;
    //A raw native buffer to hold the texture coordinates for the cube.
    private FloatBuffer mFTextureBuffer;
    private static final int FLOAT_SIZE_BYTES = 4;

    //variables to control rotation
    //if stopFlag = true stop the rotation
    private boolean stopFlag = false;
    //what is the current angle of rotation
    private float curAngle = 0;
    //At the last stop what was the angle
    //to restart.
    private float stoppedAtAngle = 0;

    //What are the vertex and fragment shader source code files
    private static final String VERTEX_SHADER_FILENAME
        = "tex_vertex_shader_1.txt";
    private static final String FRAGMENT_SHADER_FILENAME
        = "tex_fragment_shader_1.txt";

//front-face: f1,f2,f3,f4
//starting top-right-anti-clockwise
//f1(1,1) f2(-1,1) f3(-1,-1) f4(1,-1): z plane 0

//back-face: b1,b2,b3,b4
//starting bottom-right-anti-clockwise
//b1(1,-1) b2(1,1) b3(-1,1) b4(-1,-1) : z plane 2
    private float z = 2.0f;
    private final float[] mTriangleVerticesData = {
            //1. front-triangles
            //f1,f2,f3
            1,1,0,           -1,1,0,          -1,-1,0,

            //f3,f4,f1
            -1,-1,0,          1,-1,0,          1,1,0,

            //2. back-triangles
            //b1,b2,b3
```

```
              1,-1,z,              1,1,z,              -1,1,z,
              //b3,b4,b1
              -1,1,z,              -1,-1,z,            1,-1,z,

              //3. right-triangles
              //b2,f1,f4
              1,1,z,               1,1,0,              1,-1,0,
              //b2,f4,b1
              1,1,z,               1,-1,0,             1,-1,z,

              //4. left-triangles
              //b3, f2, b4
              -1,1,z,              -1,1,0,             -1,-1,z,
              //b4 f2 f3
              -1,-1,z,             -1,1,0,             -1,-1,0,

              //5. top-triangles
              //b2, b3, f2
              1,1,z,               -1,1,z,             -1,1,0,
              //b2, f2, f1
              1,1,z,               -1,1,0,             1,1,0,

              //6. bottom-triangles
              //b1, b4, f3
              1,-1,z,           -1,-1,z,      -1,-1,0,
              //b1, f3, f4
              1,-1,z,           -1,-1,0,      1,-1,0
      };

//Follow each face and the triangle set.
//Takes into account the upside down nature of bitmaps and
//texture coordinates.
      private final float[] mTextureData = {
              //1. front face: f1(10) f2(00) f3(01) f4(11)
              //front-triangles
              //f1,f2,f3
              1,0,     0,0,     0,1,
              //f3,f4,f1
              0,1,     1,1,     1,0,

              //2. back face: b2(10) b3(00) b4(01) b1(11)
              //back-triangles:
              //b1,b2,b3
              1,1,     1,0,     0,0,
              //b3,b4,b1
              0,0,     0,1,     1,1,

              //3. Right face: b2(10) f1(00) f4(01) b1(11)
              //right-triangles
              //b2,f1,f4
```

```
        1,0,    0,0,    0,1,
        //b2,f4,b1
        1,0,    0,1,    1,1,


        //4. Left face: f2(10) b3(00) b4(01) f3(11)
        //left-triangles
        //b3, f2, b4
        0,0,    1,0,    0,1,
        //b4 f2 f3
        0,1,    1,0,    1,1,


        //5. Top face: b2(10) b3(00) f2(01) f1(11)
        //top-triangles
        //b2, b3, f2
        1,0,    0,0,    0,1,
        //b2, f2, f1
        1,0,    0,1,    1,1,


        //6. Bottom face: b1(10) b4(00) f3(01) f4(11)
        //bottom-triangles
        //b1, b4, f3
        1,0,    0,0,    0,1,
        //b1, f3, f4
        1,0,    0,1,    1,1
        };
public ES20ControlledAnimatedTexturedCubeRenderer()
{
    //Turn java points to native buffer points
    setupVertexBuffer();
    //Turn java texture points to native buffer texture points.
    setupTextureBuffer();
}
//Convert to a native buffer
private void setupTextureBuffer()
{
    //Allocate and handle texture buffer
    ByteBuffer vbb1 = ByteBuffer.allocateDirect(mTextureData.length
            * FLOAT_SIZE_BYTES);
    vbb1.order(ByteOrder.nativeOrder());
    mFTextureBuffer = vbb1.asFloatBuffer();
    mFTextureBuffer.put(mTextureData);
    mFTextureBuffer.position(0);
}
//Convert to a native buffer
private void setupVertexBuffer()
{
    //Allocate and handle vertex buffer
    ByteBuffer vbb = ByteBuffer.allocateDirect(mTriangleVerticesData.length
            * FLOAT_SIZE_BYTES);
    vbb.order(ByteOrder.nativeOrder());
    mFVertexBuffer = vbb.asFloatBuffer();
```

```
        mFVertexBuffer.put(mTriangleVerticesData);
        mFVertexBuffer.position(0);
}
//Transfer the vertices from the vertex buffer
//to the shader.
private void transferVertexPoints(int vertexPositionHandle)
{
    GLES20.glVertexAttribPointer(
            vertexPositionHandle, //bound address in the vertex shader
            3, //how may floats for this attribute: x, y, z
            GLES20.GL_FLOAT, //what is type of each attribute?
            false, // not normalized
            0, //stride
            mFVertexBuffer); //local client pointer to data
    //Check to see if this caused any errors
    checkGlError("glVertexAttribPointer maPosition");

    //You have to call this to enable the arrays to be
    //used by glDrawArrays or glDrawElements.
    GLES20.glEnableVertexAttribArray(vertexPositionHandle);
    checkGlError("glEnableVertexAttribArray maPositionHandle");
}


//Same as above but for transferring texture attributes
//Notice how textures and vertices use the same concept
//of attributes and the same APIs.
private void transferTexturePoints(int texturePositionHandle)
{
    GLES20.glVertexAttribPointer(texturePositionHandle, 2,
            GLES20.GL_FLOAT, false,
            0, mFTextureBuffer);
    checkGlError("glVertexAttribPointer texture array");
    GLES20.glEnableVertexAttribArray(texturePositionHandle);
    checkGlError("glEnableVertexAttribArray textures");
}


//Drawing operation
@Override
protected void draw(GL10 gl, int positionHandle)
{
    //Hide the hidden surfaces using these APIs
    GLES20.glEnable(GLES20.GL_DEPTH_TEST);
    GLES20.glDepthFunc(GLES20.GL_LESS);

    //Transfer vertices to the shader
    transferVertexPoints(positionHandle);
    //Transfer texture points to the shader
    transferTexturePoints(getTextureHandle());

    //Implement rotation from 0 to 360 degrees
    //Stop when asked and restart when the stopFlag
    //is set to false.
```

```
        //Decide what the current angle to apply
        //for rotation is.
        if (stopFlag == true)        {
            //stop rotation
            curAngle = stoppedAtAngle;
        }
        else        {
            curAngle += 1.0f;
        }
        if (curAngle > 360)        {
            curAngle = 0;
        }

        //Tell the base class to start their
        //matrices to unit matrices.
        this.initializeMatrices();

        //The order of these model transformations matter
        //Each model transformation is specified with
        //respect to the last one, and not the very first.

        //Center the cube
        this.translate(0,0,-1);
        //Rotate it around y axis
        this.rotate(curAngle, 0,-1,0);
        //Decenter it to where ever you want
        this.trnslate(0,-2,2);

        //Go ahead calculate the ModelViewMatrix as
        //we are done with ALL of our model transformations
        this.setupMatrices();

        //Call glDrawArrays to use the vertices and draw
        int vertexCount = mTriangleVerticesData.length/3;
        GLES20.glDrawArrays(GLES20.GL_TRIANGLES, //what primitives to use
                0, //at what point to start
                vertexCount); //Starting there how many points to use
        //Check if there are errors
        checkGlError("glDrawArrays");
    }

//Indicate how big of a viewing volume we desire
//This is just a simple homegrown class
//@see FrustumDimensions
@Override
protected FrustumDimensions getFrustumDimensions()        {
    return FrustumDimensions.getMedium();
}
//Indicate the fragment shader source code
@Override
```

```
    protected String getFragmentShaderCodeString()    {
        return this.getStringFromAssetFile(FRAGMENT_SHADER_FILENAME);
    }
    //Give out the vertex shader source code
    @Override
    protected String getVertexShaderCodeString()    {
        return this.getStringFromAssetFile(VERTEX_SHADER_FILENAME);
    }

    //Stop the rotation. Called by a client
    //on a button click or other user actions.
    public void stop()    {
        this.stopFlag = true;
        this.stoppedAtAngle = curAngle;
    }
    //Restart the rotation
    public void start()    {
        this.stopFlag = false;
        this.curAngle = this.stoppedAtAngle;
    }//eof-function
}//eof-class
```

We have extensively commented in the source code shown in Listing 9-57. A key portion of this code is defining all vertices of the cube. Each face needs six vertices, so we end up repeating the vertex as it participates in forming the multiple triangles making up each face.

When you are defining the vertices, pay attention to the triangles that form on each face. The winding is important for figuring out which is the outside-facing surface. As we have explained in the key concepts section at the beginning of the chapter, the way you do this is by imagining you are turning a right-hand screw (RHS) along the vertices (following the path of their definition order) of the triangle. The RHS should advance out of the surface and not into the surface.

This class also indicates that it wants a medium frustum by overriding the getFrustumDimensions() method. See thefrustum class in Listing 9-50 for the dimensions of a medium-size frustum. This class also indicates the vertex shader and fragment shader filenames to match those in Listings 9-55 and 9-56

This class uses glVertexAttribArray() to transfer the vertex and texture points to the shaders. This class also shows how to use rotation correctly. The class first positions the cube at the center and rotates it, then it moves the cube to the final position. Why is this important? Because you have to keep three things in mind when you do model transformations:

1. Each vertex goes through all of the model transformations alone. The cumulative effect of all the vertices going through this process will be a transformed model. But it is good to think of one vertex when you are transforming OpenGL figures.

2. Rotation as indicated in Listing 9-57 is around the axis extending from the origin to the specified point.

3. Each model transformation uses the output coordinates from the previous model transformation, not the first. So if your point is at 5 and it ends up at 7 after rotation, then moving it down by 1 will result in 6 (with respect to the last point) and not in 4 (with respect to its original point). Transformations have no historical memory. They only act on the last position, so the order of model transformations can give you different results.

If you run the sample program and invoke the menu "Controlled Spinning Cube," you will see the activity shown in Figure 9-11. We have taken this picture by using the DDMS from the eclipse APT connected to a real device. In the References, we have a URL where we have documented how to use DDMS to take on device pictures.

Figure 9-11. Controlling the rotation of a textured cube with mixed views

The activity shown in Figure 9-11 is a composite view where we are mixing a OpenGL view with a regular Android view. The regular Android view can have controls that rotate the cube. But keep in mind that as you mix the views, the painting on a GL suface view is done by a background thread. The side effect of this is that, if you are using background drawables that are drawn by the main thread, they may not show up, as the GL seems to take precedence and may overrwrite the surface.

You can see the code for the activity and the layout of Figure 9-11 in the downloadable project for this chapter (see References). Or you can visit this URL to a take a quick peek at the source code: http://androidbook.com/item/4254

References

You will find the following OpenGL resources quite useful:

Author's notes on OpenGL Books and Resources: `http://androidbook.com/item/3173`.

Various notes on OpenGL research from the authors: `http://androidbook.com/opengl`.

- *OpenGL ES 2.0 Programming Guide* by Aaftab Munshi, etc. This is one of the best books we have found that explains the shading language really well. However, you will be wise to have the OpenGL Super Bible along with it to understand the basics of OpenGL.

- *OpenGL Super Bible* by Richard S. Wright Jr., etc. This book is good for learning the basics of OpenGL. However, you will need at least another book that explains the shading language well.

- *OpenGL Shading Language* by Randi J Rost, etc. You could use this as a reference book on shading language. If you are serious about spending sometime on OpenGL you will need this book as well. However, the book by Aaftab does a much better job of explaining the shading language to a beginner. You may want to own all three books. A couple of supplementary books are listed below.

- *OpenGL Programming Guide* (the red book): `www.glprogramming.com/red/`. Although this online reference is handy, it stops at OpenGL 1.1. You will need to buy the 7th edition for information on the recent stuff, including OpenGL shaders.

- *The RenderMan Companion*: *A Programmer's Guide to Realistic Computer Graphics* by Steve Upstill. This book comes highly recommended in the graphics circles. RenderMan is the software produced by Pixar.

- Android's primary document on OpenGL: `http://developer.android.com/guide/topics/graphics/opengl.html`.

- Android's tutorial on OpenGL ES 2.0 (Drawing Graphics with OpenGL): `http://developer.android.com/training/graphics/opengl/index.html`.

- Android's `android.opengl` package reference URL: `http://developer.android.com/reference/android/opengl/GLSurfaceView.html`.

- The Khronos Group's OpenGL ES Reference Manual: `www.khronos.org/opengles/documentation/opengles1_0/html/index.html`.

- The following is a very good article on texture mapping from Microsoft: `http://msdn.microsoft.com/en-us/library/ms970772(printer).aspx`.

- You will find insightful course material on OpenGL from Wayne O. Cochran from Washington State University at this URL: `http://ezekiel.vancouver.wsu.edu/~cs442/`.

- Documentation for JSR 239 (Java Binding for the OpenGL ES API) is at: `http://java.sun.com/javame/reference/apis/jsr239/`.

- The man pages at khronos.org for OpenGL ES 2.0 are useful as a reference but not a guide: www.khronos.org/opengles/sdk/docs/man/.

- Understanding shading language is essential to understanding the new OpenGL direction, including the OpenGL ES 2.0: www.opengl.org/documentation/glsl/.

- GLES20 API reference from the Android SDK: http://developer.android.com/reference/android/opengl/GLES20.html.

- GLSurfaceView Reference: http://developer.android.com/reference/android/opengl/GLSurfaceView.html.

- You can find one of the authors of this book's research on OpenGL textures here: http://www.androidbook.com/item/3190.

- Version numbers for OpenGL, OpenGL ES, and GLSL: http://androidbook.com/item/4243.

- How to run Android applications on the device from Eclipse ADB: http://androidbook.com/item/3574.

- How to capture OpenGL ES 2.0 screens on the device from EclipseADT and DDMS: http://androidbook.com/item/4255.

- How to debug OpenGL ES 2.0 programs: http://androidbook.com/item/4231.

- Understand OpenGL winding: http://androidbook.com/item/4230.

- Sample code for a spinning cube using OpenGL ES 2.0: http://androidbook.com/item/4254.

- To download the test project dedicated for this chapter: http://www.androidbook.com/expertandroid/projects. The name of the ZIP file is ExpertAndroid_Ch09_OpenGL.zip.

Summary

This is a much-improved presentation of OpenGL on Android from the previous editions of our book. This chapter is a culmination of fabulous research on introducing OpenGL on Android to you. We have covered the basics of OpenGL, ES 1.0, and ES 2.0. We have explained the basic vocabulary of OpenGL that is necessary to understand the OpenGL literature. We have covered textures, drawing multiple figures, model transformations, and GLSL. We have given you a basic set of shader programs and how to use them for a lot of simple OpenGL exercises. We have used GLSL and ES 2.0 to draw a spinning cube in a mixed activity containing both GL views and normal views. We have shown you how to control the OpenGL drawing and animation from simple Android controls, such as buttons.

Reveiw Questions

The following questions should act as landmarks to what you have learned in this chapter

1. What is the difference between OpenGL and OpenGL ES?

2. What is the difference between ES 1.0 and ES 2.0?

3. Why is ES 2.0 not backward compatible with ES 1.0?

4. What is a fixed-function graphics pipeline?

5. What are GLUT, GLEW, and EGL?

6. What are color, depth, and stencil buffers?

7. What buffers make up a frame buffer?

8. What is Android Renderscript?

9. What are the three key characteristics of Android Renderscript?

10. What is OpenCL?

11. What is CUDA?

12. What are object, model, world, eye, and device coordinates?

13. What are model, view, and projection matrices?

14. How many transforamtion matrices are there in ES 1.0?

15. How do methods related to matrix operations in ES 1.0 target a specific matrix?

16. What is the need for a push-and-pop operations for a matrix in OpenGL?

17. What is a frustum?

18. What is an OpenGL view port?

19. How do you explain position and color as ES 2.0 vertex attributes?

20. Can you pass an arbitrary set of values as vertex attributes in ES 2.0?

21. How do you know which side of an OpenGL surface is outside and which is inside?

22. Does it matter in what order you specify vertices?

23. Does it matter where you start the vertices as long as they satisfy the winding?

24. Provide a rudimentary understanding of blending, dithering, and anti-aliasing.

25. How do you use indices to draw geometry in OpenGL?

26. What is orthographic and perspective projections in OpenGL?

27. Explain how GLSurfaceView and Renderer are used to do a basic drawing?

28. How do you do animation with GLSurfaceView?

29. What is glMatrixMode() and how does it affect model transformations like glRotate?

30. Why do you need shapes for defining vertices for complex objects?

31. How do you specify texture coordinates for an OpenGL surface?

32. How are texture coordinates related to vertex coordinates?

33. What are texels?

34. What is the difference between a texture ID and a texture name?

35. What is GLSL?

36. What are shaders?

37. How do you compile and link shaders?

38. How often does a vertex shader get called?

39. How often does a fragment shader get called?

40. Why is glVertexAttribPointer() a generic method?

41. What APIs are available to debug ES 2.0 issues?

42. What Is a varyIng varIable?

43. What are reserved variables in GLSL?

44. How do you bind to the attribute and uniform variables in a shader?

45. What is the right order to transform using model, view, and projection matrices?

46. How do you load shader source code from assets?

47. What are attributes in GLSL?

48. What are uniform variables in GLSL?

49. What is the role of texture samplers in GLSL?

50. Why do you need to turn a texture coordinates upside down when attaching to a surface geometry?

51. How do you associate a texture sampler with a texture unit?

52. How do you debug compiler errors for the shading programs?

53. How do you debug linking errors from linking the shaders in a program?

54. What would you do if your texture appears upside down?

55. Can you have a texture coordinate larger than 1?

56. What is the difference between GL_REPEAT and GL_CLAMP?

Introduction to Android Search

Search capabilities in Android extend the familiar web-based Google search bar to search both device-based local content and Internet-based external content. You can further use this search mechanism to discover and invoke applications directly from the search results on the home page. Android makes these features possible by providing a search framework that allows all applications to participate in the search.

Android search involves a single search box to let users enter search data. This is true whether you are using the global search box on the home page or searching through your own application: you use the same search box.

This search box can take one of three forms: a search widget, a search dialog, or a search view. A search widget is an Android widget that you can drag and drop onto your home screen. A search dialog is what an application can invoke to help the user enter search text. This search dialog can be invoked by the search widget on the home page or inside an application. A search view is a special case of search dialog that is embedded in your views, espcially in the action bar of your application to search data that is specific to that application.

As a user enters text in a search view or a search dialog, Android takes the text and passes it to various applications that have registered to respond to a search. Applications will respond by returning a collection of responses. Android aggregates these responses from multiple applications and presents them as a list of possible suggestions. When the user clicks one of these responses, Android invokes the application that presented the suggestion to properly respond as designed by the application that presented the suggestion. In this sense, Android search is a federated search among a set of participating applications.

In this chapter, you will learn three things: (1) What the end user experience is of a search on the Android platform, (2) how activities interact with the search framework to either invoke or respond to a search, and (3) how to address device variations when writing searchable applications. This is also an introductory chapter on Android search and it forms the basis for material on writing your own search providers that is covered in the next two chapters.

Exploring Android Global Search

You can't miss the search box on an Android device; it is usually displayed on the home page, as shown in Figure 10-1. This search box is also referred to as the quick search box (QSB) or the search widget. In some releases of Android, or depending on the device manufacturer or carrier, you may not see this search widget by default on the home screen. All of the figures in this chapter are captured using the emulator in Android 4.0.

Figure 10-1. Android home page with a search widget

If you don't see the search widget on your home pane, or If you had deleted it earlier, being like any other Android widget, you can locate it by going to the catalog of widgets and choosing the search widget to be placed on any home screen you may have. You can also remove the search widget from the home page by dragging it to the trash can. Of course, you can redrag it from the widgets tab/screen again.

A side effect of QSB's being a widget is that shifting focus to the search widget on the home page in order to enter data will basically launch you into a global search dialog (see Figure 10-2), whereby you leave the home page context and are in the context of the search dialog.

Figure 10-2. Global search dialog spawned from the home search widget

You can also invoke the search dialog of Figure 10-2 by clicking the physical Search key, if it is available on your device. When the Search key is available, much like the Home key, you can click the Search key at any time, irrespective of the application that is visible.

The trend is to not have the physical Search key. The Search key may be virtual, or it may not even be there as a global icon. In that case, you will have to rely on the search widget. As a good pattern, applications are advised to use their own search menu item or put a search view in the action bar of the application. In short, you can reliably assume that the search widget will always be available and your application should explicitly provide the search experience by offering a menu item (which can be turned into a search view if there is an action bar).

The tricky thing is that a virtual or physical Search key may be present but you have to program for it if you want to take advantage of it. When this key is present, and when an application is in focus, there is an opportunity for the application to specialize the search (which we will go into later). This customized search is called a local search. The more general, common, and noncustomized search is called a *global search*.

Note   When the Search key is pressed while an application is in focus, it is up to the application to allow
or disallow both local and global searches. In releases prior to 2.0, the default action is to allow the global
search. In releases 2.2 and later, the default behavior is to disable the global search. This means that when
an activity is in focus, the user has to click the Home key first and then click the Search key or the search
widget if he or she wants a global search.

Prior to release 2.2, the Android global search box did not offer a choice of searching data only in
individual applications. All applications that are enabled for search are considered the context for the
global search.

Starting in 2.2, the Android search allows users to pick a particular search context (or application).
They can do this by clicking the left-hand side icon of the global search activity, and this opens up a
selection of individual search applications that are providing searches (see Figure 10-3).

Figure 10-3. Global search dialog with various applications' search contexts

What you see in Figure 10-3 is the default set of search applications that are enabled for 4.0. This list
may vary with subsequent releases. The search context "All" behaves much like the global search of
prior releases. You can also create your own search context by registering your application as one
of the possible searchable applications. We will cover this aspect in greater detail in the next two
chapters, and focus here on the user's search experience.

Let us refer back to Figure 10-2 for a moment. Depending on your usage of the device in the past, the image shown in Figure 10-2 may vary, since Android guesses what you are searching for based on your past actions. When there is no text entered in the QSB, this search mode is called *zero suggestions mode*. This is because the searchable applications have not been given any input in order to provide suggestions.

Depending on the search text that is entered, Android provides a number of suggestions to the user, as shown in Figure 10-4. These suggestions show up below the QSB as a list and are called *search suggestions*. As you type each letter into the search box, Android dynamically replaces the search suggestions to reflect new information. When there is no search text, Android will display what are called *zero suggestions*. In Figure 10-2, Android has determined that none of the search applications has volunteered any *zero suggestions*. However, you may see some suggestions as you start using the device, as the default suggestion provider may pull up your last search strings as possible suggestions for you to search again. Figure 10-4 show the search suggestions that appear when you type some text into the QSB.

Figure 10-4. Search suggestions

There are six areas of focus shown in Figure 10-4. These are:

1. The left-side search context/application icon

2. The search box

3. The search arrow on the right

4. The list of suggestions

5. The pencil icon next to each suggestion

6. The Go button on the keyboard

The left-side search context/application icon indicates what your search context is. For "All," it is typically an icon presented by the device manufacturer. For example, it could be Google or it could be Bing or just a standard search icon.

The search box, or QSB, is the edit control in which you enter the search text. If the search context is "All," and if some search text is present, you can click the search arrow on the right and it will fire off a default search as controlled by the device manufacturer, which more often than not is the browser search. Input for this search will be the search text you've entered in the search box. If the context of the search is a specific application, then an activity in that application is called with input provided by the search box.

In Figure 10-4, each item in the suggestion list is also a set of words. This doesn't have to be the case all the time, however. The suggestions could be the names of applications that can be directly invoked (shown in Figure 10-5, a bit later). When a suggestion is a web-searchable text, such as shown in Figure 10-4, the pencil icon on the right allows you to tap it and that moves the suggestion text into the search edit box, and thereby modifies it.

See also in Figure 10-4 that the Enter button on the keyboard has become the Go button. This behavior is manufacturer-dependent in the global dialog for the "All" context. When the search context is your application, you can use a relevant icon.

Let's look at the suggestion list one more time. Android takes the search text that has been typed into the box so far and looks for what are called *suggestion providers,* which are supplied by the searchable applications. Android calls each suggestion provider asynchronously and in parallel to retrieve a set of matching suggestions as a set of rows. Android expects that these rows (called *search suggestions*) conform to a set of predefined columns (*suggestion columns*). By exploring these well-known columns, Android paints the suggestion list.

When the search text changes, Android repeats the process. This interaction of calling all suggestion providers for search suggestions and receiving suggestions is true for the "All" search context. However, if you were to choose a specific search application context (as shown in Figure 10-3), only the suggestion provider defined for that application will be invoked to retrieve search suggestions.

> **Note** The set of search suggestions is also called the *suggestions cursor*. This is because the content provider representing the suggestion provider returns a `cursor` object.

Figure 10-5 shows an example of a suggestion list in which some of the suggestions are pointers to applications that have been installed on the device. For the input text of "se," there are two applications that match this name: Search and Settings. The icons for the respective applications are also presented in the suggestions list, as shown on the left. If you choose one of these applications (Search or Settings), the respective application is invoked.

Figure 10-5. *Search suggestions for applications*

Enabling Searchable Applications for Global Search

As we have said, you can write applications that specify searching particular data sets. These applications then need to register in their manifest file that they are to be considered for a search. Even after that, an end user has to choose a subset or all of these applications to have it (or them) be part of the searchable context.

To be able to select or deselect these search applications, you have to access the search settings. To get to the search settings, click the search widget on the home page. This takes you to the global search dialog, as we have been showing so far. Now, click the menu (virtual or physical) icon. Most phones so far seem to carry a hardware Menu button; on tablets, you may see the software menu icon on the top right-hand corner of the screen. This screen will display the single menu item available for the global search activity, as shown in Figure 10-6.

Figure 10-6. *Global search activity/dialog menu*

If you click the search settings menu, as shown in Figure 10-6, you will see the search-setting options available; see Figure 10-7.

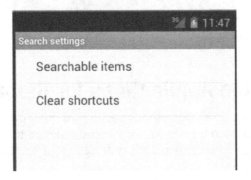

Figure 10-7. *Global search settings*

The option "Clear shortcuts" removes the search history. Instead, choose "Searchable items" to see the set of search applications available, as shown in Figure 10-8.

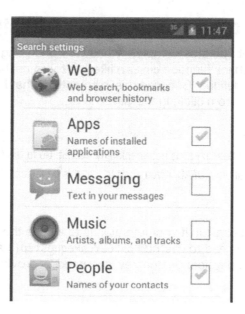

Figure 10-8. Available searchable applications

As you can see in Figure 10-8, a set of searchable applications is available or installed on the device. You can check/uncheck the applications, as you desire.

That wraps up the discussion of high-level usage of search features in Android. You can also search the Web to find dedicated user guides for each device. These specific guides will further show how the search experience can vary slightly among devices. We have included a URL reference to the Nexus user guide for Android 4.0.

We now examine how activities interact with the search framework.

Activities and Search Key Interaction

What happens when a user clicks the Search key when an activity is in focus? The answer depends on a number of things. Assuming there is a Search key, we can explore its impact on the following types of activities:

- A regular activity that is unaware of a current search
- An activity that explicitly disables a search
- An activity that explicitly invokes a global search
- An activity that uses a local search

Behavior of the Search Key on a Regular Activity

If there is a regular activity that operates completely unaware of an ongoing search, clicking the Search key will invoke the callback function onSearchRequested() callback. By default, this invokes a local search unless otherwise defined. Because this is an activity that hasn't defined a local search, there is no the impact resulting from clicking the Search key.

> **Note**   In the 4.0 emulator, the Search key is not enabled by default. Go to the AVD definition and choose to enable the physical keyboard and the DPAD, if you want to test this behavior.

There are implications to this behavior. If your intention is to invoke the global search when you press the Search key, then you need to override onSearchRequested() and explicitly invoke the global search. Or, if there is no physical Search key, you need to provide a search menu item in your application.

Behavior of an Activity that Disables Search

An activity has the option of entirely disabling the search (both global and local) by returning false from the onSearchRequested()callback method of the activity class. Listing 10-1 shows an example of this disabling.

Listing 10-1. Disabling Search Programmatically

```
//filename: NoSearchActivity.java
public class NoSearchActivity extends Activity
{
    .....other code
    @Override
    public boolean onSearchRequested()
    {
        return false;
    }
}
```

Explicitly Invoking Search through a Menu

In addition to being able to respond to the Search key, an activity can choose to explicitly invoke a search through a search menu item. This is useful when there is no longer a physical Search key. Instead, you provide an explicit menu item. If there is enough real estate, this menu item can be embedded in the action bar. When the search is a menu item, you need to process it as you would any other menu item and invoke the search explicitly by calling onSearchRequested() yourself.

Listing 10-2 shows the source code for an activity (SearchInvokerActivity) that invokes a search when a menu item is pressed.

Listing 10-2. Invoking Search through a Menu

```
public class SearchInvokerActivity extends Activity
{
    .....other stuff
    @Override
    public boolean onOptionsItemSelected(MenuItem item)
    {
        if (item.getItemId() == R.id.mid_si_search)
        {
            this.onSearchRequested();
            return true;
        }
        return super.onOptionsItemSelected(item);
    }
    @Override
    public boolean onSearchRequested()
    {
        this.startSearch("test",true,null,true);
        return true;
    }
}
```

Key portions of the source code are highlighted in bold. Notice how a menu ID (R.id.mid_si_search) is calling the function onSearchRequested(). This method, onSearchRequested(), invokes the search.

The base method "startSearch" has the following arguments:

> initialQuery: Text to search for.

> selectInitialQuery: A Boolean indicating whether to highlight the search text or not. In this case, we use "true" to hightlight the text so that it can be deleted in favor of a new text, if desired.

> appSearchData: A bundle object to pass to the search activity. In this case, we are not targeting any particular search activity. In listing 10-2 we passed null for this argument instead.

> globalSearch: If this is true, the global search is invoked. If it is false, a local search is invoked if available; otherwise, a global search is invoked.

SDK documentation recommends calling the base onSearchRequested(), unlike what we have shown in Listing 10-2. However, the default onSearchRequested() is using "false" for the last argument of startSearch(). According to the documentation, this should invoke the global search if no local search is available. However, in recent releases (from 2.2, on), the global search is not being invoked. This could either be a bug or it was designed that way and requires a documentation update.

In this example, we have forced a global search by passing "true" to this last argument of startSearch().

Understanding Local Search

Now, let's look at the circumstances under which the Search key or a specialized search icon in your application will *not* invoke a global search but, instead, invokes a local search. But first, we have to explain a local search a bit further.

A local search has four components:

1. A search dialog (with a QSB in it) or a search view

2. A search results activity

3. A searchable info XML file (search configuration)

4. An invoker activity that starts the search

The first component is a search dialog or a search view that contains a search box very similar to, if not the same as, the global search QSB. This QSB, whether local or global, provides an edit text control to enter text and a search icon to click. A local QSB is invoked instead of the global one when an activity declares, in the manifest file, that it wants a local search. You can distinguish the invoked local QSB from the global one by looking at the icon in Figure 10-10 and see the hint (the text inside the search box) in the QSB. These two values, as you will see, come from a search configuration metadata XML file.

The second component of a local search is an activity that can receive the search string from the QSB (local or global) and show a set of results or any other output that is related to the search text. Often this activity is called *search activity* or *search results activity*.

The third component is a XML search metadata file called `SearchableInfo` that defines how the QSB should behave and if there is any suggestion provider tied to this search.

The fourth component of a local search is an activity that is allowed to invoke the search results activity just described (the second component). This invoking activity is often called *search invoker* or *search invoking activity*. This search invoker activity is optional because it is possible to have the global search directly invoke the local search activity (the second component) through a suggestion.

In Figure 10-9, you can see these four components and how they interact in context.

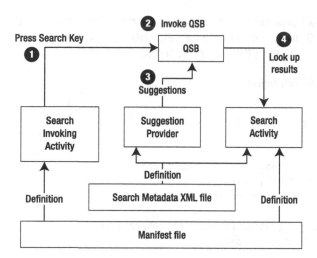

Figure 10-9. Local search activity interaction

In Figure 10-9, important interactions are shown as annotated arrows (circled numbers). Here's a more detailed explanation:

- SearchActivity (or search results activity) is the kingpin in Android search. Both the search metadata XML file and the suggestion provider hang off of this activity. A SearchActivity needs to be defined in the manifest file as an activity that is capable of receiving search requests. SearchActivity also uses a mandatory XML file to declare how the local QSB should be presented (such as with a title, hint, and so on), and if there is an associated suggestion provider (see Listing 10-6). In Figure 10-9, you can see this as a couple of "definition" lines that go between the SearchActivity and the two XML files (manifest file and the search metadata file).

- Once the SearchActivity is defined in the manifest file (see Listing 10-5), the Search InvokingActivity indicates in the manifest file that it is associated with the SearchActivity through a metadata definition android.app.default_searchable(Listing 10-8).

- With the definitions for both activities in place, when the SearchInvokingActivity is in focus, the press of the Search key will invoke the local QSB. You can see this in Figure 10-9—the circles numbered 1 and 2. You can tell that the invoked QSB is a local QSB by looking at the caption and hint of the QSB. These two values are set up in the mandatory search metadata XML definition. Once QSB is invoked through the Search key, you will be able to type query text in the QSB. This local QSB, similar to the global QSB, is capable of suggestions.

- Once the query text is entered and the search icon is clicked, the local QSB will transfer the search to the SearchActivity that is responsible for doing something with it, such as displaying a set of results.

We examine these interactions further by looking at code snippets for each of the files involved. We start with Listing 10-3, the source code for SearchActivity, (which, again, is responsible for receiving the query and displaying the search results).

Listing 10-3. A Simple Search Results Activity

```java
//filename: SearchActivity.java
public class SearchActivity extends Activity
{
    @Override
    protected void onCreate(Bundle savedInstanceState) {
        super.onCreate(savedInstanceState);
        setContentView(R.layout.search_activity);

        .....
        //Use the invoking intent to receive the search text
        //and do present what is needed
        ......
        return;
    }
}
```

This is a very simple activity with a text control in it. Listing 10-4 shows its layout.

Listing 10-4. Layout File for a Simple Search Results Activity

```xml
<?xml version="1.0" encoding="utf-8"?>
<LinearLayout
    xmlns:android="http://schemas.android.com/apk/res/android"
    android:orientation="vertical"
    android:layout_width="fill_parent" android:layout_height="fill_parent"
    >
<TextView
    android:id="@+id/text1"
    android:layout_width="fill_parent" android:layout_height="wrap_content"
    android:text="@string/search_activity_prompt"
    />
</LinearLayout>
```

We used the simplest possible search activity. In the next chapter, you'll see how search text or search queries are retrieved by this activity. For now, we show how this activity is invoked by the QSB. Listing 10-5 shows how SearchActivity is defined as a search activity responsible for the search results in the manifest file.

Listing 10-5. Defining a Search Results Activity in the Manifest File with Search Metadata

```xml
<activity android:name=".SearchActivity"
    android:label="Activity/QSB Interaction::Search Results">
    <intent-filter>
        <action android:name="android.intent.action.SEARCH"/>
        <category android:name="android.intent.category.DEFAULT"/>
    </intent-filter>
```

```
        <meta-data android:name="android.app.searchable"
                android:resource="@xml/searchable"/>
</activity>
```

> **Note** There are two things that need to be specified for a search activity. The activity needs to indicate that
> it can respond to SEARCH actions. It also needs to specify an XML file that describes the metadata required to
> interact with this search activity.

Listing 10-6 shows the search metadata XML file for this SearchActivity.

Listing 10-6. SearchableInfo for a Search Results Activity

```
<!-- /res/xml/searchable.xml -->
<searchable xmlns:android="http://schemas.android.com/apk/res/android"
    android:label="@string/search_label"
    android:hint="@string/search_hint"
    android:searchMode="showSearchLabelAsBadge"
/>
```

> **Tip** The various options available in this XML are documented in the SDK at
> http://developer.android.com/guide/topics/search/searchable-config.html.

We cover more of these searchable info XML attributes in the next two chapters. For now, the attribute android:label is used to label the search box. The attribute android:hint is used to place the initial text in the search box (see Figure 10-10). The android:searchMode attribute in Listing 10-6 is indicating to label the search box using the android:label attribute. This option used to look nice on phones in which the label is on a line by itself and the search box is underneath. However, in 4.0, this label is in line with the search box; that looks terrible, as it takes space from the search box. It is better to use showSearchIconAsBadge instead.

Now let's examine how an activity can specify this SearchActivity as its search. We called this invoking activing LocalSearchEnabledActivity. Listing 10-7 shows the source code for this LocalSearchEnbaledActivity.

Listing 10-7. LocalSearchEnabledActivity source code

```
public class LocalSearchEnabledActivity extends Activity
{
    @Override
    protected void onCreate(Bundle savedInstanceState) {
        super.onCreate(savedInstanceState);
```

```
            setContentView(R.layout.local_search_enabled_activity);
            return;
    }
    @Override
    public boolean onCreateOptionsMenu(Menu menu)        {
            super.onCreateOptionsMenu(menu);
            MenuInflater inflater = getMenuInflater();
            inflater.inflate(R.menu.search_invoker_menu, menu);
            return true;
    }
    @Override
    public boolean onOptionsItemSelected(MenuItem item)        {
            if (item.getItemId() == R.id.mid_si_search)
            {
                onSearchRequested();
                return true;
            }
            return super.onOptionsItemSelected(item);
    }
}
```

Notice, in Listing 10-7, that we have defined a menu item for the search called R.id.mid_si_search. This menu item is part of a menu file, indicated in Listing 10-7, by R.menu.search_invoker_menu. We will leave it to you to create a menu file that satisfies the R.id.mid_si_search and R.menu.search_invoker_menu. If the menu item R.id.mid_si_search is chosen, then we call the onSearchRequested(). How does Android know to invoke the local search at this point? The definition of the LocalSearchEnabledActivity in the manifest file clarifies this relationship to SearchActivity for Android, as shown in Listing 10-8.

Listing 10-8. Tying a Search Results Activity Through metadata

```
<activity android:name=".LocalSearchEnabledActivity"
    android:label="Activity/QSB Interaction::Local Search">
      <meta-data android:name="android.app.default_searchable"
          android:value=".SearchActivity" />
</activity>
```

Notice how this LocalSearchEnabledActivity is pointing to the kingpin SearchActivity. SearchActivity in turn tells how the local QSB should be presented and the search text is passed to that SearchActivity.

Note   You can use this metadata definition at the application level as well, so that all activities will inherit this search activity. Individual activities can further override the application-level search activity, if needed. Prior releases used to accept a "*" in this place to indicate a global search; this "*" specification is deprecated now.

When the `LocalSearchEnabledActivity` is in focus, if you click on the device search, or use a menu item as identified in Listing 10-7, both will invoke a local search box (local QSB), as shown in Figure 10-10.

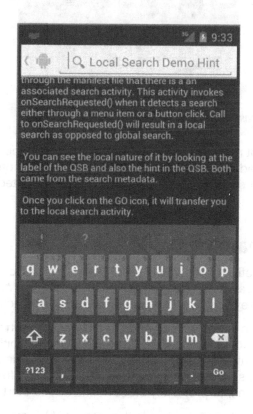

Figure 10-10. Local search QSB

Notice the icon on this search box and the hint of this search box. See how they differ from the global search (see Figure 10-2). The icon comes from the icon of the application package as defined in the manifest file for your application package. The hint comes from the search metadata (searchable.xml, Listing 10-6) specified for the `SearchActivity`. Now, if you type text in the QSB and click the search icon, you will end up invoking the `SearchActivity` (see Listing 10-3). Figure 10-11 shows what this `SearchActivity` looks like.

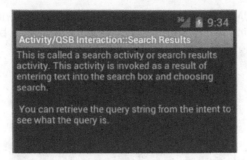

Figure 10-11. Search results in response to the local search QSB

Although this activity does not make use of any query search text to pull up results, it demonstrates how a search activity is defined and gets invoked. In the next two chapters, we'll show how this SearchActivity makes use of search queries and various search-related actions to which it needs to respond.

Enabling Type-to-Search

When you are looking at an activity such as the LocalSearchInvokerActivity shown in Figure 10-10, there is a way to invoke the search by typing a random letter (such as "t"). This mode is called *type-to-search* because any key you type that is not handled by the activity will invoke a search.

The intention of type-to-search is this: on any Android activity, you can tell Android that any key press can invoke a search—except for the keys that the activity explicitly handles. For example, if an activity handles "x" and "y," but doesn't care about any other keys, the activity can choose to invoke the search for any other keys, such as "z" or "a." This mode is useful for an activity that is already displaying search results; it can interpret a key press as the cue to start the search again.

Here are a couple of lines of code you can use in the onCreate() method of the activity to enable this behavior (the first line is used to invoke the global search and the second is used to invoke the local search):

```
this.setDefaultKeyMode(Activity.DEFAULT_KEYS_SEARCH_GLOBAL);
```

or

```
this.setDefaultKeyMode(Activity.DEFAULT_KEYS_SEARCH_LOCAL);
```

Using SearchView in the Action Bar

So far we have seen a search widget on the home page, a global search dialog, and a local search dialog. There is another way to make use of the search function. This is through a SearchView that is exposed through an action bar, and it is the recommended pattern now for both phones and tablets.

Figure 10-12 shows how a search view looks on a phone, along with the application icon in the title/action bar at the top.

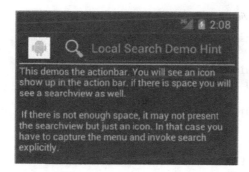

Figure 10-12. Search view in the action bar of a phone

Figure 10-13 shows how an action bar with a search view looks on a tablet.

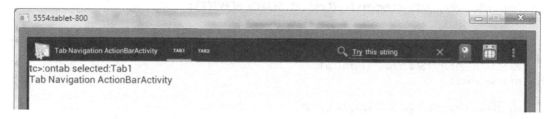

Figure 10-13. Search view in the action bar of a tablet

Defining the Search View Widget as a Menu Item

To define a search view to show up in the action bar of your activity, you need to define a menu item in one of your menu XML files, as shown in Listing 10-9.

Listing 10-9. Search View Menu Item Definition

```
<item android:id="@+id/menu_search"
    android:title="Search"
    android:showAsAction="ifRoom"
    android:actionViewClass="android.widget.SearchView"
    />
```

The key element in Listing 10-9 is the `actionViewClass` attribute pointing to `android.widget.SearchView`. The other attributes are merely the usual menu item attributes.

Identifying the Search Target for the Search View Widget

So far you have the search view in your action bar, and you have the activity (SearchActivity) that can respond to the search. We need to tie these two pieces together, and this is done in Java code. You will need to do this in the `onCreateOptions()` callback of the search invoking activity as part of setting up your menu. The function in Listing 10-10 can be called from `onCreateOptions()` to tie the search view widget and the search results activity.

Listing 10-10. Tying the Search View Widget to the Search Results Activity

```
private void setupSearchView(Menu menu)
{
    //Locate the search view widget
    //as indicated by the menu item of listing 10-9
    SearchView searchView =
        (SearchView) menu.findItem(R.id.menu_search).getActionView();
    if (searchView == null)
    {
        Log.d(tag, "Failed to get search view");
        return;
    }

    //setup searchview
    SearchManager searchManager =
        (SearchManager) getSystemService(Context.SEARCH_SERVICE);
    ComponentName cn =
        new ComponentName(this,SearchActivity.class);
    SearchableInfo info =
        searchManager.getSearchableInfo(cn);
    if (info == null)
    {
        Log.d(tag, "Failed to get search info");
        return;
    }

    searchView.setSearchableInfo(info);

    // Do not iconify the widget; expand it by default
    searchView.setIconifiedByDefault(false);
}
```

We have included an activity called ActionBarSearchActivity in the sample project for this chapter so as to exercise this code. This is the activity we have shown in Figure 10-12.

It is possible that the menu item in Listing 10-9 may not have space in an activity's action bar. In that case, it will merely remain as a menu item and you have to explicitly call onSearchRequested() to invoke the search dialog, as opposed to the search view. You can see code Listing 10-7 for this example.

Owing to space limitations, we have not included every file necessary to test the concepts presented in this chapter. You can download the dedicated project for this chapter; we give the URL for that project in the References.

References

Here is a list of resources we found valuable in writing this chapter.

- `http://static.googleusercontent.com/external_content/untrusted_dlcp/` `www.google.com/en/us/help/hc/images/android/android_ug_42/Nexus-7-` `Guidebook.pdf`: This is both a Nexus 7 user guide and also talks about search user experiencee in Android 4.0. You can also search Google for terms like "Android Jellybean Userguide." You may find guides that are dedicated to each device on the market.

- `http://developer.android.com/guide/topics/search/index.html`: Search overview and entry document to Android search at Google.

- `http://developer.android.com/guide/topics/search/searchable-config.html`: This URL at Google is a key document that outlines the attributes available in the searchableinfo xml file.

- `http://developer.android.com/reference/android/app/SearchManager.html`: API reference for the main Android search facility, namely `SearchManager`.

- `http://www.androidbook.com/notes_on_search`: At this URL you can find the authors' notes on Android search. We will continue to update the content after this book goes to press. You will find here code snippets, summaries, key URLs for search, and what changes in each release.

- Download the test project for this chapter at `www.androidbook.com/` `expertandroid/projects`. The name of the ZIP file is `ExpertAndroid_Ch10_AndroidSearch.zip`.

Summary

This is an introductory chapter on Android search, covering the user experience. We have shown how to work with the Search key for invoking a search. We have showed the basics of creating search results activities that can respond to searches. We explained how to tie applications or search invoking activities to search results activities. We have shown how a search results activity defines its search needs through a searchable info XML file. We have demonstrated how to use a searchview in an action bar. And we have listed the various ways a search capability can be made available on devices and how to code to cover all those cases.

The next two chapters further explore the search results activity to retrieve search text and produce results. We will also cover how to write simple and custom suggestion providers that can provide search suggestions in search dialogs.

Review Questions

The following questions act as landmarks for what you have learned in this chapter.

1. What is QSB?

2. What is a search widget, a search dialog, and a search view?

3. What is searchable info?

4. What is a global search and a local search?

5. What is a search results activity?

6. How do you attach a search results activity to an application or an activity?

7. What is search metadata?

8. What are search suggestions? What are suggestion columns? What is a suggestion cursor?

9. What is a suggestions provider? What is zero suggestions mode?

10. How do you craft a search so that it works well when the phyical search key is present and when it is not?

11. How do you craft a search so that it works well on both tablets and phones?

12. How does a search interact with the action bar?

13. How do you attach searchable info to a search view in the action bar?

14. How do you define the search icon for an action bar?

15. What is the class name you would use for a search view in the menu.xml?

16. How do you enable the Search key in the emulator if it is disabled by default?

11

Simple Search Suggestion Provider

We explored the user experience of the Android search in Chapter 10. There, we explained how search applications can offer suggestions in response to user-entered search text. The components of the search applications that respond with suggestions are called *suggestion providers*. This chapter introduces the suggestion providers and explores a pre-built suggestion provider called SearchRecentSuggestionsProvider. In the next chapter, we will show you how to write a custom search suggestion provider from scratch.

When you are writing a suggestion provider, there are three main pieces to be concerned with. The first is a suggestion provider Java class that is responsible for returning those suggestions to the Android search. The second is a search results activity (similar to the one discussed in Chapter 10), which takes a query or suggestion and turns it into search results. We use the terms *search activity* and *search results activity* interchangeably in this chapter.

The third piece involved in writing a suggestion provider is the metadata XML file (also introduced in Chapter 10), which is defined in the context of the search activity. This search metadata XML file is also called searchableinfo XML file, because, in Java source code, this file is typically referred to as "getting and setting searchableinfo on the SearchActivity object."

We describe the responsibilities of each of these search application pieces, and show how they are implemented to form a simple suggestion provider through snippets of source code. In the References at the end of this chapter, we also give you a link to download the complete working application.

Planning a Simple Suggestion Provider

The goal of all search suggestion providers is the same: receive partial or full search text from the Android search facility (the quick search box, also called the QSB, introduced in Chapter 10), and reply with a set of suggestions in terms of a suggestion cursor (a set of search suggestion rows).

A suggestion provider is a content provider. Thus, implementing a suggestion provider is essentially the same as implementing a content provider, albeit with a fixed set of inputs and outputs.

To demonstrate a suggestion provider, the easiest route is to extend the pre-built SearchRecentSuggestionsProvider. The SearchRecentSuggestionsProvider allows you to replay (or suggest) the queries that were previously presented to the search results activity from the QSB. Once these queries are saved by the search results activity, they are prompted back to the QSB through the suggestion provider as the user starts typing text into the QSB.

The SearchRecentSuggestionsProvider starts with an empty set of suggestions. The user types some text into the search box. This text is given to the search activity, which looks for results. The search activity also saves the search text as a possible suggestion for next time. This save operation is essentially a save into the SearchRecentSuggestionsProvider; it allows the suggestion provider to represent those previous searches as suggestions. But again, this is the protocol specific to SearchRecentSuggestionsProvider. In the next chapter, when you learn to write a custom suggestion provider, you are free to define how you will respond with suggestions.

Although this protocol is already implemented by the SearchRecentSuggestionsProvider, you need to initialize and specialize the SearchRecentSuggestionsProvider to your specific search needs. In the derived suggestion provider, you initialize the base SearchRecentSuggestionsProvider by indicating what portions of the search text need to be replayed.

In our simple demonstration application, we use a minimal search results activity that is just a text view in order to show that the search results activity has been invoked. Inside the search results activity, we also show you the methods to retrieve and save the search queries so that they are available to the search suggestion provider next time.

Once the application is complete, we should see the previous queries prompted as suggestions in the local and global QSB. We have figures showing this user experience in the last section of this chapter.

Implementing the Simple Suggestion Provider

Because the simple suggestion provider is derived from the SearchRecentSuggestionsProvider, most of the responsibilities are handled by this base class. Because a suggestion provider is a content provider, you need to have a unique string identifying the authority for this content provider. Read up on content providers, as we assume in this chapter that you are already aware of content providers. An authority for a content provider is its weblike invocation URL.

The base SearchRecentSuggestionsProvider needs to be initialized with an authority string that is unique to this application. Android search then invokes this suggestion provider based on the unique content provider URL. Once the derived suggestion provider is implemented using this simple call to the base SearchRecentSuggestionsProvider class, it needs to be configured in the manifest file as a regular content provider with an authority. It is tied (indirectly via the searchable metadata XML file) to a search activity. The search activity definition refers to the searchable XML file, which in turn points to the suggestion provider.

We will show all these steps now in detail, with annotated code snippets. The full source code and the working application are available for download at the URL indicated in the References at the end of this chapter. Because we are inheriting from the SearchRecentSuggestionsProvider, the source code for the simple suggestions provider is going to be quite simple, and this is shown in Listing 11-1.

Listing 11-1. SimpleSuggestionProvider.java

```
//SimpleSuggestionProvider.java
public class SimpleSuggestionProvider
extends SearchRecentSuggestionsProvider {

final static String AUTHORITY =
  "com.androidbook.search.simplesp.SimpleSuggestionProvider";

    final static int MODE =
        DATABASE_MODE_QUERIES | DATABASE_MODE_2LINES;

    public SimpleSuggestionProvider() {
        super();
        setupSuggestions(AUTHORITY, MODE);
    }
}
```

There are a couple of things noteworthy in Listing 11-1:

1. The parent class is initialized.

2. The base provider is set up with an authority and mode, indicating what portions of a search text need to be remembered.

The suggestion content provider authority string needs to be unique. The unique authority string in Listing 11-1 needs to match its content provider definition in the manifest file. This SimpleSuggestionProvider (Listing 11-1) is registered in the manifest file as is any other content provider. Listing 11-2 shows this definition.

Listing 11-2. SimpleSuggestionProvider in the Manifest File

```
<?xml version="1.0" encoding="utf-8"?>
<manifest xmlns:android=http://schemas.android.com/apk/res/android..>
<application...>
    <provider android:name=".SimpleSuggestionProvider"
            android:authorities
        ="com.androidbook.search.simplesp.SimpleSuggestionProvider" />
</application>
</manifest>
```

Notice how the authority of the simple suggestion provider matches in the source code (Listing 11-1) and the manifest file (Listing 11-2). In both cases, the value of this authority is

```
com.androidbook.search.simplesp.SimpleSuggestionProvider
```

A key functionality of the Android-supplied SearchRecentSuggestionsProvider facility is to store/replay queries from the database so that they are available as future suggestions. A suggestion has two text strings with it (see Figure 11-6, later in this chapter). One string is the query, and the other string is the description line that shows up in the suggestion display item. Only the first string is mandatory. As you use SearchRecentSuggestionsProvider to replay these strings, you need to tell it whether you want to use one string or two strings.

To accommodate this, there are two modes (mode bits) supported by the base suggestion provider.

```
DATABASE_MODE_QUERIES (value of binary 1)
DATABASE_MODE_2LINES (value of binary 2)
```

The search activity is responsible for saving these two string values when it is called to respond to queries. The search activity would call the method shown in Listing 11-3 to store the query strings. (We will cover this in greater detail when we discuss the search activity.).

Listing 11-3. How to Save Recent Queries

```
pulbic class SearchRecentSuggestions
{
    ...
    public void saveRecentQuery (String queryString, String line2);
    ...
}
```

> **Note** The class SearchRecentSuggestions is an SDK class, and we will cover more of this when we discuss the search activity code (Listing 11-4).

In Listing 11-3, the queryString is the string as typed by the user. This string is displayed as the suggestion, and if the user clicks on the suggestion, this string will be sent to the search activity (as a new search query).

Here is what the Android docs say about the line2 argument:

If you have configured your recent suggestions provider with DATABASE_MODE_2LINES, you can pass a second line of text here. It will be shown in a smaller font, below the primary suggestion. When typing, matches in either line of text will be displayed in the list. If you did not configure two-line mode, or if a given suggestion does not have any additional text to display, you can pass null here.

You can see that Android Developer reference at

```
http://developer.android.com/reference/android/provider/SearchRecentSuggestions.html
```

In our example, we would like to save both the query and the helpful text that shows along with the query in a suggestion. Or at least, we want to show helpful text such as SSSP (search simple suggestion provider) at the bottom of the suggestion, so that when suggestions from this provider appear in the global search, we can see what application is responsible for searching the text in the suggestion.

The way you specify this mode so that you can save the suggestion and the helpful text is to set the two mode bits as indicated in the source code of the SimpleSuggestionProvider (see Listing 11-1). If you just set the mode bit to saving two lines, you will get an invalid argument exception. The mode bits must include at least the DATABASE_MODE_QUERIES bit. Essentially, you need to do a bitwise OR so the modes are complementary in nature, not exclusive.

> **Tip**   You can learn more about this prefabricated suggestions provider at
> http://developer.android.com/reference/android/provider/SearchRecentSuggestions.html.

Search Results Activity

A search results activity is invoked by Android search (QSB) with a query string. The search activity
in turn needs to read this query string from the intent, do what is necessary, and perhaps show
results. Because a search results activity is an activity, it is possible that it can be invoked by other
intents and other actions. For this reason, it is good practice to check the intent action that invoked
it. In our case, when the Android search invokes the search results activity, the action attribute that
is passed in with the invoking intent is ACTION_SEARCH.

Under some circumstances, a search results activity can invoke itself. When this is likely to happen,
you should define the search activity launch mode as a singleTop. The activity will also need to deal
with the firing of onNewIntent(). (We will cover this as well in the upcoming section "Understanding
onCreate () and onNewIntent().") When it comes to the query string, we just log it. Once the query
is logged, we need to save it in the SearchRecentSuggestionsProvider so that it is available as a
suggestion for future searches.

Now let's look at the source code of the search results or search activity class that carries out these
responsibilities. Listing 11-4 shows the source code for this SearchActivity class.

Listing 11-4. Java Code for the Search Activity

```java
public class SearchActivity extends Activity
{
    private final static String tag ="SearchActivity";
    @Override
    protected void onCreate(Bundle savedInstanceState) {
        super.onCreate(savedInstanceState);

        setContentView(R.layout.layout_search_activity);
        //this.setDefaultKeyMode(Activity.DEFAULT_KEYS_SEARCH_GLOBAL);
        this.setDefaultKeyMode(Activity.DEFAULT_KEYS_SEARCH_LOCAL);

        // get and process search query here
        final Intent queryIntent = getIntent();
        final String queryAction = queryIntent.getAction();
        if (Intent.ACTION_SEARCH.equals(queryAction))
        {
            Log.d(tag,"new intent for search");
            this.doSearchQuery(queryIntent);
        }
        else {
            Log.d(tag,"new intent NOT for search");
        }
        return;
    }
```

```java
@Override
public void onNewIntent(final Intent newIntent)
{
    super.onNewIntent(newIntent);
    Log.d(tag,"new intent calling me");

    // get and process search query here
    // Notice we are using the newIntent and not the one
    // from the activity.
    final Intent queryIntent = newIntent;
    final String queryAction = queryIntent.getAction();
    if (Intent.ACTION_SEARCH.equals(queryAction))
    {
        this.doSearchQuery(queryIntent);
        Log.d(tag,"new intent for search");
    }
    else {
        Log.d(tag,"new intent NOT for search");
    }
}
private void doSearchQuery(final Intent queryIntent)
{
    final String queryString =
    queryIntent.getStringExtra(SearchManager.QUERY);

    // Record the query string in the recent
    // queries suggestions provider.
    SearchRecentSuggestions suggestions =
    new SearchRecentSuggestions(this,
        SimpleSuggestionProvider.AUTHORITY,
        SimpleSuggestionProvider.MODE);
    String helpfullHint = "SSSP";
    suggestions.saveRecentQuery(queryString, helpfullHint);
}
}
```

Listing 11-5 quickly notes the layout file that goes with the search results activity of Listing 11-4.

Listing 11-5. Search Activity Layout File

```xml
<?xml version="1.0" encoding="utf-8"?>
<!-- /res/layout/layout_search_activity.xml -->
<LinearLayout
  xmlns:android="http://schemas.android.com/apk/res/android"
    android:orientation="vertical"
    android:layout_width="fill_parent"    android:layout_height="fill_parent"
    >
<TextView
    android:id="@+id/text1"
    android:layout_width="fill_parent"  android:layout_height="wrap_content"
    android:text="Test Search Activity view"
    />
</LinearLayout>
```

Listing 11-6 shows how to define SearchActivity activity in the manifest file and tie it to its searchableinfo xml file.

Listing 11-6. Defining SearchActivity along with its SearchableInfo

```
<activity android:name=".SearchActivity"
        android:label="SSSP: Search Activity"
        android:launchMode="singleTop">
        <intent-filter>
            <action android:name="android.intent.action.SEARCH" />
            <category android:name="android.intent.category.DEFAULT" />
        </intent-filter>
    <meta-data android:name="android.app.searchable"
                    android:resource="@xml/searchable" />
</activity>

<meta-data android:name="android.app.default_searchable"
                android:value=".SearchActivity" />
```

In Chapter 10, we covered how a search activity is defined in the manifest file. All those aspects are present in the search activity manifest file, shown in Listing 11-6. To reiterate, we defined the search activity as being able to respond to search action. Then we attached a searchable XML file to define the nature of the search. (We will go into the details of this XML file later in this chapter in the section "Search Metadata".) We also indicated that, at the application-level, this (SearchActivity of Listing 11-4) is the search activity that is designated. This means that searching in any activity in this application will target this search activity.

Let us return to the Implmentation source code of the search activity of Listing 11-4 to see how the search activity checks the action and retrieves the query string.

Working with Search Query String

The search activity code checks for the invoking action by looking at the invoking intent and comparing it to the constant intent.ACTION_SEARCH. If the action matches, then it invokes the doSearchQuery() function.

In the doSearchQuery() function, the search activity retrieves the query string using an intent extra. Listing 11-7 shows this code:

Listing 11-7. How to Read the Query String from a Search Intent

```
final String queryString =
    queryIntent.getStringExtra(SearchManager.QUERY);
```

Notice that the intent extra is defined as SearchManager.QUERY. As you work through this chapter, you will see a number of these extras defined in the SearchManager API reference. (Its URL is included in the Resources at the end of this chapter.)

Understanding onCreate() and onNewIntent()

A search activity is kicked off by Android when a user enters text into a search box and clicks either a suggestion or the Go arrow. This results in creating the search activity and calling its onCreate() method. The intent that is passed to this onCreate() will have the action set to ACTION_SEARCH.

There are times when the activity is not created, but instead would be passed the new search criteria through the onNewIntent() method. How does this happen? The callback onNewIntent() is closely related to the launching mode of an activity.

When an activity is set up as a singleTop (see the manifest file definition of SearchActivity in Listing 11-6), it instructs Android not to create a new activity when that activity is already on top of the stack. In that case, Android calls onNewIntent() instead of onCreate(). This is why, in the SearchActivity source in Listing 11-4, we have two places where we examine the intent. Note that, in the onNewIntent() method, you should be using the new intent to retrieve the query and not the intent that started the activity.

Testing for onNewIntent()

Once you have onNewIntent() implemented, you start noticing that it doesn't get invoked in the normal flow of things. This suggests the question, When will the search activity be on top of the stack? This usually doesn't happen.

Here's why: Say a search-invoker Activity A invokes a search and that causes a search Activity B to come up. Activity B then displays the results, and the user hits a Back button to go back, at which time the Activity B, which is the user's search activity, is no longer on top of the stack, Activity A is. Or the user may click the Home key and use the global search on the home screen, in which case home activity is the activity on top.

One way the search activity can be on top is this: Say Activity A results in Activity B, owing to the search. If Activity B defines a type-to search, then when you are focused on Activity B, a search will invoke Activity B again with the new criteria. Listing 11-4 shows how we have set up the type-to search to demonstrate. Here is the code again:

```
this.setDefaultKeyMode(Activity.DEFAULT_KEYS_SEARCH_LOCAL);
```

Saving the Search Query

We have talked about how the search activity needs to save the queries that it has encountered so that they can be played back as suggestions through the suggestion provider. Listing 11-8 is the code segment that saves these queries:

Listing 11-8. Saving Recent Search Queries for Future Suggestions

```
final String queryString =
    queryIntent.getStringExtra(SearchManager.QUERY);

// Record the query string in the
// recent queries suggestions provider.
```

```
SearchRecentSuggestions suggestions =
    new SearchRecentSuggestions(this,
        SimpleSuggestionProvider.AUTHORITY,
        SimpleSuggestionProvider.MODE);
String helpfullHint = "SSSP";
suggestions.saveRecentQuery(queryString, helpfullHint);
```

From this code you see that Android passes the query information as an EXTRA (SearchManager.QUERY) through the intent.

Once you have the query available, you can make use of the SDK utility class SearchRecentSuggestions to save the query and a hint ("SSSP") by instantiating a new suggestions object and asking it to save. Because we have chosen to use the two-line mode and the query mode, the second argument to the saveRecentQuery is SSSP (again, this stands for simple search suggestion provider). You will see this help text appear at the bottom of each each suggestion from this provider. (See Figure 11-6 later in chapter).

Now, we look at the search metadata definition (also called searchableinfo), where we tie the search activity with the search suggestion provider. (On the other hand, see the manifest file Listing 11-6, where we tie the search metadata to the search activity.)

Exploring Search Metadata

The definition of *search* in Android starts with a search activity. You first define a search activity in the manifest file. As part of this definition, you tell Android where to find the search metadata XML file. See Listing 11-6, where our search activity is defined along with a path to the search metadata XML file (searchable.xml). Listing 11-9 shows this corresponding search metadata XML file.

Listing 11-9. SimpleSuggestionProvider Search Metadata

```
<!-- filename: /res/xml/searchable.xml -->
<searchable
 xmlns:android="http://schemas.android.com/apk/res/android"
    android:label="@string/search_label"
    android:hint="@string/search_hint"
    android:searchMode="showSearchLabelAsBadge"
    android:queryAfterZeroResults="true"

    android:includeInGlobalSearch="true"
      android:searchSuggestAuthority=
          "com.androidbook.search.simplesp.SimpleSuggestionProvider"
      android:searchSuggestSelection=" ? "
/>
```

Let's work through some of the key attributes in Listing 11–9.

To begin, in Listing 11-9, the attribute searchSuggestAuthority, points to the authority of the suggestion provider as defined in the manifest file for that suggestion provider (see Listing 11-2). The attribute includeInGlobalSearch tells Android to use this suggestion provider as one of the sources in a global QSB.

The attribute queryAfterZeroResults indicates whether the QSB should send more letters to a suggestion provider if the current set of letters did not return any results. Because we are testing, we don't want to leave any stones unturned, so we set this attribute to True so that we give every opportunity to the provider to respond.

When you are deriving from the recent search suggestion provider, the attribute searchSuggestSelection, is always the character string represented by " ?," This string is passed to the suggestion provider as the selection string (where clause) of the content provider query method. Typically, this represents the "where" clause that goes into a select statement of any content provider.

Specific to suggestion providers, when there is a value specified for searchSuggestSelection (as a protocol), Android passes the search query string (entered in the QSB) as the first entry in the select arguments array of the content provider query method.

The code to respond to these nuances (how these strings are used internally by the provider) is hidden in the recent search suggestion provider; we won't be able to show you how these arguments are used in the query method of the content provider. (We go into this in more detail in the next chapter, in which you will see the full picture of the string " ?.") In fact, it is quite unlikely that this string is used at all to narrow the results of SearchRecentSuggestionsProvider because it doesn't qualify any field to query on such as "someid == ?" It is likely that its sheer presence prompts Android to pass the QSB string as the first argument to the provider. And the SDK search suggestion provider merely relies on this protocol to receive the QSB string in a convenient array provided by the select argument list of the content provider query() method.

Now let us talk about a search invoker activity that we will use as the main entry point for this application. This main activity allows us to test the local search.

Search Invoker Activity

So far we have developed two key assets: a search suggestion provider and a search activity. Then we have tied them together through the searchableinfo.xml. We have also indicated in Listing 11-6 that the SearchActivity is the target activity for search in this application.

> **Note**   You can take advantage of an application-level search activity to invoke onNewIntent() by clicking on the Search key when you are examining the results on the SearchActivity. This won't be the case if you were to define the default search only for a single activity and not the whole application.

Now with these (search activity, suggestion provider, searchableinfo xml, and the specified entries in the manifest file) in place, you can test the search functionality by using any simple activity as the Search Invoker Activity. In the next section, we outline this search experiencee using the sample program we have developed for this chapter.

Simple Suggestion Provider User Experience

The sample application contains a very simple main activity, as shown in Figure 11-1. This activity is bare bones and is not aware of any search context.

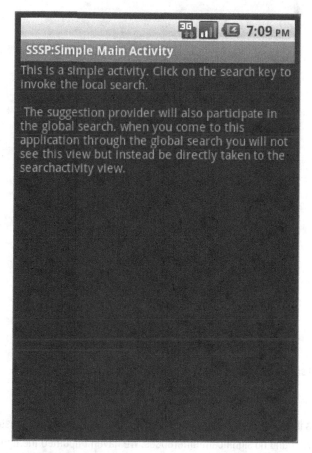

Figure 11-1. A simple main activity (enabled for local search)

However, because we have defined our search activity (see Listing 11-6) as global to the application, if we click the Search key while the simple main activity in Figure 11-1 is in focus, we will see the local search invoked, as in Figure 11-2.

Figure 11-2. Local search QSB shown on top of the main activity

Note   All of the figures in this chapter were captured using Android 2.3. We have tested the application in 4.0 as well, and we have found no significant differences. We haven't updated the figures for 4.0, but the application download for this chapter uses Android 4.0.

As you can see, there are no suggestions in Figure 11-2 because we haven't searched for any so far. You can also see that this is a local search—the label and hint of the search are as we specified in the search metadata XML file.

Let us go ahead and search for string test1. This will take you to the Search Activity screen, as shown in Figure 11-3.

Figure 11-3. Local search results activity

As you can see from the SearchActivity source in Listing 11-4, SearchActivity does nothing spectacular on the screen, but behind the scenes it is saving the query strings in the database. Now if you navigate back to the main screen (by pressing the Back button) and invoke the search again, you will see the screen as shown in Figure 11-4, where the search suggestions are populated with the previous query text. You can also see in Figure 11-4 the bottom part of the suggestion "SSSP." This may seem extraneous here, as this is a local search and clearly indicates that it comes from our application. However, this string "SSSP" will distinguish the test1 search string when it is displayed as part of the global search suggestions.

Figure 11-4. Retrieved local suggestion

This is a good moment to see how you can invoke onNewIntent(). When you are on the search activity (Figure 11-3), you can type a letter like *t* and it will invoke the search again using type-to-search and you will see onNewIntent() called in the debug log.

Let us see what we need to do for these suggestions to show up in the global QSB. Because we have enabled includeInGlobalSearch in searchable.xml, you should be able to see these suggestions in the global QSB as well. However, before you can do that, you need to enable this application for global QSB suggestions, as shown in Figure 11-5.

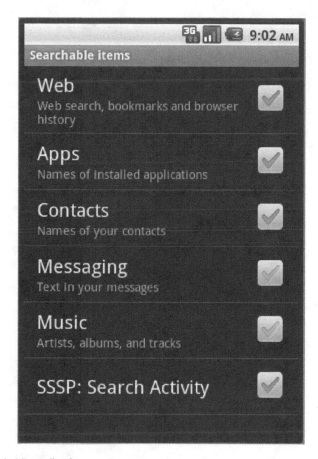

Figure 11-5. Enabling a Searchable application

In Chapter 10, we showed you how to reach this screen. The simple custom suggestion provider we have coded is now available in the list of searchable applications as "SSSP:Search Activity." This text string comes from the activity name for the SearchActivity (see Listing 11-6). With this selection in place, you can see the global search as shown in Figure 11-6, working with our suggestion provider.

Figure 11-6. Global suggestions from simple suggestion provider

In the global search of Figure 11-6, if you type a text like *t*, it will bring up the suggestions from the suggestion provider of this section. However, you may want to test this with a long word such as *testsuperb* so that the general facility doesn't have other suggestions that start with a *t*. Or you have to scroll all the way down. Or you can filter and choose this provider explicitly to search from. In Figure 11-6, when you navigate through the global search to the specific item, you will see the local search activity as shown in Figure 11-3.

References

The following resources will be useful as you work through this chapter.

- http://developer.android.com/guide/topics/search/index.html: Search overview and entry document to Android search at Google.

- http://developer.android.com/guide/topics/search/searchable-config.html: This URL at Google is a key document that outlines the attributes available in the searchableinfo xml file.

- `http://developer.android.com/reference/android/app/SearchManager.html`:
  API reference for the main Android search facility, namely SearchManager. You
  will see here some of the constants that you use while coding the suggestion
  provider.

- `http://developer.android.com/reference/android/provider/`
  `SearchRecentSuggestions.html`: API reference for the class that allows you to
  save recent search suggestions.

- `http://www.androidbook.com/notes_on_search`: At this URL you can find the
  authors' notes on Android search. We will continue to update the content even
  after this book goes to press. You will find here code snippets, summaries, key
  URLs for search, and what changed in each release.

- Download the test project dedicated for this chapter at: `www.androidbook.com/`
  `expertandroid/projects`. The name of the ZIP file is Expert
  `Android_ch11_SimpleSuggestionProvider.zip`.

Summary

You have learned about using the built-in `RecentSearchSuggestionProvider` to remember searches
that are specific to your application. Using this approach, with minimal code, you should be able to
take local searches and make them available as suggestions even in a global context. We have also
explained how to take advantage of `singleTop` activities using `onNewIntent()` callbacks.

However, this simple exercise hasn't shown you how to write suggestion providers from scratch.
More important, we haven't given you the slightest clue as to how a suggestion provider returns a
set of suggestions and what columns are available in this suggestion set. To understand this and
more, we need to implement a custom suggestions provider from scratch.

That has to wait until the next chapter.

Review Questions

The following questions should serve as landmarks for what you have learned in this chapter:

1. What are suggestion providers?

2. How do you code a very simple suggestion provider?

3. What is `SearchRecentSuggestionProvider`?

4. How do you save recent suggestions so that the
    `SearchRecentSuggestionProvider` could use them?

5. What are the basic attributes of `searchableinfo` xml that are relevent to a
    `SearchRecentSuggestionProvider`?

6. How do you test `singleTop` and `onNewIntent()`?

7. How do you enable suggestion providers to show up in a global search?

Custom Search Suggestion Provider

Android search is too flexible not to customize it. Because we used a pre-built suggestion provider in the last chapter, many customizable features of a suggestion provider were hidden in the SearchRecentSuggestionsProvider and not discussed. We explore these details in this chapter by implementing a custom suggestion provider called a SuggestUrlProvider.

We start by explaining how SuggestUrlProvider is expected to work. We will give you all the necessary code snippets to implement the provider, and these snippets should provide a detailed idea of how to build a custom suggestion provider. We will also show you how this custom suggestion provider is put to use by showing it in a sample application.

Planning the Custom Suggestion Provider

We are going to call our custom suggestion provider SuggestURLProvider. The objective of this provider is to monitor what is being typed into the QSB. If the search query has text that looks something like "great.m" (the suffix ".m" is chosen to represent meaning), our custom suggestion provider will interpret the first part of the query as a word and suggest an Internet-based URL that can be invoked to look up the meaning of that word.

For every word that is recognized using this pattern, the SuggestURLProvider offers two URLs. The first is a URL that allows the user to search for the word using http://www.thefreedictionary.com and the second URL uses http://www.google.com. Choosing one of these suggestions takes the user directly to one of those sites.

Implementing the custom SuggestUrlProvider

You have seen in Chapter 11 that, at the core, a suggestion provider is a content provider. So implementing a custom suggestion provider is the same as implementing a content provider. We will go through the steps of implementing a content provider and show you what is done differently to make it a custom suggestion provider. It would certainly help if you have a general background on content providers so you can quickly draw the parallels. But even if you don't have that knowledge, you should be able to follow the argument and the code presented here— and in the process may get to know content providers as well!

Implementing a custom suggestion provider involves implementing the virtual methods defined by a content provider, especially the query() method, as we extend the base provider class. The following details are important as you extend the base ContentProvider class methods:

1. Understand the URIs honored by your suggestion provider.

2. Understand how to implement the getType() method that is expected to return MIME types for the search results. This involves recognizing the incoming URIs from item 1 above through the URIMatcher class. Then based on the URI type use the SearchManager defined MIME types for identifying the MIME type of the search results.

3. Understand how to implement the query() method that is expected to return the search results. This involves (a) recognizing the incoming URIs through the URIMatcher class, (b) understanding how to retrieve and use the query search text that was entered, and (c) returning a collection of rows with the required columns as defined by the SearchManager.

4. Understand how to construct the necessary columns required by the SearchManager into a cursor as defined by the suggestion provider's suggestion cursor contract.

We now cover these details roughly in the same order as above, along with source code snippets where needed. At the end, we present the entire source code for the planned SuggestUrlProvider.

Understanding Suggestion Provider URIs

Central to a content provider is its set of URIs that are used to read and update that content provider. In that sense, a content provider is a website that has content or data. A URI is a way to read or update that content.

Android search uses two kinds of URIs to invoke the suggestion provider. The first is called the *search URI*. This URI is used by the suggestion provider to offer up the set of suggestions. The response to this search URI needs to be one or more search suggestion rows, with each row containing a set of well-known columns containing search suggestion data. This search URI could take the form of either of the two shown in Listing 12-1.

Listing 12-1. Structure of Suggestion Provider Search URIs

```
content://com.androidbook.search.suggesturlprovider/search_suggest_query
content://com.androidbook.search.suggesturlprovider/search_suggest_query/<your-query>
```

In this search URI, the first part, represented in Listing 12-2, is the content provider authority that is unique to our suggestion provider.

Listing 12-2. Base Authority of Our Custom Suggestion Provider

```
com.androidbook.search.custom.suggesturlprovider
```

The second URI is called a *suggest shortcut URI*. This URI is used to update a suggestion that is previously cached. These cached suggestions are called *Android suggestion shortcuts*. The response to this type of URI needs to be a single row containing the same set of well-known search suggestions columns. This suggest shortcut URI could take the form of either of the two shown in Listing 12-3.

Listing 12-3. Structure of Suggest Shortcut URIs

```
content://com.androidbook.search.suggesturlprovider/search_suggest_shortcut
content://com.androidbook.search.suggesturlprovider/search_suggest_shortcut/<shortcut-id>
```

This suggest shortcut URI is issued by Android when it tries to determine if the shortcuts that it had cached are still valid. If the provider returns a single row, it will replace the current shortcut with the new one. If the provider sends a null, then Android assumes that this suggestion is no longer valid.

The SearchManager class in Android defines two constants to represent these URI segments that distinguish them (search_suggest_search and search_suggest_shortcut). These constants are shown in Listing 12-4.

Listing 12-4. SearchManager Suggest URI Definitions

```
SearchManager.SUGGEST_URI_PATH_QUERY
SearchManager.SUGGEST_URI_PATH_SHORTCUT
```

It is the responsibility of the provider to recognize these incoming URIs in its query() method. To compare the incoming URI string with one of the constants above, Android provides a utility class called UriMatcher. Listing 12-5 shows how to initialize the UriMatcher so that it could be used later for discerning the incoming search URI structure.

Listing 12-5. Building a UriMatcher with SearchManager Suggest URI Definitions

```
private static UriMatcher buildUriMatcher(String AUTHORITY)
{
    UriMatcher matcher =
        new UriMatcher(UriMatcher.NO_MATCH);
    matcher.addURI(AUTHORITY,
        SearchManager.SUGGEST_URI_PATH_QUERY, SEARCH_SUGGEST);
    matcher.addURI(AUTHORITY,
        SearchManager.SUGGEST_URI_PATH_QUERY + "/*", SEARCH_SUGGEST);
```

```
matcher.addURI(AUTHORITY, SearchManager.SUGGEST_URI_PATH_SHORTCUT,
    SHORTCUT_REFRESH);
matcher.addURI(AUTHORITY,
    SearchManager.SUGGEST_URI_PATH_SHORTCUT + "/*",
    SHORTCUT_REFRESH);
return matcher;
}
```

In Listing 12-5, we are creating a UriMatcher object that knows how to identify an incoming string If it looks like one of our suggestion provider's search URIs. To do this, the UriMatcher needs to know the *authority* of the suggestion provider and the URI path string pattern that follows the authority, much like a web URI and the corresponding path segment. Once we have a UriMatcher object that is initialized with an authority and the structure of expected URIs, we can use it, as shown in Listing 12-6, to distinguish content provider URIs based on their authority.

Listing 12-6. Outline of query() Method Using a UriMatcher

```
@Override
public Cursor query(Uri uri, String[] projection, String selection,
        String[] selectionArgs, String sortOrder)
{
    ...other stuff
    switch (sURIMatcher.match(uri))
    {
        case SEARCH_SUGGEST:
        //Return a series of suggestions
        case SHORTCUT_REFRESH:
        //Return the updated suggestion
    }//eof-switch
    ....other stuff
}
```

In Listing 12-6, the query() method is a signature required by all content providers. This method is called when any URI is issued against this content provider. (We will cover a bit later how this query() method is fully implemented.)

Implementing getType() to specify MIME Types

Because a suggestion provider is ultimately a content provider, it has the responsibility of implementing a content provider contract, which includes defining an implementation for the getType() method to return the MIME types for the respective URIs. Listing 12-7 presents the getType() implementation.

Listing 12-7. Implementing getType() for Suggest UrlProvider

```
....other stuff
//Initialize the declared object below first using code in listing 12-5
private static URIMatcher sURIMatcher;
....other stuff
```

```
public String getType(Uri uri) {
  switch (sURIMatcher.match(uri)) {
    case SEARCH_SUGGEST:
      return SearchManager.SUGGEST_MIME_TYPE;
    case SHORTCUT_REFRESH:
      return SearchManager.SHORTCUT_MIME_TYPE;
    default:
      throw new IllegalArgumentException("Unknown URL " + uri);
  }
}
```

Notice in Listing 12-7 how we are making use of the `UriMatcher` class. Through its `SearchManager` class, the Android search framework provides a couple of constants to help with these MIME types. The MIME type constants are shown in Listing 12-8.

Listing 12-8. SearchManager MIME Type Constants

```
SearchManager.SUGGEST_MIME_TYPE
SearchManager.SHORTCUT_MIME_TYPE
```

The constants in Listing 12-8 translate to the strings shown in Listing 12-9.

Listing 12-9. SearchManager MIME Type Constant Values

```
vnd.android.cursor.dir/vnd.android.search.suggest
vnd.android.cursor.item/vnd.android.search.suggest
```

MIME types are important to content providers, much as they are important to web URLs. They indicate the data type that is returned by the URI so that the caller will know what kind of data is coming back. Although we don't use the string values given in Listing 12-9 directly, they are useful in understanding how MIME types are mapped in Android and also for debugging purposes when looking at the log files.

Implementing Content Provider Query Method

When it uses one of the search URIs to call the suggestion provider, Android ends up calling the `query()` method of the suggestion provider (being a content provider) to receive a suggestion cursor. Listing 12-10 shows the outline implementation of `query()` method for our `SuggestUrlProvider`.

Listing 12-10. Implementing query() Method for SuggestUrlProvider

```
public Cursor query(Uri uri, String[] projection,
        String selection,
        String[] selectionArgs, String sortOrder)
{
   Log.d(tag,"query called with uri:" + uri);
   Log.d(tag,"selection:" + selection);

   String query = selectionArgs[0];
   Log.d(tag,"query:" + query);
```

```
switch (sURIMatcher.match(uri)) {

    case SEARCH_SUGGEST:
        Log.d(tag,"search suggest called");
        return getSuggestions(query);

    case SHORTCUT_REFRESH:
        Log.d(tag,"shortcut refresh called");
        return null;

    default:
        throw new IllegalArgumentException("Unknown URL " + uri);
    }
}
```

Let's look at the arguments in the query() method shown in Listing 12-10. The "uri" argument is one of the search URIs we have talked about: it has a type of Uri. The class Uri is just a thin wrapper around the URI string value. The "projection" argument carries a list of columns that the caller is interested in retrieving from a content provider, such as our suggestion provider. In the case of a suggestion provider, we can ignore this argument because the list of columns expected of a suggestion provider is fixed and known.

The "selection" argument is a string indicating a clause with a question mark (?) in it. The question mark is expected to be replaced by values in the selectionArgs array. In the case of a suggestion provider, the selection argument is usually "?" and the selectionArgs array contains a single element carrying the query string that was typed into the QSB.

Alhough what goes into the selection argument is "?," you can alter it, as the searchableinfo XML file makes provisions for it. Listing 12-11 shows how our custom suggestion provider is configured through the searchableinfo XML file.

Listing 12-11. *CustomSuggestionProvider Searchableinfo Metadata XML File*

```
//xml/searchable.xml
<searchable
  xmlns:android="http://schemas.android.com/apk/res/android"
    android:label="@string/search_label"
    android:hint="@string/search_hint"
    android:searchMode="showSearchLabelAsBadge"
    android:searchSettingsDescription="suggests urls"
    android:includeInGlobalSearch="true"
    android:queryAfterZeroResults="true"

    android:searchSuggestAuthority=
            "com.androidbook.search.custom.suggesturlprovider"

    android:searchSuggestIntentAction=
            "android.intent.action.VIEW"
    android:searchSuggestSelection=" ? "
/>
```

> **Note**   Please note the `searchSuggestAuthority` string value. It should match the corresponding content provider URL definition in the Android manifest file.

Notice the `searchSuggestSelection` attribute in the search metadata definition file shown in Listing 12-11. It directly corresponds to the selection argument of the content provider's `query()` method in Listing 12-10.

When you specify `searchSuggestSelection` in the `searchableinfo` XML file, Android assumes that you don't want to receive the search text through the URI but, instead, want it through the selection argument of the `query()` method. In that case, Android search will send the " ? " (notice the spaces before and after the question mark) as the value of the selection argument and will pass the query text as the first element of the selection argument (`selectionArgs`, in Listing 12-10) array. If you don't specify the `searchSuggestSelection`, then it will pass the search text as the last path segment of the URI. You can choose one or the other. In our example, we have chosen the selection approach and not the URI approach.

Now, if you notice the body of the `query()` method in Listing 12-10, you will see that we are first deciding what kind of a URI has invoked the `query()` method. As before, we use the `UriMatcher` class to know this. If the URI is a suggestions URI, then we call `getSuggestions()` to return a cursor. If it is a shortcut URI, we simply return null to indicate that the suggestion has expired. Of course, you can change this logic if you want to specialize this behavior based on your need for what is to be returned.

Exploring Suggestion Cursor Columns

While implementing the `query()` method in Listing 12-10, we have made use of a method `getSuggestions()` to return a cursor worth of columns. So this `getSuggestions()` method needs a set of columns with well-defined names to be returned. The cursor returned by the `getSuggestions()` method is called a *suggestion cursor.*

A suggestion cursor is, after all, a cursor. It is no different from the database cursors that are defined by Android. The suggestion cursor acts as the contract between the Android search facility and the suggestion provider. This means that the names and types of columns that the cursor returns are fixed and known to both parties. To provide flexibility to the search, Android search offers a large number of columns in this cursor. Many, if not most, of these columns are optional. A suggestion provider does not need to return all of these columns; it can ignore sending columns that are not relevant to the suggestion provider. Let's look at the columns that are available for a suggestion provider to return, what each column means, and how it affects the search.

Like all cursors, a suggestion cursor has to have an `_id` column. This is mandatory. Every other column starts with a `SUGGEST_COLUMN_` prefix. These constants are defined as part of the `SearchManager` API reference. Here, we review the most frequently used columns. (For the complete list, use the API sources in the References at the end of this chapter.) In the following description of the columns, the words *search activity* refer to the activity that is invoked to show the results for the search text.

- `text_1`: The first line of text in the presented suggestion (see the list of search suggestions based on what is typed, shown in Figure 12-1, later in chapter).

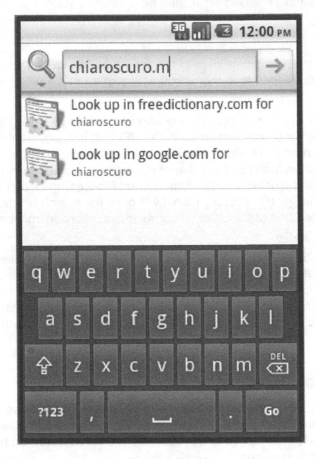

Figure 12-1. Suggestions from the custom SuggestUrlProvider

- `text_2`: The second line of text in the presented suggestion (see Figure 12-1, later in chapter).

- `icon_1`: The icon on the left side in a suggestion and is typically a resource ID.

- `icon_2`: The icon on the right side in a suggestion and is typically a resource ID.

- `intent_action`: What is passed to the `SearchActivity` when it is invoked as the intent action. This will override the corresponding intent action when available in the search metadata (see Listing 12-11).

- `intent_data`: What is passed to the `SearchActivity` when it is invoked as the intent data. This will override the corresponding intent action when available in the search metadata (see Listing 12-11). This is a data URI.

- intent_data_id: Gets appended to the data URI. It is especially useful if you want to mention the root part of the data in the metadata one time and then change this for each suggestion. It is a bit more efficient that way.

- query: The query string to be used to send to the search activity.

- shortcut_id: As indicated earlier, Android search caches suggestions provided by a suggestion provider. These cached suggestions are called *shortcuts*. If this column is not present, Android will cache the suggestion and will never ask for an update. If this contains a value equivalent to SUGGEST_NEVER_MAKE_SHORTCUT, then Android will not cache this suggestion. If it contains any other value, this ID is passed as the last path segment of the shortcut URI. (See the section "Understanding Suggestion Provider URIs.")

- spinner_while_refreshing: This Boolean value tells Android if it should use a spinner when it is in the process of updating the shortcuts.

There is a variable set of additional columns for responding to action keys. We cover that in the later section on action keys. Now, let's see how our custom suggestion provider chooses what columns to return and how they are returned.

Populating and Returning the Suggestion Cursor

Each custom suggestion provider is not required to return all of these columns. For our suggestion provider, we will return only a subset of the columns based on the functionality indicated in the "Planning the Custom Suggestion Provider" section at the beginning of this chapter.

The method getSuggestions() relies on the array of column names that we define, as shown in Listing 12-12.

Listing 12-12. Defining Suggestion Cursor Columns for SuggestUrlProvider

```
private static final String[] COLUMNS = {
        "_id",  // must include this column
        SearchManager.SUGGEST_COLUMN_TEXT_1,
        SearchManager.SUGGEST_COLUMN_TEXT_2,
        SearchManager.SUGGEST_COLUMN_INTENT_DATA,
        SearchManager.SUGGEST_COLUMN_INTENT_ACTION,
        SearchManager.SUGGEST_COLUMN_SHORTCUT_ID
};
```

As you can see, the names of the columns are not hard-coded but, rather, are taken from the column name definitions available in the SearchManager API. These columns are chosen so that the following functionality is met:

First, the user enters a word with a hint, like "great.m," in the QSB. Our suggestion provider will not respond until there is a ".m" in the search text. Once it is recognized, the suggestion provider extracts the word from it (in this case, "great") and then provides two suggestions.

Next, the first suggestion is to invoke the thefreewebdictionary.com with this word and a second suggestion is to search Google with a pattern of define:great. To accomplish this, the provider loads up the column intent_action as intent.action.view (defined by the constant intent.ACTION_VIEW) and the intent data containing the entire URI. The hope is that Android will launch the browser when it sees the data URI starting with http://.

Then, we populate the text 1 column with search some-website with: and the text 2 column with the word itself (again, "great," in this case). We also set the shortcut ID to SUGGEST_NEVER_MAKE_SHORTCUT to simplify things. This setting disables caching and also prevents the suggest shortcut URI from being fired.

Once we have these columns identified in an array like the COLUMNS in Listing 12-12, we can define a cursor, as shown in Listing 12-13.

Listing 12-13. Using a MatrixCursor

```
MatrixCursor cursor = new MatrixCursor(COLUMNS);
String[] rowData;
//insert values for each column in rowData
cursor.addRow(rowData);
```

The class MatrixCursor is from the Android API. Once we have this cursor object, we can add each suggestion row by calling addRow() on the MatrixCursor object.

Overall Source Code for SuggestUrlProvider

We have covered all the background necessary to now show you the full code for our custom SuggestUrlProvider. Listing 12-14 shows the entire source code for the SuggestUrlProvider class.

Listing 12-14. Custom Suggestion Provider Full Source Code

```
public class SuggestUrlProvider extends ContentProvider
{
    private static final String tag = "SuggestUrlProvider";
    public static String AUTHORITY =
        "com.androidbook.search.custom.suggesturlprovider";

    private static final int SEARCH_SUGGEST = 0;
    private static final int SHORTCUT_REFRESH = 1;
    private static final UriMatcher sURIMatcher = buildUriMatcher();

    private static final String[] COLUMNS = {
            "_id",  // must include this column
            SearchManager.SUGGEST_COLUMN_TEXT_1,
            SearchManager.SUGGEST_COLUMN_TEXT_2,
            SearchManager.SUGGEST_COLUMN_INTENT_DATA,
            SearchManager.SUGGEST_COLUMN_INTENT_ACTION,
            SearchManager.SUGGEST_COLUMN_SHORTCUT_ID
    };
```

```java
private static UriMatcher buildUriMatcher()
{
    UriMatcher matcher =
        new UriMatcher(UriMatcher.NO_MATCH);

    matcher.addURI(AUTHORITY,
        SearchManager.SUGGEST_URI_PATH_QUERY,
        SEARCH_SUGGEST);
    matcher.addURI(AUTHORITY,
        SearchManager.SUGGEST_URI_PATH_QUERY +
        "/*",
        SEARCH_SUGGEST);
    matcher.addURI(AUTHORITY,
        SearchManager.SUGGEST_URI_PATH_SHORTCUT,
        SHORTCUT_REFRESH);
    matcher.addURI(AUTHORITY,
        SearchManager.SUGGEST_URI_PATH_SHORTCUT +
        "/*",
        SHORTCUT_REFRESH);
    return matcher;
}

@Override
public boolean onCreate() {
    //lets not do anything in particular
    Log.d(tag,"onCreate called");
    return true;
}

@Override
public Cursor query(Uri uri, String[] projection,
                    String selection, String[] selectionArgs,
                    String sortOrder)
{
    Log.d(tag,"query called with uri:" + uri);
    Log.d(tag,"selection:" + selection);

    String query = selectionArgs[0];
    Log.d(tag,"query:" + query);

    switch (sURIMatcher.match(uri)) {
        case SEARCH_SUGGEST:
            Log.d(tag,"search suggest called");
            return getSuggestions(query);
        case SHORTCUT_REFRESH:
            Log.d(tag,"shortcut refresh called");
            return null;
        default:
         throw new IllegalArgumentException("Unknown URL " + uri);
    }
}
```

```java
    private Cursor getSuggestions(String query)
    {
        if (query == null) return null;
        String word = getWord(query);
        if (word == null)
            return null;

        Log.d(tag,"query is longer than 3 letters");

        MatrixCursor cursor = new MatrixCursor(COLUMNS);
        cursor.addRow(createRow1(word));
        cursor.addRow(createRow2(word));
        return cursor;
    }
    private Object[] createRow1(String query)
    {
        return columnValuesOfQuery(query,
            "android.intent.action.VIEW",
            "http://www.thefreedictionary.com/" + query,
            "Look up in freedictionary.com for",
            query);
    }

    private Object[] createRow2(String query)
    {
        return columnValuesOfQuery(query,
            "android.intent.action.VIEW",
"http://www.google.com/search?hl=en&source=hp&q=define%3A/"
            + query,
            "Look up in google.com for",
            query);
    }
    private Object[] columnValuesOfQuery(String query,
                                        String intentAction,
                                        String url,
                                        String text1,
                                        String text2)
    {
        return new String[] {
            query,          // _id
            text1,          // text1
            text2,          // text2
            url,
            // intent_data (included when clicking on item)
            intentAction, //action
            SearchManager.SUGGEST_NEVER_MAKE_SHORTCUT
        };
    }
```

```java
    private Cursor refreshShortcut(String shortcutId,
                                  String[] projection) {
        return null;
    }

    public String getType(Uri uri) {
        switch (sURIMatcher.match(uri)) {
            case SEARCH_SUGGEST:
                return SearchManager.SUGGEST_MIME_TYPE;
            case SHORTCUT_REFRESH:
                return SearchManager.SHORTCUT_MIME_TYPE;
            default:
             throw
             new IllegalArgumentException("Unknown URL " + uri);
        }
    }

    public Uri insert(Uri uri, ContentValues values) {
        throw new UnsupportedOperationException();
    }

    public int delete(Uri uri, String selection,
                    String[] selectionArgs) {
        throw new UnsupportedOperationException();
    }

    public int update(Uri uri, ContentValues values,
                    String selection,
                    String[] selectionArgs) {
        throw new UnsupportedOperationException();
    }

    private String getWord(String query)
    {
        int dotIndex = query.indexOf('.');
        if (dotIndex < 0)
            return null;
        return query.substring(0,dotIndex);
    }
}
```

In summary, Listing 12-14 brings together all the code snippets. Here, you will see how we have satisfied the complete contract imposed by the base class ContentProvider.

Exploring Search Metadata

We have covered some of the details of the search metadata XML file in the last two chapters on Android search. We have also introduced the contents of this search metadata XML file in Listing 12-11, where we showed how the search query is sent to our custom suggestion provider. We are at a point where we could cover a few more attributes of this searchableinfo XML file that are often used. For a complete list of the attributes of this file, refer to the search configuration document from Google, available at:

http://developer.android.com/guide/topics/search/searchable-config.html

To aid in the discussion of these additional attributes, let's reproduce Listing 12-11 here, as Listing 12-15 so as to have a quick reference.

Listing 12-15. Searchableinfo XML File

```
//xml/searchable.xml
<searchable
  xmlns:android="http://schemas.android.com/apk/res/android"
    android:label="@string/search_label"
    android:hint="@string/search_hint"
    android:searchMode="showSearchLabelAsBadge"
    android:searchSettingsDescription="suggests urls"
    android:includeInGlobalSearch="true"
    android:queryAfterZeroResults="true"

    android:searchSuggestAuthority=
          "com.androidbook.search.custom.suggesturlprovider"

    android:searchSuggestIntentAction=
          "android.intent.action.VIEW"
    android:searchSuggestSelection=" ? "
/>
```

Understanding SearchSuggestAction Attribute

In Listing 12-15, the searchSuggestIntentAction attribute is used to pass or specify the intent action when the SearchActivity is invoked. This allows the SearchActivity to do something other than the default search. Listing 12-16 shows how an intent action is used in the onCreate() method of a responding search activity:

Listing 12-16. Responding to Action_View and Action_Search

```
//Body of onCreate

// get and process search query here
final Intent queryIntent = getIntent();
//query action
final String queryAction = queryIntent.getAction();
```

```
if (Intent.ACTION_SEARCH.equals(queryAction))
{
    this.doSearchQuery(queryIntent);
}
else if (Intent.ACTION_VIEW.equals(queryAction))
{
    this.doView(queryIntent);
}
else {
    Log.d(tag,"Create intent NOT from search");
}
```

You will see the code in Listing 12-16 used in context, as Listing 12-17 shows how the SearchActivity is looking for either a view action or a search action by examining the action value of the intent.

Understanding searchSuggestIntentData Attribute

Just as with the intent action, you can specify the intent data using the searchSuggestIntentData attribute. This is a data URI that can be passed along the action to the search activity, as part of the intent, when invoked.

Understanding searchSuggestPath Attribute

Another attribute that we are not using here, but that is available to suggestion providers, is called searchSuggestPath. If specified, this string value is appended to the search suggest URI (one that invokes the suggestion provider). It allows a single custom suggestion provider to offer suggestions targeted for two different search activities. Each search activity uses the same suggestion provider authority, but employs a different searchSuggestPath. The suggestion provider can use this path suffix to return a different set of suggestions for each targeted search activity.

Understanding searchSuggestThreshold Attribute

The attribute called searchSuggestThreshold indicates the number of characters that have to be typed into a QSB before invoking this suggestion provider. The default threshold value is zero.

Understanding queryAfterZeroResults Attribute

The attribute queryAfterZeroResults (true or false) indicates whether the provider should be contacted if the current set of characters returns a zero set of results, as more characters are being typed. In our particular SuggestUrlProvider, it is important to turn this flag on so that we can get a look at the whole query text every time.

Implementing the Search Activity

Now that we have our SuggestUrlProvider fully coded, we need a search activity that responds to the suggestions put forward by this provider. During the simple suggestion provider implementation discussed in Chapter 11, we covered only some of the responsibilities of a search activity. Now let's look at the aspects we overlooked.

Android search invokes a search activity in order to respond to search actions that come in one of two ways. This happens either when a search icon is clicked from the QSB or when the user directly clicks on a suggestion. When invoked, a search activity needs to examine why it is invoked. This information is available in the intent action. That is, the search activity examines intent action so as to do the right thing. In many cases, this action is ACTION_SEARCH. However, a suggestion provider has the option of overriding this by specifying action either through the search metadata XML file or through a suggestion cursor column. This type of action can be anything. In our case, we are going to use a view action as well.

As we pointed out in the discussion of the simple suggestion provider in Chapter 11, it is also possible to set up the launch mode of the search activity as a singleTop. In this case, the search activity has the added responsibility of responding to onNewIntent() as well as to onCreate(). Let's look at both of these cases and show how similar they are.

We use both onNewIntent() and onCreate() to examine both ACTION_SEARCH and ACTION_VIEW. In the case of search action ACTION_SEARCH, we simply display the query text back to the user. (Look at Figure 12-2 to see what this text looks like.). In the case of view action, we transfer control to a browser and call the finish() method on the current activity so that the user has the impression of invoking the browser by directly clicking on the suggestion.

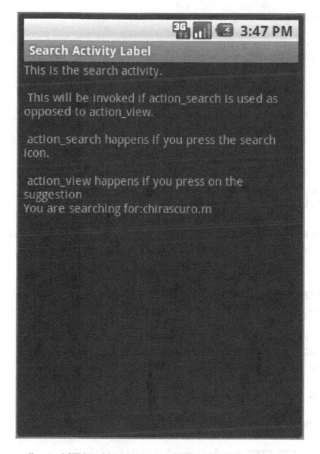

Figure 12-2. SearchActivity responding to ACTION_SEARCH

Note   This `search activity` does not need to be a launchable activity from the main applications menu of Android. Make sure you don't inadvertently set intent filters for this activity as you would other activities that need to be invoked from the device's main applications screen.

With that, let's examine the source code of SearchActivity.java.

SearchActivity Source Code

Now that we have outlined the responsibilities of a search activity, we can look at the source code of this search activity, shown in Listing 12-17.

Listing 12-17. Full Source Code of SearchActivity

```java
//file: SearchActivity.java
public class SearchActivity extends Activity
{
    private final static String tag ="SearchActivity";
    @Override
    protected void onCreate(Bundle savedInstanceState) {
        super.onCreate(savedInstanceState);

        Log.d(tag,"I am being created");
        //See the downloadable project if you want the following layout file
        //Or copy it from Listing 12-19.
        setContentView(R.layout.layout_test_search_activity);

        // get and process search query here
        final Intent queryIntent = getIntent();

        //query action
        final String queryAction = queryIntent.getAction();
        Log.d(tag,"Create Intent action:"+queryAction);

        final String queryString =
            queryIntent.getStringExtra(SearchManager.QUERY);
        Log.d(tag,"Create Intent query:"+queryString);

        if (Intent.ACTION_SEARCH.equals(queryAction))
        {
            this.doSearchQuery(queryIntent);
        }
        else if (Intent.ACTION_VIEW.equals(queryAction))
        {
            this.doView(queryIntent);
        }
        else {
            Log.d(tag,"Create intent NOT from search");
        }
        return;
    }

    @Override
    public void onNewIntent(final Intent newIntent)
    {
        super.onNewIntent(newIntent);
        Log.d(tag,"new intent calling me");

        // get and process search query here
        final Intent queryIntent = newIntent;

        //query action
        final String queryAction = queryIntent.getAction();
        Log.d(tag,"New Intent action:"+queryAction);
```

```
    final String queryString =
        queryIntent.getStringExtra(SearchManager.QUERY);
    Log.d(tag,"New Intent query:"+queryString);

    if (Intent.ACTION_SEARCH.equals(queryAction))
    {
        this.doSearchQuery(queryIntent);
    }
    else if (Intent.ACTION_VIEW.equals(queryAction))
    {
        this.doView(queryIntent);
    }
    else {
        Log.d(tag,"New intent NOT from search");
    }
    return;
}
private void doSearchQuery(final Intent queryIntent)
{
    final String queryString =
        queryIntent.getStringExtra(SearchManager.QUERY);
    appendText("You are searching for:" + queryString);
}
private void appendText(String msg)
{
    TextView tv = (TextView)this.findViewById(R.id.text1);
    tv.setText(tv.getText() + "\n" + msg);
}
private void doView(final Intent queryIntent)
{
    Uri uri = queryIntent.getData();
    String action = queryIntent.getAction();
    Intent i = new Intent(action);
    i.setData(uri);
    startActivity(i);
    this.finish();
}
}
```

We start our analysis of this source code (Listing 12-17) by first examining how this search activity is invoked.

Details of Search Activity Invocation

Like all activities, we know that a search activity must have been invoked through an intent. However, it would be wrong to assume that it is always the action of the intent that is responsible for this. As it turns out, the search activity is invoked explicitly through its component name specification.

You might ask why this is important. Well, we know that in our suggestion provider, we are explicitly specifying an intent *action* in the suggestion row. If this intent action is view and the intent data is an http URL, then an unsuspecting programmer would think that a browser will be launched in response, and not the search activity. That would certainly be desirable. But because the ultimate intent is also loaded with the component name of SearchActivity in addition to the intent action and data, the component name will take precedence.

We are not sure why this restriction is there or how to overcome it. But the fact is that, irrespective of the intent action that your suggestion provider specifies in the suggestion, SearchActivity is the one that is going to be invoked. In our case, we simply launch the browser from the search activity and close the search activity.

To demonstrate this, here is the intent that Android fires off to invoke our search activity when we click on a suggestion:

```
launching Intent {
act=android.intent.action.VIEW
dat=http://www.google.com
flg=0x10000000
cmp=com.androidbook.search.custom/.SearchActivity (has extras)
}
```

Notice the component spec of the intent. It is directly pointing to the search activity. So no matter what intent action you indicate, Android will always invoke SearchActivity. As a result, it becomes the responsibility of the search activity to invoke the browser. Now, let's look at what we do with these intents in the search activity.

Responding to ACTION_SEARCH and ACTION_VIEW

We know that Android search explicitly invokes a search activity by name. However, the invoking intent also carries with it the action that is specified. When QSB invokes this activity through the search icon, this action is ACTION_SEARCH. The action could be different if it were invoked by a search suggestion. It depends on how the suggestion provider sets up the suggestion. In our case, the suggestion provider sets this up as an ACTION_VIEW.

As a result, a search activity needs to examine the type of action. Listing 12-18 shows how we examine this type of action to see whether to call a search query method or the view method. (This code segment is extracted from Listing 12-17.)

Listing 12-18. Responding to Action_Search and Action_View

```
if (Intent.ACTION_SEARCH.equals(queryAction))
{
   this.doSearchQuery(queryIntent);
}
else if (Intent.ACTION_VIEW.equals(queryAction))
{
   this.doView(queryIntent);
}
```

From the code in Listing 12-18, you can see that we invoke doView() for a view action and doSearchQuery() in the case of a search action.

In the doView() function, we retrieve the action and the data URI and populate a new intent with them and then invoke the activity. This will invoke the browser. We also call the method finish() on the activity so that the Back button takes you back to whatever search invoked it.

In the doSearchQuery(),we are just logging the search query text to the view. Let us take a look at the layout that is used to support doSearchQuery().

Search Activity Layout

Listing 12-19 is a simple layout that is used by a search activity in case of doSearchQuery().

Listing 12-19. SearchActivity Layout XML

```xml
<?xml version="1.0" encoding="utf-8"?>
<!-- file: layout/layout_test_search_activity.xml -->
<LinearLayout xmlns:android="http://schemas.android.com/apk/res/android"
    android:orientation="vertical"
    android:layout_width="fill_parent"
    android:layout_height="fill_parent"
    >
<TextView
    android:id="@+id/text1"
    android:layout_width="fill_parent"
    android:layout_height="wrap_content"
    android:text="@string/search_activity_main_text"
    />
</LinearLayout>
```

It is appropriate at this point to mention the strings.xml that is responsible for some of the text needs of this application, as also indicated in Listing 12-19. (See the android:text attribute.) You will see the strings we used for Listing 12-9 in Figure 12-2 (SearchActivity view). You can also see all the files used in this chapter in the corresponding downloadable application identified in the references section. There is not much to gain by listing the long string values here.

Responding to onCreate() and onNewIntent()

In Listing 12-17, you will see that the code in onCreate() and onNewIntent() is almost identical. This is not an uncommon pattern. When a search activity is invoked, depending on the launch mode of the search activity, either onCreate() or onNewIntent() is called. These methods were discussed in detail in Chapter 11.

Notes on Finishing a Search Activity

Earlier in this discussion we briefly mentioned how to respond to doView(). Listing 12-20 shows excerpts from the code for this doView() function (excerpted from Listing 12-17).

Listing 12-20. Finishing the Search Activity

```
private void doView(final Intent queryIntent)
{
    Uri uri = queryIntent.getData();
    String action = queryIntent.getAction();
    Intent i = new Intent(action);
    i.setData(uri);
    startActivity(i);
    this.finish();
}
```

The goal of this function is to invoke the browser. If we were not doing the finish() at the end, the user would be taken back to the search activity from the browser after clicking the Back button, instead of back to the search screen where they came from, as expected. Ideally, to give the best user experience, the control should never pass through the search activity. Finishing this activity solves that problem. Listing 12-20 also gives an opportunity to examine how we transfer the intent action and intent data from the original intent (which are set by the suggestion provider) and then pass them on to a new browser intent.

So far, we have a suggestion provider, a search activity, and a searchableinfo XML file. Now, we cover how the manifest file looks for this application.

Custom Suggestions Provider Manifest File

The manifest file is where you bring together many components of your application. For our custom suggestions provider application, as in other examples, this is where you declare its components, such as the search activity and the suggestion provider. You also use the manifest file to declare that this application is enabled for local search by declaring Search Activity as the default search. Also, pay attention to the intent filters defined for the search activity. These details are highlighted in bold in the manifest file code, Listing 12-21.

Listing 12-21. Custom Suggestion Provider Manifest File

```
//file:AndroidManifest.xml
<?xml version="1.0" encoding="utf-8"?>
<manifest xmlns:android="http://schemas.android.com/apk/res/android"
      package="com.androidbook.search.custom"
      android:versionCode="1"
      android:versionName="1.0.0">
   <application android:icon="@drawable/icon"
                        android:label="Custom Suggestions Provider">
<!--
***************************************************************
* Search related code: search activity
***************************************************************
 -->
   <activity android:name=".SearchActivity"
                     android:label="Search Activity Label"
                     android:launchMode="singleTop">
      <intent-filter>
```

```
        <action
        android:name="android.intent.action.SEARCH" />
        <category
        android:name="android.intent.category.DEFAULT" />
      </intent-filter>

    <meta-data android:name="android.app.searchable"
        android:resource="@xml/searchable" />
    </activity>

<!-- Declare default search -->
    <meta-data android:name="android.app.default_searchable"
      android:value=".SearchActivity" />

<!-- Declare Suggestion Provider -->
    <provider android:name="SuggestUrlProvider"
        android:authorities=
        "com.androidbook.search.custom.suggesturlprovider" />
</application>
    <uses-sdk android:minSdkVersion="4" />
</manifest>
```

As you can see, we have highlighted three things in Listing 12-21:

- Defining the search activity along with its search metadata XML file

- Defining SearchActivity as the default search for the application

- Defining the suggestion provider and its authority

With all of the source code in place, it is time to take a tour of the application and see how it looks in the emulator.

Custom Suggestion Provider User Experience

In this section, we show you how the custom suggestion provider we have developed can be put to use. If you would like to see this in your emulator or device, you can download the Android Eclipse project for this chapter from the URL, included in the References at the end of this chapter. This section is a quick walk-through of that experience.

Once you build and deploy the downloaded application through ADT, you will not see any activity pop up because there is no activity to start in this application. The custom suggestion provider is simply a behind-the-scenes engine. So, instead of starting any activity by the installer, all you will see is that the application is successfully installed in the Eclipse console. Of course, the application is included in your list of applications on the emulator or the device.

Successful Installation means that that the suggestion provider is ready to respond to the global QSB. But before that can take place, you will need to enable this suggestion provider to participate in global search. We have shown in Chapters 10 and 11 how to enable custom search applications.

To start the user experience tour of this custom search provider, open the global QSB and type "chiaroscur.m" in the QSB.

Notice in Figure 12-1 how search suggestions from the custom suggestions provider are presented. If there are too many suggestions from other search applications, our suggestions might be under them and beyond the view, and you may need to scroll. Or you can click on the search icon on the top left and change the search application to the "custom suggestion provider" application. This will filter the search suggestions to our suggestions list.

Now, navigate to one of the suggestions provided by our custom suggestions provider as shown in Figure 12-1 and click the QSB search icon. Android will take you to the search activity directly, without invoking any browser, as shown in Figure 12-2.

This example demonstrates the ACTION_SEARCH as opposed to the ACTION_VIEW. Now instead, if you touch the free dictionary suggestion in Figure 12-1, our search activity gets the ACTION_VIEW, and the search activity invokes the browser, as shown in Figure 12-3. This demonstrates the two types of intent actions discussed: the search activity and the view.

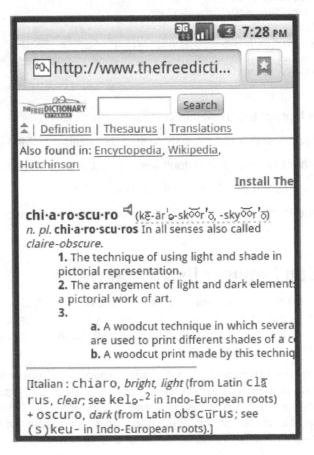

Figure 12-3. SearchActivity transferring to free dictionary

Similarly, in Figure 12-1, if you touch the Google suggestion item, you will see the browser change as shown in Figure 12-4.

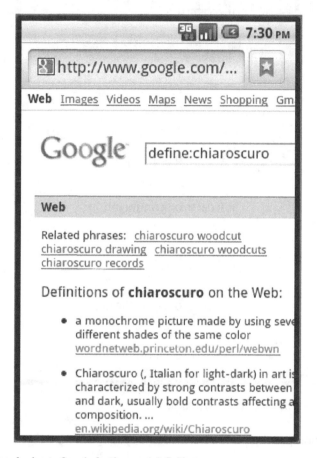

Figure 12-4. SearchActivity transferring to Google for the word definition

Figure 12-5 shows what happens if you don't type the suffix ".m" into the global search.

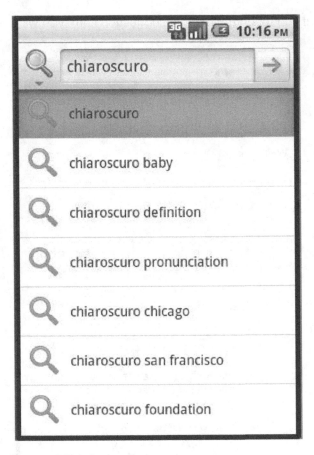

Figure 12-5. Custom provider with no contributed suggestions

Notice how the suggestion provider hasn't provided anything back.

This concludes the discussion of building a functional custom suggestions provider from scratch. Although we've covered many aspects of search, there are still a couple of topics not covered yet. These are the action keys and application-specific search data.

Using Action Keys and Application-Specific Search Data

Action keys and application-specific search data add flexibility to the Android search. *Action keys* allow you to employ specialized device keys for search-related functionality. *Application-specific search data* allow an activity to pass additional data to the search activity. Let's begin with action keys.

Using Action Keys in Android Search

So far, we've shown a number of ways to invoke a search:

- The search icon available in the QSB
- The search key that is part of a set of action keys
- An explicit icon or button that is displayed by an activity
- Any key press based on a type-to-search declaration

In this section, we look at invoking a search through use of action keys. Action keys are a set of keys available on the device that are tied to specific actions. Some examples of action keys are shown in Listing 12-22.

Listing 12-22. List of Action Keycodes

```
keycode_dpad_up
keycode_dpad_down
keycode_dpad_left
keycode_dpad_right
keycode_dpad_center
keycode_back
keycode_call
keycode_camera
keycode_clear
kecode_endcall
keycode_home
keycode_menu
keycode_mute
keycode_power
keycode_search
keycode_volume_up
keycode_volume_down
```

You can see these action keys defined in the API for KeyEvent, which is available at
http://developer.android.com/reference/android/view/KeyEvent.html.

> **Note** Not all of these action keys can be co-opted for search, but some can, such as keycode_call.
> You will have to try each and see which is suitable for your need.

Once you know which action key you want to use, you can tell Android that you are interested in this key by dropping it into the metadata using the XML segment, as shown in Listing 12-23.

Listing 12-23. Action Key Definition Example

```xml
<searchable xmlns:android="http://schemas.android.com/apk/res/android"
    android:label="@string/search_label"
    android:hint="@string/search_hint"
    android:searchMode="showSearchLabelAsBadge"
```

```
          android:includeInGlobalSearch="true"
          android:searchSuggestAuthority=
             "com.androidbook.search.simplesp.SimpleSuggestionProvider"
          android:searchSuggestSelection=" ? "
>
     <actionkey
          android:keycode="KEYCODE_CALL"
          android:queryActionMsg="call"
          android:suggestActionMsg="call"
          android:suggestActionMsgColumn="call_column" />

     <actionkey
          android:keycode="KEYCODE_DPAD_CENTER"
          android:queryActionMsg="doquery"
          android:suggestActionMsg="dosuggest"
          android:suggestActionMsgColumn="my_column" />
     .....
</searchable>
```

You can also have multiple action keys for the same search context. Here is what each attribute of the actionKey element stands for and how it is used to respond to an action key press.

- *keycode*: This is the keycode as defined in the KeyEvent API class that should be used to invoke the search activity. There are two times when this key identified by the keycode can be pressed. The first is when the user enters query text in the QSB but hasn't navigated to any suggestions. Typically, the user, without an action key implementation, will have pressed the search icon of the QSB. With an action key specified in the metadata of the search, Android allows the user to click the action key instead of the QSB search Go icon. The second is when the user navigates to a specific suggestion and then clicks the action key. In both cases, the search activity is invoked with an action of ACTION_SEARCH. To know that this action is invoked through an action key, look for an extra string called SearchManager.ACTION_KEY. If you see a value here, you know that you are being called in response to an action key press.

- *queryActionMsg*: Any text you enter in this element is passed to the search activity, invoking intent as an extra string called SearchManager.ACTION_MSG. This is done when the user has entered text into the QSB and pressed the action key.

- *suggestActionMsg*: Any text you enter in this element is passed to the search activity, invoking intent as an extra string called SearchManager.ACTION_MSG. This is done when a suggestion is in focus and the user has pressed the action key. As you can see, in the intent the "extra" keys for this and the queryActionMsg are the same. If you give the same value for both of these fields, such as call, then you will not know in what way the user has invoked the action key. In many cases, this is irrelevant so you can just give the same value for both. But if you have a need to distinguish one from the other, you will have to specify a value that is different from the queryActionMsg.

- *suggestActionMsgColumn*: The values queryActionMsg and suggestActionMsg apply globally to this search activity and the suggestion provider. There isn't a way to alter the action meaning based on the suggestion. If you would like to do that, then you will need to tell the metadata that there is an extra column to carry this message in the suggestion cursor for each suggestion. This will allow Android to pick up the text from that extra column and send it to the activity as part of the invoking ACTION_SEARCH intent. Interestingly, the value of this additional column from the cursor is sent through the same extra key in the intent, namely SearchManager.ACTION_MSG.

Among these attributes, the keycode is mandatory. In addition, there needs to be at least one of the additional three attributes present for the action key to fire.

If you were to use the suggestActionMsgColumn, you would need to populate this column in the suggestion provider class. In the searchableinfo XML file of Listing 12-23, if you were to use both of the action keys indicated, then you would need to have the specified two additional string columns defined in the suggest cursor (see Listing 12-12), namely call_column and my_column. In that case, your cursor column array from Listing 12-12 would instead be as shown in Listing 23-24.

Listing 12-24. Example of Action Key Columns in the Suggestion Cursor

```
private static final String[] COLUMNS = {
        "_id",  // must include this column
        SearchManager.SUGGEST_COLUMN_TEXT_1,
        SearchManager.SUGGEST_COLUMN_TEXT_2,
        SearchManager.SUGGEST_COLUMN_INTENT_DATA,
        SearchManager.SUGGEST_COLUMN_INTENT_ACTION,
        SearchManager.SUGGEST_COLUMN_SHORTCUT_ID,
        "call_column",
        "my_column"
};
```

Working with Application-Specific Search Context

Android search allows an activity to pass additional search data to the search activity when it is invoked. Let's walk through the details of this.

As we showed in Chapter 11, an activity in your application can override the onSearchRequested() method to disable search by returning false. Interestingly, the same method can be used to pass additional application-specific data to the search activity. Listing 12-25 shows this as an example.

Listing 12-25. Passing Additional Application Data to Search Activity

```
public boolean onSearchRequested()
{
    Bundle applicationData = new Bundle();
    applicationData.putString("string_key","some string value");
    applicationData.putLong("long_key",290904);
    applicationData.putFloat("float_key",2.0f);
```

```
    startSearch(null,          // Initial Search search query string
       false,                  // don't "select initial query"
       applicationData,        // extra data
       false                   // don't force a global search
       );
    return true;
}
```

> **Note**   You can use the following Bundle API reference to see the various functions available on the
> bundle object: `http://developer.android.com/reference/android/os/Bundle.html`.

Once the search has started this way, the activity can use the extra called `SearchManager.APP_DATA`
to retrieve the application data bundle. Listing 12-26 shows how you can retrieve each of the above
application data fields (set in Listing 12-27) from the search intent, in either your `onCreate()` or
`onNewIntent()` method of the search activity responsible for the search results.

Listing 12-26.   Retrieving Additional Application Data Context

```
Bundle applicationData =
  queryIntent.getBundleExtra(SearchManager.APP_DATA);
if (applicationData != null)
{
  String s = applicationData.getString("string_key");
  long   l = applicationData.getLong("long_key");
  float  f = applicationData.getFloat("float_key");
}
```

Let us return to the `startSearch()` method shown in Listing 12-25. We introduced this `startSearch()`
method in Chapter 11, and you can find more about it at the following URL as part of the Activity API:

`http://developer.android.com/reference/android/app/Activity.html`

It may be beneficial to quickly provide an overview of this method. It takes the following four
arguments:

- `initialQuery`   // a string argument
- `selectInitialQuery`   // boolean
- `applicationDataBundle` //Bundle
- `globalSearchOnly`   //boolean

The first argument, if available, will populate the query text in the QSB. The second Boolean argument will highlight the text if true. Doing so will enable the user to replace all of the selected query text with what is typed over. If false, then the cursor will be at the end of the query text. The third argument is, of course, the bundle that we are preparing. And the fourth argument, if true, will always invoke a global search. If it is false, then the local search is invoked first, if available; otherwise, it will use the global search.

References

Here is a list of resources that we found valuable while writing this chapter:

- `http://developer.android.com/guide/topics/search/index.html`: Search overview and entry document to Android search at Google.

- `http://developer.android.com/guide/topics/search/searchable-config.html`: This URL at Google is a key document that outlines the attributes available in the searchableinfo XML file.

- `http://developer.android.com/reference/android/app/SearchManager.html`: API reference for the main Android search facility, namely `SearchManager`. You will see here some of the constants that you use while coding the suggestion provider.

- `http://developer.android.com/reference/android/os/Bundle.html`: You can use this bundle API reference to see the various functions available on the bundle object. This is useful for application-specific search data.

- `http://www.androidbook.com/notes_on_search`: At this URL, you can find the authors' notes on Android search. We will continue to update the content even after this book goes to press. You will find here code snippets, summaries, key URLs for search, and what changed in each release.

- `http://developer.android.com/reference/android/view/KeyEvent.html`: To understand what the constants are for coopting them as search keys.

- Download the test project dedicated for this chapter at `www.androidbook.com/expertandroid/projects`. The name of the ZIP file is `ExpertAndroid_ch12_CustomSuggestionProvider.zip`.

Summary

In this chapter, we presented in a fair amount of detail the internal workings of Android search by coding a custom suggestion provider from scrach. In the process, we demonstrated the suggestion cursor and its columns in detail, explored the URIs that are responsible for getting data from suggestion providers, and presented a lot of sample code that should make it easy to devise and implement your own creative search strategies.

Review Questions

The following questions should act as landmarks for what you have learned in this chapter:

1. How do you specialize a content provider to become a suggestion provider?

2. How many types of search URIs are there?

3. Why and how do you differentiate various search URIs?

4. How do you know the names of the suggestion cursor columns?

5. What Java class do you use to construct a cursor from the names of the cursor columns?

6. How do you add rows to a `MatrixCursor`?

7. How do you co-opt action keys to be search keys?

8. How do you pass application-specific data to a search activity?

Chapter

13

Introduction to Cloud Storage with Parse

Some of your mobile applications may require the ability to store data on a server. This data may be as simple as the user profiles. Or, if your application is a game, you may want to store user scores. Or, your application might be collaborative, in which case one user may need to see data created by another user. Or, you may want to provide your mobile application with cross-device synching features.

These types of data use need a server available to your mobile application as a service. This server-side technology space, especially for mobile needs, now has a name. It is called BaaS: Backend As A Service. There are now a large number of companies in this BaaS space. Typical features offered by such a BaaS platform are:

- User registration
- Ability to allow users from well-known sites such as Facebook or Twitter to directly log in
- Ability to store arbitrary objects in the cloud
- Ability to work with schema-less objects (Like NoSQL)
- Ability to save immediately or with a certain time lapse
- Ability to query objects
- Ability to cache queries on the local device
- Having Web consoles to manage users and their data
- Ability to deliver push notifications

- Abillity to categorize users and their behavior and accordingly delivery of push notifications

- Ability to write executable services in the cloud in addition to storing data, giving rise to a three-tier architecture for mobile applications

In this and the next few chapters, we will cover some of these features by using one of the popular BaaS plaform `Parse.com` as an example. Other emerging players in the BaaS space are:

- ACS Appcelerator Cloud Services (previously Cocoafish)

- Applicasa

- Stackmob

- Microsoft Azure Mobile Services

- Kinvey

- Fatfractal

In this chapter, we will explore the Parse cloud API by writing a simple Android application that goes through the basic features of Parse. That should give you enough information on the Parse API to get started. The next chapter will focus on key nuances regarding dependent objects and how to pass Parse objects through parcels. And in the chapter after that, we will cover Push notifications to your users to engage them on a continuing basis.

Let's now turn to the sample application we have been planning for working with Parse.

Planning a Sample Parse Application

The sample application we create here is a multiuser mobile application. That is, each user is able to create a word and see the words created by other users. In addition to working with words, this app needs to have the basic user-management features, such as signup, login, reset password, and logout.

Figure 13-1 shows the home screen the user will be presented with when the user first encounters the application.

Figure 13-1. Parse sample application signup/login activity

So, when the user sees the application for the first time, he or she has the option to either sign up or log in if that user is already signed up, as shown in Figure 13-1.

> **Note** Parse also allows logins from other websites such as Facebook and Twitter. However, we are not covering those integrations in this chapter.

Designing the Signup Activity

Let's plan the signup page first. Figure 13-2 shows what the signup page could look like.

Figure 13-2. Parse sample application signup activity

As part of the signup activity, you would collect the user ID, email address, and password as shown in Figure 13-2. You would then call the Parse API to register the user with those details.

Designing the Login Screen

Once the signup is complete, the user can use the following login activity as shown in Figure 13-3 to log in. (However, note that when the user signup is successful, the user is automatically logged in! The user needs to logout to see and make use of this login screen.)

Figure 13-3. Parse sample application login activity

Nothing should be surprising with the login screen shown in Figure 13-3. You are collecting user ID and password, so that you can call the Parse API to log in. As there is likely to be delay when contacting Parse on the server for login, it is best to put a progress dialog. This interaction is shown in Figure 13-4.

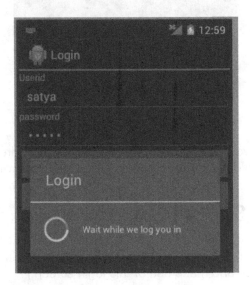

Figure 13-4. Waiting for login to complete

Most Parse APIs come with their asynchronous variants. These APIs provide a callback to be invoked when the call returns. In this callback, we can programmatically turn off the progress dialog.

Designing the Password Reset Activity

It is possible that a user may not have remembered the password that was used before. Using Parse, it is quite easy to implement the Reset Password capability. The screen for the reset password facility could look as shown in Figure 13-5.

Figure 13-5. An activity to reset password

All the user needs as an input to reset the password is the email address. The form in Figure 13-5 collects the email address, and once the user clicks the *Send a Password Reset* button, you can call the Parse API to reset the password by passing the email. Parse would subsequently send a web link to the email address in order to reset the password.

Planning the Homepage of the Application

Once the user is logged in, the screen you would show for this application is a welcome screen that looks like the one shown in Figure 13-6.

Figure 13-6. Welcome activity after a successful login

Using this welcome screen, we will demonstrate three things. The first is to show the list of users who have registered so far. This will explore the Parse APIs available to query for users.

We will then explore how to create a data object and store it in the Parse cloud. To do this we will create a "word" object that we can store in the Parse cloud.

Using the *Create Word* button shown in Figure 13-6, we will create a number of words and then use the *Show Word List* button to see all the words that are created so far.

Showing the Users

Figure 13-7 shows the activity that lists all the registered users.

Figure 13-7. An activity that shows a list of users

In Figure 13-7, there is only one user shown because there is only one user registered so far. If there were more registered users, the query would show all of them. It is also possible to page through the users if there are too many. However, for this chapter we are not going to show paging. Refer to Parse documentation for details on paging queries.

Creating and Storing a Data Object

Figure 13-8 shows the activity that allows you to create a word and store it in the Parse cloud.

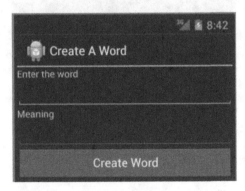

Figure 13-8. Creating a word Parse object

Once you collect the word and its meaning, you can call the Parse API to store it in the Parse cloud. A goal of this application is to develop a simple-minded community-based dictionary in which meanings are provided by other users.

Querying for Words

Once a user creates a word, that user can browse for all existing words. Figure 13-9 shows the list activity that displays the available set of words.

Figure 13-9. Querying for the list of registered users

The activity in Figure 13-9 lists the words created, which user has created that word, and when it was created. This screen also provides the ability to delete a word. The *Meanings* button allows multiple users to provide individual meanings for a word. In this chapter, we won't go into the additional screens that are used to create and browse meanings. Those concepts are similar to that for creating words and browsing words, as both words and meanings are Parse objects.

That completes the quick overview of the application we are planning to implement with Parse. We will now cover a few basic concepts in Parse and then go into setting up your mobile application for Parse.

Exploring Parse Basics

In Parse, objects are stored as a set of key value pairs. Objects don't have to stick to a predefined schema like columns in a relational table or attributes in a class definition. Once you have a Parse object, you can add as many columns as you want; values for all those columns get stored in that object against those column names. However, you have to specify the column names (attribute names) every time you store their values in that Parse object.

Understanding the Base ParseObject

A Parse object has a type name associated with it. It is like a table name in a relational database. However, many objects that belong to this type or table name can have a varied set of columns and respective values. This is in contrast to types in typed languages and tables in relational databases.

Each object in Parse is guranteed to have an object ID. The Parse object also keeps the fields (a) when that object is created and (b) when that object is last updated. You can place most types of objects as values for a particular key. These objects (those specified as values) are typically converted to some stream representation and stored against their respective key names. When these object values are retrieved, they are retrieved as their original type of object. So, a Parse object can store other Parse objects as the target value for a given key. This means that a Parse object can have relationships with other Parse objects, especially its parents.

Say, your application has 30 types of Java objects. When stored in Parse, they are all represented as typeless key-value-pair–based Parse objects. It is up to you to map them to your respective Java objects for type safety when needed.

Although it is the right thing to do, lots of times, to convert typeless objects into typed objects, keep in mind that there are occasions where typeless collections allow lot more dynamism and flexibility, especially when you are crafting a framework where these objects have to be passed through various firewalls.

Understanding a ParseUser Object

A ParseUser is also a ParseObject and it provides some additional typed features, such as username, email, etc., without reverting to the underlying key names. A ParseUser also provides methods necessary to login, logout, and so on.

Because a ParseUser is a ParseObject, you can put additional attributes into a ParseUser object if you want.

Understanding a ParseQuery Object

Unlike a relational database, there is no SQL for querying Parse objects. There is a Java API provided that you can use to retrieve Parse objects.

Using the Parse query API, you can retrieve only one type of object at a time. This means you cannot selectively join multiple Parse object types and retrieve both of them.

However, some types of joins can be accomplished through other means while honoring the constraint that there is only one type of root-level object you can retrieve through Parse. For example, if we have a Word and if that word has many meanings, then we represent the word and word meaning as two types of objects. Then the WordMeaning will have a relationship to its Word as an additional attribute. Now, we can say "get all the WordMeanings whose Word is so and so."

When you retrieve a primary object, you can tell the query to include the associated Parse objects, if needed. You can also set caching policies on a Parse query to save on latency. You can do this either while saving the object or while retriving the objects through queries.

These basics should be sufficient to implement the application that we have suggested at the start of this chapter.

Setting up a Parse-Enabled Android Application

The sample application we have described so far is a good candidate for development with the Parse API. We will implement all of the features indicated in the stated use cases. That will give you an excellent introduction to the Parse platform and its API.

Before we implement the sample application, let us first cover how to set up Parse and get started with it.

Creating a Parse Account and Application

Starting with parse.com is very simple. Visit parse.com and create an account. Within that account, create an application. Once you create an application, you will be the owner of that application. You can create as many applications as you would like.

> **Note**   The links needed to create the account and create the application may change on the Parse.com site. You should be able to navigate and do those basic tasks.

Once an application is created, Parse creates a set of keys with which you need to initialize your mobile application. Parse provides a dashboard for your application to easily copy and paste these keys. Figure 13-10, shows that dashboard for the first sample app we have created.

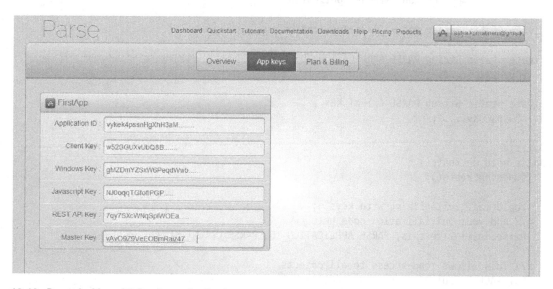

Figure 13-10. Parse dashboard to locate application keys

We have truncated the keys as shown in Figure 13-10 for security purposes. From this panel, you will be able to copy and paste these keys into your mobile application.

We will show you very shortly how to use these keys so that your application is allowed to communicate with Parse in the cloud. But first you should download the necessary jar files and create the Android mobile application. To bootstrap the application development with Parse, Parse has provided a sample Android application, called *Parse Starter* (or *Android Blank Project*) that you can download and use as a starting point.

> **Note**   As Parse goes through multiple releases, it may change the name of this starter application or it might provide an entirely different mechanism to get you started. Nevertheless, what we cover here should apply.

You can download this sample starter template application from this URL:
https://www.parse.com/apps/quickstart

Once you are at this URL, choose your platform (for example, Android) and download and set up the Parse starter application in your eclipse ADT. Depending on the release of Parse download, what we cover in this chapter may be slightly different from what you download, but the general prinicples and directions should apply.

Once you download and set up the Parse starter application in your prefered IDE, it will most likely fail with errors in a file called ParseApplication.java. This is because Parse has intentionally left the placeholders for putting the keys that we have shown earlier. Once you place those keys, this file will look something like what is shown in Listing 13-1 (taking into account that later releases of Parse may have additional code segments!).

Listing 13-1. Initializing Application with Parse Keys

```
public class ParseApplication extends Application {

    private static String tag = "ParseApplication";

    private static String PARSE_APPLICATION_ID
        = "vykek4ps.....";

    private static String PARSE_CLIENT_KEY
        = "w52SGUXv....";

    @Override
    public void onCreate() {
        super.onCreate();

        Log.d(tag,"initializing with keys");
        // Add your initialization code here
        Parse.initialize(this, PARSE_APPLICATION_ID, PARSE_CLIENT_KEY);

        // This allows read access to all objects
        ParseACL defaultACL = new ParseACL();
        defaultACL.setPublicReadAccess(true);

        ParseACL.setDefaultACL(defaultACL, true);
        Log.d(tag,"initializing app complete");
    }
}
```

After plugging in the application ID and the client key in the code as shown above, the Parse starter application is ready for us to work with Parse on the server. The ACL in the code stands for "access control lists." For this book, we set this to the default read access for all objects created by users. Outside of that, this book doesn't cover the security aspects of Parse and the reader is advised to check the Parse documentation.

We are almost ready to start implementing the application we have described. Before we do that, though, let's cover a few basic concepts of Parse.

Implementing the Sample Application

In this part of the chapter, we are going to use each screen presented so far and show the key code snippets that demonstrate how the parse API is used to accomplish that use case. If you are interested in the entire application source code, you can download it from the project download URL that is given in the References section at the end of this chapter.

Implementing Signup

Let's start with the signup activity (see Figure 13-2). In that signup activity we are gathering username, password, and email address. Using these values, the code in Listing 13-2 demonstrates how we use the Parse API to sign up the user.

Listing 13-2. Parse APIs for User Signup

```
private void signup(String userid, String email, String password)
{
    ParseUser user = new ParseUser();
    user.setUsername(userid);
    user.setPassword(password);
    user.setEmail(email);

    //Show the progress dialog
    turnOnProgressDialog("Signup", "Please wait while we sign you up");

    //Go for signup with a callback
    user.signUpInBackground(new SignUpCallback() {
      public void done(ParseException e) {
        turnOffProgressDialog();
        if (e == null) {
          // Hooray! Let them use the app now.
            signupSuccessful();
        } else {
          // Sign up didn't succeed. Look at the ParseException
          // to figure out what went wrong
          signupFailed(e);
        }
      }
    });
    return;
}//signup-method

private void signupSuccessful()
{
    //Go to signup successful page
    //finish
    gotoActivity(SignupSuccessActivity.class);
    finish();
}
```

```
private void signupFailed(ParseException x)
{
    //stay on the page
    //Put an error message for the exception
    String message = x.getMessage();
    alert("Signup", "Failed:" + message);
}
```

Note that as this code (and the other code snippets in this chapter) is taken from the middle of a larger code base. It will help you understand how the Parse APIs are used.

Don't try to compile, because the code refers to some methods that are not listed in this chapter. However, the intention of these methods should be clear from their naming. For example, the alert() method is there to put an alert dialog. The gotoActivity() method is there to transfer control to another activity. The turnOnProgressDialog() method is there to show the progress dialog until the Parse method returns through its callback.

Now, turn your attention back to the main flow of the Parse signup code in Listing 13-2. We first create a new Parse object called ParseUser and fill it with user-related information that we have collected through the user registration form. We then call the progress dialog in anticipation of the call to the Parse API signUpInBackground. This signup API is asynchronous. This method takes a callback object that provides a done() callback method. In the done() method, we first turn off the progress dialog. We then figure out if the signup method is a success or failure. If the signup is successful, Parse automatically logs in the user on the device.

With this step the user is signed up. Now the user can do things like login, logout, and so on.

Detecting if the User Is Logged in or Not

To know if the user is logged in, you can use the code snippet in Listing 13-3:

Listing 13-3. To Show if a User Is Logged in or Not

```
private void setViewsProperly()
{
    ParseUser pu = ParseUser.getCurrentUser();
    if (pu == null)
    {
        //User is not logged in
        showLoggedOutView();
        return;
    }
        //User is logged in
        showLoggedInView();
}
```

We called the static method on the ParseUser class getCurrentUser(). If this method returns a valid user, then the user is logged in. If not, the user is not logged in.

Logging Out

You can use the code snippet in Listing 13-4 to log out a user from the current session.

Listing 13-4. Logging out from Parse

```
private void logoutFromParse()
{
    ParseUser.logOut();
}
```

Once you call this logout method, the `ParseUser.getCurrentUser()` will return a null, indicating that no user is in the current session.

Implementing Logging in

To understand login, turn your attention to the login activity presented in the beginning of the chapter and see Figure 13-3. In the login activity we are collecting user ID and password. Once we have these fields, the code to log in is straightforward and provided in Listing 13-5.

Listing 13-5. Parse API to Log in

```
public void login(View v)
{
    if (validateForm() == false){
        return;
    }
    //form is valid
    String sUserid = getUserid();
    String sPassword = getPassword();

    turnOnProgressDialog("Login","Wait while we log you in");
    ParseUser.logInInBackground(sUserid, sPassword, new LogInCallback() {
            public void done(ParseUser user, ParseException e) {
              turnOffProgressDialog();
              if (user != null) {
                reportSuccessfulLogin();
              } else {
                reportParseException(e);
              }
            }
        });
}//eof-login

private void reportParseException(ParseException e)
{
    String error = e.getMessage();
    reportTransient("Login failed with:" + error);
}
```

```
private void reportSuccessfulLogin()
{
    gotoActivity(ParseStarterProjectActivity.class);
    finish();
}
```

Again, the login call is available on the `ParseUser` object as a static method. We are also using this method in the background by providing a callback, as is the usual pattern for Android for talking to server-side content. This pattern is very similar to the pattern of using the signup API and almost every other Parse API, as they all have the callbacks so that they don't stop the main thread.

Implementing Reset Password

What if one forgets the password? Of course, you provide a way to reset it. See the reset activity presented an the beginning of this chapter, shown in Figure 13-5. We use this activity to collect the email address of the account and we call the `requestPasswordResetInBackground()` static method on the `ParseUser` class. The code in Listing 13-6 shows how this Parse reset password API is used.

Listing 13-6. Resetting Password Through Parse API

```
public void resetPassword(View v)
{
    if (validateForm() == false){
        return;
    }
    String sEmail = email.getText().toString();
    turnOnProgressDialog("Reset Password","Wait while we send you email with password reset");
    //userid is there
    ParseUser.requestPasswordResetInBackground(sEmail,
            new RequestPasswordResetCallback() {
                public void done(ParseException e) {
                    turnOffProgressDialog();
                    if (e == null) {
                        reportSuccessfulReset();
                    } else {
                        reportResetError(e);
                    }
                }
        });
 }//eof-reset

private void reportSuccessfulReset(){
    gotoActivity(PasswordResetSuccessActivity.class);
    finish();
}
private void reportResetError(ParseException e)
{
    //stay on the page
    //Put an error message for the exception
    String message = e.getMessage();
    alert("Reset Password", "Failed:" + message);
}
```

The pattern of the reset password Parse API is similar to other Parse APIs. You call the method, provide a callback, and deal with success and failure. If the reset password call is successful, Parse will send an email to the user with a web URL to enter a new password.

Querying for Users

Listing 13-7 shows the code you can use to see the users that have registered so far. Refer to the List of Users activity presented at the begining of the chapter, shown in Figure 13-7.

Listing 13-7. Querying for Users

```
private void populateUserNameList()
{
    ParseQuery query = ParseUser.getQuery();
    this.turnOnProgressDialog("Going to get users", "Patience. Be Right back");
    query.findInBackground(new FindCallback() {
      public void done(List<ParseObject> objects, ParseException e) {
        turnOffProgressDialog();
        if (e == null) {
            // The query was successful.
            successfulQuery(objects);
        } else {
            // Something went wrong.
            queryFailure(e);
        }
      }
    });
}
private void successfulQuery(List<ParseObject> objects)
{
    ArrayList<ParseUserWrapper> userList = new ArrayList<ParseUserWrapper>();
    for(ParseObject po: objects)
    {
        ParseUser pu = (ParseUser)po;
        ParseUserWrapper puw = new ParseUserWrapper(pu);
        userList.add(puw);
    }

  ArrayAdapter<ParseUserWrapper> listItemAdapter =
      new ArrayAdapter<ParseUserWrapper>(this
              ,android.R.layout.simple_list_item_1
              ,userList);
  this.setListAdapter(listItemAdapter);
}
private void queryFailure(ParseException x)
{
    this.setErrorView(x.getMessage());
}
```

First use the `ParseUser` object to get a `ParseQuery` object. Then use a find method on that query object to look for the users. Once this method returns through a callback, you retrieve the collection of `ParseUser` objects and populate the user list shown in Figure 13-7. We will revisit the query object when we talk about querying for the `Word` objects.

Storing a Data Object in Parse: Create a Word

You know now how to sign up, log in, log out, and reset the password when needed. The next two things shown here are how to create other objects in Parse and how to query for them.

Let's start with creating an object and storing it in the Parse cloud. For this, recall the screens presented in the begining (Figure 13-8) for creating a word. In that create word activity you collect a word and its meaning and store it in the Parse cloud. To do this using the Parse API, all you have to do is show in the psuedo code, as given in Listing 13-8.

Listing 13-8. Psuedocode for Saving an Object in the Cloud

```
ParseObject po = new ParseObject("word_table");
po.put("word", "prow");
po.put("word","I think it means something to do with boats and ships!");
po.saveInTheBackground(...withsomecallback-method...)
```

This is the level of API provided by Parse. In the Java pseudocode given in Listing 13-8, you can see that we are using the `ParseObject` as primarily a typeless collection of key value pairs. It may be worthwhile to create a typed class called `Word` with two fields in it. Here is some psuedocode for it (Listing 13-9) showing how it could be done.

Listing 13-9. Idea of Crafting a Typed Object as a Stand-in for a Typeless Parse Object

```
public class Word extends ParseObjectWrapper
{
    public Word(String word, String meaning);
    public String getWord();
    public String setWord(String word);
    public String getMeaning();
    public String setMeaning();
}
```

This type of formal class definition for a `Word` allows us to treat words as Java objects and not merely as a collection of strings. The base class `ParseObjectWrapper` can hold the underlying Parse object and store the field values in that Parse object as the key value pairs.

Here is the actual code for the `ParseObjectWrapper` taken from our downloadable sample project and presented in Listing 13-10.

Listing 13-10. Source Code for a ParseObjectWrapper Class

```
public class ParseObjectWrapper
{
    public static String f_createdAt = "createdAt";
    public static String f_createdBy = "createdBy";
```

```java
public static String f_updatedAt = "updatedAt";
public static String f_updatedBy = "updatedBy";

public ParseObject po;
public ParseObjectWrapper(String tablename)
{
    po = new ParseObject(tablename);
    po.put(f_createdBy, ParseUser.getCurrentUser());
}
public ParseObjectWrapper(ParseObject in)
{
    po = in;
}
//Accessors
public ParseObject getParseObject() { return po; }
String getTablename()
{
    return po.getClassName();
}
public ParseUser getCreatedBy()
{
    return po.getParseUser(f_createdBy);
}
public void setCreatedBy(ParseUser in)
{
    po.put(f_createdBy, in);
}
public void setUpdatedBy()
{
    po.put(f_updatedBy, ParseUser.getCurrentUser());
}
public ParseUser getLastUpdatedBy()
{
    return (ParseUser)po.getParseObject(f_updatedBy);
}
}//eof-class
```

Listing 13-10 shows how we have designed this Parse object wrapper class as a first attempt. It will hold a reference to an actual ParseObject. There are two ways a Parse object wrapper can acquire a ParseObject. When you are creating a Parse object for the first time, you can simply tell what the table name for that Parse object is. Or, if you happen to have retrieved a Parse object from the cloud and want to alter it, then you can pass in that Parse object directly.

Here's another feature we have built into this Parse object wrapper: the native ParseObject doesn't carry with it which user created it or last updated it. So the Parse object wrapper provides field names for these two additional attributes, starting with "f_...". These additional fields allow us to store these two types of users (created by, and last updated by) with every ParseObject. Given this Parse object wrapper, Listing 13-11 shows how we can craft the Word class.

Listing 13-11. Using ParseObjectWrapper to Represent a Typed Object Word

```java
public class Word
extends ParseObjectWrapper
{
    //Name of the table or class for this type of object
    public static String t_tablename = "WordObject";

    //Only two fileds
    public static String f_word = "word";
    public static String f_meaning = "meaning";

    public Word(String word, String meaning)
    {
        super(t_tablename);
        setWord(word);
        setMeaning(meaning);
    }
    public Word(ParseObject po)
    {
        super(po);
    }

    public String getWord()
    {
        return po.getString(f_word);
    }
    public void setWord(String in)
    {
        po.put(f_word,in);
    }

    public String getMeaning()
    {
        return po.getString(f_meaning);
    }
    public void setMeaning(String in)
    {
        po.put(f_meaning,in);
    }

    public String toString()
    {
        String word = getWord();
        String user = getCreatedBy().getUsername();
        return word + "/" + user;
    }
}//eof-class
```

Code for the Word class in Listing 13-11 is straightforward. We have used the convention of "t_" for table names and "f_" for field names. These static constants just are as important as the methods that they are used in. This is because when you provide queries for this object, you will be using these string names for the fields to query by.

With the right class definition for a Word, you are now ready to create a Word and store it in the Parse cloud, as shown in Listing 13-12.

Listing 13-12. Creating and Savind a Word Parse Object in the Cloud

```
public void createWord(View v){
    if (validateForm() == false) {
        return;
    }
    //form is valid
    String sWord = getWord();
    String sMeaning = getMeaning();

    Word w = new Word(sWord, sMeaning);
    turnOnProgressDialog("Saving Word", "We will be right back");
    w.po.saveInBackground(new SaveCallback() {
        @Override
        public void done(ParseException e) {
            turnOffProgressDialog();
            if (e == null)    {
                //no exception
                wordSavedSuccessfully();
            }
            else    {
                wordSaveFailed(e);
            }
        }
    });
}//eof-login

private void wordSaveFailed(ParseException e)
{
    String error = e.getMessage();
    alert("Saving word failed", error);
}
private void wordSavedSuccessfully()
{
    gotoActivity(WordListActivity.class);
    //Don't finish it as back button is valid
    //finish();
}
```

Notice how, in this code shown in Listing 13-12, you are able to create a Word object through its constructor and not worry about setting the field names explicitly on the Parse object. Where needed, this also ensures that you are not mistyping field names every time they are needed. Because a Parse object allows any field name, if you were to mistype, you would end up creating new attributes that you don't intend. Of course, there may be places that you legitimately want to do this, but at least for the most common cases, this is a good firewall to have.

Also notice in Listing 13-12 that you are using the real ParseObject from the underlying Parse object wrapper (w.po) to fire off the Parse APIs such as save.

> **Note**   The code presented here for the `ParseObjectWrapper` and the `Word` are stripped down to show you the minimum necessary for our current needs. If you were to look up the downloadable project, you will see that these classes have a bit more code. The additional code was necessary when you start passing objects like "Word" through Android parcels. (That is a topic for the next chapter.) So keep that in mind when you see the original code in the downloaded project.

Now, let's turn our attention to how to query for these word objects and paint them in a list by using Android list adapters.

Querying and Populating Parse Objects

Listing 13-13 shows how to query for objects of type Word. This code is slightly different from querying for Parse users.

Listing 13-13. Querying for a List of Parse Objects

```
private void populateWordList()
{
    ParseQuery query = new ParseQuery(Word.t_tablename);
    query.orderByDescending(Word.f_createdAt);
    query.include(Word.f_createdBy);

    query.setCachePolicy(ParseQuery.CachePolicy.CACHE_ELSE_NETWORK);
    //Milliseconds
    query.setMaxCacheAge(100000L);

    this.turnOnProgressDialog("Going to get words", "Patience. Be Right back");
    query.findInBackground(new FindCallback() {
      public void done(List<ParseObject> objects, ParseException e) {
        turnOffProgressDialog();
        if (e == null) {
            // The query was successful.
            successfulQuery(objects);
        } else {
```

```
            // Something went wrong.
            queryFailure(e);
        }
      }
   });
}
private void successfulQuery(List<ParseObject> objects)
{
    ArrayList<Word> wordList = new ArrayList<Word>();
    for(ParseObject po: objects)
    {
        Word puw = new Word(po);
        wordList.add(puw);
    }

  WordListAdapter listItemAdapter =
      new WordListAdapter(this
               ,wordList
               ,this);
  this.setListAdapter(listItemAdapter);
}
private void queryFailure(ParseException x)
{
    this.setErrorView(x.getMessage());
}
```

As indicated before, Parse uses an object called `ParseQuery` to perform queries. A Parse query object is initialized with the type of object you are querying, and you used the `Word` class to indicate what this type is. In our case, the variable `Word.t_tablename` points to the name of the table. In Parse, this table name is refered as a "class" in line with object databases, as opposed to relational databases.

You then set the order clause on the query using the field name by which you are ordering. `Word.f_createdBy`. Notice again how the static field definitions on the `Word` and `ParseObjectWrapper` are used here to avoid typing the string names directly.

You then set the cache policy in milliseconds so that you don't go to the server too often. Then you call the `findInBackground()` method on the query object. Also, see that when you are called back, you take the returned Parse objects and stuff them into a `Word` through its constructor. This allows you to call regular Java methods on the `Word` object and not worry about string-based field names.

> **Note**   All the utility functions and classes that are not listed in this chapter, but are referenced in the code, are available in the downloadable project that is mentioned in the References section.

That basically covers the general mode of working with Parse and documents how the application we have presented as a use case is implemented.

What's Next

This chapter is just scratching the surface with Parse. It represents probably about a fourth or fifth of what Parse offers. Although we cover push notifications using Parse in chapter 15, we don't have space or time to cover all of the Parse topics in this book, so we refer you to the Parse documentation, which is quite excellent. Also, the Parse forum is one of the best we have seen, including how quick the responses are.

Further, we would like to point out a few things that are worth considering before completing this chapter. First, the approach we have taken for translating Parse object to Java objects is a basic one. You may want to consider enhancing it to suit your needs. There are some efforts, like *ParseFacade* and *BaaSFacade,* that are trying to do this more cleverly, using less code and more type safety. Consider those options and see how they fit your needs. For instance, *BaaSFacade* provides not only a facade for Parse backend but also to other sources/sinks, such as *StackMob* and even local SQLLite.

Second, a key drawback with straight Parse objects is that they don't provide a way to serialize them to strings. This is a problem when you try to pass them through intent extras to other activities. Without this ability you have only two options: either completely convert them to plain Java objects and then pass them through intent firewalls or pass the ID of the object across and requery the real object based upon its ID. We hope that, with caching properly tuned, the latter option is not that bad. But it is unnatural to have an object in hand but be unable to use it because you can't pass it to another activity through an intent.

Third, keep in mind that you can use JSON to serialize plain Java objects quite effectively and transport them as intent extras. However, note that `ParseObjects` cannot be converted to JSON strings. So you may have to first convert Parse objects to plain Java objects manually and then use JSON to transport them as parcelables. Chapter 4 on JSON for local storage is equally applicable for implementing JSON parcelables. Yes, JSON is a bit more verbose than pure parcelables that are hand coded; however, if your objects are small, this approach works really well and saves you from doing a lot of error-prone code.

In Chapter 14 we will provide a reasonable work-around whereby we show you a middle-of-the-road approach to using `ParseObjects` directly for parceling. If you can't wait, you can look at the downloadable project for this chapter and see how the Parse object wrapper is enhanced to implement parcelable and how it makes the necessary provisions so that this approach works.

As we have implemented the sample application for this chapter, we have made use of the form processing framework mentioned in Chapter 6. That advanced form processing framework saved us a lot of time, as this application has a number of forms for such things as log in, sign up, create words, and so on.

References

We found the following links helpful in our research for this chapter.

- Parse home page: `http://parse.com`

- Parse documentation: `https://www.parse.com/docs/index`

- Parse Android Guide: `https://www.parse.com/docs/android_guide`

- Parse Java API: `https://www.parse.com/docs/android/API/`

- Research log for this chapter on Parse: `http://androidbook.com/item/4458`. You can use this web page to follow the research and discover other links related to Parse development.

- How to use GSON for persistence: `http://androidbook.com/item/4440`. You can use this article also to use GSON for parceling pure Java objects. Chapter 4 of this book also covers this topic of GSON and JSON in great depth.

- Advanced Form Processing and Validations: `http://androidbook.com/item/4494`. You can use this article to find out how to validate forms effectively. Chapter 6 of this book also covers this topic of form processing in great depth.

- Download the test project dedicated for this chapter at `www.androidbook.com/expertandroid/projects.` The name of the ZIP file is `ExpertAndroid_Ch13_ParseStarterProject.zip.`

Summary

Collaborative mobile applications are ubiquitous. Storing data in the cloud is an essential need for these types of applications. This chapter gave an excellent introduction to one of the popular cloud-storage platforms, Parse. The chapter also laid out a standard pattern for signing up users and working with users. It provided the necessary Parse APIs for user management and also explained how to store and retrieve Parse objects. Lastly, the chapter briefly contrasted the relational joins with No-SQL approaches.

Review Questions

The following questions should help you consolidate what you have learned in this chapter:

1. What is a Parse application key and a client key?

2. How do you get the keys in question 1?

3. How do you initialize an application that needs to talk with Parse with the Parse generated keys?

4. What Parse APIs do you use to sign up a user?

5. What Parse APIs do you use to log in a user?

6. How do you reset a user password with Parse?

7. How do you log out using Parse?

8. Are you logged in when the signup is successful?

9. How is a Parse object different from a relational table?

10. Does a Parse object maintain the user that has either created the object or last updated it?

11. Why do you need to use progress dialogs when you are issuing Parse methods?

12. How do you cache Parse objects?

13. How do you tell a Parse query to include dependent objects?

14. Can you change an Android package name while keeping the Parse keys intact?

Enhancing Parse with Parcelables

In Chapter 13 we documented the basic features of Parse. We showed you how to create an account with Parse and how to use that account to sign up users and store objects in the cloud on behalf of those users. We also showed you the basic mechanism to query Parse objects.

In this chapter we will cover two more topics related to Parse. First is the need to pass Parse objects as parcelables through intent extras. The second is the ability to query for Parse objects based on their relationship to other Parse objects.

Let's talk about the first topic in a bit more detail. If you recall the dictionary-like application we introduced to explain Parse, there were two types of objects that are specific to that application: words and their meanings. Each word can have a number of meanings provided by various users. We now want to create a screen where we show the meanings for a given word. As it turns out, this is a bit tricky because of Android and also because of Parse.

Let's understand what is tricky about displaying the screen that shows meanings for a given word. Ideally we would choose a Word Parse object and pass it to the activity that lists meanings for that word. Once we have this Word object in the receiving meanings activity, we can run a query on word meanings whose parent word is the word that is passed in.

However, Android SDK has a stipulation whereby you cannot easily pass references to in-memory objects to another activity. Only certain ceremonial objects can be done this way (for example, those implementing IBinder). Word and WordMeaning objects are not the least bit ceremonial! They are just plain Java objects holding a few attributes. So in Android, you pass data (as opposed to object references) to other activities through intent extras. You can try this by doing the following:

```
ParseObject wordObject;
Intent i = new Intent(this,MeaningsListActivity.classname);
i.putExtra("word-parse-object", wordObject);
this.startActivity(i);
```

In this code, the variable this points to the current activity. If this were to be successful, then the receiving activity can retrieve the word object this way:

```
Intent i = this.getIntent();
ParseObject parceledWord = (ParseObject)i.getParcelableExtra();
```

However, for this method to work the type ParseObject needs to implement the Android SDK interface Parcelable, and the ParseObject does not do this! So, in order to over come this limition, we'll show you:

- How to pass a ParseObject through intents
- How to use the parceled ParseObject in a query to retrieve its children

Before we start exploring these two topics, however, let's look at the screens we will use to implement and illustrate these concepts.

User Experience of the Sample Application

We start with the list of words that was shown in Chapter 13, now given below in Figure 14-1.

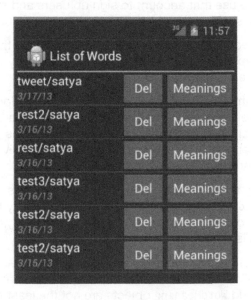

Figure 14-1. List of words activity

What you see in Figure 14-1 is a list of words. By tapping the Meanings button for a word, you are taken to the activity that shows the meaning for that word, if there is any. Figure 14-2 is that screen.

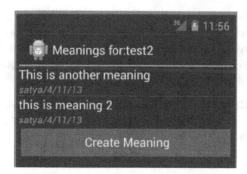

Figure 14-2. List of meanings activity

What you see in Figure 14-2 is a list of available meanings for a word that is passed in from the previous screen (Figure 14-1). Clearly, this activity needs a word object to paint itself. So when we implement this activity later, we will show how parcelables play a role here. This screen also shows a button to create a new meaning for the current word. Figure 14-3 shows the screen to create that new meaning for the word.

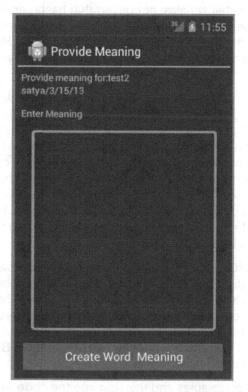

Figure 14-3. Create a word meaning activity

Although the Figure 14-3 screen is quite simple, we need to solve the problem of passing the parent word object as a parcelable so that the meaning we create belongs to the right Parse word object. Also, because this screen is invoked from the word meanings list screen (Figure 14-2), we need to parcel a word Parse object that is already passed in parceled from Figure 14-1. So any solution here should pass a Parse object multiple times as an intent extra.

Let us turn now to examining the parcelable in more detail. We will also cover the theory behind parcels and parcelables in the Android SDK. Then, we will show how to implement the solution for passing ParseObjects as parcelables.

Passing ParseObjects as Parcelables

To send a ParseObject through an intent is to make it a Parcelable. But ParseObject is a type that is already defined and frozen by the Parse SDK. To further complicate the matter, the ParseObject is not only not parcelable but also not serializable. Also, it cannot be converted to a JSON string. Had it bean serializable or converted to a JSON string, we could have passed it through the parcelable in that form.

So here is one of the possible options. Read all the values from a Parse object and put them in a hashmap ourselves, and then either serialize or convert that hashmap to a string that can then be passed throught the parcelable. On the other side, you take that parceled hashmap and construct a Parse object—to the extent that you can construct it as the original Parse object. It is possible, though, that the original Parse object may have an internal state that you are not aware of and hence it cannot be replicated as is.

However, we haven't used that approach of mapping Parse objects into hashmaps for transport. One reason why not is that, in Chapter 13, we already had an object that is wrapping the original Parse object. (It is called the ParseObjectWrapper.) So, we wanted to use this wrapper to go across as a parcelable even with some limitations. One limitation is when this ParseWrapperObject is recreated on the other side, it will have a recreated ParseObject at its core and not be the original ParseObject. We could compensate for this a bit as the methods on the ParseObjectWrapper can detect that the embedded ParseObject is a cloned one and do the adjustments as needed to give the impression that you are as close as possible to dealing with a real Parse object. In addition, the end user objects such as Word and WordMeaning are already extending the ParseObjectWrapper, so it is easier to recreate them from ParseObjectWrapper.

So, we have started with ParseObjectWrapper, and it seem to be doable at that level. Therefore, we are going to stick to extending the ParseObjectWrapper with parcelable support. The research to see if the hashmap method is better in other ways was not done. Those advantages are not too apparent at the moment, nor do they have a possibility of being better, so we stick to using ParseObjectWrapper as a vehicle for parcelables. Also, as indicated in Chapter 13, if you were to use reflection- and interface-based approaches, such as ParseFacade or BaaSFacade, you may have better options. We will leave that research to you.

Let's cover the theory behind parcelables and then dig into the code to see how to make the ParseObjectWrapper parcelable.

Revisiting Parcelables

In Android, `Parcel`s are used to pass messages between processes. It is an IPC (inter process communication) mechanism in Android. A `Parcel`, as a result, is a stream of message data that can be communicated and stored either in real time or at a later point through a store-and-forward mechanism between processes.

A `Parcel` can contain data from objects that is flattened on one side and then unflattened on the other side, back into objects. It can be used also to carry object references or proxies to services or file streams. A `Parcel` may contain the following:

- Primitives
- Arrays (4 byte length + data)
- Objects that implement the parcelable interface
- Bundles (key value pairs where values reflect any of the above)
- Proxy objects using IBinder interfaces
- File descriptor objects that are proxies

You can learn more about `Parcel`s and `Parcelable`s at the Android SDk link: `http://developer.android.com/reference/android/os/Parcel.html`.

When an object implements the `Parcelable` interface, the object is promising the Android SDK that it knows how to write itself to a `Parcel`, field by field. Such a `Parcelable` object also knows how to create and read itself field by field from the `Parcel`.

A Simple Example of Implementing a Parcelable

Let us consider a simple object and see how it goes about implementing a parcelable if it wants to be transported across. This simple object, a `User`, is presented in Listing 14-1.

Listing 14-1. A Simple Parcelable Implementation Example: A User Class

```
public class User
implements Parcelable
{
    //Add more field types later
    public String userid;
    public String username;

    public User(String inuserid, String inusername)
    {
        userid = inuserid;
        username = inusername;
    }
    public static final Parcelable.Creator<User> CREATOR
        = new Parcelable.Creator<User>() {
            public User createFromParcel(Parcel in) {
                return new User(in);
            }
```

```
            public User[] newArray(int size) {
                return new User[size];
            }
    }; //end of creator

    //
    @Override
    public int describeContents() {
        return 0;
    }

    public User(Parcel in)
    {
        userid = in.readString();
        username = in.readString();
    }
    @Override
    public void writeToParcel(Parcel dest, int flags)
    {
        dest.writeString(userid);
        dest.writeString(username);
    }
}//eof-class
```

This class User has just two fields: username and userid. When this class implements the Parcelable interface, it needs to be able to do the following:

1. Understand to see if it needs to handle describeContents()

2. Know how to read and write its constituent attributes

3. Understand flags to alter the behavior of what and how to write if needed

Describing Contents and File Descriptors

Apparently for Android SDK, it is important to know if a Parceled object contains file descriptors. This information is used to implement the method Bundle.hasFileDescriptors(). The method in turn is used to prevent objects with descriptors from being given to the system process.For example, code like this can be seen in the core Android SDK source:

```
//Taken from ActivityManagerService.java
if (intent.hasFileDescriptors()) {
        throw new IllegalArgumentException("File descriptors passed in Intent");
}
```

In our case, the User object does not even remotely deal with file descriptors, so we can safely return a zero indicating that we don't need any special handling by the OS. (If you want to see how to work with objects containing file descriptors, refer to the source code of the Android SDK class ParcelFileDescriptor.)

Reading and Writing Members to a Parcel

The second responsibility of the parcelable class is to read and write its members from and to the parcel object. If you see the writeToParcel() method in Listing 14-1, you note that we are writing the string objects to the parcel stream. Similarly, to read the members of the User class, take a look at the constructor User(Parcel p). This constructor simply reads the values back into its local variables.

Unlike the writeParcel() method, there is no equivalent readParcel() in the User class. Instead, the Android SDK requires that the class implementing the parcelable interface provide a static reference to a CREATOR object that knows how to instantiate objects of the specific type, such as User in our case. This CREATOR object has the createFromParcel() method that is responsible for instantiating the User object by calling its appropriate constructor that takes ths parcel object as input.

The Write Time Parcelable Flags

Now let's consider the finer points of the parcelable flag. When you write an object to a parcel using the parcel.writeParcelable(Parcelable p, int flags), you can pass flags so that the parcelable that is being written can alter what to write.The only flag defined and recognized by the Android SDK is:

PARCELABLE_WRITE_RETURN_VALUE

To know if a Parcelable does anything differently when this flag is passed, you need to check its documentation. For example, the ParcelableFileDescriptor uses this flag, and if passed in it will close the file descriptor and merely pass its value through the parcel. In our case, the User class does not use this flag at all.

Another recommendation from the API is that if your parcelable represents a stateful object—say, a file descriptor or a reference to a service—you may want to reclaim the resources and just pass the proxies or values to those underlying resources. In such cases, Android API recommends this as a good way to recognize this flag. So while parceling core Android objects, pay attention to the documentation of those objects to see if they honor this flag and if the behavior would be affected by the flag. In the case of the User example, there is really no reason to recognize or react to the flag. For most cases when you are writing parcelables, you can always return 0 for describeContents() and ignore the flags while writing to the parcelables.

Now that you have an understanding of what parcelables are and how they work, let's see how to go about implementing the ParseObjectWrapper as a parcelable.

Implementing Parcelable ParseObjectWrapper

Listing 14-2 presents the source code for the ParseObjectWrapper. The code in this listing is best understood when it is all in one place, but we'll discuss the relevant portions subsequently. The listing is lengthy; scan it quickly, going through the various sections to see how they all fit together first. We explain all the key sections following the listing. Once you read through the explanations, you can revisit the listing to consolidate the structural composition of this class.

Listing 14-2. Source Code for ParseObjectWrapper

```java
public class ParseObjectWrapper
implements Parcelable
{
    public static String f_createdAt = "createdAt";
    public static String f_createdBy = "createdBy";

    public static String f_updatedAt = "updatedAt";
    public static String f_updatedBy = "updatedBy";

    //The parse object that is being wrapped
    public ParseObject po;

    //Constructors
    //Use this when you are creating a new one from scratch
    public ParseObjectWrapper(String tablename)    {
        po = new ParseObject(tablename);
        po.put(f_createdBy, ParseUser.getCurrentUser());
    }
    //Use this to create proper shell
    //For example you can do this in parcelable
    public ParseObjectWrapper(String tablename, String objectId)  {
        po = ParseObject.createWithoutData(tablename, objectId);
    }

    //Use this when you are creating from an exsiting parse obejct
    public ParseObjectWrapper(ParseObject in)  {
        po = in;
    }

    //To create derived objects like Word using the
    //ParseObjectWrapper that is unparceled
    public ParseObjectWrapper(ParseObjectWrapper inPow)    {
        //Parseobject underneath
        po = inPow.po;

        //parseobject essentials if it has it
        poe = inPow.poe;
    }

    //Accessors
    public ParseObject getParseObject() { return po; }
    String getTablename(){return po.getClassName();      }
    public ParseUser getCreatedBy(){return po.getParseUser(f_createdBy);}
    public void setCreatedBy(ParseUser in){po.put(f_createdBy, in);}
    public void setUpdatedBy(){po.put(f_updatedBy, ParseUser.getCurrentUser());}
    public ParseUser getLastUpdatedBy(){return
            (ParseUser)po.getParseObject(f_updatedBy);      }
```

```
//Parcelable stuff
@Override
public int describeContents() {
    return 0;
}
public static final Parcelable.Creator<ParseObjectWrapper> CREATOR
    = new Parcelable.Creator<ParseObjectWrapper>() {
        public ParseObjectWrapper createFromParcel(Parcel in) {
            return create(in);
        }
        public ParseObjectWrapper[] newArray(int size) {
            return new ParseObjectWrapper[size];
        }
};   //end of creator

@Override
public void writeToParcel(Parcel parcel, int flags)
{
    //Order: tablename, objectId, fieldlist, field values, essentials

    //write the tablename
    parcel.writeString(this.getTablename());

    //write the object id
    parcel.writeString(this.po.getObjectId());

    //write the field list and write the field names
    List<ValueField> fieldList = getFieldList();
    //See how many
    int i = fieldList.size();
    parcel.writeInt(i);

    //write each of the field types
    for(ValueField vf: fieldList)        {
        parcel.writeParcelable(vf, flags);
    }

    //You need to write the field values now
    FieldTransporter ft =
        new FieldTransporter(this.po,
                    parcel,FieldTransporter.DIRECTION_FORWARD);
    for(ValueField vf: fieldList)        {
        //This will write the field from parse object to the parcel
        ft.transfer(vf);
    }

    //get the essentials and write to the parcel
    ParseObjectEssentials lpoe = this.getEssentials();
    parcel.writeParcelable(lpoe, flags);
}
//
```

```java
private static ParseObjectWrapper create(Parcel parcel)
{
    //Order: tablename, objectid, fieldlist, field values, essentials

    String tablename = parcel.readString();
    String objectId = parcel.readString();

    ParseObjectWrapper parseObject =
        new ParseObjectWrapper(tablename, objectId);

    //Read the valuefiled list from parcel
    List<ValueField> fieldList = new ArrayList<ValueField>();
    int size = parcel.readInt();
    for(int i=0;i<size;i++)
    {
        ValueField vf = (ValueField)
                parcel.readParcelable(
                        ValueField.class.getClassLoader());
        fieldList.add(vf);
    }
    //add the field values
    FieldTransporter ft =
        new FieldTransporter(
                parseObject.po, parcel,
                IFieldTransport.DIRECTION_BACKWARD);
    for(ValueField vf: fieldList)
    {
        ft.transfer(vf);
    }
    //read essentials
    ParseObjectEssentials poe =
        (ParseObjectEssentials)parcel.readParcelable(
                    ParseObjectEssentials.class.getClassLoader());

    parseObject.setParseObjectEssentials(poe);
    return parseObject;
}

//have the derived classes override this
public List<ValueField> getFieldList()
{
    return new ArrayList<ValueField>();
}

//To represent createdby and lastupdatedby user objects
//when parceled. We don't recreate them as ParseObjects but save their
//essential attributes in separate objects.
private ParseObjectEssentials poe;
public void setParseObjectEssentials(ParseObjectEssentials inpoe)   {
    poe = inpoe;
}
```

```
    public ParseObjectEssentials getEssentials()
    {
        if (poe != null) return poe;

        Date cat = po.getCreatedAt();
        Date luat = po.getUpdatedAt();
        ParseUser cby = getCreatedBy();
        ParseUser luby = getLastUpdatedBy();
        return new ParseObjectEssentials(
                cat, User.fromParseUser(cby),
                luat, User.fromParseUser(luby));
    }
    public boolean isParcelled()
    {
        if (poe != null) return true;
        return false;
    }


    //Utility methods that take into account if this
    //object is parceled or not
    public User getCreatedByUser()     {
        if (!isParcelled())
        {
            //it is not parcelled so it is original
            return User.fromParseUser(getCreatedBy());
        }
        //it is parcelled
        return poe.createdBy;
    }
    public Date getCreatedAt()     {
        if (!isParcelled())
        {
            //it is not parcelled so it is original
            return po.getCreatedAt();
        }
        //it is parcelled
        return poe.createdAt;
    }
}//eof-class
```

You have seen the basics of this class in the previous chapter. This same class is now extended in Listing 14-2 to implement the parcelable methods required to send a ParseObjectWrapper through a parcel. Also, the code in Listing 14-2 assumes that the User class shown in Listing 14-1, has the following two additional static methods:

```
public static User getAnnonymousUser() {
    return new User("0","Annonynous");
}
public static User fromParseUser(ParseUser pu) {
    if (pu == null) return getAnnonymousUser();
```

```
  //pu is available
  String userid = pu.getObjectId();
  String username = pu.getUsername();
  return new User(userid,username);
}
```

Now, let's dissect the code of parcelable `ParseObjectWrapper` in Listing 14-2. As indicated during the discussion of parcelable, the `describeContents()` method of this class returns 0, and this class also ignores the write time parcelable flags.

Most of the code in this class `ParseObjectWrapper` comes from the desire to do what is shown in the pseudo code in Listing 14-3 below.

Listing 14-3. Psuedocode for a Parcelable ParseObjectWrapper

```
public class Word extends ParseObjectWrapper {}
public class WordMeaning extends ParseObjectWrapper {}

//On the sending side
Word wordObject;
Intent i;
i.putExtra(Word.t_tablename, wordObject);
startActivity(i,...);

//In the receiving activity
Intent i = getIntent();
Word parceledWordObject = (Word)i.getExtra(Word.t_tablename);
//Use the parceledWordObject
```

Now, the solution provided by the parcelable `ParseObjectWrapper` code in Listing 14-2 is not as exact, precise, or pure as it could be but it's pretty close, as you will see. This high-level understanding as shown in Listing 14-3 is key to quickly grasping the code for the `ParseObjectWrapper` (Listing 14-2).

Implementing writeToParcel()

The key methods of Listing 14-2 are the `writeToParcel()` method and the static counterpart method `createFromParcel()`. We start the discussion with `writeToParcel()`. In this method, you write the following elements to the parcel in that order:

```
tablename, objectId, fieldlist, field values, essentials
```

The table name and the Parse object ID are required to recreate the `ParseObject` on the other side. As indicated, there is no way to clone or serialize a `ParseObject`. So you end up creating a new `ParseObject` using merely the table name and its Parse object ID. You then put in the parcel each of the attributes held by a Parse object.

To transport these field values from the Parse object to the parcel, you need some help on two accounts. First, the philosophy behind our parcelable implementation is such that we don't need derived classes like `Word` and `WordMeaning` to implement the `Parceleble` and stream their own fields. We want the base class `ParseObjectWrappper` to do this job for us. This keeps the burden on the derived classes to a minimum.

To allow the base class to parcel the attributes, we want the derived classes to declare their fields using a method called getFieldList(). This method returns a list of field names and their types. We can then store those field names and types in the parcel and retrieve them back on the other side to set them on the targeted newly created Parse object. These field definitions are encapsulated in a class called ValueField with two attributes: a field name and its type. Listing 14-4 is the code for the ValueField.

Listing 14-4. ValueField: A Class to Represent Field Name and Type

```java
public class ValueField
implements Parcelable
{
    public static String FT_int = "Integer";
    public static String FT_string = "String";
    public static String FT_Object = "Object";
    public static String FT_unknown = "Unknown";

    //Add more field types later
    public String name;
    public String type;

    public ValueField(String inName, String inFieldType)
    {
        name = inName;
        type = inFieldType;
    }
    public static final Parcelable.Creator<ValueField> CREATOR
        = new Parcelable.Creator<ValueField>() {
            public ValueField createFromParcel(Parcel in) {
                return new ValueField(in);
            }

            public ValueField[] newArray(int size) {
                return new ValueField[size];
            }
        }
}; //end of creator

    //
    @Override
    public int describeContents() {
        return 0;
    }
    public ValueField(Parcel in)    {
        name = in.readString();
        type = in.readString();
    }
    @Override
    public void writeToParcel(Parcel dest, int flags)    {
        dest.writeString(name);
        dest.writeString(type);
    }
```

```
    public String toString()   {
        return name + "/" + type;
    }
    public static ValueField getStringField(String fieldName)  {
        return new ValueField(fieldName, ValueField.FT_string);
    }
}//eof-class
```

Because a ValueField needs to be stored in the parcel, we have made the ValueField to be a Parcelable by implementing the respective methods of the Parcelable. This ValueField class also defines the constants for the required field types. For now we have defined only a couple of types; you can extend this by adding other allowed primitive types.

So, refering back to the writeParcel() method of the ParseObjectWrapper, you can see that it is pretty simple to write the field names and their type names to the parcel.

Field Transporters

The next task is to write the values of each attribute or field of the ParseObject into the parcel. Both Parcel and the ParseObject provide typed methods to get and set the values. So you need a matchmaker to take the value from one to the other. To do this translation, you use an interface and a couple of classes.These are presented in Listing 14-5.

Listing 14-5. Supporting Classes for Transporting Fields Between a ParseObject and a Parcel

```
//Transfer value from one source to another
public interface IFieldTransport
{
    public static int DIRECTION_FORWARD = 1;
    public static int DIRECTION_BACKWARD= 2;

    //Transfer from one mode to another
    public void transfer(ValueField f);
}


//A class to transport an integer between a
//ParseObject and a Parcel
//ParseObject is source and Parcel is target
//Direction indicates how this value should be transported
public class IntegerFieldTransport
implements IFieldTransport
{
    ParseObject po;
    Parcel p;
    int d = IFieldTransport.DIRECTION_FORWARD;

    public IntegerFieldTransport(ParseObject inpo, Parcel inp){
        this(inpo,inp,DIRECTION_FORWARD);
    }
```

```java
    public IntegerFieldTransport(ParseObject inpo, Parcel inp, int direction)
    {
        po = inpo;
        p = inp;
        d = direction;
    }
    @Override
    public void transfer(ValueField f)
    {
            //1
        if (d == DIRECTION_BACKWARD) {
            //parcel to parseobject
            int i = p.readInt();
            po.put(f.name, i);
        }
        else {
            //forward
            //parseobject to parcel
            int i = po.getInt(f.name);
            p.writeInt(i);
        }
    }
}

public class StringFieldTransport
implements IFieldTransport
{
    ParseObject po;
    Parcel p;
    int d = IFieldTransport.DIRECTION_FORWARD;

    public StringFieldTransport(ParseObject inpo, Parcel inp){
        this(inpo,inp,DIRECTION_FORWARD);
    }

    public StringFieldTransport(ParseObject inpo, Parcel inp, int direction)
    {
        po = inpo;
        p = inp;
        d = direction;
    }
    @Override
    public void transfer(ValueField f) {
        if (d == DIRECTION_BACKWARD)
        {
            //parcel to parseobject
            String s = p.readString();
            po.put(f.name, s);
        }
```

```
        else
        {
            //forward
            //parseobject to parcel
            String s = po.getString(f.name);
            p.writeString(s);
        }
    }
}
```

Given this interface and the type translators, you can gather them in a registry and have the registry handle the transfer for all the types. Listing 14-6 is the code for a FieldTransporter that can transfer all field types that are known to it.

Listing 14-6. FieldTransporter: A Registry for Individual Field Transports

```
public class FieldTransporter
implements IFieldTransport
{
    ParseObject po;
    Parcel p;
    int d = IFieldTransport.DIRECTION_FORWARD;

    Map<String,IFieldTransport> transporterMap;

    public FieldTransporter(ParseObject inpo, Parcel inp, int direction){
        po = inpo;
        p = inp;
        d = direction;

        //Register the all the translators/tranporters
        register();
    }
    private void register()
    {
        transporterMap = new HashMap<String,IFieldTransport>();
        //register integers
        transporterMap.put(
                ValueField.FT_int,
                new IntegerFieldTransport(po,p,d));

        //register string transporter
        transporterMap.put(
                ValueField.FT_string,
                new StringFieldTransport(po,p,d));

        //Other missing transporters
    }
```

```
    private IFieldTransport getTransportFor(String fieldType)
    {
        IFieldTransport ift = transporterMap.get(fieldType);
        if (ift == null)
        {
            throw new RuntimeException("Problem with locating the type");
        }
        return ift;
    }

    @Override
    public void transfer(ValueField f)
    {
        IFieldTransport ift = getTransportFor(f.type);
        ift.transfer(f);
    }
}//eof-class
```

Using this `FieldTransporter`, you can now easily see how the `writeParcel()` method does its magic of writing the values for all the fields from the `parseobject` to the `parcel`. That code is repeated in Listing 14-7 for quick review.

Listing 14-7. How to Use a Field Transporter

```
//add the field values
FieldTransporter ft =
    new FieldTransporter(
            parseObject.po, parcel, IFieldTransport.DIRECTION_BACKWARD);
for(ValueField vf: fieldList)
{
    ft.transfer(vf);
}
```

See how the `FieldTransporter` in Listing 14-7 is instantiated with source, target, and direction; then for each `ValueField` given by the `ParseObjectWrapper`, the field values are transfered. This approach keeps the type safety of the writes between the `ParseObject` and the `parcel`. Keep in mind, though, that as you are likely to have more field types, you will need to create transporters for those and add them to the `FieldTransporter` registration above.

What Is ParseObjectEssentials?

So far we have gathered the primitive attributes of the source `ParseObject` and have transfered over. However, the source Parse object has some attributes that point to other Parse objects. This especially includes the two user objects: the user who created the Parse object and the user who last updated it.

Potentially, you can extend the parcelables concept to these child objects as well. For our purposes here, however, we take a simpler approach. We strip out the essentials of these two user objects and encapsulate them into a homegrown `User` object, as laid out in the begining of the chapter. Then we capture both users in a consolidated object called ParseObjectEssentials. Once we have this ParseObjectEssentials extracted from the current ParseObject that is being parceled, we can instead parcel the ParseObjectEssentials in place of the child or the dependent Parse objects. Listing 14-8 gives the definition for the ParseObjectEssentials.

Listing 14-8. Idea of ParseObjectEssentials

```
public class ParseObjectEssentials
implements Parcelable
{
    //Add more fields if desired from their respective ParseObjects
    public Date createdAt;
    public User createdBy;
    public Date lastUpdatedAt;
    public User lastUpdatedBy;

    public ParseObjectEssentials(Date createdAt, User createdBy,
            Date lastUpdatedAt, User lastUpdatedBy) {
        super();
        this.createdAt = createdAt;
        this.createdBy = createdBy;
        this.lastUpdatedAt = lastUpdatedAt;
        this.lastUpdatedBy = lastUpdatedBy;
    }
    public static final Parcelable.Creator<ParseObjectEssentials> CREATOR
        = new Parcelable.Creator<ParseObjectEssentials>() {
            public ParseObjectEssentials createFromParcel(Parcel in) {
                return new ParseObjectEssentials(in);
            }

            public ParseObjectEssentials[] newArray(int size) {
                return new ParseObjectEssentials[size];
            }
    }; //end of creator

    @Override
    public int describeContents() {
        return 0;
    }

    public ParseObjectEssentials(Parcel in)
    {
        createdAt = new Date(in.readLong());
        createdBy = (User)in.readParcelable(User.class.getClassLoader());
        lastUpdatedAt = new Date(in.readLong());
        lastUpdatedBy = (User)in.readParcelable(User.class.getClassLoader());
    }
    @Override
    public void writeToParcel(Parcel dest, int flags)
    {
        dest.writeLong(this.createdAt.getTime());
        dest.writeParcelable(createdBy, flags);
```

```
        dest.writeLong(lastUpdatedAt.getTime());
        dest.writeParcelable(lastUpdatedBy, flags);
    }
    public static ParseObjectEssentials getDefault()
    {
        Date cat = new Date(0);
        User auser = User.getAnnonymousUser();
        Date luat = new Date(0);
        return new ParseObjectEssentials(cat,auser,luat,auser);
    }
}//eof-class
```

To finish the writeToParcel() of the ParseObjectWrapper, you save one of these ParseObjectEssentials in the parcel.

Next, we look at the ParseObjectWrapper code to see how to obtain this ParseObjectEssentials from the core embedded ParseObject of the ParseObjectWrapper.

The Other Side: Recreating the ParseObjectWrapper

As a parcelable, the ParseObjectWrapper needs to be able to recreate itself from the parcel. See the static create() function that returns the ParseObjectWrapper from a given parcel. In this method, you read things in reverse, as follows.

First, read the table name and the object ID belonging to the old Parse object that was parceled. From these two arguments, you create a Parse shell object. Next, you read the field definitions to see how many attributes are available and parceled for this Parse object. Then you use the field transporters to transfer each field and its value to the newly creaed ParseObject. You take this ParseObject and create a new ParseObjectWrapper. At this point, you have the ParseObjectWrapper ready to be returned. However, you also need to read the ParseObjectEssentials and set it on the ParseObjectWrapper.

The ParseObjectWrapper becomes quite context-sensitive as it sits in possibly multiple states. When it is originally created, it is just holding to a ParseObject that is created with merely its table name (even without an ID) as the ParseObject has not even been saved in the Parse cloud. At a next state, the ParseObjectWrapper could be holding a ParseObject that is fully saved in the Parse cloud. Then, in the third state, the ParseObjectWrapper could have been parceled and recreated on the other side. In this last state the ParseObject it holds is merely a stand-in and is not tied to the server. The ParseObjectWrapper also holds a ParseObjectEssentials, so it is possible to ask the ParseObjectWrapper if it is parceled.

I have created some methods on the ParseObjectWrapper, such as the last created user and last updated by, so that they take into account which state the ParseObjectWrapper is in and will accordingly return the right values.

Parceling the Word

Let's see how to package a Word object into a parcel and bring it back. Listing 14-9 shows the definition for the Word based on our new ParseObjectWrapper.

Listing 14-9. Extending the Parcelable ParseObjectWrapper

```java
public class Word
extends ParseObjectWrapper
{
    public static String t_tablename = "WordObject";
    public static String PARCELABLE_WORD_ID = "WordObjectId";

    //Only two fileds
    public static String f_word = "word";
    public static String f_meaning = "meaning";

    //Constructors: A new word from scratch
    public Word(String word, String meaning){
        super(t_tablename);
        setWord(word);
        setMeaning(meaning);
    }
    //Wrapping from a ParseObject gotten from the cloud
    public Word(ParseObject po)    {
        super(po);
    }
    //Recreated using a previously Parceled word
    public Word(ParseObjectWrapper inPow)    {
        super(inPow);
    }

    //Accessors
    public String getWord()    {
        return po.getString(f_word);
    }
    public void setWord(String in)    {
        po.put(f_word,in);
    }
    public String getMeaning()    {
        return po.getString(f_meaning);
    }
    public void setMeaning(String in)    {
        po.put(f_meaning,in);
    }
    public String toString()
    {
        String word = getWord();
        String user = getCreatedBy().getUsername();
        return word + "/" + user;
    }
    //have the children override this
    @Override
    public List<ValueField> getFieldList()
    {
        ArrayList<ValueField> fields = new ArrayList<ValueField>();
        fields.add(ValueField.getStringField(Word.f_word));
```

```
        fields.add(ValueField.getStringField(Word.f_meaning));
        return fields;
    }
}//eof-class
```

If you look back to Chapter 13, you'll see that this version of Word is very similar. The main addition is that the Word class now provides its field list by overriding getFieldList(). It also has a constructor that accepts the ParseObjectWrapper as an input. This constructor is useful in recreating the Word once it is passed through the parcel.

We are now ready to implement the WordMeanings activity that was introduced in the begining of the chapter (see Figure 14-2).

Implementing the Word Meanings List Activity

The subject of implementing the WordMeaningsListActivity includes the following:

1. How to invoke this activity by passing a Word through an intent

2. How to retrieve that word from the intent

3. How to access the word so that you can change the title of the activity based on the input word

4. How you use the word to query for its word meanings

Passing Word as an Intent Extra

The word list activity screen in Figure 14-1 shows that each row represents a Word object defined by the Word class that was given in Listing 14-9. If you tap the Meanings button in that figure, it will need to invoke the WordMeaningsListActivity shown in Figure 14-2. Listing 14-10 indicates how to invoke this activity.

Listing 14-10. Passing Word as an Intent Extra

```
private void respondToClick(WordListActivity activity, Word wordRef)
{
    Intent i = new Intent(activity,WordMeaningsListActivity.class);
    i.putExtra(Word.t_tablename,wordRef);
    activity.startActivity(i);
}
```

Recreating the Word from the Intent Extra

Notice how the word object is passed to the intent extra as a parcelable. Let's see how get the Word object back on the other side. Listing 14-11 shows the code snippet from WordMeaningsListActivity for obtaining the Word object again.

Listing 14-11. Retrieving Typed Word from an Intent Extra

```
private Word getParceledWordFromIntent()
{
    Intent i = this.getIntent();
    ParseObjectWrapper pow =
        (ParseObjectWrapper)i.getParcelableExtra(Word.t_tablename);
    Word parceledWord = new Word(pow);
    return parceledWord;
}
```

Notice how a `ParseObjectWrapper` is first retrieved from the intent extra and then is used to wrap the Word object.

Using the Retrieved Word Object in the target Activity

You can use the Word object to access all its attributes and use its methods. Listing 14-12 shows how to set the title of the activity.

Listing 14-12. Psuedocode for Using the Word Accessor Methods

```
Word parceledWord;
activity.setTitle(parceledWord.getWord());
```

Notice that you are able to transfer the word through the intent and use it without resorting to the underlying Parse object. Had you not been able to pass the word via the intent, you would have had to pass just the Parse object ID of the word and do a query again to the Parse backend to retrieve the word object so as to get its word string value and determine who created it and when. It is to avoid this second query to the server that we go to the trouble of writing this much parceling code.

Using the Retrieved Word to Search for Its Meanings

Let's see how to use this parceled Word object to retrieve WordMeanings. First, let's look at how a Word and a WordMeaning are connected, as indicated in Listing 14-13.

Listing 14-13. Source Code for WordMeaning

```
public class WordMeaning extends ParseObjectWrapper
{
    //Design the table first
    public static String t_tablename = "WordMeaningObject";
    public static String f_word = "word";
    public static String f_meaning = "meaning";

    public WordMeaning(String wordMeaning, Word inParentWord)
    {
        super(t_tablename);
        setMeaning(wordMeaning);
        setWord(inParentWord);
    }
```

```
    //Make sure there is a way to construct with a straight
    //Parse object
    public WordMeaning(ParseObject po)
    {
        //Create a check in the future if it is not of the same type
        super(po);
    }
    public void setMeaning(String meaning)   {
        po.put(f_meaning, meaning);
    }
    public void setWord(Word word)   {
        po.put(f_word, word.po);
    }
    public String getMeaning()   {
        return po.getString(f_meaning);
    }
    public Word getWord()   {
        return new Word(po.getParseObject(f_word));
    }
}
```

A WordMeaning carries an attribute pointing to its parent word. You use this property to query all the word meanings for a given word, as shown in Listing 14-14.

Listing 14-14. Using Parceled Word to Query for its Meanings

```
private void populateWordMeaningsList(Word word)
{
    ParseQuery query = new ParseQuery(WordMeaning.t_tablename);
    query.whereEqualTo(WordMeaning.f_word, word.po);
    query.orderByDescending(WordMeaning.f_createdAt);

    //Include who created me
    query.include(WordMeaning.f_createdBy);

    //Include who the parent word is
    query.include(WordMeaning.f_word);

    //How can We include the owner of the word
    query.include(WordMeaning.f_word + "." + Word.f_createdBy);

    this.turnOnProgressDialog("Going to get word meanings for:" + word.getWord(),
            "Patience. Be Right back");
    query.findInBackground(new FindCallback() {
      public void done(List<ParseObject> objects, ParseException e) {
        turnOffProgressDialog();
        if (e == null) {
            // The query was successful.
            successfulQuery(objects);
        } else {
```

```
            // Something went wrong.
            queryFailure(e);
        }
    }
});
}
private void successfulQuery(List<ParseObject> objects)
{
    this.setEmptyViewToNoRows();
    ArrayList<WordMeaning> wordMeaningList = new ArrayList<WordMeaning>();
    for(ParseObject po: objects)
    {
        WordMeaning wordMeaning = new WordMeaning(po);
        wordMeaningList.add(wordMeaning);
    }

  WordMeaningListAdapter listItemAdapter =
      new WordMeaningListAdapter(this
              ,wordMeaningList
              ,this);
    this.setListAdapter(listItemAdapter);
}
private void queryFailure(ParseException x)
{
    this.setErrorView(x.getMessage());
}
```

This code is very similar to the code given in the previous chapter to query for words. The difference here is in how you specify the "where" clause that involves a parent word Parse object. Here is that line from the code just given:

```
query.whereEqualTo(WordMeaning.f_word, word.po);
```

Notice that you are able to use the parceled word object as you would on any other occasion. The rest of the code is very similar to those given in Chapter 13.

Creating the Meaning for a Word

Let's turn attention to the *Create Meaning* button in Figure 14-2, which invokes the create word activity. Here also you can benefit directly from the parceled word. Listing 14-15 shows how to transport the already parceled word one more time through the intent to the create word meaning activity.

Listing 14-15. Transfering an Already Parceled Word to Another Activity

```
public void createWordMeaning(View v)
{
    Intent i = new Intent(this,CreateAMeaningActivity.class);
    i.putExtra(Word.t_tablename,parceledWord);
    startActivity(i);
}
```

Notice how the parceled word is parceled again through the intent extra. This means that the `ParseObjectWrapper` needs to be aware of its state and parcel successfully both when it had not been parceled before and also when it had already been parceled. You can see this in the `writeToParcel()` method and also when creating the `ParseObjectWrapper` from the parcel in the `create()` method of the `ParseObjectWrapper`.

Listing 14-16 show how to retrieve the parceled word for the `CreateWordMeaning` activity. Notice that this code is identical to the one used to retrieve the parceled word the first time, as given in Listing 14-11.

Listing 14-16. Retrieving a Word That Is Parceled Twice

```
private Word getParceledWordFromIntent()
{
    Intent i = this.getIntent();
    ParseObjectWrapper pow =
        (ParseObjectWrapper)i.getParcelableExtra(Word.t_tablename);
    Word parceledWord = new Word(pow);
    return parceledWord;
}
```

Listing 14-17 shows how to use the retrieved word to populate the word detail necessary to display in the `CreateWordMeaning` activity.

Listing 14-17. Using the ParseObjectEssentials Accessor Methods

```
private String getWordDetail(Word pword)
{
    String by = pword.getCreatedByUser().username;
    Date d = pword.getCreatedAt();

    DateFormat df = SimpleDateFormat.getDateInstance(DateFormat.SHORT);
    String datestring =  df.format(d);

    return by + "/" + datestring;
}
```

Finally, Listing 14-18 shows how to use the passed in Word to create a WordMeaning in the Parse cloud.

Listing 14-18. Further Use of Parceled ParseObjects

```
public void createMeaning(View v)
{
    if (validateForm() == false)   {
        return;
    }
    //get meaning from the text box
    String meaning = getUserEnteredMeaning();

    WordMeaning wm = new WordMeaning(meaning, parceledWord);
    turnOnProgressDialog("Saving Word Meaning", "We will be right back");
```

```
        wm.po.saveInBackground(new SaveCallback() {
            @Override
            public void done(ParseException e) {
                turnOffProgressDialog();
                if (e == null)     {
                    wordMeaningSavedSuccessfully();
                }
                else {
                    wordMeaningSaveFailed(e);
                }
            }
        });
    }
    private void wordMeaningSaveFailed(ParseException e) {
        String error = e.getMessage();
        alert("Saving word failed", error);
    }
    private void wordMeaningSavedSuccessfully(){
        alert("word meaning saved", "Success");
    }
```

Notice in this code that the twice-parceled word is used as the direct target for the parent word attribute of the word meaning being saved.

References

The references for Parse given in Chapter 13 are applicable here. The following additional links further support the material in this chapter.

- Understanding parcelables: http://androidbook.com/item/3814

- Android SDK documentation on parcelables:
  http://developer.android.com/reference/android/os/Parcel.html

- Download the test project dedicated for this chapter at
  www.androidbook.com/expertandroid/projects. The name of the zip file is
  ExpertAndroid_Ch13_ParseStarterProject.zip. This is the same zip file as in the
  previous chapter. Same application supports both chapters.

Summary

This chapter covers the critical topic of how to use parcelables to effectively develop with Parse. We have presented the detail architecture of how parcelables work in Android. We have reasoned why parcelables are important when coding with Android and Parse. And we have presented a workable framework that you can use as is or tweak to create a brand new framework to meet the stated guidelines. In Chapter 15 we will cover Parse Push notifications.

Review Questions

The following questions should help consolidate what you have learned in this chapter:

1. Why are parcelables important while working with Parse in Android?

2. How do you implement a parcelable?

3. What is `Parcelable.describeContents()`?

4. What are parcelable flags?

5. What is the creator static method in a parcelable?

6. Are `ParseObjects` parcelable?

7. Are `ParseObjects` serializable?

8. Can `ParseObjects` be converted to JSON strings?

9. How can you query for Parse objects where an attribute points to another Parse object?

10. Can you create a Parse object using its Parse object ID?

15

Exploring Push Notifications with Parse

When you publish mobile applications you want a way to communicate with users of your mobile applications. For some applications, you may even want to facilitate communication among the users themselves. These features of a mobile application are generally facilitated through *push notifications*.

In Chapters 13 and 14, we covered how the Parse cloud is used to manage users and how to store objects on their behalf. In this chapter, we cover the push notiifcations API of Parse. The features we cover are:

1. How to intialize a mobile appplication so that it is enabled for Parse push notifications

2. How to send notifications using the Parse dashboard from the server

3. How to send notifications using the Parse dashboard to specific channels

4. How to allow mobile client applications, to send notifications to specific channels subscribed by other users, instead of using the server-side dashboard

5. How to capture push notifications through Android broadcast receivers

To demonstrate these concepts, we will expand the application that was developed for the last two chapters by adding an activity that can both respond to push notifications and also send push notifications. We start with the user experience of the application that we then implement in this chapter.

Demonstrating Parse Push Notifications

If you were to run the application we use as an example for this chapter, you would see a screen like the one shown in Figure 15-1. This screen lists the options available for a logged-in user.

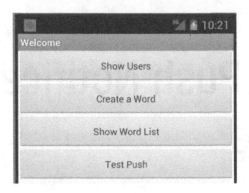

Figure 15-1. *Welcome screen to invoke the test push activity*

Note that the welcome screen in Figure 15-1 is the same as the one shown in Chapter 13 (Figure 13-6) except that there is an additional button to invoke the activity that will be used to both receive and send push notifications.

Responding to a Push Notification

The activity in Figure 15-2 shows the user controls that demonstrate how to respond to and send push notifications. In the Java code (shown later), this activity is called RespondToPushActivity.

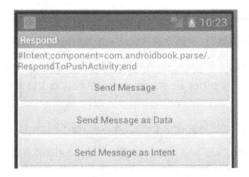

Figure 15-2. *Activity to respond to and send push notifications*

Let's look at a few things about this RespondToPushActivity, as it is a multipurpose activity.

At the top, there is a text view that displays the contents of the intent that invoked this activity as a result of a push notification. When you push a notification message from the Parse cloud, the notification message shows up in the notification bar at the top of the Android device (or wherever that notifications bar lies depending on the Android device and model). When you pull down that notification message and tap or click it, the activity shown in Figure 15-2, the RespondToPushActivity, is invoked.

The first thing this activity does is to display the intent that invoked it, with its details, at the top in the "read only" text view. Looking at this intent text view, you can see how Parse has delivered the message to the activity in your mobile application. When we push a message like this from server, it is a server-side push and is done through the Parse dashboard. In contrast, the activity in Figure 15-2 has a couple of other buttons to trigger a push from the user side. We will talk about these Send buttons next.

Push Notifications from a Client Program

As shown in Figure 15-2, there are three additional buttons in the RespondToPushActivity screen. The first button sends a message from the client program to other client programs using a simpler typed message API of Parse. The second button sends a message from the client program to other client prorgrams using a somewhat typeless JSON data object. Both are similar, but you will see the subtle differences very soon. Also, both of these options utilize something called *push channels* and each channel can be associated with an activity. In the sample application, we have used the RespondToPushActivity (Figure 15-2) as the target for the push notifications coming from the channels. Because the RespondToPushActivity also investigates the intent that invoked it, this allows you to see what type of message is received when client programs push notifications.

The third button sends a similar message from the client program to other client programs using channels, but instead of targeting an activity, the message targets a broadcast receiver. The broadcast receiver can then choose to notify via the Android notification manager. This broadcast receiver–based approach gives more flexibility, if needed, regarding how and what is shown in the notification.

Supporting Screens

There are a few supporting screens. Figure 15-3 is a screen shot of the server-side Parse dashboard from where you can send messages to all users (or clients).

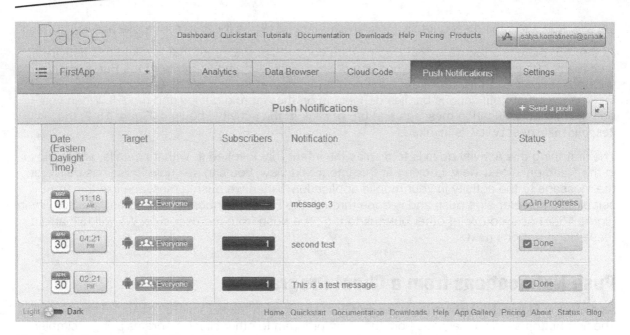

Figure 15-3. Parse push notification dashboard

Figure 15-4 is a screen shot of the page of the Parse push notification dashboard that is responsible for constructing and pushing a message to all Android clients of this application.

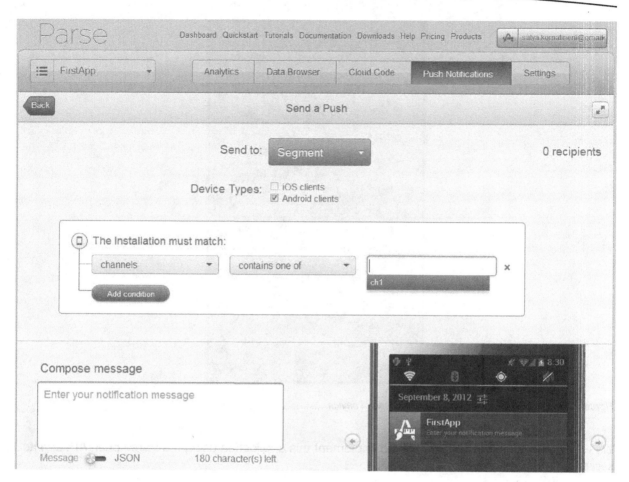

Figure 15-4. Constructing a push message

Figure 15-5 is a screen shot of how the message shows up on an Android device. More specifically, Figure 15-5 is the view of the notification when the user drags down the notification panel to examine the notification in the notifications bar.

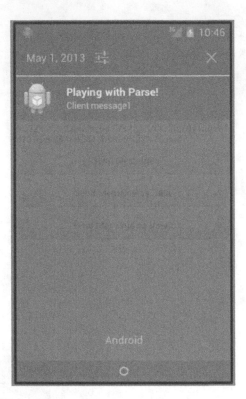

Figure 15-5. Push notification displayed on an Android device

We will now move on to discuss how to implement this application using the Parse push API and its server-side facilities.

Implementing Parse Push

Implementing the push notifications with Parse is really simple. Parse maintains an Android service that is in constant touch with the Parse cloud. This enables Parse to push messages to clients from the server directly and also from other clients, ofcourse, via the server.

Each application installed on a device is represented by an "installation" Parse object. (Refer to Chapters 13 and 14 for what Parse objects are and how to install the Parse SDK.) The installation object needs to be initialized when your application starts. It is stored in the Parse cloud for each application, and it tells the Parse cloud what type of a device it is and if it is ready to receive messages, and so on.

Listing 15-1 shows how a mobile application is initialized with an installation object. This code is quite similar to the initialization code used in the last two chapters, except that the last section contains the push-related initialization.

Listing 15-1. Intializing an application for Parse push notifications

```java
public class ParseApplication extends Application {

    private static String tag = "ParseApplication";

    private static String PARSE_APPLICATION_ID
        = "....wqHaD2m";

    private static String PARSE_CLIENT_KEY
        = "....WGd2p";

    @Override
    public void onCreate() {
        super.onCreate();

        // Add your initialization code here
        Parse.initialize(this, PARSE_APPLICATION_ID, PARSE_CLIENT_KEY);

        //Security of data
        ParseACL defaultACL = new ParseACL();
        // If you would like objects to be private by default, remove this line.
        defaultACL.setPublicReadAccess(true);
        ParseACL.setDefaultACL(defaultACL, true);

        //Enable to receive push
        PushService.setDefaultPushCallback(this, RespondToPushActivity.class);
        ParseInstallation pi = ParseInstallation.getCurrentInstallation();

        //Register a channel to test push channels
        Context ctx = this.getApplicationContext();
        PushService.subscribe(ctx, "ch1", RespondToPushActivity.class);

        pi.saveEventually();
    }
}
```

We have made use of the PushService class to indicate the default activity that should be invoked when the user taps the received message. (We will show you shortly what the RespondToPushActivity code looks like.) We have also used the PushService to subscribe to all messages that are targeted for a user-defined channel, called ch1.

Channels are merely a way to classify messages and allow a publish/subscribe kind of functionality. It is important to note that the Parse dashboard has no explicit place to create or maintain these channel strings (their names). It is up to the developer to design these channel string names as needed. In fact, there is no formal API to create these channels; by merely subscribing to a string, the string becomes a channel!

For example, you can devise three activities that you want to target when you receive messages. Then you create (or subscribe to) three channels and call them "ch1," "ch2," and "ch3." And when you target messages to those channels, the respective activities are invoked.

Another way to use channels is that a user of your application may create channels through your application and other users could subscribe to those channels. In that case, as a developer you are responsible for keeping track of this channel metadata (channel names and how they are subscribed to), as you would any other Parse object.

Now back to the installation object. At the end of the code segment in Listing 15-1, you get the current installation object and save it to the Parse cloud by calling saveEventually() or saveInTheBackground(). Earlier versions of Parse had some problems with saveInTheBackground() while another server-side call may be in progress, like the Parse.initialize()or an earlier saveInTheBackground()that was not completed yet on the same thread. This could happen easily when you write a method that calls multiple Parse SDK methods that either directly or indirectly begin a save in the background operation. This problem was rectified in recent releases, such as the one we have used: Parse 1.2.3.

To complete the initialization, in addition to the code in Listing 15-1, you also need the following entries (Listing 15-2) in the manifest file of your application.

Listing 15-2. Permissions Required for Parse Push Notifications

```
<uses-permission android:name="android.permission.INTERNET" />
<uses-permission android:name="android.permission.ACCESS_NETWORK_STATE" />
<uses-permission android:name="android.permission.RECEIVE_BOOT_COMPLETED" />
<uses-permission android:name="android.permission.VIBRATE" />
```

These permission tags usually go right above the application tag and are siblings of the application tag.

Inside the application tag, you need the lines in Listing 15-3.

Listing 15-3. Registering Parse Push Service and Parse Broadcast Receiver

```
<service android:name="com.parse.PushService" />
<receiver android:name="com.parse.ParseBroadcastReceiver">
  <intent-filter>
    <action android:name="android.intent.action.BOOT_COMPLETED" />
    <action android:name="android.intent.action.USER_PRESENT" />
  </intent-filter>
</receiver>
```

Both PushService and the ParseBroadcastReceiver in this code are part of the Parse SDK. Listings 15-1, 15-2, and 15-3 complete the initialization process. We will now describe how to send and receive a Parse push message.

Sending a Push Notification from the Parse Dashboard

In Figures 15-2, 15-3, and 15-4, while describing the user experience of this application, we showed how to construct a push message and send it to all the Android clients. This pushed message will be received by the RespondToPushActivity class. Let's now see the code for the RespondToPushActivity class that is targeted by the push notification of the sample application. This code is presented in Listing 15-4.

Listing 15-4. RespondToPushActivity: Responding to and Sending Push Notifications

```
public class RespondToPushActivity
extends BaseActivity
{
    public RespondToPushActivity() {
        super("RespondToPushActivity");
    }
    public void onCreate(Bundle savedInstanceState) {
        super.onCreate(savedInstanceState);
        setContentView(R.layout.rtp_respond_to_push);
        examineIntent(getIntent());
    }
    //This activity is setup as a singletop
    @Override
    protected void onNewIntent(Intent intent) {
        examineIntent(intent);
    }

    //Populate the textview with the intent that has the message
    private void examineIntent(Intent i)
    {
        String u = i.toURI(0);
        TextView tv = (TextView)findViewById(R.id.rtp_welcomeMessage);
        tv.setText(u);
    }
}//eof-class
```

The layout used for this RespondToPushActity was shown in Figure 15-2. Note the display of the incoming intent text and the three buttons to send messages.

Listing 15-4 for the onCreate() method takes the invoking intent and populates the intent text view that is at the top. You can see this in the method examineIntent(). We have used the toUri(0) method on the intent to get a string representation of the intent. This tell us how Parse is constructing the message to be delivered to the activity.

Also, as you may receive other messages targeted for this same activity, we have indicated the activity as singletop in the manifest file. Listing 15-5 shows this code.

Listing 15-5. Registering RespondToPushActivity as a Singletop

```
<activity android:name="com.androidbook.parse.RespondToPushActivity"
    android:launchMode="singleTop"
    android:label="Respond"/>
```

The implication of being a singletop is that onCreate() won't be called if this activity is on the top of the stack. Instead, the onNewIntent() method is called. That is why the code in Listing 15-4 takes onNewIntent() into consideration. If we didn't do this, every time a new message arrives and the user taps on it, a new activity is created on the stack. But by specifying it as singletop, you avoid multiple activities on the stack.

With this `RespondToPushActivity` in place, you can send a message from the server that will appear first as an alert at the top of your Android device. Then you choose the notification after dragging the notification panel down (Figure 15-5) and clicking it, and you are taken to this `RespondToPushActivity` (Figure 15-2), with the intent displayed at the top. You will be able to see the message that you typed in the dashboard, available in the intent. You may likely want to take some action using this message text.

Sending a Message to a Channel Using the Dashboard

Because you will have subscribed to a channel called "ch1" in the initialization process (Listing 15-1), Parse knows that there is a channel "ch1" that can be targeted. In the Parse push notification dashboard, you can choose this channel as the target. That message will then go to all the users who have subscribed to this channel and will end up invoking the same `RespondToPushActivity`, as this activity is registered as the target activity for that channel.

Sending a Message Through a Client Program

Take a look at the `sendMessage()` method in Listing 15-6. You can add this code to the `RespondToPushActivity` in order to respond to the Send Message button in Figure 15-2.

Listing 15-6. Sending a Push Notification from a User (Client)

```
//A useful counter to distinguish messages
private int i = 0;

//Use Java methods to push a message
public void sendMessage(View v)
{
    ParsePush push = new ParsePush();
    String message = "Client message" + Integer.toString(i++);
    push.setChannel("ch1");
    push.setMessage(message);
    push.sendInBackground();
}
```

In this code snippet, you are using an object called `ParsePush` to set the channel and set a message, and then send it in the background. This message will show up and ultimately result in invoking the same `RespondToPushActivity` (Figure 15-2). However, on the Parse dashboard, you need to enable the client-side push first. You go to `parse.com` and access the dashboard for your application. Then, you will see the settings for push where you will find this client-side push setting.

Sending a Message as Data from a Client Program

When you are using the `ParsePush` object, you may be wondering whether it is possible to send additional data other than a message. The answer is yes. This is done by using the `setData()` method on the `ParsePush` object. This method takes a JSON object as its input. Being a JSON object, the data object then allows any number of key value pairs that could be sent to the receivers.

Even when you use the ParsePush.setMessage() method, underneath it gets converted to a JSON object with a set of predefined keys. The message that is used as part of the setMessage() goes as the key alert. (We will cover another reserved key called action later in the chapter. For the full list of these keys, see the online Parse documentation.)

Now let's send an extra data element called customdata and see if this field becomes accessible in the RespondToPushActivity.

Note You may be wondering what size message you can deliver to clients. There is a hard limit of about 199 characters for IOS. For Android devices, this can be large and unspecified at this time. So you can try pushing much larger payloads if you know that your receivers are Android. However, a better option is to send a limited message and then have the receiver pull it back from Parse to avoid this limitation!

The code in Listing 15-7 shows how to create a JSON data object and then send it as a Parse push message.

Listing 15-7. Sending a Push Notification Using JSON Data

```
//Use a JSON object to send a message
public void sendMessageAsData(View v)
{
    JSONObject data = getJSONDataMessage();
    ParsePush push = new ParsePush();
    push.setChannel("ch1");
    push.setData(data);
    push.sendInBackground();
}
private JSONObject getJSONDataMessage()
{
    try
    {
        JSONObject data = new JSONObject();
        data.put("alert", "Main Message");
        data.put("customdata", "custom data value");
        return data;
    }
    catch(JSONException x)
    {
        throw new RuntimeException("Something wrong with JSON", x);
    }
}
```

When you are using a JSON data object, it is important what keys or attributes you use to send the data. Refer to the Parse documentation to get a handle on the available keys.

There doesn't appear to be a way to send push messages from the client side to *all* the other clients. User-side push messages seem to require a channel to publish on. But if all of your mobile applications subscribe to a single, well-known channel, anything published on that channel will go to all clients.

Using the client-side push, you can also give a collection of Installation objects to ParsePush. We do not cover that in this chapter, however it is quite easy to do that. You get a query object on the Installation class and then specify the "where" clause of all the types of installation objects you want to target.

Using Broadcast Receivers as Targets for Push Notifications

By setting a different attribute (action attribute) on the JSON data object being sent through the push message, you can make Parse invoke a broadcast receiver instead of triggering a notification that shows up in the notification bar. When you use this approach, Parse does not send a notification to the notification manager. Instead, Parse invokes a broadcast receiver indicated by the action attribute.

To prompt Parse to do this, construct a JSON data object with a key called action that points to an Android intent whose action invokes a broadcast receiver. The code in Listing 15-8 shows how to create such a JSON data object and send it as a push notification.

Listing 15-8. Sending a Push Notification to Invoke a Broadcast Receiver

```java
//Use JSON data to send a message to a broadcast receiver
public void sendMessageAsIntent(View v)
{
    JSONObject data = getJSONDataMessageForIntent();
    ParsePush push = new ParsePush();
    push.setChannel("ch1");
    push.setData(data);
    push.sendInBackground();
}
//Notice how the 'action' attribute enables the
//broadcast receiver behavior.
private JSONObject getJSONDataMessageForIntent()
{
    try
    {
        JSONObject data = new JSONObject();
        //Notice alert is not required
        //data.put("alert", "Message from Intent");
        //instead action is used
        data.put("action", TestBroadcastReceiver.ACTION);
        data.put("customdata", "custom data value");
        return data;
    }
    catch(JSONException x)
    {
        throw new RuntimeException("Something wrong with JSON", x);
    }
}
```

When you use the action attribute, make sure not to use the alert at the same time. If you do, Parse will seem to do both—invoke the broadcast receiver and also send the notification.

In Listing 15-8, the action attribute of the JSON object is pointing to the constant TestBroadcastReceiver.ACTION. This is a string defined in the code for TestBroadcastReceiver. Listing 15-9 shows the code for the TestBroadcastReceiver. Notice that the value of the action is com.androidbook.parse.TestPushAction

Listing 15-9. Source Code for TestBroadcastReceiver

```java
public class TestBroadcastReceiver
extends BroadcastReceiver
{
    public static final String ACTION="com.androidbook.parse.TestPushAction";
    public static final String PARSE_EXTRA_DATA_KEY="com.parse.Data";
    public static final String PARSE_JSON_ALERT_KEY="alert";
    public static final String PARSE_JSON_CHANNELS_KEY="com.parse.Channel";

    private static final String TAG = "TestBroadcastReceiver";

    @Override
    public void onReceive(Context context, Intent intent)
    {
        try
        {
          String action = intent.getAction();

          //"com.parse.Channel"
          String channel =
              intent.getExtras()
                  .getString(PARSE_JSON_CHANNELS_KEY);

          JSONObject json =
              new JSONObject(
                      intent.getExtras()
                        .getString(PARSE_EXTRA_DATA_KEY));

          Log.d(TAG, "got action " + action + " on channel " + channel + " with:");
          Iterator itr = json.keys();
          while (itr.hasNext())
          {
              String key = (String) itr.next();
              Log.d(TAG, "…" + key + " => " + json.getString(key));
          }
          notify(context,intent,json);
        }
        catch (JSONException e)
        {
            Log.d(TAG, "JSONException: " + e.getMessage());
        }
    }
    private void notify(Context ctx, Intent i, JSONObject dataObject)
    throws JSONException
```

```
            {
                    NotificationManager nm = (NotificationManager)
                        ctx.getSystemService(Context.NOTIFICATION_SERVICE);

                    int icon = R.drawable.robot;
                    String tickerText =
                        dataObject.getString("customdata");
                    long when = System.currentTimeMillis();
                    Notification n = new Notification(icon, tickerText, when);

                    //Let the intent invoke the respond activity
                    Intent intent = new Intent(ctx, RespondToPushActivity.class);
                    //Load it with parse data
                    intent.putExtra("com.parse.Data",
                            i.getExtras().getString("com.parse.Data"));

                    PendingIntent pi = PendingIntent.getActivity(ctx, 0, intent, 0);

                    n.setLatestEventInfo(ctx, "Parse Alert", tickerText, pi);
                    n.flags |= Notification.FLAG_AUTO_CANCEL;

                    nm.notify(1, n);
            }
}//eof-class
```

Following the rules of broadcast receivers, this receiver needs to be registered in the Android manifest file, as shown in Listing 15-10.

Listing 15-10. Registering the TestBroadcastReceiver

```
<receiver
    android:name=".TestBroadcastReceiver"
    android:exported="false"
    >
    <intent-filter>
      <action android:name="com.androidbook.parse.TestPushAction" />
    </intent-filter>
</receiver>
```

Notice that the action name in the JSON object matches the action filter for the test broadcast receiver. This is how the TestBroadcastReceiver is invoked when this message is pushed to the Android devices.

You are doing two things in using this broadcast receiver (Listing 15-9). First, you are retrieving the JSON data object that Parse sends through the intent. From this JSON object, you can extract the standard fields and also any custom fields you may have prepared. Next, you are constructing your own notification and sending it to the notification manager. (You may be tempted to pop out an activity from the broadcast receiver, but that is not a good practice as the user gets jolted out of context from whatever that user is doing. Also, imagine what would happen if multiple broadcast receivers start doing this. The good practice to alert the user from a broadcast receiver is to send a notification to the notification manager.) You have also set a new intent on the notification so that the same RespondToPushActivity is invoked when the user taps on the notification.

References

The references for Parse given in Chapters 13 and 14 are applicable here. The following additional links further support the material in this chapter.

- Push notification guide from Parse:
  https://www.parse.com/docs/push_guide#top/Android

- Author's research log on Parse push notifications:
  http://androidbook.com/item/4547. You will see here the basic research for this chapter and also a number resources, code snippets, etc.

- Working with broadcast receivers: http://androidbook.com/item/3482

- Working with the Android notification manager:
  http://androidbook.com/item/3506

- Download the test project dedicated for this chapter at
  www.androidbook.com/expertandroid/projects. The name of the zip file is
  ExpertAndroid_Ch15_ParsePushProject.zip.

Summary

Parse.com can take your mobile applications to places where they haven't gone before. Using Parse, you will be better able communicate with your user base. It is possible to write collaborative applications that can bring the power of groups and community to the fore.

Parse.com enables this communication by providing storage, user management, and push notifications through a really nice API and a web-based dashboard. With Facebook acquiring Parse, we expect to see this platform mature quickly and even possibly leapfrog ahead of others with new ideas in the next year.

This chapter gives an excellent inroduction to some of the things that you can do with Parse push notifications. For more features, see the Parse website for additional things that either we have mentioned in passing or haven't covered at all.

Review Questions

The following questions should consolidate what you have learned in this chapter:

1. How does Parse accomplish push notifications?

2. How do you set up your application to work with Parse push notifications?

3. What kind of dashboard support is there to work with push notifications in Parse?

4. What are installation objects?

5. What are the Parse services and receivers that need to be registered in your application?

6. What are channels?

7. How do you manage channels? Do they need to be predefined?

8. How do you send messages only to certain devices based on a query?

9. How do you write broadcast receivers that can be triggered by push messages?

10. What is the difference between mobile clients sending push messages and a server using a dashboard to send push messages?

11. Is there a message size limitation for Push notifications?

12. What is the role of JSON data objects in sending and receiving push notifications?

13. How do you retrieve and construct a JSON data object using intent extras?

Index